THE COLD WAR
THROUGH DOCUMENTS
A Global History

Third Edition

Edited by

Edward H. Judge
Le Moyne College

John W. Langdon
Le Moyne College

ROWMAN & LITTLEFIELD
Lanham • Boulder • New York • London

Executive Editor: Susan McEachern
Assistant Editor: Rebeccah Shumaker
Senior Marketing Manager: Kim Lyons

Credits and acknowledgments for material borrowed from other sources, and
reproduced with permission, appear on the appropriate page within the text.

Published by Rowman & Littlefield
A wholly owned subsidiary of The Rowman & Littlefield Publishing Group, Inc.
4501 Forbes Boulevard, Suite 200, Lanham, Maryland 20706
www.rowman.com

Unit A, Whitacre Mews, 26-34 Stannary Street, London SE11 4AB, United Kingdom

British Library Cataloguing in Publication Information Available

Library of Congress Cataloging-in-Publication Data

Names: Judge, Edward H., editor. | Langdon, John W., editor.
Title: The Cold War through documents : a global history / edited by Edward
  H. Judge, Le Moyne College, John W. Langdon, Le Moyne College.
Description: Third edition. | Lanham : Rowman & Littlefield, 2017. | Previous
  edition entered under: Judge, Edward H. | Title of previous edition: The
  Cold War : a global history with documents.
Identifiers: LCCN 2017033810 (print) | LCCN 2017039855 (ebook) | ISBN
  9781538109274 (electronic) | ISBN 9781538109250 (cloth : alk. paper) |
  ISBN 9781538109267 (pbk. : alk. paper)
Subjects: LCSH: Cold War—Sources. | World politics—1945–1989—Sources. |
  World politics—1985–1995—Sources.
Classification: LCC D839.3 (ebook) | LCC D839.3 .C65 2017 (print) | DDC
  909.82/5—dc23
LC record available at https://lccn.loc.gov/2017033810

♾™ The paper used in this publication meets the minimum requirements of
American National Standard for Information Sciences—Permanence of Paper
for Printed Library Materials, ANSI/NISO Z39.48-1992.

Printed in the United States of America

Contents

Part II: The Global Confrontation, 1950–1960

Part IV: The Era of Détente, 1969–1979

I

THE ORIGINS OF
THE COLD WAR, 1945–1950

1

The Yalta Conference, February 1945

D URING WORLD WAR II, DESPITE mutual distrust, the Soviet Union and the Western powers cooperated in a Grand Alliance to defeat Nazi Germany. From 1941 to 1944 the Soviets bore the brunt of this struggle, reversing the German onslaught, while the British and Americans, who were also fighting Japan without Soviet help, delayed opening a second front in the west—much to Moscow's dismay. Not until June 1944 did they finally launch their "D-day" invasion of Nazi-occupied France.

In February 1945 the "Big Three" leaders—US president Franklin Roosevelt, British prime minister Winston Churchill, and Soviet premier Joseph Stalin—convened at Yalta in the Soviet Crimea. By then the Anglo-American forces had driven the Germans from France, the Soviets had occupied Poland, and German defeat was in sight. The war against Japan, however, seemed far from over. Anxious to secure Soviet cooperation in this conflict, Roosevelt was willing to concede Russian dominance in Poland, which was already occupied by the Red Army and administered by a Soviet-sponsored provisional government. He and Churchill tried to get the best bargain they could, but the final agreement on Poland, regardless of its language, would be implemented by the occupying Soviets. Later, as the Communists assumed full control, the Western leaders would be accused of having sold out the Poles.

The Yalta agreements on Poland and Japan are reproduced in the following section. The statement on Poland was released at the end of the conference, but the secret agreement on Japan was not made public until several years later.

A. DECLARATION ON POLAND

A new situation has been created in Poland as a result of her complete liberation by the Red Army. This calls for the establishment of a Polish Provisional Government which can be more broadly based than was possible before the recent liberation of the Western part of Poland. The Provisional Government which is now functioning in Poland should therefore be reorganized on a broader democratic basis with the inclusion of democratic leaders from Poland itself and from Poles abroad. This new government should then be called the Polish Provisional Government of National Unity.

M. Molotov, Mr. Harriman, and Sir A. Clark Kerr are authorized as a mission to consult . . . with members of the present Provisional Government and with other Polish democratic leaders from within Poland and from abroad, with a view to the reorganization of the present Government along the above lines. This Polish Provisional Government of National Unity shall be pledged to the holding of free and unfettered elections as soon as possible on the basis of universal suffrage and secret ballot. In these elections all democratic and anti-Nazi parties shall have the right to take part and to put forward candidates.

When a Polish Provisional Government of National Unity has been properly formed in conformity with the above, the Government of the USSR, which now maintains diplomatic relations with the present Provisional Government of Poland, and the Government of the United Kingdom and the Government of the USA will establish diplomatic relations with the new Polish Provisional Government of National Unity, and will exchange Ambassadors by whose reports the respective Governments will be kept informed about the situation in Poland.

The three Heads of Government consider that the Eastern frontier of Poland should follow the Curzon Line with digressions from it in some regions of five to eight kilometers in favor of Poland. They recognize that Poland must receive substantial accessions of territory in the north and west. They feel that the opinion of the new Polish Provisional Government of National Unity should be sought in due course on the extent of these accessions and that the final delimitation of the Western frontier of Poland should thereafter await the peace conference.

B. AGREEMENT REGARDING SOVIET
ENTRY INTO THE WAR AGAINST JAPAN

The leaders of the three great powers—the Soviet Union, the United States of America, and Great Britain—have agreed that in two or three months after

Germany has surrendered and the war in Europe has terminated the Soviet Union shall enter into the war against Japan on the side of the Allies on condition that:

1. The status quo in Outer Mongolia (The Mongolian People's Republic) shall be preserved,
2. The former rights of Russia violated by the treacherous attack of Japan in 1904 shall be restored, viz . . . :
   (A) the southern part of Sakhalin, as well as all the islands adjacent to it, shall be returned to the Soviet Union,
   (B) the commercial port of Dairen shall be internationalized, the pre-eminent interests of the Soviet Union in this port being safeguarded and the lease of Port Arthur as a naval base of the USSR restored,
   (C) the Chinese-Eastern Railroad and the South-Manchurian Railroad which provides an outlet to Dairen shall be jointly operated by the establishment of a joint Soviet-Chinese Company, it being understood that the pre-eminent interests of the Soviet Union shall be safeguarded and that China shall retain full sovereignty in Manchuria;
3. The Kurile islands shall be handed over to the Soviet Union. . . .

The heads of the three great powers have agreed that these claims of the Soviet Union shall be unquestionably fulfilled after Japan has been defeated.

For its part the Soviet Union expresses its readiness to conclude with the National Government of China a pact of friendship and alliance between the USSR and China in order to render assistance to China with its armed forces for the purpose of liberating China from the Japanese yoke.

Discussion Questions

1. Why did Roosevelt and Churchill agree to allow the Soviet-sponsored Provisional Government to continue in power in Poland?
2. Why did they want it reorganized to include democratic leaders and committed to "free and unfettered" elections?
3. What factors would make it possible for the Soviets to establish Communist control in Poland, despite these provisions?
4. Why did the conference assert that Poland should receive substantial accessions of territory in the north and west?

5. Why did the agreement on Japan promise the Soviet Union so much territory in East Asia?
6. Why would many Americans have been disappointed with the Yalta agreements?
7. To what extent were Roosevelt and Churchill guilty of having "sold out" Poland at Yalta? What other choice did they have?

2

The Potsdam Conference, July–August 1945

GERMANY'S SURRENDER IN MAY 1945 was followed by its division into zones of occupation, with the Soviets in the east and the other Allies in the west, and by another major conference of Allied leaders. From 17 July through 2 August 1945, at the city of Potsdam near the German capital of Berlin, Stalin met again with Western leaders—but they were not the same ones he had dealt with at Yalta. Roosevelt's death in April meant that a new president, Harry Truman, would represent the United States. Churchill was present at the start of the Potsdam Conference, but he and his cabinet were soon turned out of power as the result of elections, and he was replaced at Potsdam by a new prime minister, Clement Attlee.

The conference saw growing contention between the Soviets and the West but resulted in what seemed a reasonable compromise. The Soviet Union would take the $10 billion in reparations it demanded from Germany from its occupation zone alone, rather than from the entire country. In return, the Americans and British would agree to the new Polish-German borders favored by Moscow and would grant the Soviets a percentage of capital equipment from the Western-occupied zones. As the conference closed on 2 August, it was clear that the Grand Alliance was functioning less smoothly now that Germany had been defeated, but at this stage no government was yet talking about Cold War.

EXCERPTS FROM THE BERLIN (POTSDAM) CONFERENCE REPORT, 2 AUGUST 1945

III. *Germany*
The Political and Economic Principles to Govern the Treatment of Germany in the Initial Control Period

A. **POLITICAL PRINCIPLES**

   1. In accordance with the Agreement on Control Machinery in Germany, supreme authority in Germany is exercised, on instructions from their respective Governments, by the Commanders-in-Chief of the armed forces of the United States of America, the United Kingdom, the Union of Soviet Socialist Republics, and the French Republic, each in his own zone of occupation, and also jointly, in matters affecting Germany as a whole, in their capacity as members of the Control Council. . . .

B. **ECONOMIC PRINCIPLES**

  11. In order to eliminate Germany's war potential, the production of arms, ammunitions and implements of war as well as all types of aircraft and sea-going ships shall be prohibited and prevented. Production of metals, chemicals, machinery and other items that are directly necessary to a war economy shall be rigidly controlled and restricted. . . .

IV. *Reparations From Germany*

   1. Reparation claims of the USSR shall be met by removals from the zone of Germany occupied by the USSR, and from appropriate German external assets.

   2. The USSR undertakes to settle the reparation claims of Poland from its own share of reparations.

   3. The reparation claims of the United States, the United Kingdom and other countries entitled to reparations shall be met from the Western Zones and from appropriate German external assets.

   4. In addition to the reparations to be taken by the USSR from its own zone of occupation, the USSR shall receive additionally from the Western zones:

     (a) 15 percent of such usable and complete industrial capital equipment from the metallurgical, chemical and machine manufacturing industries as is unnecessary for the German peace economy and should be removed from the Western Zones of Germany, in exchange for an equivalent value of food, coal, potash, zinc, timber, clay products, petroleum products, and such other commodities as may be agreed upon.

     (b) 10 percent of such industrial capital equipment as is unnecessary for the German peace economy and should be removed from the Western Zones, to be transferred to the Soviet Government on reparations account without payment or exchange of any kind in return. . . .

8. The Soviet Government renounces all claims in respect of reparations to shares of German enterprises which are located in the Western Zones of occupation in Germany as well as to German foreign assets in all countries except those specified in paragraph 9 below.

9. The Governments of the UK and USA renounce their claims in respect of reparations to shares of German enterprises which are located in the Eastern Zone of occupation in Germany, as well as to German foreign assets in Bulgaria, Finland, Hungary, Rumania and Eastern Austria. . . .

IX. *Poland*

A. We have taken note with pleasure of the agreement reached among representative Poles from Poland and abroad which has made possible the formation, in accordance with the decisions reached at the Crimea Conference, of a Polish Provisional Government of National Unity recognized by the Three Powers. The establishment by the British and the United States Governments of diplomatic relations with the Polish Provisional Government of National Unity has resulted in the withdrawal of their recognition from the former Polish Government in London, which no longer exists. . . .

The Three Powers note that the Polish Provisional Government of National Unity, in accordance with the decisions of the Crimea Conference, has agreed to the holding of free and unfettered elections as soon as possible on the basis of universal suffrage and secret ballot in which all democratic and anti-Nazi parties shall have the right to take part and to put forward candidates, and that the representatives of the Allied press shall enjoy full freedom to report to the world upon developments in Poland before and during the elections.

B. The following agreement was reached on the western frontier of Poland:

In conformity with the agreement on Poland reached at the Crimea Conference the Three Heads of Government have sought the opinion of the Polish Provisional Government of National Unity in regard to the accession of territory in the north and west which Poland should receive. . . .

The Three Heads of Government agree that, pending the final determination of Poland's western frontier, the former German territories east of a line running from the Baltic Sea immediately west of Swinemunde, and thence along the Oder River to the confluence of the western Neisse River and along the western Neisse to the Czechoslovak frontier . . . shall be under the administration of the Polish State and for such purposes should not be considered as part of the Soviet zone of occupation in Germany. . . .

XIII. Orderly Transfer of German Populations
The Three Governments . . . recognize that the transfer to Germany of German populations, or elements thereof, remaining in Poland, Czechoslovakia, and Hungary, will have to be undertaken. They agree that any transfers that take place should be effected in an orderly and humane manner. . . .

Discussion Questions

1. What factors might have encouraged the members of the Grand Alliance to continue working together at Potsdam despite their differences?
2. Who was assigned supreme authority in occupied Germany? Why was this done?
3. Why were the Soviets determined to receive industrial reparations from defeated Germany?
4. Why did the Americans insist that the USSR could take reparations only from the Soviet-occupied zone and not from the rest of Germany?
5. Why did the Western leaders agree to the new Polish-German borders favored by Moscow?
6. Why did they agree to transfer to Germany the German populations remaining in Poland, Czechoslovakia, and Hungary?
7. In what ways did the Potsdam agreements set the stage for the future division of Europe into Eastern and Western blocs?

3

The Atomic Bombing
of Hiroshima, August 1945

O N 6 AUGUST 1945 THE UNITED STATES dropped an atomic bomb on the city of Hiroshima in Japan, obliterating that city and inaugurating the Atomic Age. This bomb, and the one dropped on Nagasaki three days later, helped bring the Pacific War to an expeditious end, without the need for an

Allied invasion of Japan. It also thus prevented the Soviets, who on 8 August declared war on Japan in accordance with their Yalta commitment, from invading and occupying part of Japan. And it left them scrambling to catch up with the Americans in atomic weaponry.

The impact of Hiroshima and Nagasaki on Soviet-American relations was profound. The Truman administration, delighted with its new weapon, became less willing to compromise with Moscow; as Truman put it to his secretary of state in early 1946, "I'm tired of babying the Soviets." Stalin promptly diverted massive Soviet resources, desperately needed to repair the devastation caused by the German invasion, to an all-out program to build a comparable bomb as quickly as possible. After the Soviet bomb was tested successfully in 1949, Truman made the decision to begin development of a much more powerful hydrogen-fusion (or thermonuclear) bomb; the Soviets followed suit, and the nuclear arms race was on. The resulting Cold War would be far more dangerous to the ultimate survival of the human race than any "hot war" in history.

STATEMENT BY PRESIDENT TRUMAN, 6 AUGUST 1945

Sixteen hours ago an American airplane dropped one bomb on Hiroshima, an important Japanese Army base. That bomb had more power than 20,000 tons of T.N.T. It had more than two thousand times the blast power of the British "Grand Slam," which is the largest bomb ever yet used in the history of warfare.

The Japanese began the war from the air at Pearl Harbor. They have been repaid many fold. And the end is not yet. With this bomb we have now added a new and revolutionary increase in destruction to supplement the growing power of our armed forces. In their present forms these bombs are now in production and even more powerful forms are in development.

It is an atomic bomb. It is a harnessing of the basic power of the universe. The force from which the sun draws its power has been loosed against those who brought war to the Far East.

Before 1939, it was the accepted belief of scientists that it was theoretically possible to release atomic energy. But no one knew any practical method of doing it. By 1942, however, we knew that the Germans were working feverishly to find a way to add atomic energy to the other engines of war with which they hoped to enslave the world. But they failed. We may be grateful to Providence that the Germans got the V–1's and the V–2's late and in limited quantities and even more grateful that they did not get the atomic bomb at all.

The battle of the laboratories held fateful risks for us as well as the battles of the air, land, and sea, and we have now won the battle of the laboratories as we have won the other battles. . . . We have spent two billion dollars on the greatest scientific gamble in history—and won.

But the greatest marvel is not the size of this enterprise, its secrecy, nor its cost, but the achievement of scientific brains in putting together infinitely complex pieces of knowledge held by many men in different fields of science into a workable plan. And hardly less marvelous has been the capacity of industry to design, and of labor to operate, the machines and methods to do things never done before so that the brain child of many minds came forth in physical shape and performed as it was supposed to do. . . . What has been done is the greatest achievement of organized science in history. It was done under high pressure and without failure.

We are now prepared to obliterate more rapidly and completely every productive enterprise the Japanese have above ground in any city. We shall destroy their docks, their factories, and their communications. Let there be no mistakes; we shall completely destroy Japan's power to make war.

It was to spare the Japanese people from utter destruction that the ultimatum of July 26 was issued at Potsdam. Their leaders promptly rejected that ultimatum. If they do not now accept our terms, they may expect a rain of ruin from the air, the like of which has never been seen on this earth. Behind this air attack will follow sea and land forces in such numbers and power as they have not yet seen and with the fighting skill of which they are already well aware. . . .

The fact that we can release atomic energy ushers in a new era in man's understanding of nature's forces. Atomic energy may in the future supplement the power that now comes from coal, oil, and falling water, but at present it cannot be produced on a basis to compete with them commercially. Before that comes, there must be a long period of intensive research.

It has never been the habit of the scientists of this country or the policy of this Government to withhold from the world scientific knowledge. Normally, therefore, everything about the work with atomic energy would be made public.

But under present circumstances it is not intended to divulge the technical processes of production or all the military applications, pending further examination of possible methods of protecting us and the rest of the world from the danger of sudden destruction.

I shall recommend that the Congress of the United States consider promptly the establishment of an appropriate commission to control the production and use of atomic power within the United States. I shall give further consideration and make further recommendations to the Congress as to how atomic power can become a powerful and forceful influence towards the maintenance of world peace.

Discussion Questions

1. Why was Truman so pleased with the development and use of the atomic bomb? What benefits did he expect from it?
2. How did Truman justify the use of atomic weapons? Why did he call Hiroshima a "Japanese Army base"? Why did he mention Pearl Harbor and Germany's effort to build an atomic bomb?
3. Truman announced that the United States had won "the battle of the laboratories." What implications would this have for future scientific research on weapons systems?
4. Did Truman assume that the dropping of the bomb on Hiroshima would make an invasion of Japan unnecessary? How do you know?
5. What impact was the atomic bomb likely to have on Soviet-American relations? Why might Stalin be less than pleased that his American allies had developed such a powerful weapon?

4

Ho Chi Minh's Declaration of Independence for Vietnam, 2 September 1945

ON 2 SEPTEMBER 1945, the same day the formal Japanese surrender finally ended World War II, a man called Ho Chi Minh ("he who brings enlightenment"), addressing a huge crowd in the Southeast Asian city of Hanoi, declared independence for a new nation that he called the Democratic Republic of Vietnam. In retrospect, Ho's speech marked not just an assertion of Vietnamese freedom from French colonial rule but also the onset of the postwar wave of anti-imperialist struggles, rooted in prewar and wartime events, that destroyed the global colonial empires forged by the great European powers in the preceding centuries.

Ho's declaration was also a foreshadowing of the Cold War. For Ho Chi Minh was a Communist, wedded to the Marxist-Leninist views that Western imperialism was a natural outgrowth of industrial capitalism, that capitalism and imperialism were thus one and the same, and hence that colonized nations fighting for independence were natural allies of the global Communist movement. Although Ho's declaration cited the ideals of the American and French Revolutions, and made no mention of world communism or the USSR, the declaration was directed primarily against Western imperialism as practiced by the French in Southeast Asia. And France, which in 1949 would become a founding member of NATO (Document 17), the Western anti-Communist alliance led by the United States, was determined to restore its colonial rule in Southeast Asia. The logic of Ho's situation and ideals would soon compel him to lead his small nation into long and devastating wars, first against the French and later against the Americans. And Vietnam's anti-imperialist quest for national independence would become part of the global Cold War, bringing Southeast Asia decades of almost constant conflict.

EXCERPTS FROM HO CHI MINH'S SPEECH DECLARING INDEPENDENCE FOR VIETNAM, 2 SEPTEMBER 1945

"All men are created equal. They are endowed by their Creator with certain inalienable rights, among these are Life, Liberty, and the pursuit of Happiness." This immortal statement was made in the Declaration of Independence of the United States of America in 1776. In a broader sense, this means: All the peoples on the earth are equal from birth, all the peoples have a right to live, to be happy and free.

The Declaration of the French Revolution made in 1791 on the Rights of Man and the Citizen also states: "All men are born free and with equal rights, and must always remain free and have equal rights." Those are undeniable truths.

Nevertheless, for more than eighty years, the French imperialists . . . have violated our Fatherland and oppressed our fellow-citizens. . . .

In the field of politics, they have deprived our people of every democratic liberty. They have enforced inhuman laws. . . . They have built more prisons than schools. They have . . . drowned our uprisings in rivers of blood. They have fettered public opinion. . . .

In the fields of economics, they have fleeced us to the backbone, impoverished our people, and devastated our land. They have robbed us of our rice fields, our mines, our forests, and our raw materials. . . . They have . . . reduced our people . . . to a state of extreme poverty. They have . . . mercilessly exploited our workers.

In the autumn of 1940, when the Japanese Fascists violated Indochina's territory . . . the French imperialists went down on their bended knees and handed over our country to them. . . . The result was that . . . more than two million of our fellow-citizens died from starvation. . . . After the Japanese had surrendered to the Allies, our whole people rose to regain our national sovereignty. . . .

The French have fled, the Japanese have capitulated. . . . Our people have broken the chains which for nearly a century have fettered them and have won independence for the Fatherland. . . .

For these reasons, we . . . declare that from now on we break off all relations of a colonial character with France. . . . The whole Vietnamese people . . . are determined to fight to the bitter end against any attempt by the French colonialists to re-conquer their country.

We are convinced that the Allied nations, which at Tehran and San Francisco have acknowledged the principles of self-determination and equality of nations, will not refuse to acknowledge the independence of Vietnam.

A people who have courageously opposed French domination . . . , who have fought side by side with the Allies against the Fascists . . . , such a people must be free and independent.

For these reasons, we, members of the Provisional Government of the Democratic Republic of Vietnam, solemnly declare to the world that Vietnam has the right to be a free and independent country and in fact it is so already. The entire Vietnamese people are determined to mobilize all their physical and mental strength, to sacrifice their lives and property in order to safeguard their independence and liberty.

Discussion Questions

1. Why did Ho Chi Minh cite the US Declaration of Independence and the French Declaration on the Rights of Man and the Citizen in declaring independence for Vietnam?
2. Why did Ho's declaration avoid mention of Marxist-Leninist Communism or the USSR?
3. What reasons did Ho have to hope that his quest for independence might receive support from the United States and the Allied powers? In retrospect, why did such hopes prove unrealistic?
4. How did Ho's quest for independence help set the stage for other such liberation movements?
5. Why and how was Ho's quest for independence likely to become intertwined with the emerging Cold War?

5

Stalin's Election Speech, February 1946

ON 9 FEBRUARY 1946 JOSEPH STALIN delivered an "election" speech to an assembly of voters in Moscow. In the USSR, elections were not designed to give voters a choice between competing candidates or programs. There was only one candidate for each position, and that candidate always endorsed the Communist Party's positions on questions facing the nation. Election speeches were therefore used to inform citizens of those positions, to defend and justify them, and to identify the candidate as a person worthy of trust and responsibility. When one of the party leaders spoke, everyone listened attentively, for the speech might contain hints as to the future actions of the Soviet government.

On this occasion, Stalin reasserted the validity of Marxist-Leninist thought, blamed World War II on conflicts among capitalists, and painted the contrast between capitalism and Communism in vivid colors not used in official Soviet pronouncements since 1941. Although it was intended largely to rally the Soviet peoples for continued sacrifices in rebuilding their war-torn country, his speech was viewed by many in the West as a declaration of Cold War against the capitalist world.

HIGHLIGHTS OF STALIN'S ELECTION SPEECH, 9 FEBRUARY 1946

Comrades! Eight years have elapsed since the last elections. This is a period rich in events of a decisive character. The first four years passed in strenuous work of the Soviet people in the fulfillment of the Third Five-Year Plan. During the past four years the events of the struggle against the German and Japanese aggressors developed—the events of the Second World War. Doubtless the war was the main event of that period.

It would be incorrect to think that the war arose accidentally or as the result of the fault of some of the statesmen. Although these faults did exist, the war arose in reality as the inevitable result of the development of the world economic and political forces on the basis of monopoly capitalism.

Our Marxists declare that the capitalist system of world economy conceals elements of crisis and war, that the development of world capitalism does not follow a steady and even course forward, but proceeds through crises and catastrophes. The uneven development of the capitalist countries leads in time to sharp disturbances in their relations, and the group of countries which consider themselves inadequately provided with raw materials and export markets try usually to change this situation and to change the position in their favor by means of armed force. As a result of these factors, the capitalist world is sent into two hostile camps and war follows.

Perhaps the catastrophe of war could have been avoided if the possibility of periodic redistribution of raw materials and markets between the countries existed in accordance with their economic needs, in the way of coordinated and peaceful decisions. But this is impossible under the present capitalist development of world economy.

Thus, as a result of the first crisis in the development of the capitalist world economy, the First World War arose. The Second World War arose as a result of the second crisis. . . .

What about the origin and character of the Second World War? In my opinion, everybody now recognizes that the war against fascism was not, nor could it be, an accident in the life of the people; that the war turned into a war of the peoples for their existence; that precisely for this reason it could not be a speedy war, a "lightning war."

As far as our country is concerned, this war was the most cruel and hard of all wars ever experienced in the history of our motherland. But the war has not only been a curse; it was at the same time a hard school of trial and a testing of all the people's forces. . . .

And so, what is the balance of the war; what are our conclusions? . . .

Now victory means, first of all, that our Soviet social system has won, that the Soviet social system has successfully stood the test in the fire of war and has proved its complete vitality. . . .

The war has shown that the Soviet multinational state system has successfully stood the test, has grown still stronger during the war and has proved a completely vital state system. . . .

Third, our victory implies that it was the Soviet armed forces that won. Our Red Army had won. The Red Army heroically withstood all the adversities of the war, routed completely the armies of our enemies and emerged victoriously from the war. . . .

Now a few words on the plans for the work of the Communist Party in the near future. . . . The fundamental task of the new Five-Year Plan consists in restoring the areas of the country which have suffered, restoring the pre-war level in industry and agriculture, and then exceeding this level by more or less considerable amounts. . . .

1. How did Stalin explain the outbreak of World War II?
2. How can you tell that Stalin's explanation is based on Marxist principles?
3. Why did Stalin emphasize so strongly that the Soviet social and state systems had triumphed, in addition to the obvious victory of the Red Army?
4. Why was this speech viewed with alarm in Washington and London?
5. If an American or British politician had been making a similar speech, how would his or her reasoning and explanations have differed from those of Stalin?

6

Churchill's Iron Curtain Speech, March 1946

IN FEBRUARY 1946, SEVERAL WEEKS after Stalin's election speech, former British prime minister Winston Churchill visited the United States. Increasingly concerned over Soviet behavior, he confided his fears to President Truman. The two men decided that Churchill should deliver a major address in Fulton, Missouri, to alert the world to the Soviet threat. That candid speech, in which Churchill used the term "iron curtain" to describe the barrier Moscow had placed between the West and the Communist-dominated nations of Eastern Europe, startled many Americans and infuriated Stalin. Churchill issued a ringing call for the continuation of Anglo-American wartime cooperation, this time against a Soviet Union he viewed as bent on world domination. Although he was no longer prime minister, his dramatic and quotable speech made headlines throughout the world and came to be considered a declaration of Cold War.

Stalin's reaction to the "iron curtain" speech was vigorous and direct. In a subsequent interview in the Soviet newspaper *Pravda*, he characterized Churchill as a man bent on war against the Soviet Union. He defended Soviet actions in Eastern Europe, pointing out the importance of that region to Soviet security and insisting that the governments there were democratic. Considering it unlikely that Truman would have appeared on the platform with Churchill had he disagreed with the latter's remarks, Stalin also asserted that the Americans and British were banding together against their wartime Soviet allies.

A. HIGHLIGHTS OF CHURCHILL'S "IRON CURTAIN" SPEECH, 5 MARCH 1946

The United States stands at this time at the pinnacle of world power. It is a solemn moment for the American democracy. For with this primacy in power is also joined an awe-inspiring accountability to the future. . . . Opportunity is here now, clear and shining, for both our countries. To reject it or ignore it or fritter it away will bring upon us all the long reproaches of the after-time. It is necessary that constancy of mind, persistency of purpose, and the grand simplicity of decision shall guide and rule the conduct of the English-speaking peoples in peace as they did in war. We must and I believe we shall prove ourselves equal to this severe requirement. . . .

A shadow has fallen upon the scenes so lately lighted by the Allied victory. Nobody knows what Soviet Russia and its Communist international organization intends to do in the immediate future, or what are the limits, if any, to their expansive and proselytizing tendencies. I have a strong admiration and regard for the valiant Russian people and for my wartime comrade, Marshal Stalin. There is sympathy and good-will in Britain—and I doubt not here also—toward the peoples of all the Russias and a resolve to persevere through many differences and rebuffs in establishing lasting friendships.

We understand the Russian need to be secure on her western frontiers . . . by the removal of all possibility of German aggression. We welcome Russia to her rightful place among the leading nations of the world. . . . Above all, we welcome or should welcome constant, frequent, and growing contacts between the Russian people and our own people on both sides of the Atlantic. It is my duty, however . . . to place before you certain facts about the present position in Europe.

From Stettin in the Baltic to Trieste in the Adriatic, an iron curtain has descended across the Continent. Behind that line lie all the capitals of the ancient states of central and eastern Europe. Warsaw, Berlin, Prague, Vienna, Budapest, Belgrade, Bucharest, and Sofia, all these famous cities and the populations around them lie in what I might call the Soviet sphere, and all are subject, in one form or another, not only to Soviet influence but to a very high and increasing measure of control from Moscow. . . .

The Russian-dominated Polish Government has been encouraged to make enormous and wrongful inroads upon Germany, and mass expulsions of millions of Germans on a scale grievous and undreamed of are now taking place. The Communist parties, which were very small in all these eastern states of Europe, have been raised to preeminence and power far beyond their numbers and are seeking everywhere to obtain totalitarian control. Police governments are prevailing in nearly every case, and so far, except in Czechoslovakia, there is no true democracy. Turkey and Persia are both profoundly alarmed and disturbed at the claims which are made upon them and at the pressure being exerted by the Moscow government.

An attempt is being made by the Russians in Berlin to build up a quasi-Communist party in their zone of occupied Germany by showing special favors to groups of left-wing German leaders. . . .

If now the Soviet Government tries, by separate action, to build up a pro-Communist Germany in their areas, this will cause new serious difficulties in the British and American zones, and will give the defeated Germans the power of putting themselves up to auction between the Soviets and the Western democracies. Whatever conclusions may be drawn from these facts—and facts they are—this is certainly not the liberated Europe we fought to build up. Nor is it one which contains the essentials of permanent peace. . . .

In front of the iron curtain which lies across Europe are other causes for anxiety. In Italy the Communist Party is seriously hampered by having to support the Communist-trained Marshal Tito's claims to former Italian territory at the head of the Adriatic. Nevertheless, the future of Italy hangs in the balance. Again, one cannot imagine a regenerated Europe without a strong France. . . .

However, in a great number of countries, far from the Russian frontiers and throughout the world, Communist fifth columns are established and work in complete unity and absolute obedience to the directions they received from the Communist center. Except in the British Commonwealth, and in the United States, where Communism is in its infancy, the Communist parties or fifth columns constitute a growing challenge and peril to Christian civilization. These are somber facts for anyone to have to recite on the morrow of a victory gained by so much splendid comradeship in arms and in the cause of freedom and democracy, and we should be most unwise not to face them squarely while time remains.

The outlook is also anxious in the Far East, and especially in Manchuria. The agreement which was made at Yalta, to which I was a party, was extremely favorable to Soviet Russia, but it was made at a time when no one could say that the German war might not extend all through the summer and autumn of 1945 and when the Japanese war was expected to last for a further eighteen months from the end of the German war. In this country you are so well informed about the Far East, and such devoted friends of China, that I do not need to expatiate on the situation there. . . .

On the other hand . . . I repulse the idea that a new war is inevitable; still more that it is imminent. It is because I am sure that our fortunes are still in our hands, in our own hands, and that we hold the power to save the future, that I feel the duty to speak out now that I have an occasion to do so.

I do not believe that Soviet Russia desires war. What they desire is the fruits of war and the indefinite expansion of their power and doctrines.

But what we have to consider here today while time remains, is the permanent prevention of war and the establishment of conditions of freedom and democracy as rapidly as possible in all countries. Our difficulties and dangers will not be removed by closing our eyes to them; they will not be removed by more waiting to see what happens; nor will they be relieved by a policy of appeasement. What is needed is a settlement, and the longer this is delayed, the more difficult it will be and the greater our dangers will become.

From what I have seen of our Russian friends and allies during the war, I am convinced that there is nothing they admire so much as strength, and there is nothing for which they have less respect than for military weakness. For that . . . reason the old doctrine of a balance of power is unsound. We cannot afford, if we can help it, to work on narrow margins, offering temptations to a trial of strength. If the western democracies stand together in strict adherence to the principles of the United Nations Charter, their influence for furthering these principles will be immense and no one is likely to molest them. If, however, they become divided or falter in their duty, and if these all-important years are allowed to slip away, then indeed catastrophe may overwhelm us all.

Last time I saw it all coming, and cried aloud to my own fellow countrymen and to the world, but no one paid any attention. Up till the year 1933 or even 1935, Germany might have been saved from the awful fate which has overtaken her and we might all have been spared the miseries Hitler let loose upon mankind. There never was a war in all history easier to prevent by timely action than the one which has just desolated such great areas of the globe. It could have been prevented without the firing of a single shot, and Germany might be powerful, prosperous, and honored today, but no one would listen and one by one we were all sucked into the awful whirlpool.

We surely must not let that happen again. This can only be achieved by reaching now, in 1946 . . . a good understanding on all points with Russia under the general authority of the United Nations . . . , supported by the whole strength of the English-speaking world and all its connections. . . .

If the population of the English-speaking Commonwealth be added to that of the United States, with all such cooperation implies in the air, on the seas all over the globe, and in science and in industry, and in moral force, there will be no quivering, precarious balance of power to offer its temptation to ambition or adventure. On the contrary there will be an overwhelming assurance of security. If we adhere faithfully to the Charter of the United Nations and walk forward in sedate and sober strength, seeking no one's land or treasure, seeking to lay no arbitrary control upon the thoughts of men, if all British moral and material forces and convictions are joined with your own in fraternal association, the high roads of the future will be clear, not only for us but for all, not only for our time but for a century to come.

B. EXCERPTS FROM *PRAVDA*'S INTERVIEW WITH STALIN, MARCH 1946

Q. How do you assess the last speech of Mr. Churchill which was made in the United States?

A. I assess it as a dangerous act calculated to sow the seed of discord among the Allied governments and hamper their cooperation.

Q. Can one consider that the speech of Mr. Churchill is damaging to the cause of peace and security?

A. Undoubtedly, yes. In substance, Mr. Churchill now stands in the position of a firebrand of war. And Mr. Churchill is not alone here. He has friends not only in England but also in the United States of America.

In this respect, one is reminded remarkably of Hitler and his friends. Hitler began to set war loose by announcing his racial theory, declaring that only people speaking the German language represent a fully valuable nation. Mr. Churchill begins to set war loose also by a racial theory, maintaining that only nations speaking the English language are fully valuable nations, called upon to decide the destinies of the entire world.

The German racial theory brought Hitler and his friends to the conclusion that the Germans, as the only fully valuable nation, must rule over other nations. The English racial theory brings Mr. Churchill and his friends to the conclusion that nations speaking the English language, being the only fully valuable nations, should rule over the remaining nations of the world. . . .

But the nations have shed their blood during five years of cruel war for the sake of liberty and the independence of their countries, and not for the sake of exchanging the lordship of Hitler for the lordship of Churchill. . . .

There is no doubt that the set-up of Mr. Churchill is a set-up for war, a call to war with the Soviet Union. . . .

Q. How do you assess that part of Mr. Churchill's speech in which he attacks the democratic regime of the European countries which are our neighbors and in which he criticizes the good neighborly relations established between these countries and the Soviet Union?

A. This part of Mr. Churchill's speech is a mixture of the elements of the libel with the elements of rudeness and lack of tact. Mr. Churchill maintains that Warsaw, Berlin, Prague, Vienna, Budapest, Belgrade, Bucharest, and Sofia, all these famous cities and the population of those areas, are within the Soviet sphere and are all subjected to Soviet influence and to the increasing control of Moscow.

Mr. Churchill qualifies this as the "boundless expansionist tendencies of the Soviet Union." It requires no special effort to show that Mr. Churchill rudely and shamelessly libels not only Moscow but also the above-mentioned States neighborly to the USSR.

To begin with, it is quite absurd to speak of the exclusive control of the USSR in Vienna and Berlin, where there are Allied control councils with representatives of four States, where the USSR has only one fourth of the voices. . . .

Secondly, one cannot forget the following fact: the Germans carried out an invasion of the USSR through Finland, Poland, Rumania, Bulgaria and Hungary. The Germans were able to carry out the invasion through these countries by reason of the fact that these countries had governments inimical to the Soviet Union.

As a result of the German invasion, the Soviet Union has irrevocably lost in battles with the Germans, and also during the German occupation and through the expulsion of Soviet citizens to German slave labor camps, about 7,000,000 people. In other words, the Soviet Union has lost in men several times more than Britain and the United States together.

It may be that some quarters are trying to push into oblivion these sacrifices of the Soviet people which insured the liberation of Europe from the Hitlerite yoke. But the Soviet Union cannot forget them. One can ask, therefore, what can be surprising in the fact that the Soviet Union, in a desire to ensure its security for the future, tries to achieve that these countries should have governments whose relations to the Soviet Union are loyal? How can one, without having lost one's reason, qualify these peaceful aspirations of the Soviet Union as "expansionist tendencies" of our Government?

. . . As for Mr. Churchill's attack on the Soviet Union in connection with the extending of the western boundaries of Poland, as compensation for the territories seized by the Germans in the past, there it seems to me that he quite blatantly distorts the facts. As is known, the western frontiers of Poland were decided upon at the Berlin conference of the three powers, on the basis of Poland's demands. The Soviet Union repeatedly declared that it considered Poland's demands just and correct. It may well be that Mr. Churchill is not pleased with this decision. But why does Mr. Churchill, not sparing his darts against the Russians in the matter, conceal from his readers the fact that the decision was taken at the Berlin conference unanimously, that not only the Russians voted for this decision but also the British and Americans?

... Mr. Churchill further maintains that the Communist parties were very insignificant in all these Eastern European countries but reached exceptional strength, exceeding their numbers by far, and are attempting to establish totalitarian control everywhere; that police-government prevailed in almost all these countries, even up to now, with the exception of Czechoslovakia, and that there exists in them no real democracy....

The growth of the influence of Communism cannot be considered accidental. It is a normal function. The influence of the Communists grew because during the hard years of the mastery of fascism in Europe, Communists showed themselves to be reliable, daring and self-sacrificing fighters against fascist regimes for the liberty of peoples....

Discussion Questions

1. What evidence did Churchill give of Soviet expansionism? What developments made him so insistent that Anglo-American cooperation must be preserved after World War II?
2. If Churchill recognized "the Russian need to be secure on her western frontiers," why did he object so strongly to what the Russians were doing in Eastern Europe?
3. Why did Churchill assert that "the old doctrine of the balance of power is unsound"? With what did he propose to replace it?
4. Was Stalin justified in his accusation that Churchill's speech reflected Anglo-American racism? Why or why not?
5. How did Stalin justify the extension of Soviet influence into many Eastern European countries? How did he explain the growth of Communist parties in those countries?

7

The Baruch and Gromyko Plans for Control of Atomic Weapons, 1946

IN 1946 THE UNITED STATES enjoyed a monopoly on the production of atomic weapons, but no one believed it would last forever. Conscious that sooner or later the Soviet Union would develop its own nuclear capability, Washington sought to devise a policy that would simultaneously internationalize atomic energy, forestall Soviet acquisition of atomic weapons, and prevent a nuclear arms race. Bernard Baruch, a well-known consultant and advisor to American presidents, was selected by President Truman to present the American plan to the UN Atomic Energy Commission on 14 June 1946.

On its face, the Baruch Plan appeared to be a generous proposal, with its unprecedented willingness to place an American technology under international control. The Russians, however, saw it as a carefully conceived ploy to maintain the US nuclear monopoly and open secret Soviet facilities to international inspection. But they could not simply reject it without damaging their standing in the eyes of the world. On 19 June 1946 Soviet delegate Andrei Gromyko presented a draft treaty designed to prohibit the manufacture and deployment of atomic weapons. All such weapons would be destroyed three months after the conclusion of the convention; punishment for violators would be fixed by mutual agreement three months after that. Inspection of plants and stockpiles was not mentioned at all. As a result of the fundamental differences between the American and Soviet approaches, neither plan was approved, and efforts to prevent a nuclear arms race proved futile.

A. SPEECH BY BERNARD BARUCH
TO THE UN ATOMIC ENERGY COMMISSION, 14 JUNE 1946

My fellow-members of the United Nations Atomic Energy Commission, and my fellow-citizens of the world:

We are here to make a choice between the quick and the dead. That is our business.

Behind the black portent of the new atomic age lies a hope which, seized upon with faith, can work our salvation. If we fail, then we have damned every man to be the slave of fear. Let us not deceive ourselves: We must elect world peace or world destruction.

Science has torn from nature a secret so vast in its potentialities that our minds cower from the terror it creates. Yet terror is not enough to inhibit the use of the atomic bomb. The terror created by weapons has never stopped man from employing them. For each new weapon a defense has been produced, in time. But now we face a condition in which adequate defense does not exist.

Science, which gave us this dread power, shows that it can be made a giant help to humanity, but science does not show us how to prevent its baleful use. So we have been appointed to obviate that peril by finding a meeting of the minds and the hearts of our peoples. Only in the will of mankind lies the answer.

It is to express this will and make it effective that we have been assembled. We must provide the mechanism to assure that atomic energy is used for peaceful purposes and preclude its use in war. To that end, we must provide immediate, swift, and sure punishment of those who violate the agreements that are reached by the nations. Penalization is essential if peace is to be more than a feverish interlude between wars. . . .

The United States proposes the creation of an International Atomic Development Authority, to which should be entrusted all phases of the development and use of atomic energy, starting with the raw material and including—

(1) Managerial control or ownership of all atomic-energy activities potentially dangerous to world security.
(2) Power to control, inspect, and license all other atomic activities.
(3) The duty of fostering the beneficial uses of atomic energy.
(4) Research and development responsibilities of an affirmative character intended to put the Authority in the forefront of atomic knowledge and thus to enable it to comprehend, and therefore to detect, misuse of atomic energy. . . .

I offer this as a basis for beginning our discussion.

But I think the peoples we serve would not believe—and without faith nothing counts—that a treaty, merely outlawing possession or use of the atomic bomb, constitutes effective fulfillment of the instructions of this Commission. Previous failures have been recorded in trying the method of simple renunciation, unsupported by effective guaranties of security and armament limitation. No one would have faith in that approach alone. . . . If I read the signs aright, the peoples want a program not composed merely of pious thoughts but of enforceable sanctions—an international law with teeth in it.

We of this nation, desirous of helping to bring peace to the world and realizing the heavy obligations upon us, arising from our possession of the means for producing the bomb and from the fact that it is part of our armament, are prepared to make our full contribution toward effective control of atomic energy.

When an adequate system for control of atomic energy, including the renunciation of the bomb as a weapon, has been agreed upon and put into effective operation and condign punishments set up for violations of the rules of control which are to be stigmatized as international crimes, we propose that:

(1) Manufacture of atomic bombs shall stop;
(2) Existing bombs shall be disposed of pursuant to the terms of the treaty, and
(3) The Authority shall be in possession of full information as to the know-how for the production of atomic energy. . . .

Now as to violations: in the agreement, penalties of as serious a nature as the nations may wish and as immediate and certain in their execution as possible, should be fixed for:

(1) Illegal possession or use of an atomic bomb;
(2) Illegal possession, or separation, of atomic material suitable for use in an atomic bomb;
(3) Seizure of any plant or other property belonging to or licensed by the Authority;
(4) Willful interference with the activities of the Authority;
(5) Creation or operation of dangerous projects in a manner contrary to, or in the absence of, a license granted by the international control body.

It would be a deception, to which I am unwilling to lend myself, were I not to say to you and to our peoples, that the matter of punishment lies at the very heart of our present security system. It might as well be admitted, here and now, that the subject goes straight to the veto power contained in the Charter of the United Nations so far as it relates to the field of atomic energy. The Charter permits penalization only by concurrence of each of the five great powers—Union of Soviet Socialist Republics, the United Kingdom, China, France and the United States. I want to make very plain that I am concerned here with the veto power only as it affects this particular problem. There must be no veto to protect those who violate their solemn agreements not to develop or use atomic energy for destructive purposes. . . .

And now I end. I have submitted an outline for present discussion. Our consideration will be broadened by the criticism of the United States proposals and by the plans of the other nations, which, it is to be hoped, will be submitted at their early convenience. . . .

B. DRAFT INTERNATIONAL AGREEMENT TO FORBID THE PRODUCTION AND USE OF ATOMIC WEAPONS, PROPOSED BY ANDREI GROMYKO ON 19 JUNE 1946

Article 1
The high contracting parties solemnly declare that they will forbid the production and use of a weapon based upon the use of atomic energy, and with this in view take upon themselves the following obligations:

- (a) Not to use, in any circumstance, an atomic weapon;
- (b) To forbid the production and keeping of a weapon based upon the use of atomic energy;
- (c) To destroy within a period of three months from the entry into force of this agreement all stocks of atomic energy weapons, whether in a finished or semi-finished condition.

Article 2
The high contracting parties declare that any violation of Article 1 of this agreement shall constitute a serious crime against humanity.

Article 3
The high contracting parties, within six months of the entry into force of the present agreement, shall pass legislation providing severe punishment for the violation of the terms of this agreement.

Article 4
The present agreement shall be of indefinite duration.

Article 5
The present agreement is open for signature to all states, whether or not they are members of the United Nations. . . .

Article 7

After the entry into force of the present agreement, it shall be an obligation upon all states, whether members or not of the United Nations. . . .

Discussion Questions

1. What were the main differences between the American and Soviet approaches to control of nuclear weapons?
2. Why did Baruch insist that the veto rights enjoyed by great powers in the UN Security Council must not protect violators of nuclear control agreements? Why might the Soviets disagree?
3. Why would the Americans be willing to permit international inspection of their facilities? Why would the Soviet Union object to such inspections of its facilities?
4. Why did the Gromyko Plan recommend outright prohibition and destruction of atomic weapons rather than international control of nuclear materials?
5. Which aspects of the Baruch and Gromyko Plans appear to be designed to appeal to world opinion? Why were the United States and the USSR so sensitive to such opinion?
6. Do you accept Baruch's assertion that "the terror created by weapons has never stopped man from employing them"? Why or why not?

8

The Truman Doctrine, 1947

AMERICA'S DECLARATION OF COLD WAR was issued on 12 March 1947. Ever since the end of World War II, Britain had supported the government of Greece in its attempts to suppress a Communist insurgency. That internal uprising was soon supported by Yugoslavia, and by February 1947 the British found themselves unable to bear the financial and military burdens involved in aiding the Greeks. The US State Department, led by George

Marshall and Dean Acheson, worked with President Truman to formulate a policy that would assist not only Greece but also its similarly endangered neighbor, Turkey. Advised by congressional leaders to take his case to the public, Truman did precisely that, addressing a joint session of Congress and a nationwide radio audience on 12 March.

Truman asked Congress for legislation to permit the administration to step into the protector's position being vacated by Great Britain. Following the suggestion of Senator Vandenberg, Truman identified the Communist threat as a global one, applicable not only to Greece and Turkey but to Western Europe and Asia as well. This policy, which came to be called the Truman Doctrine, set the stage for US aid to regimes that were threatened by Communist insurgencies throughout the Cold War era.

PRESIDENT TRUMAN'S SPEECH TO THE NATION, 12 MARCH 1947

Mr. President, Mr. Speaker, Members of the Congress of the United States:

The gravity of the situation which confronts the world today necessitates my appearance before a joint session of the Congress. The foreign policy and the national security of this country are involved.

One aspect of the present situation, which I wish to present to you at this time for your consideration and decision, concerns Greece and Turkey. . . .

The very existence of the Greek state is today threatened by the terrorist activities of several thousand armed men, led by Communists, who defy the Government's authority at a number of points, particularly along the northern boundaries. . . .

Greece's neighbor, Turkey, also deserves our attention. . . . Since the war Turkey has sought additional financial assistance from Great Britain and the United States for the purpose of effecting that modernization necessary for the maintenance of its national integrity. That integrity is essential to the preservation of order in the Middle East. . . .

One of the primary objectives of the foreign policy of the United States is the creation of conditions in which we and other nations will be able to work out a way of life free from coercion. This was a fundamental issue in the war with Germany and Japan. Our victory was won over countries which sought to impose their will, and their way of life, upon other nations. . . .

At the present moment in world history nearly every nation must choose between alternative ways of life. The choice is too often not a free one.

One way of life is based upon the will of the majority, and is distinguished by free institutions, representative government, free elections, guarantees of individual liberty, freedom of speech and religion, and freedom from political oppression.

The second way of life is based upon the will of a minority forcibly imposed upon the majority. It relies upon terror and oppression, a controlled press and radio, fixed elections, and the suppression of personal freedoms.

I believe that it must be the policy of the United States to support free peoples who are resisting attempted subjugation by armed minorities or by outside pressures. I believe that we must assist free peoples to work out their own destinies in their own way. I believe that our help should be primarily through economic and financial aid which is essential to economic stability and orderly political processes.

The world is not static, and the *status quo* is not sacred. But we cannot allow changes in the *status quo* in violation of the Charter of the United Nations by such methods as coercion, or by such subterfuges as political infiltration. In helping free and independent nations to maintain their freedom, the United States will be giving effect to the principles of the Charter of the United Nations.

It is necessary only to glance at a map to realize that the survival and integrity of the Greek nation are of grave importance in a much wider situation. If Greece should fall under the control of an armed minority, the effect upon its neighbor, Turkey, would be immediate and serious. Confusion and disorder might well spread throughout the entire Middle East. . . .

I therefore ask the Congress to provide authority for assistance to Greece and Turkey in the amount of $400,000,000 for the period ending June 30, 1948. . . .

In addition to funds, I ask the Congress to authorize the detail of American civilian and military personnel to Greece and Turkey, at the request of those countries, to assist in the tasks of reconstruction, and for the purpose of supervising the use of such financial and material assistance as may be furnished. I recommend that authority also be provided for the instruction and training of selected Greek and Turkish personnel.

Finally, I ask that the Congress provide authority which will permit the speediest and most effective use, in terms of needed commodities, supplies, and equipment, of such funds as may be authorized.

If further funds, or further authority, should be needed for purposes indicated in this message, I shall not hesitate to bring the situation before the Congress. On this subject the executive and legislative branches of the Government must work together.

This is a serious course upon which we embark. I would not recommend it except that the alternative is much more serious. . . .

The seeds of totalitarian regimes are nurtured by misery and want. They spread and grow in the evil soil of poverty and strife. They reach their full growth when the hope of a people for a better life has died. We must keep that hope alive. The free peoples of the world look to us for support in maintaining their freedoms. If we falter in our leadership, we may endanger the peace of the world—and we shall surely endanger the welfare of this nation. . . .

Discussion Questions

1. How did Truman underscore the gravity of the situation in Greece and Turkey?
2. What reasoning did Truman use to convince his listeners that economic aid would help prevent the spread of communism?
3. This speech has been characterized as America's "declaration of Cold War." Do you consider this an accurate description? Why or why not?
4. How might Stalin have reacted to Truman's speech? Why?
5. What aspects of this speech suggest that the Truman Doctrine could become part of a global strategy, with implications going far beyond Greece and Turkey?

9

The Marshall Plan, 1947

SHORTLY AFTER THE PROCLAMATION of the Truman Doctrine, US secretary of state George Marshall traveled to Moscow to attend a conference of foreign ministers. There he spoke extensively with Stalin and learned that the Soviet leader was convinced that European capitalism was in its death throes. War-torn Europe had never recovered from the devastation of World War II, and in France and Italy, it appeared that widespread economic misery would enable Communists to win the 1948 elections. Returning to Washington, DC, Marshall informed Truman of his concerns and set the State Department to work on measures designed to promote European economic recovery.

On 5 June 1947 Marshall embodied the final version of these measures in a commencement address at Harvard University. Although the proposal was officially called the European Recovery Program, it became widely known as the Marshall Plan, in hopes that Marshall's immense popularity would help win congressional approval for the large expenses involved. As matters developed, approval came easily, both because of widespread fear of communism and because of the plan's preference for grants of credits to purchase American goods rather than outright gifts of money. The purchases stimulated the prosperous US economy even further, and the Marshall Plan fueled spectacular economic recovery in Western Europe during the following decade.

MARSHALL'S COMMENCEMENT ADDRESS AT HARVARD UNIVERSITY, 5 JUNE 1947

I need not tell you gentlemen that the world situation is very serious. That must be apparent to all intelligent people. I think one difficulty is that the problem is one of such enormous complexity that the very mass of facts presented to the public by press and radio make it exceedingly difficult for the man in the street to reach a clear appraisement of the situation. Furthermore, the people of this country are distant from the troubled areas of the earth and it is hard for them to comprehend the plight and consequent reactions of the long-suffering peoples, and the effect of those reactions on their governments in connection with our efforts to promote peace in the world.

In considering the requirements for the rehabilitation of Europe, the physical loss of life, the visible destruction of cities, factories, mines, and railroads was correctly estimated, but it has become obvious during recent months that this visible destruction was probably less serious than the dislocation of the entire fabric of European economy. For the past ten years conditions have been highly abnormal. The feverish preparation for war and the more feverish maintenance of the war effort engulfed all aspects of national economies. Machinery has fallen into disrepair or is entirely obsolete. Under the arbitrary and destructive Nazi rule, virtually every possible enterprise was geared into the German War machine. Long-standing commercial ties, private institutions, banks, insurance companies, and shipping companies disappeared, through loss of capital, absorption through nationalization, or by simple destruction.

In many countries, confidence in the local currency has been severely shaken. The breakdown of the business structure of Europe during the war was complete. Recovery has been seriously retarded by the fact that two years after the close of hostilities a peace settlement with Germany and Austria has not been agreed upon. But even given a more prompt solution of these difficult problems, the rehabilitation of the economic structure of Europe quite evidently will require a much longer time and greater effort than had been foreseen. . . .

Aside from the demoralizing effect on the world at large and the possibilities of disturbances arising as a result of the desperation of the people concerned, the consequences to the economy of the United States should be apparent to all. It is logical that the United States should do whatever it is able to do to assist in the return of normal economic health in the world, without which there can be no political stability, and no assured peace.

Our policy is directed not against any country or doctrine but against hunger, poverty, desperation, and chaos. Its purpose should be the revival of a working economy in the world so as to permit the emergence of political and social conditions in which free institutions can exist. Such assistance, I am convinced, must not be on a piecemeal basis as various crises develop. Any assistance that this Government may render in the future should provide a cure rather than a mere palliative. Any government that is willing to assist in the task of recovery will find full cooperation, I am sure, on the part of the United States Government. Any government which maneuvers to block the recovery of other countries cannot expect help from us. Furthermore, governments, political parties, or groups which seek to perpetuate human misery in order to profit therefrom politically or otherwise will encounter the opposition of the United States.

It is already evident that, before the United States Government can proceed much further in its efforts to alleviate the situation and help start the European world on its way to recovery, there must be some agreement among the countries of Europe as to the requirements of the situation and the part those countries themselves will take in order to give proper effect to whatever action might be undertaken by this Government. It would be neither fitting nor efficacious for this Government to undertake to draw up unilaterally a program designed to place Europe on its feet economically. This is the business of the Europeans. The initiative, I think, must come from Europe. The role of this country should consist of friendly aid in the drafting of a European program and of later support of such a program so far as it may be practical for us to do so. The program should be a joint one, agreed to by a number, if not all, of European nations.

An essential part of any successful action on the part of the United States is an understanding on the part of the people of America of the character of the problem and the remedies to be applied. Political passion and prejudice should have no part. With foresight, and a willingness on the part of our people to face up to the vast responsibility which history has clearly placed upon our country, the difficulties I have outlined can and will be overcome.

Discussion Questions

1. Why was Marshall so concerned about the economic situation in Europe? Why did he think American aid was essential?
2. Why was it likely that destitute Europeans might turn to communism if nothing was done to alleviate their poverty?

3. What arguments might have been advanced in 1947 by Americans opposed to helping Europe recover?

4. Why did Marshall insist that Europeans take a principal role in the plan's implementation? Why did the plan favor grants to purchase US goods rather than outright gifts of money?

10

George F. Kennan, "The Sources of Soviet Conduct," 1947

GEORGE FROST KENNAN WAS A CAREER foreign service officer in the US Department of State and a highly regarded student of Russian and Soviet affairs. Early in 1946, while serving at the American embassy in Moscow, he sent a lengthy message to Washington providing an expert analysis of Soviet behavior. Placing Soviet expansionism squarely within the context of traditional Russian suspicion and insecurity, he argued that the USSR could not be fully trusted or reasoned with by the West and must instead be treated with firm resistance and strength. This "Long Telegram" made a deep impression on Kennan's superiors and helped shape their thinking about US foreign policy.

Returning to Washington later that year, Kennan wrote a paper entitled *Psychological Background of Soviet Foreign Policy*. Early in 1947, following an impressive public lecture, he was asked to submit an article for publication in the journal *Foreign Affairs*. The State Department authorized him to do so, as long as he did not use his own name. He took the paper he had written, signed it with an "X," and sent it to the journal.

Kennan was now becoming a very influential man. That spring he was placed at the head of the State Department's Policy Planning Staff, which was instrumental in developing the Marshall Plan. In July his article, now titled "The Sources of Soviet Conduct," appeared in *Foreign Affairs*. The "X-article," as it came to be known (despite the fact that its writer's identity was soon disclosed in the *New York Times*), is excerpted below. It provided a conceptual basis for the new US foreign policy embodied in the Truman

Doctrine and Marshall Plan. Describing Soviet expansion as "a fluid stream which moves constantly, wherever it is permitted to move," Kennan called for "a policy of firm containment, designed to confront the Russians with unalterable counter-force at every point where they show signs of encroaching upon the interests of a peaceful and stable world. . . ." This "containment" policy would serve as a foundation of American Cold War behavior for the next four decades.

"THE SOURCES OF SOVIET CONDUCT"*

The political personality of Soviet power as we know it today is the product of ideology and circumstances: ideology inherited by the present Soviet leaders from the movement in which they had their political origin, and circumstances of the power which they now have exercised for nearly three decades in Russia. There can be few tasks of psychological analysis more difficult than to try to trace the interaction of these two forces and the relative role of each in the determination of official Soviet conduct. Yet the attempt must be made if that conduct is to be understood and effectively countered.

It is difficult to summarize the set of ideological concepts with which the Soviet leaders came into power. Marxian ideology, in its Russian-Communist projection, has always been in process of subtle evolution. The materials on which it bases itself are extensive and complex. But the outstanding features of Communist thought as it existed in 1916 may perhaps be summarized as follows: (a) that the central factor in the life of man, the fact which determines the character of public life and the "physiognomy of society," is the system by which material goods are produced and exchanged; (b) that the capitalist system of production is a nefarious one which inevitably leads to the exploitation of the working class by the capital-owning class and is incapable of developing adequately the economic resources of society or of distributing fairly the material goods produced by human labor; (c) that capitalism contains the seeds of its own destruction and must, in view of the inability of the capital-owning class to adjust itself to economic change, result eventually and inescapably in a revolutionary transfer of power to the working class; and (d) that imperialism, the final phase of capitalism, leads directly to war and revolution.

The rest may be outlined in Lenin's own words: "Unevenness of economic and political development is the inflexible law of capitalism. It follows from

---

* George F. Kennan, "The Sources of Soviet Conduct," *Foreign Affairs* 25 (July 1947), 566–82. Reprinted by permission of *Foreign Affairs*, July 1947. Copyright 1947 by the Council on Foreign Relations, Inc.

this that the victory of Socialism may come originally in a few capitalist countries or even in a single capitalist country. The victorious proletariat of that country, having expropriated the capitalists and having organized Socialist production at home, would rise against the remaining capitalist world, drawing to itself in the process the oppressed classes of other countries." It must be noted that there was no assumption that capitalism would perish without proletarian revolution. A final push was needed from a revolutionary proletariat movement in order to tip over the tottering structure. But it was regarded as inevitable that sooner or later that push be given. . . .

The circumstances of the immediate post-Revolution period—the existence in Russia of civil war and foreign intervention, together with the obvious fact that the Communists represented only a tiny minority of the Russian people—made the establishment of dictatorial power a necessity. . . .

Lenin, had he lived, might have proved a great enough man to reconcile these conflicting forces to the ultimate benefit of Russian society, though this is questionable. But be that as it may, Stalin, and those whom he led in the struggle for succession to Lenin's position of leadership, were not the men to tolerate rival political forces in the sphere of power which they coveted. Their sense of insecurity was too great. Their particular brand of fanaticism, unmodified by any of the Anglo-Saxon traditions of compromise, was too fierce and too jealous to envisage any permanent sharing of power. From the Russian-Asiatic world out of which they had emerged they carried with them a skepticism as to the possibilities of permanent and peaceful coexistence of rival forces. Easily persuaded of their own doctrinaire "rightness," they insisted on the submission or destruction of all competing power. . . .

Let it be stressed again that subjectively these men probably did not seek absolutism for its own sake. They doubtless believed—and found it easy to believe—that they alone knew what was good for society and that they would accomplish that good once their power was secure and unchallengeable. But in seeking that security of their own rule they were prepared to recognize no restrictions, either of God or man, on the character of their methods. And until such time as that security might be achieved, they placed far down on their scale of operational priorities the comforts and happiness of the peoples entrusted to their care.

Now the outstanding circumstance concerning the Soviet regime is that down to the present day this process of political consolidation has never been completed and the men in the Kremlin have continued to be predominantly absorbed with the struggle to secure and make absolute the power which they seized in November 1917. They have endeavored to secure it primarily against forces at home, within Soviet society itself. But they have also endeavored to secure it against the outside world. For ideology, as we have seen, taught them that the outside world was hostile and that it was their duty eventually to overthrow the political forces beyond their borders. . . .

Now it lies in the nature of the mental world of the Soviet leaders, as well as in the character of their ideology, that no opposition to them can be officially recognized as having any merit or justification whatsoever. Such opposition can flow, in theory, only from the hostile and incorrigible forces of dying capitalism. As long as remnants of capitalism were officially recognized as existing in Russia, it was possible to place on them . . . part of the blame for the maintenance of a dictatorial form of society. But as these remnants were liquidated, little by little, this justification fell away. . . . And this fact created one of the most basic of the compulsions which came to act upon the Soviet regime: since capitalism no longer existed in Russia and since it could not be admitted that there could be serious or widespread opposition to the Kremlin springing spontaneously from the liberated masses under its authority, it became necessary to justify the retention of the dictatorship by stressing the menace of capitalism abroad.

This began at an early date. In 1924, Stalin specifically defended the retention of the "organs of suppression," meaning, among others, the army and the secret police, on the ground that "as long as there is a capitalist encirclement there will be danger of intervention with all the consequences that flow from that danger." In accordance with that theory, and from that time on, all internal opposition forces in Russia have consistently been portrayed as the agents of foreign forces of reaction antagonistic to Soviet power.

By the same token, tremendous emphasis has been placed on the original Communist thesis of a basic antagonism between the capitalist and Socialist worlds. It is clear, from many indications, that this emphasis is not founded in reality. The real facts concerning it have been confused by the existence abroad of genuine resentment provoked by Soviet philosophy and tactics and occasionally by the existence of great centers of military power, notably the Nazi regime in Germany and the Japanese government of the late 1930s, which did indeed have aggressive designs against the Soviet Union. But there is ample evidence that the stress laid in Moscow on the menace confronting Soviet society from the world outside its borders is founded not in the realities of foreign antagonism but in the necessity of explaining away the maintenance of dictatorial authority at home. . . .

II. So much for the historical background. What does it spell in terms of the political personality of Soviet power as we know it today?

Of the original ideology, nothing has been officially junked. Belief is maintained in the basic badness of capitalism, in the inevitability of its destruction, in the obligation of the proletariat to assist in that destruction and to take power into its own hands. But stress has come to be laid primarily on those concepts which relate most specifically to the Soviet regime itself: to its position as the sole truly Socialist regime in a dark and misguided world, and to the relationship of power within it.

The first of these concepts is that of the innate antagonism between capitalism and Socialism. We have seen how deeply that concept has become imbedded in foundations of Soviet power. It has profound implications for Russia's conduct as a member of international society. It means that there can never be on Moscow's side any sincere assumption of a community of aims between the Soviet Union and powers which are regarded as capitalist. It must invariably be assumed in Moscow that the aims of the capitalist world are antagonistic to the Soviet regime and, therefore, to the interests of the peoples it controls. If the Soviet government occasionally sets its signature to documents which would indicate the contrary, this is to be regarded as a tactical maneuver permissible in dealing with the enemy (who is without honor) and should be taken in the spirit of *caveat emptor*. Basically, the antagonism remains. . . . And from it flow many of the phenomena which we find disturbing in the Kremlin's conduct of foreign policy: the secretiveness, the lack of frankness, the duplicity, the war suspiciousness, and the basic unfriendliness of purpose. These phenomena are there to stay, for the foreseeable future. There can be variations of degree and of emphasis. When there is something the Russians want from us, one or the other of these features of their policy may be thrust temporarily into the background; and when that happens there will always be Americans who will leap forward with gleeful announcements that "the Russians have changed," and some will even try to take credit for having brought about those "changes." But we should not be misled by tactical maneuvers. These characteristics of Soviet policy . . . are basic to the internal nature of Soviet power, and will be with us, whether in the foreground or the background, until the internal nature of Soviet power is changed.

This means that we are going to continue for a long time to find the Russians difficult to deal with. It does not mean that they should be considered as embarked upon a do-or-die program to overthrow our society by a given date. The theory of the inevitability of the eventual fall of capitalism has the fortunate connotation that there is no hurry about it. The forces of progress can take their time in preparing the final *coup de grace*. Meanwhile, what is vital is that the "Socialist fatherland"—that oasis of power which has been already won for Socialism in the person of the Soviet Union—should be cherished and defended by all good Communists at home and abroad, its fortunes promoted, its enemies badgered and confronted. The promotion of premature, "adventuristic" revolutionary projects abroad which might embarrass Soviet power in any way would be an inexcusable, even a counterrevolutionary act. The cause of Socialism is the support and promotion of Soviet power, as defined in Moscow.

This brings us to the second of the concepts important to contemporary Soviet outlook. That is the infallibility of the Kremlin. The Soviet concept of power, which permits no focal points of organization outside the Party itself, requires that the Party leadership remain in theory the sole repository of truth. For if truth were to be found elsewhere, there would be justification for its expression in organized activity. But it is precisely that which the Kremlin cannot and will not permit.

The leadership of the Communist Party is therefore always right, and has been always right ever since in 1929 Stalin formalized his personal power by announcing that decisions of the Politburo were being taken unanimously.

On the principle of infallibility there rests the iron discipline of the Communist Party. In fact, the two concepts are mutually self-supporting. Perfect discipline requires recognition of infallibility. Infallibility requires the observance of discipline. And the two together go far to determine the behaviorism of the entire Soviet apparatus of power. But their effect cannot be understood unless a third factor be taken into account: namely, the fact that the leadership is at liberty to put forward for tactical purposes any particular thesis which it finds useful to the cause at any particular moment and to require the faithful and unquestioning acceptance of that thesis by the members of the movement as a whole. This means that truth is not a constant but is actually created, for all intents and purposes, by the Soviet leaders themselves. It may vary from week to week, from month to month. It is nothing absolute and immutable—nothing which flows from objective reality. It is only the most recent manifestation of the wisdom of those in whom the ultimate wisdom is supposed to reside, because they represent the logic of history. The accumulative effect of these factors is to give to the whole subordinate apparatus of Soviet power an unshakable stubbornness and steadfastness in its orientation. This orientation can be changed at will by the Kremlin but by no other power. Once a given party line has been laid down on a given issue of current policy, the whole Soviet governmental machine, including the mechanism of diplomacy, moves inexorably along the prescribed path, like a persistent toy automobile wound up and headed in a given direction, stopping only when it meets some unanswerable force. The individuals who are the components of this machine are unamenable to argument or reason which comes to them from outside sources. Their whole training has taught them to mistrust and discount the glib persuasiveness of the outside world. . . .

But we have seen that the Kremlin is under no ideological compulsion to accomplish its purposes in a hurry. Like the Church, it is dealing in ideological concepts which are of long-term validity, and it can afford to be patient. . . . Again, these precepts are fortified by the lessons of Russian history: of centuries of obscure battles between nomadic forces over the stretches of a vast unfortified plain. Here caution, circumspection, flexibility and deception are the valuable qualities. . . . Thus the Kremlin has no compunction about retreating in the face of superior force. And being under the compulsion of no timetable, it does not get panicky under the necessity for such retreat. Its political action is a fluid stream which moves constantly, wherever it is permitted to move, toward a given goal. Its main concern is to make sure that it has filled every nook and cranny available to it in the basin of world power. But if it finds unassailable barriers in its path, it accepts these philosophically and accommodates itself to them. The main thing is that there should always be pressure, increasing constant pressure, toward the desired goal. There is no trace of any feeling in Soviet psychology that that goal must be reached at any given time.

These considerations make Soviet diplomacy at once easier and more difficult to deal with than the diplomacy of individual aggressive leaders like Napoleon and Hitler. On the one hand it is more sensitive to contrary force, more ready to yield on individual sectors of the diplomatic front when that force is felt to be too strong, and thus more rational in the logic and rhetoric of power. On the other hand it cannot be easily defeated or discouraged by a single victory on the part of its opponents. And the patient persistence by which it is animated means that it can be effectively countered not by sporadic acts which represent the momentary whims of democratic opinion but only by intelligent long-range policies on the part of Russia's adversaries—policies no less steady in their purpose, and no less variegated and resourceful in their application, than those of the Soviet Union itself.

In these circumstances it is clear that the main element of any United States' policy toward the Soviet Union must be that of a long-term, patient but firm and vigilant containment of Russian expansive tendencies. It is important to note, however, that such a policy has nothing to do with outward histrionics: with threats or blustering or superfluous gestures of outward "toughness." While the Kremlin is basically flexible in its reaction to political realities, it is by no means unamenable to considerations of prestige. Like almost any other government, it can be placed by tactless and threatening gestures in a position where it cannot afford to yield even though this might be dictated by its sense of realism. The Russian leaders are keen judges of human psychology, and as such they are highly conscious that loss of temper and of self-control is never a source of strength in political affairs. They are quick to exploit such evidences of weakness. For these reasons, it is a *sine qua non* of successful dealing with Russia that the foreign government in question should remain at all times cool and collected and that its demands on Russian policy should be put forward in such a manner as to leave the way open for a compliance not too detrimental to Russian prestige.

III. In the light of the above, it will be clearly seen that the Soviet pressure against the free institutions of the Western world is something that can be contained by the adroit and vigilant application of counter-force at a series of constantly shifting geographical and political points, corresponding to the shifts and maneuvers of Soviet policy, but which cannot be charmed or talked out of existence. The Russians look forward to a duel of infinite duration, and they see that already they have scored great successes. It must be borne in mind that there was a time when the Communist Party represented far more of a minority in the sphere of Russian national life than Soviet power today represents in the world community.

But if ideology convinces the rulers of Russia that truth is on their side and that they can afford to wait, those of us on whom that ideology has no claim are free to examine objectively the validity of that premise. The Soviet thesis not only implies complete lack of control by the west over its own economic destiny, it likewise assumes Russian unity, discipline and patience over an indefinite period. Let us . . . suppose that the western world finds the strength and resourcefulness to contain Soviet power over a period of ten to fifteen years. What does that spell for Russia itself?

The Soviet leaders, taking advantage of the contributions of modern technique to the arts of despotism, have solved the question of obedience within the confines of their power. Few challenge their authority; and even those who do are unable to make that challenge valid against the organs of suppression of the state. The Kremlin also proved able to accomplish its purpose of building up in Russia, regardless of the interests of the inhabitants, an industrial foundation of heavy metallurgy, which is . . . continuing to grow and is approaching those of the other major industrial countries. All of this, however, both the maintenance of internal political security and the building of heavy industry, has been carried out at a terrible cost of human life and in human hopes and energies. It has necessitated the use of forced labor on a scale unprecedented in modern times under conditions of peace. It has involved the neglect or abuse of other phases of Soviet economic life, particularly agriculture, consumers' goods production, housing and transportation.

To all that, the war has added its tremendous toll of destruction, death and human exhaustion. In consequence of this, we have in Russia today a population which is physically and spiritually tired. The mass of the people are disillusioned, skeptical, and no longer as accessible as they once were to the magical attraction which Soviet power still radiates to its followers abroad. The avidity with which people seized upon the slight respite accorded to the Church for tactical reasons during the war was eloquent testimony to the fact that their capacity for faith and devotion found little expression in the purposes of the regime.

In these circumstances, there are limits to the physical and nervous strength of the people themselves. These limits are absolute ones, and are binding even for the cruelest dictatorship, because beyond them people cannot be driven. The forced labor camps and the other agencies of constraint provide temporary means of compelling people to work longer hours than their own volition or mere economic pressure would dictate; but if people survive them at all they become old before their time and must be considered as human casualties to the demands of dictatorship. In either case their best powers are no longer available to society and can no longer be enlisted in the service of the state. . . .

In addition to this . . . Soviet economic development . . . has been precariously spotty and uneven. Russian Communists who speak of the "uneven development of capitalism" should blush at the contemplation of their own national economy. Here is a nation striving to become in a short period one of the great industrial nations of the world while it still has no highway network worthy of the name and only a relatively primitive network of railways. Much has been done to increase efficiency of labor and to teach primitive peasants something about the operation of machines. But maintenance is still a crying deficiency of all Soviet economy. Construction is hasty and poor in quality. . . . And in vast sectors of economic life it has not yet been possible to instill into labor anything like that general culture of production and technical self-respect which characterizes the skilled worker of the west.

It is difficult to see how these deficiencies can be corrected at an early date by a tired and dispirited population working largely under the shadow of fear and compulsion. And as long as they are not overcome, Russia will remain economically a vulnerable, and in a certain sense an impotent, nation, capable of exporting its enthusiasm and radiating the strange charm of its primitive political vitality but unable to back up those articles of export by the real evidences of material power and prosperity.

Meanwhile, a great uncertainty hangs over the political life of the Soviet Union. That is the uncertainty involved in the transfer of power from one individual or group of individuals to others.

This is, of course, outstandingly the problem of the personal position of Stalin. We must remember that his succession to Lenin's pinnacle of preeminence in the Communist movement was the only such transfer of individual authority which the Soviet Union has experienced. That transfer took 12 years to consolidate. It cost the lives of millions of people and shook the state to its foundations. The attendant tremors were felt all through the international revolutionary movement, to the disadvantage of the Kremlin itself.

It is always possible that another transfer of pre-eminent power may take place quietly and inconspicuously, with no repercussions anywhere. But again, it is possible that the questions involved may unleash, to use some of Lenin's words, one of those "incredibly swift transitions" from "delicate deceit" to "wild violence" which characterize Russian history, and may shake Soviet power to its foundations. . . .

Thus the future of Soviet power may not be by any means as secure as Russian capacity for self-delusion would make it appear to the men in the Kremlin. That they can keep power themselves, they have demonstrated. That they can quietly and easily turn it over to others remains to be proved. Meanwhile, the hardships of their rule and vicissitudes of international life have taken a heavy toll of the strength and hopes of the great people on whom their power rests. It is curious to note that the ideological power of Soviet authority is strongest today in areas beyond the frontiers of Russia, beyond the reach of its police power. . . . And who can say with assurance that the strong light still cast by the Kremlin on the dissatisfied peoples of the western world is not the powerful afterglow of a constellation which is in actuality on the wane? This cannot be proved. And it cannot be disproved. But the possibility remains . . . that Soviet power, like the capitalist world of its conception, bears within it the seeds of its own decay, and that the sprouting of these seeds is well advanced.

IV. It is clear that the United States cannot expect in the foreseeable future to enjoy political intimacy with the Soviet regime. It must continue to regard the Soviet Union as a rival, not a partner, in the political arena. It must continue to expect that Soviet policies will reflect no abstract love of peace and stability, no real faith in the possibility of a permanent happy coexistence of the Socialist and capitalist worlds, but rather a cautious, persistent pressure toward the disruption and weakening of all rival influence and rival power.

Balanced against this are the facts that Russia, as opposed to the Western world in general, is still by far the weaker party, that Soviet policy is highly flexible, and that Soviet society may well contain deficiencies which will eventually weaken its own total potential. This would of itself warrant the United States entering with reasonable confidence upon a policy of firm containment, designed to confront the Russians with unalterable counter-force at every point where they show signs of encroaching upon the interests of a peaceful and stable world.

But in actuality the possibilities for American power are by no means limited to holding the line and hoping for the best. It is entirely possible for the United States to influence by its actions the internal developments, both within Russia and throughout the international Communist movement, by which Russian policy is largely determined. This is not only a question of the modest measure of informational activity which this government can conduct in the Soviet Union and elsewhere. . . . It is rather a question of the degree to which the United States can create among the peoples of the world generally the impression of a country which knows what it wants, which is coping successfully with the problems of its internal life and with the responsibilities of a world power, and which has a spiritual vitality capable of holding its own among the major ideological currents of the time. To the extent that such an impression can be created and maintained, the aims of Russian Communism must appear sterile and quixotic, the hopes and enthusiasm of Moscow's supporters must wane, and added strain must be imposed on the Kremlin's foreign policies. For the palsied decrepitude of the capitalist world is the keystone of Communist philosophy. Even the failure of the United States to experience the early economic depression which the ravens of Red Square have been predicting . . . since hostilities ceased would have deep and important repercussions throughout the Communist world.

By the same token, exhibitions of indecision, disunity and internal disintegration within this country have an exhilarating effect on the whole Communist movement. At each evidence of these tendencies, a thrill of hope and excitement goes through the Communist world; . . . new groups of foreign supporters climb onto what they can only view as the bandwagon of international politics; and Russian pressure increases all along the line in international affairs.

It would be an exaggeration to say that American behavior unassisted and alone could exercise a power of life and death over the Communist movement and bring about the early fall of Soviet power in Russia. But the United States has it in its power to increase enormously the strains under which Soviet policy must operate, to force upon the Kremlin a far greater degree of moderation and circumspection than it has had to observe in recent years, and in this way to promote tendencies which must eventually find their outlet in either the breakup or the gradual mellowing of Soviet power. For no mystical, Messianic movement—and particularly not that of the Kremlin—can face frustration indefinitely without eventually adjusting itself in one way or another to the logic of that state of affairs.

Thus the decision will really fall in large measure in this country itself. The issue of Soviet-American relations is in essence a test of the over-all worth of the United States as a nation among nations. To avoid destruction the United States need only measure up to its own best traditions and prove itself worthy of preservation as a great nation.

Surely there was never a fairer test of national quality than this. In the light of these circumstances, the thoughtful observer of Russian-American relations will find no cause for complaint in the Kremlin's challenge to American society. He will rather experience a certain gratitude to a Providence which, by providing the American people with this implacable challenge, has made their entire security as a nation dependent on their pulling themselves together and accepting the responsibilities of moral and political leadership that history plainly intended them to bear.

Discussion Questions

1. What did Kennan consider to be the main principles of Communist ideology?
2. What did Kennan see as the main reasons for Soviet hostility toward the West?
3. Why did Kennan believe that Soviet leaders could never be fully trusted by the West?
4. What did Kennan think the West should do to counter Soviet expansionism? Why did he caution Western leaders to avoid gestures of outward "toughness" toward the USSR?
5. How did Kennan think that US policy could contribute to the breakup or mellowing of Soviet power?
6. Why did Kennan's ideas have such an important influence on US policymakers?

11

The Rio Treaty, September 1947

IN 1823 US PRESIDENT JAMES MONROE proclaimed, in what later came to be called the Monroe Doctrine, that any efforts by European powers to conquer or reconquer any independent state in the Western Hemisphere would be viewed by the United States as an unfriendly act. More than eight decades later, in 1904, US president Theodore Roosevelt added the Roosevelt Corollary to the Monroe Doctrine, declaring that the United States reserved the right to intervene in Latin American nations guilty of "flagrant and chronic wrongdoing" to prevent European intervention to collect debts owed by those nations to European banks. The Roosevelt Corollary became a tool for

Roosevelt's "Big Stick" diplomacy. It led to repeated US interventions in Latin America and was widely resented there.

During the 1930s, Washington became increasingly concerned with the possibility that the Axis powers, Germany and Italy, might attempt to take advantage of the presence in nations like Argentina, Brazil, and Chile of significant populations of German and Italian descent to build close military relationships with those countries. Should the United States ever become involved in war against the Axis, such relationships could pose strategic threats to the Panama Canal and to US shipping throughout the hemisphere. Once war actually broke out in 1941, the United States obtained commitments of support from every Latin American nation except Uruguay and Argentina, which remained neutral in World War II. In February and March 1945, the nations of the hemisphere agreed in the Act of Chapultepec to assist one another in case of aggression by foreign powers. After the 1947 proclamation of the Truman Doctrine (Document 8), the United States acted to formalize the Act of Chapultepec (which had technically lapsed with the end of the war), aim it at Communist aggression rather than the now-defeated Axis powers, and link its commitments of mutual assistance to the Charter of the United Nations. The result was the Inter-American Treaty of Reciprocal Assistance, signed in Rio de Janeiro in 1947 and commonly referred to as the Rio Treaty.

THE INTER-AMERICAN TREATY OF RECIPROCAL ASSISTANCE (RIO TREATY), 2 SEPTEMBER 1947

In the name of their Peoples, the Governments represented at the Inter-American Conference for the Maintenance of Continental Peace and Security, desirous of consolidating and strengthening their relations of friendship and good neighborliness, and

Considering:

That Resolution VIII of the Inter-American Conference on Problems of War and Peace, which met in Mexico City, recommended the conclusion of a treaty to prevent and repel threats and acts of aggression against any of the countries of America;

That the High Contracting Parties reiterate their will to remain united in an inter-American system consistent with the purposes and principles of the United Nations, and reaffirm the existence of the agreement which they have concluded concerning those matters relating to the maintenance of international peace and security which are appropriate for regional action;

That the High Contracting Parties reaffirm their adherence to the principles of inter-American solidarity and cooperation, and especially to those set forth in the preamble and declarations of the Act of Chapultepec, all of which should be understood to be accepted as standards of their mutual relations and as the juridical basis of the Inter-American System;

That the American States propose, in order to improve the procedures for the pacific settlement of their controversies, to conclude the treaty concerning the "Inter-American Peace System" envisaged in Resolutions IX and XXXIX of the Inter-American Conference on Problems of War and Peace;

That the obligation of mutual assistance and common defense of the American Republics is essentially related to their democratic ideals and to their will to cooperate permanently in the fulfillment of the principles and purposes of a policy of peace;

That the American regional community affirms as a manifest truth that juridical organization is a necessary prerequisite of security and peace, and that peace is founded on justice and moral order and, consequently, on the international recognition and protection of human rights and freedoms, on the indispensable well-being of the people, and on the effectiveness of democracy for the international realization of justice and security;

Have resolved, in conformity with the objectives stated above, to conclude the following Treaty, in order to assure peace, through adequate means, to provide for effective reciprocal assistance to meet armed attacks against any American State, and in order to deal with threats of aggression against any of them:

Article 1
The High Contracting Parties formally condemn war and undertake in their international relations not to resort to the threat or the use of force in any manner inconsistent with the provisions of the Charter of the United Nations or of this Treaty.

Article 2
As a consequence of the principle set forth in the preceding Article, the High Contracting Parties undertake to submit every controversy which may arise between them to methods of peaceful settlement and to endeavor to settle any such controversy among themselves by means of the procedures in force in the Inter-American System before referring it to the General Assembly or the Security Council of the United Nations.

Article 3
1. The High Contracting Parties agree that an armed attack by any State against an American State shall be considered as an attack against all the American States and, consequently, each one of the said Contract-

ing Parties undertakes to assist in meeting the attack in the exercise of the inherent right of individual or collective self-defense recognized by Article 51 of the Charter of the United Nations.

2. On the request of the State or States directly attacked and until the decision of the Organ of Consultation of the Inter-American System, each one of the Contracting Parties may determine the immediate measures which it may individually take in fulfillment of the obligation contained in the preceding paragraph and in accordance with the principle of continental solidarity. The Organ of Consultation shall meet without delay for the purpose of examining those measures and agreeing upon the measures of a collective character that should be taken.

3. The provisions of this Article shall be applied in case of any armed attack which takes place within the region described in Article 4 or within the territory of an American State. When the attack takes place outside of the said areas, the provisions of Article 6 shall be applied.

4. Measures of self-defense provided for under this Article may be taken until the Security Council of the United Nations has taken the measures necessary to maintain international peace and security. . . .

Article 5

The High Contracting Parties shall immediately send to the Security Council of the United Nations, in conformity with Articles 51 and 54 of the Charter of the United Nations, complete information concerning the activities undertaken or in contemplation in the exercise of the right of self-defense or for the purpose of maintaining inter-American peace and security.

Article 6

If the inviolability or the integrity of the territory or the sovereignty or political independence of any American State should be affected by an aggression which is not an armed attack or by an extra-continental or intra-continental conflict, or by any other fact or situation might endanger the peace of America, the Organ of Consultation shall meet immediately in order to agree on the measures which must be taken in case of aggression to assist the victim of the aggression or, in any case, the measures which should be taken for the common defense and for the maintenance of the peace and security of the Continent.

Article 7

In the case of a conflict between two or more American States, without prejudice to the right of self-defense in conformity with Article 51 of the Charter of the United Nations, the High Contracting Parties, meeting in consultation shall call upon the contending States to suspend hostilities and restore mat-ters to the *status quo ante bellum*, and shall take in addition all other neces-sary measures to reestablish or maintain inter-American peace and security and for the solution of the conflict by peaceful means. The rejection of the pacifying action will be considered in the determination of the aggressor and in the application of the measures which the consultative meeting may agree upon.

Article 8

For the purposes of this Treaty, the measures on which the Organ of Con-sultation may agree will comprise one or more of the following: recall of chiefs of diplomatic missions; breaking of diplomatic relations; breaking of consular relations; partial or complete interruption of economic relations or of rail, sea, air, postal, telegraphic, telephonic, and radiotelephonic or radio-telegraphic communications; and use of armed force.

Article 9

In addition to other acts which the Organ of Consultation may characterize as aggression, the following shall be considered as such:

a. Unprovoked armed attack by a State against the territory, the people, or the land, sea or air forces of another State;
b. Invasion, by the armed forces of a State, of the territory of an American State, through the trespassing of boundaries demarcated in accordance with a treaty, judicial decision, or arbitral award, or, in the absence of frontiers thus demarcated, invasion affecting a region which is under the effective jurisdiction of another State. . . .

Article 20

Decisions which require the application of the measures specified in Article 8 shall be binding upon all the Signatory States which have ratified this Treaty, with the sole exception that no State shall be required to use armed force without its consent. . . .

Article 26

The principles and fundamental provisions of this Treaty shall be incorpo-rated in the Organic Pact of the Inter-American System.

In witness whereof, the undersigned Plenipotentiaries, having deposited their full powers found to be in due and proper form, sign this Treaty on behalf of their respective Governments, on the dates appearing opposite their signatures.

Done in the city of Rio de Janeiro, in four texts respectively in the English, French, Portuguese and Spanish languages, on the second of September nineteen hundred forty-seven.

***

Discussion Questions

1. How did the Rio Treaty explicitly reaffirm the Act of Chapultepec?
2. In what ways did the Rio Treaty link its commitments of mutual assistance to the Charter of the United Nations?
3. The Rio Treaty was directed against the possibility of Communist aggression. Can you tell from its text that this was its intention? If so, how?
4. What would happen in the event of one hemispheric state attacking another?
5. In what way was the principle of national sovereignty reinforced by the Rio Treaty?

***

12

Zhdanov and the Cominform on the Imperialist and Anti-Imperialist Camps, 1947

***

BY FALL OF 1947, THE DIVISION of Europe into two opposing camps was virtually complete. In Eastern Europe, anxious to create a buffer zone between themselves and Germany—and to gain access to materials needed to rebuild the USSR—the Soviets had installed "friendly" governments dominated by Communists. In Western Europe, anxious to impede the spread of communism and secure their own foreign markets, the Americans had initiated the Marshall Plan, designed to foster economic recovery and stability.

In part because of its emphasis on rebuilding the economy of Germany, which had recently devastated the USSR, the Marshall Plan was seen in Moscow as a serious threat. To respond to this, and to encourage closer coordination among the European Communist parties, the Soviets called representatives of these parties to a special meeting in Poland in September 1947. There, Andrei Zhdanov, the chief Soviet spokesperson, delivered a report in which he described the whole world as divided into two main camps. One was an imperialist camp, led by the United States and including the colony-owning countries of Western Europe; the other was an anti-imperialist camp, led by the USSR and including not only other Communist countries but also countries emerging from colonial rule and fighters for national liberation in the colonies. He further called for the formation of a new international organization, designed to advance the interests of communism, to be known as the Communist Information Bureau, or Cominform.

The new organization, which would last until 1956, was in some ways a throwback to the old Communist International, or Comintern, a worldwide association of Communist parties, which had been disbanded during World War II. Like the Comintern, the Cominform could be used not only to secure socialist solidarity but also to prod Communists elsewhere to follow Moscow's lead. Among other things, the Cominform would engineer a wave of strikes in France and Italy in the fall of 1947, encourage Communist-led anticolonial uprisings in Southeast Asia, and make a futile bid to force the wayward Yugoslav Communists back into line the next spring.

A. ZHDANOV'S REPORT ON THE INTERNATIONAL SITUATION, 22 SEPTEMBER 1947

The fundamental changes caused by the war . . . [have] entirely changed the political landscape of the world. A new alignment of political forces has arisen. The more the war recedes into the past, the more distinct becomes two major trends in postwar international policy, corresponding to the division of the political forces operating on the international arena into two major camps: the imperialist and anti-democratic camp, on the one hand, and the anti-imperialist and democratic camp, on the other.

The principal driving force of the imperialist camp is the U.S.A. Allied with it are Great Britain and France. . . . The imperialist camp is also supported by colony-owning countries, such as Belgium and Holland, by countries with reactionary anti-democratic regimes, such as Turkey and Greece, and by countries politically and economically dependent upon the United States. . . . The cardinal purpose of the imperialist camp is to strengthen imperialism, to hatch a new imperialist war, to combat socialism and democracy, and to support reactionary and anti-democratic pro-fascist regimes and movements everywhere. In the pursuit of these ends the imperialist camp is prepared to rely on reactionary and anti-democratic forces in all countries, and to support its former adversaries in the war against its wartime allies.

The anti-fascist forces comprise the second camp. This camp is based on the U.S.S.R. and the new democracies. It also includes countries that have broken with imperialism and have firmly set foot on the path of democratic development, such as Rumania, Hungary and Finland. Indonesia and Vietnam are associated with it; it has the sympathy of India, Egypt and Syria. The anti-imperialist camp is backed by the labor and democratic movement and by the fraternal Communist parties in all countries, by the fighters for national liberation in the colonies and dependencies, by all progressive and democratic forces in every country. . . .

The Soviet Union is a staunch champion of liberty and independence of all nations, and a foe of national and racial oppression and colonial exploitation in any shape or form. The change in the general alignment of forces between the capitalist world and the socialist world brought about by the war has still further enhanced the significance of the foreign policy of the Soviet state and enlarged the scope of its activity on the international arena. . . .

Soviet foreign policy proceeds from the fact of the coexistence for a long period of the two systems—capitalism and socialism. From this it follows that cooperation between the U.S.S.R. and countries with other systems is possible, provided that the principle of reciprocity is observed and that obligations once assumed are honored. Everyone knows that the U.S.S.R. has always honored the obligations it has assumed. The Soviet Union has demonstrated its will and desire for cooperation.

B. MANIFESTO PROCLAIMING
THE COMINFORM, 5 OCTOBER 1947

In the international situation brought about by the Second World War and in the period that followed fundamental changes took place. The characteristic aspect of these changes is a new balance of political forces interplaying in the world arena, a shift in the relationship between states which were the victors in the Second World War, and their reevaluation.

As long as the war lasted the Allied states fighting against Germany and Japan marched in step and were one. Nevertheless, in the Allies' camp already during the war there existed differences regarding the aims of the war as well as the objectives of the post-war and world organization. The Soviet Union and the democratic countries believed that the main objective of the war was the rebuilding and strengthening of democracy in Europe, the liquidation of fascism and the prevention of a possible aggression on behalf of Germany, and that its further aim was an achievement of an all-around and lasting co-operation between the nations of Europe.

The United States of America and with them England placed as their war aim a different goal—the elimination of competition on the world market (Germany and Japan) and the consolidation of their dominant position. This difference in the definition of war aims and post-war objectives has begun to deepen in the post-war period.

Two opposite political lines have crystallized. On one extreme the USSR and the democratic countries aim at whittling down imperialism and the strengthening of democracy. On the other hand the United States of America and England aim at the strengthening of imperialism and choking democracy. . . .

In this way there arose two camps—the camp of imperialism and anti-democratic forces, whose chief aim is an establishment of a worldwide American imperialists' hegemony and the crushing of democracy; and an anti-imperialist democratic camp whose chief aim is the elimination of imperialism, the strengthening of democracy, and the liquidation of the remnants of fascism. . . .

In these conditions the anti-imperialist democratic camp has to close its ranks and draw up and agree on a common platform to work out its tactics against the chief forces of the imperialist camp, against American imperialism, against its English and French allies, against the Right-Wing Socialists above all in England and France. To frustrate those imperialistic plans of aggression we need the efforts of all democratic and anti-imperialist forces in Europe. . . .

C. RESOLUTION OF THE CONFERENCE OF COMMUNIST PARTIES ON ESTABLISHING THE COMINFORM, 5 OCTOBER 1947

The Conference states that the absence of connections between Communist parties who have taken part in this conference is in the present situation a serious shortcoming. Experience has shown that such division between Communist parties is incorrect and harmful. The requirement for an exchange of experience and voluntary coordination of actions of the separate parties has become particularly necessary now in conditions of the complicated post-war international situation and when the disunity of Communist parties may lead to damage for the working class. Because of this, members of the conference agreed upon the following:

First, to set up an Information Bureau of representatives of the Communist Party of Yugoslavia, the Bulgarian Workers Party (of Communists), the Communist Party of Rumania, the Hungarian Communist Party, the Polish Workers Party, the Communist Party of the Soviet Union (Bolshevik), the Communist Party of France, the Communist Party of Czechoslovakia, and the Communist Party of Italy.

Second, the task given to the Information Bureau is to organize and exchange experience and, in case of necessity, coordinate the activity of Communist parties on foundations of mutual agreement.

Third, the Information Bureau will have in it representatives of the Central Committees—two from each Central Committee. Delegations of the Central Committee must be appointed and replaced by the Central Committees.

Fourth, the Information Bureau is to have a printed organ—a fortnightly and later on weekly. The organ is to be published in French and Russian and, if possible, in other languages.

Fifth, the Information Bureau is to be in Belgrade.

Discussion Questions

1. How and why did Zhdanov divide the world into two main camps? How would his division support the Soviet worldview and Soviet foreign policy? How might it also aid the spread of communism?
2. Why did Zhdanov and the other Communist leaders refer to their own camp as "democratic" and the Western camp as "imperialist"? What did they claim were the main goals of the Western "imperialist" powers?
3. How did the authors of this manifesto and resolution justify the formation of the Cominform?
4. What reasons did they give for the breakdown of the wartime alliance and division of Europe into two hostile camps?
5. How did they think the Cominform could help Communists respond to the West?

13

The Communist Coup in Czechoslovakia, February 1948

O F ALL THE NATIONS OF EASTERN EUROPE, Czechoslovakia had the strongest industrial base, the most successful experience with democracy, and, thanks to its abandonment by England and France in the face of Nazi demands in 1938, the biggest beef against the West. There was general goodwill toward the USSR and much popular support for the Czechoslovak Communists. Stalin had reason to expect that communism might triumph there in free elections, and the Czechs had reason to expect that they could maintain their democratic traditions and still be friendly to Moscow.

For several years after World War II, this seemed to be a real possibility. As the rest of Eastern Europe fell under Communist control, Czechoslovakia remained democratic. President Edvard Benes, who had signed an alliance with Stalin in 1943, worked to preserve his nation as a bridge between East and West. Free elections in 1946 gave the Communists a plurality in the National Assembly, but Klement Gottwald, the new Communist premier, led a coalition government called the National Front, which included non-Communist parties and maintained close ties with the West.

All this began to change with the coming of the Marshall Plan in 1947. The Czechoslovak leaders, anxious to improve their economy, unanimously agreed to accept American aid. But Stalin, fearful that this might promote US economic hegemony in Eastern Europe, forced them to withdraw their application and instead join a Soviet-sponsored "Molotov Plan" for aid to Communist countries.

The situation quickly deteriorated. The Czechoslovak Communists began to browbeat and tyrannize the other members of the National Front, who responded in February 1948 by resigning their positions, hoping the government would fall. This was a disastrous miscalculation. Aided by their socialist allies, the Communists remained in office and carried out a coup. As the following correspondence makes clear, President Benes strove to maintain a modicum of democracy and independence, but the Communists refused to cooperate. As a result, Czechoslovakia became part of the Soviet Bloc, and Moscow consolidated its control over all of Eastern Europe.

A. LETTER FROM PRESIDENT BENES TO THE CZECHOSLOVAK COMMUNIST PARTY PRESIDIUM, 24 FEBRUARY 1948

You sent me a letter on February 21 in which you express your attitude on a solution of the crisis and ask me to agree with it. Allow me to formulate my own attitude.

I feel fully the great responsibility of this fateful hour on our national and state life. From the beginning of this crisis I have been thinking about the situation as it was forming itself, putting these affairs of ours in connection with world affairs.

I am trying to see clearly not only the present situation but also the causes that led to it and the results that a decision can have. I am aware of the powerful forces through which the situation is being formed.

In a calm, matter of fact, impassionate and objective judgment of the situation I feel, through the common will of various groups of our citizens which turn their attention to me, that the will is expressed to maintain the peace and order and discipline voluntarily accepted to achieve a progressive and really socialist life.

How to achieve this goal? You know my sincerely democratic creed. I cannot but stay faithful to that creed even at this moment because democracy, according to my belief, is the only reliable and durable basis for a decent and dignified human life.

I insist on parliamentary democracy and parliamentary government as it limits democracy. I state I know very well it is necessary to social and economic content. I built my political work on these principles and cannot—without betraying myself—act otherwise.

The present crisis of democracy here too cannot be overcome but through democratic and parliamentary means. I thus do not overlook your demands. I regard parties associated in the National Front as bearers of political responsibility. We all accepted the principle of the National Front and this proved successful up to the recent time when the crisis began.

This crisis, however, in my opinion, does not deny the principle in itself. I am convinced that on this principle, even in the future, the necessary cooperation of all can be achieved. All disputes can be solved for the benefit of the national and common state of the Czechs and the Slovaks.

I therefore have been in negotiation with five political parties. I have listened to their views and some of them also have been put in writing. These are grave matters and I cannot ignore them.

Therefore, I again have to appeal to all to find a peaceful solution and new successful cooperation through parliamentary means and through the National Front.

That much for the formal side. As far as the personal side is concerned, it is clear to me, as I have said already, that the Prime Minister will be the chairman of the strongest party element, Gottwald.

Finally, on the factual side of this matter it is clear to me that socialism is a way of life desired by an overwhelming part of our nation. At the same time I believe that with socialism a certain measure of freedom and unity is possible and that these are vital principles to all in our national life.

Our nation has struggled for freedom almost throughout its history. History also has shown us where discord can lead.

I beg of you therefore to relive these facts and make them the starting point for our negotiations. Let us all together begin negotiations again for further durable cooperation and let us not allow prolongation of the split of the nation into two quarreling parts.

I believe that a reasonable agreement is possible because it is indispensable.

B. REPLY BY THE CZECHOSLOVAK COMMUNIST PARTY PRESIDIUM TO THE LETTER OF PRESIDENT BENES, 25 FEBRUARY 1948

The Presidium of the Central Committee of the Communist Party acknowledges your letter dated February 24, and states that it cannot enter into negotiations with the present leadership of the National Socialist, People's, and Slovak Democratic Parties because this would not conform to the interests of the unity of the people nor with the interests of further peaceful development of the republic.

Recent events indisputably proved that these three parties no longer represent the interests of the working people of the cities and countryside, that their leaders have betrayed the fundamental ideas of the people's democracy and National Front . . . , and that they assumed the position of undermining the opposition.

This was shown again and again in the government, in the Constitutional National Assembly, in the press of these parties, and in actions that, with menacing levity, were organized by their central secretariats against the interests of the working people, against the security of the state, against the alliances of the republic, against state finance, against nationalized industry, against urgent agricultural reforms—in one word, against the whole constructive efforts of our people and against the very foundations, internal and external, of the security of the country.

These parties even got in touch with foreign circles hostile to our people's democratic order and our alliances, and in collaboration with these hostile foreign elements they attempted disruption of the present development of the republic.

This constantly increasing activity was crowned by an attempt to break up the government, an attempt that, as it was proved, should have been accompanied by actions aiming at a putsch.

Massive people's manifestations during the last few days clearly have shown that our working people denounce, with complete unity and with indignation, the policy of these parties and ask the creation of a government in which all honest progressive patriots devoted to the republic and the people are represented. . . .

In conformity with this powerfully expressed will of the people, the Presidium of the Central Committee of the Communist Party approved the proposals of Premier Klement Gottwald according to which the government will be filled in with prominent representatives of all parties and also big nationwide organizations.

We stress that a government filled in this way will present itself, with full agreement with the principles of parliamentary democracy, before the Constitutional National Assembly with its program and ask for its approval.

Being convinced that only such a highly constitutional and parliamentary process can guarantee the peaceful development of the republic, and at the same time that it corresponds to the ideas of a complete majority of the working people, the Presidium of the Central Committee hopes firmly after careful consideration that you will recognize the correctness of its conclusions and will agree with its proposals.

Discussion Questions

1. What reasons did President Benes advance for preserving democracy in Czechoslovakia?
2. Why did he think it was important to restore the National Front?
3. What concessions was he willing to make to the Communists?
4. What reasons did the Communists give for rejecting his pleas? What charges did they make against the non-Communist parties that resigned from the National Front?

14

The Treaty of Brussels, 1948

THE COMMUNIST TAKEOVER OF CZECHOSLOVAKIA in February 1948 helped expedite the creation of an anti-Soviet military alliance in Western Europe. On 17 March, five nations—Belgium, the Netherlands, Luxembourg, Britain, and France—met at Brussels to sign a treaty committing them to mutual consultation and cooperation in the event of aggression against any one of them. In the spirit of the Marshall Plan, the Treaty of Brussels pledged its signatories to close economic cooperation; it was designed to remain in force for fifty years.

Although the only potential enemy mentioned in the treaty was Germany, it was clear to everyone that the Soviet Union was the real target. The Marshall Plan had begun the economic reintegration of western Germany into Western Europe, and the Americans, British, and French were moving toward creation of a single currency for their three occupation zones in Germany. No one believed that a fragmented, occupied Germany posed any credible threat to the peace of Europe in 1948. The events of February 1948 in Prague, on the other hand, confirmed the Western conviction that Soviet objectives included the extension of Communist political and economic systems throughout the world. The Treaty of Brussels and the consultative council it created would serve as the embryo for the North Atlantic Treaty Organization (Document 17).

EXCERPTS FROM THE TREATY OF BRUSSELS, 17 MARCH 1948

Article I
Convinced of the close community of their interests and of the necessity of uniting in order to promote the economic recovery of Europe, the high contracting parties will so organize and coordinate their economic activities as to produce the best possible results, by the elimination of conflict in their economic policies, coordination of production and development of commercial exchanges. . . .

Article II

The high contracting parties will make every effort . . . to promote the attainment of a higher standard of living by their peoples. . . .

Article IV

If any of the high contracting parties should be the object of an armed attack in Europe, the other high contracting parties will, in accordance with the provisions of Article 51 of the Charter of the United Nations, afford the party so attacked all military and other aid and assistance in their power.

Article V

All measures taken as a result of the preceding article shall be immediately reported to the Security Council. They shall be terminated as soon as the Security Council has taken the measures necessary to maintain or restore international peace and security. . . .

Article VI

. . . None of the high contracting parties will conclude any alliance or participate in any coalition directed against any other of the high contracting parties.

Article VII

For the purpose of consulting together on all questions dealt with in the present treaty, the high contracting parties will create a consultative council which shall be so organized as to be able to exercise its functions continuously. The Council shall meet at such times as it shall deem fit. At the request of any of the high contracting parties, the Council shall be immediately convened in order to permit the high contracting parties to consult with regard to any situation which may constitute a threat to peace, in whatever area this threat should arise, with regard to the attitude to be adopted and the steps to be taken in the case of a renewal by Germany of an aggressive policy, or with regard to any situation constituting a danger to economic stability. . . .

Discussion Questions

1. Why did the Brussels treaty mention Germany but not the USSR? How can you tell that the USSR was the treaty's real target?
2. Why did the treaty assure its readers that any military measures taken by its signatories would immediately terminate once the UN Security Council took action?

3. Why did the treaty consider economic cooperation as important as military cooperation?
4. What was the purpose of the consultative council created by the treaty?
5. Do you see any similarities between the security guarantees contained in the Treaty of Brussels and those embodied in the Rio Treaty (Document 11)?

15

The Expulsion of Tito from the Communist Bloc, 1948

IN SPRING 1948, NOT LONG AFTER the Communist coup in Czechoslovakia, a crisis arose between the USSR and Communist Yugoslavia. Relations between the two socialist states had been strained for some time. As a national hero who led his country's wartime anti-Nazi resistance, Marshal Tito, the postwar Yugoslav leader, enjoyed broad popular support. Unlike other East European Communists, he did not owe his position to Moscow and thus felt free to pursue his own course. Determined to strengthen his nation's industry, he refused to let Stalin exploit its natural resources to rebuild the USSR. Bent on enhancing Yugoslav power, he demanded territory from Italy, intervened in the Greek civil war, and talked grandly of forming a federation of Balkan Communist countries. Stalin, who had little use for any Communist he could not control, grew increasingly annoyed and frustrated with Tito's independence.

Finally, in June 1948, the Soviet dictator made his move. He cut off aid to Yugoslavia, withdrew all Soviet advisors, and arranged an economic boycott by the entire Soviet Bloc. At his insistence, the recently founded Cominform (Document 12B) issued a denunciation of the Yugoslav leaders, expelled them from its membership, and called on the "healthy elements" of the Yugoslav Communist Party to throw them out. Its formal resolution, excerpted below, accused them of various harmful, arrogant, anti-Soviet behaviors.

Unfortunately for Stalin, his efforts failed. Tito moved quickly to oust the Stalinists in his own entourage, and the United States, anxious to exploit any division within the Communist ranks, provided trade and economic assistance to help him overcome the boycott. Stalin, whose Red Army forces had withdrawn from Yugoslavia after brutally liberating it in 1944, and whose attention in June 1948 was focused increasingly on the developing Berlin Blockade crisis, apparently decided that getting rid of Tito was not worth the price of invasion. At any rate, the Yugoslav leader survived and went on to guide his nation on a separate road to socialism, independent of Moscow's control.

COMINFORM RESOLUTION ON THE
SITUATION IN YUGOSLAVIA, 28 JUNE 1948

1. The Cominform asserts that the leadership of the Yugoslav Communist Party has lately undertaken an entirely wrong policy on the principal questions of foreign and internal politics, which means a retreat from Marxism-Leninism. . . .
2. The Cominform finds that the leadership of the Yugoslav Communist Party created a hateful policy in relation to the Soviet Union and to the All-Communist Union of Bolsheviks. In Yugoslavia an undignified policy of underestimating Soviet military specialists was allowed. Also, members of the Soviet Army were discredited. . . . All these facts prove that the leading persons in the Communist Party of Yugoslavia took a stand unworthy of Communists, on the line of which they began to identify the foreign policy of the Soviet Union with that of the imperialist powers, and they treat the Soviet Union in the same manner as they treat the bourgeois states. . . .
3. In their policy inside the country the leaders of the Communist Party of Yugoslavia are retreating from positions of the working class and departing from the Marxist theory of classes and class struggle. . . . Leading Yugoslav politicians are carrying out a wrong policy in the villages, ignoring the class differences in the villages . . . despite the well-known Lenin precept that a small individual economy inexorably gives birth to capitalism and the bourgeoisie. . . .
4. The Cominform is sure that the leadership of the Yugoslav Communist Party is revising the Marxist-Leninist theory about the Party. . . .
5. The Information Bureau maintains that the bureaucratic regime inside the party is pernicious to the life and the progress of the Yugoslav Communist Party. There is no intra-party democracy in the party, the electoral principle is not realized, there is no criticism and self criticism.
6. The Information Bureau maintains that the criticism of the Central Committee of the Communist Party of Yugoslavia that was made by the

Central Committee of the [Communist Party of the Soviet Union] and by the Central Committees of the other Communist parties as a brotherly help to the Yugoslav Communist Party creates for its leadership all the conditions necessary for the correction of the faults committed. But the leaders of the Communist Party of Yugoslavia, affected by exaggerated ambition, megalomania and conceit, instead of honestly accepting this criticism and taking the path of Bolshevik correction of these mistakes, received the criticism with dislike, took a hostile standpoint toward it, and in an anti-party spirit categorically and generally denied their faults. . . .

7. With regard to the situation created in the Communist Party of Yugoslavia . . . the Central Committee of the [Communist Party of the Soviet Union] and other Central Committees of the other brotherly parties, decided to discuss the situation . . . at a meeting of the Information Bureau. . . . But . . . the Yugoslav leaders answered with a refusal. . . .

The Information Bureau finds that, as a result of all this, the Central Committee of the Communist Party of Yugoslavia puts itself and the Yugoslav Communist Party outside the family of brotherly Communist parties, outside the united Communist front, and therefore outside the ranks of the Information Bureau.

The Information Bureau maintains that the basis of all these faults of the leadership of the Communist Party of Yugoslavia is the incontestable fact that in its leadership in the last five to six months openly nationalistic elements prevailed that were formerly masked. . . .

The Information Bureau does not doubt that in the core of the Communist Party of Yugoslavia there are enough sound elements that are truly faithful to Marxism-Leninism, faithful to the internationalistic traditions of the Yugoslav Communist Party, and faithful to the united Socialist front. The aim of these sound elements of the Communist Party of Yugoslavia is to force their present party leaders to confess openly and honestly their faults and correct them; to part from nationalism; to return to internationalism and in every way to fix the united Socialist front against imperialism, or if the present leaders of the Communist Party of Yugoslavia prove unable to do this task, to change them and raise from below a new internationalistic leadership of the Communist Party of Yugoslavia. . . .

Discussion Questions

1. What reasons did the Cominform give for the split between Yugoslavia and the rest of the Communist Bloc? What charges did it make against the Yugoslav leaders?
2. According to the Cominform, how did Yugoslav Marxism differ from orthodox Marxism?
3. What did the Cominform want Yugoslav Communists to do in order to resolve the situation?
4. Why did Stalin want to get rid of Tito? Why was Tito able to survive Stalin's efforts to get rid of him?

16

The Berlin Blockade, 1948–1949

THE FIRST MAJOR MILITARY CRISIS of the Cold War began in June 1948. The Western allies had responded to the Communist coup in Czecho-slovakia with the Treaty of Brussels and a decision to create an independent West German state. This threatened the Soviet objective of a permanently crippled Germany, and when the West announced the creation of a common West German currency called the deutsche mark, Moscow moved to seal off West Berlin and force the Western powers to remove their troops from the divided city.

Like Germany as a whole, Berlin had been divided into occupation zones at the end of World War II, with the Soviets in the east and the Americans, British, and French in the west. Since the city sat in the midst of Soviet-occupied East Germany, Stalin assumed that he could drive the others out simply by cutting off the roads and railways that linked it with the West. Since few believed that the West could remain in Berlin if the Soviets moved against it, Stalin surely thought his actions involved minimal risk.

The American response, however, caught him by surprise. President Truman announced that the United States would stay in Berlin, and he ordered a military airlift to supply West Berliners with food, fuel, and supplies. Secretary of State Marshall subsequently sent a protest note to the Soviet government, demanding that the blockade be lifted and categorically asserting US rights, responsibilities, and determination to remain in Berlin. The Berlin Blockade lasted eleven months, but the airlift proved effective, and the crisis ended in May 1949 when the Soviets quietly lifted their blockade.

NOTE FROM SECRETARY OF STATE
MARSHALL TO THE SOVIET AMBASSADOR, 6 JULY 1948

EXCELLENCY: The United States Government wishes to call to the attention of the Soviet Government the extremely serious international situation which has been brought about by the actions of the Soviet Government in imposing restrictive measures on transport which amount now to a blockade against the sectors in Berlin occupied by the United States, United Kingdom and France. The United States Government regards these measures of blockade as a clear violation of existing agreements concerning the administration of Berlin by the four occupying powers.

The rights of the United States as a joint occupying power in Berlin derive from the total defeat and unconditional surrender of Germany. The international agreements undertaken in connection therewith by the Governments of the United States, United Kingdom, France and the Soviet Union defined the zones in Germany and the sectors in Berlin which are occupied by these powers. They established the quadripartite control of Berlin on a basis of friendly cooperation which the Government of the United States earnestly desires to continue to pursue.

These agreements implied the right of free access to Berlin. This right has long been confirmed by usage. It was directly specified in a message sent by President Truman to Premier Stalin on June 14, 1945, which agreed to the withdrawal of United States forces to the zonal boundaries provided satisfactory arrangements could be entered into between the military commanders, which would give access by rail, road and air to United States forces in Berlin. Premier Stalin replied on June 16 suggesting a change in date but no other alteration in the plan proposed by the President. Premier Stalin then gave assurances that all necessary measures would be taken in accordance with the plan. Correspondence in a similar sense took place between Premier Stalin and Mr. Churchill. In accordance with this understanding, the United States, whose armies had penetrated deep into Saxony and Thuringia, parts of the Soviet zone, withdrew its forces to its own area of occupation in Germany and took up its position in its own sector in Berlin. Thereupon the agreements in regard to the occupation of Germany and Berlin went into effect. The United

States would not have so withdrawn its troops from a large area now occupied by the Soviet Union had there been any doubt whatsoever about the observance of its agreed right of free access to its sector of Berlin. The right of the United States to its position in Berlin thus stems from precisely the same source as the right of the Soviet Union. It is impossible to assert the latter and deny the former.

It clearly results from these undertakings that Berlin is not a part of the Soviet zone, but is an international zone of occupation. Commitments entered into in good faith by the zone commanders, and subsequently confirmed by the Allied Control Authority, as well as practices sanctioned by usage, guarantee the United States together with other powers, free access to Berlin for the purpose of fulfilling its responsibilities as an occupying power. The facts are plain. Their meaning is clear. Any other interpretation would offend all the rules of comity and reason.

In order that there should be no misunderstanding whatsoever on this point, the United States Government categorically asserts that it is in occupation of its sector in Berlin with free access thereto as a matter of established right deriving from the defeat and surrender of Germany and confirmed by formal agreements among the principal Allies. It further declares that it will not be induced by threats, pressures or other actions to abandon these rights. It is hoped that the Soviet Government entertains no doubts whatsoever on this point.

This Government now shares with the Governments of France and the United Kingdom the responsibility initially undertaken at Soviet request on July 7, 1945, for the physical well-being of 2,400,000 persons in the western sectors of Berlin. Restrictions recently imposed by the Soviet authorities in Berlin have operated to prevent this Government and the Governments of the United Kingdom and of France from fulfilling that responsibility in an adequate manner.

The responsibility which this Government bears for the physical well-being and the safety of the German population in its sector of Berlin is outstandingly humanitarian in character. This population includes hundreds of thousands of women and children, whose health and safety are dependent on the continued use of adequate facilities for moving food, medical supplies and other items indispensable to the maintenance of human life in the western sectors of Berlin. The most elemental of these human rights which both our Governments are solemnly pledged to protect are thus placed in jeopardy by these restrictions. It is intolerable that any one of the occupying authorities should attempt to impose a blockade upon the people of Berlin.

The United States Government is therefore obliged to insist that in accordance with existing agreements the arrangements for the movement of freight and passenger traffic between the western zones and Berlin be fully restored. There can be no question of delay in the restoration of these essential services, since the needs of the civilian population in the Berlin area are imperative. . . .

Discussion Questions

1. What might Stalin have hoped to accomplish by cutting off Western access to Berlin?
2. Why did the Americans decide to stay in Berlin, despite the Soviet blockade? What were the advantages and disadvantages of an airlift as a means of supplying the city?
3. According to Marshall, what were the legal and moral foundations of the American presence in West Berlin?
4. On what basis did Marshall insist that the Soviets had no right to restrict Western access to the city?
5. What were the implications of Marshall's assertion that the United States would "not be induced by threats, pressures or other actions" to abandon Berlin?

17

The NATO Alliance, 1949

THROUGHOUT ITS EXISTENCE, the United States had been reluctant to commit itself to "entangling alliances" with other nations in peacetime. One of the principal reasons for its struggle for independence from Great Britain had been the desire to keep clear of Europe's quarrels. But Soviet actions in Czechoslovakia and Berlin in 1948 convinced Washington to modify its position and conclude a military alliance with eleven other nations in Europe and North America. This alliance, known as NATO (the North Atlantic Treaty Organization), testified to America's assumption that the Cold War would last indefinitely.

The NATO alliance was constructed upon the foundations laid by the Treaty of Brussels (Document 14). The consultative council created at Brussels had organized a standing military committee, which spent much of 1948 discussing the potential threat of a Soviet invasion of Western Europe. The Berlin Blockade helped convince skeptics that this was a real danger. In such an environment, nations that only four years earlier had been allied with the Soviet Union in a desperate struggle against Nazi Germany now gave notice that they considered their former ally a greater threat than their former foe. This was underscored by NATO's inclusion of Italy, which had fought on Germany's side in World War II, and Portugal, whose fascist government had remained neutral. Neither had been part of the Treaty of Brussels, but the Berlin Blockade frightened the signatories of that accord, as well as the United States, into including them in the new alliance.

THE TREATY OF WASHINGTON
(NORTH ATLANTIC TREATY), 4 APRIL 1949

The Parties to this Treaty reaffirm their faith in the purposes and principles of the Charter of the United Nations and their desire to live in peace with all peoples and all governments.

They are determined to safeguard the freedom, common heritage, and civilization of their peoples, founded on the principles of democracy, individual liberty, and the rule of law.

They seek to promote stability and well-being in the North Atlantic area.

They are resolved to unite their efforts for collective defense and for preservation of peace and security.

They therefore agree to this North Atlantic Treaty:

Article 1
The Parties undertake, as set forth in the Charter of the United Nations, to settle any international disputes in which they may be involved by peaceful means in such a manner that international peace and security, and justice, are not endangered, and to refrain in their international relations from the threat or use of force in any manner inconsistent with the purposes of the United Nations.

Article 2
The Parties will contribute toward the further development of peaceful and friendly international relations by strengthening their free institutions, by bringing about a better understanding of the principles upon which these

institutions are founded, and by promoting conditions of stability and well-being. They will seek to eliminate conflict in their international economic policies and will encourage economic collaboration between any or all of them.

Article 3

In order more effectively to achieve the objectives of this Treaty, the Parties, separately and jointly, by means of continuous and effective self-help and mutual aid, will maintain and develop their individual and collective capacity to resist armed attack.

Article 4

The Parties will consult together whenever, in the opinion of any of them, the territorial integrity, political independence or security of any of the Parties is threatened.

Article 5

The Parties agree that an armed attack against one or more of them in Europe or North America shall be considered an attack against them all; and consequently they agree that, if such an armed attack occurs, each of them, in exercise of the right of individual or collective self-defense recognized by Article 51 of the Charter of the United Nations, will assist the Party or Parties so attacked by taking forthwith, individually and in concert with the other Parties, such action as it deems necessary, including the use of armed force, to restore and maintain the security of the North Atlantic area.

Any such armed attack and all measures taken as a result thereof shall immediately be reported to the Security Council. Such measures shall be terminated when the Security Council has taken the measures necessary to restore and maintain international peace and security.

Article 6

For the purpose of Article 5 an armed attack on one or more of the Parties is deemed to include an armed attack on the territory of any of the Parties in Europe or North America, on the Algerian dependents of France, on the occupation forces of any Party in Europe, on the islands under the jurisdiction of any Party in the North Atlantic area north of the Tropic of Cancer or on the vessels or aircraft in this area of any of the Parties.

Article 7

This Treaty does not affect, and shall not be interpreted as affecting, in any way the rights and obligations under the Charter of the Parties which are members of the United Nations, or the primary responsibility of the Security Council for the maintenance of international peace and security.

Article 8
Each Party declares that none of the international engagements now in force between it and any other of the Parties or any third state is in conflict with the provisions of this Treaty, and undertakes not to enter into any international engagement in conflict with this Treaty.

Article 9
The Parties hereby establish a council, on which each of them shall be represented, to consider matters concerning the implementation of this Treaty. The council shall be so organized as to be able to meet promptly at any time. The council shall set up such subsidiary bodies as may be necessary; in particular it shall establish a defense committee which shall recommend measures for the implementation of Articles 3 and 5.

Article 10
The Parties may, by unanimous agreement, invite any other European state in a position to further the principles of this Treaty and to contribute to the security of the North Atlantic area to accede to this Treaty. Any state so invited may become a party to the Treaty by depositing its instrument of accession with the Government of the United States of America. . . .

Signed by representatives of:

Kingdom of Belgium	Grand Duchy of Luxembourg
Canada	Kingdom of the Netherlands
Kingdom of Denmark	Kingdom of Norway
France	Portugal
Iceland	United Kingdom
Italy	United States

Discussion Questions

1. Which provisions of the Treaty of Brussels (Document 14) are reflected in the North Atlantic Treaty?
2. What were the differences between this document and the Treaty of Brussels? What might account for these differences?

3. Article 5 states that an attack upon one of the parties shall be considered an attack upon them all. Given the inclusion of the United States, and its possession of nuclear weapons, what were the main implications of this article?
4. Why would the wartime allies have been willing to include Italy and Portugal in this alliance?
5. Why did the treaty contain a provision for adding new members to the alliance? Which nations might have been considered potential members and why?
6. How can you tell that the USSR was the main target of the treaty, even though it was not mentioned by name?

18

Acheson on the Communist Triumph in China, 1949

DESPITE US EFFORTS TO ACHIEVE peace and stability in postwar China, a civil war broke out in 1946 between the Nationalist government, led by Jiang Jieshi (Chiang Kai-shek) and his Guomindang (Kuomintang) party,* and its Communist rivals. Initially the Nationalists, with some American aid, seemed to gain the upper hand, but eventually the momentum changed. Hampered by ineffective leadership and government corruption, the Nationalist forces floundered, while the Communists staged an impressive display of discipline, dedication, and zeal. By 1949 it was clear that the Communists were winning and that only a massive US military intervention could save the Nationalist regime. Facing a dangerous Soviet challenge in the West, however, including the Berlin Blockade (Document 16), US officials decided that protecting Europe was their main priority and that they must therefore not get diverted into an Asian war.

---

* Jiang Jieshi and Guomindang are modernized (pinyin) versions of the name of this man and his party. In the early Cold War, they were known in the West as Chiang Kai-shek and Kuomintang, based on an older (Wade-Giles) transliteration system.

Dean Acheson, who became secretary of state in January 1949, was deeply committed to Europe's defense, having previously been involved in implementing the Truman Doctrine and Marshall Plan. Ironically, his tenure in office was dominated by Asian events. In his first year, China fell to the Communists, and a political firestorm broke out in Washington about the American role. In this letter of transmittal for a State Department "White Paper" on China, Acheson sought to explain events in China and to justify the policies and actions of the Truman administration.

SECRETARY OF STATE ACHESON'S LETTER OF TRANSMITTAL FOR US STATE DEPARTMENT "WHITE PAPER" ON CHINA, 30 JULY 1949

Two factors have played a major role in shaping the destiny of modern China.

The population of China during the eighteenth and nineteenth centuries doubled, thereby creating an unbearable pressure upon the land. The first problem which every Chinese Government has had to face is that of feeding this population. So far none has succeeded. The Kuomintang attempted to solve it by putting many land-reform laws on the statute books. Some of these laws have failed, others have been ignored. In no small measure, the predicament in which the National Government finds itself today is due to its failure to provide China with enough to eat. A large part of the Chinese Communists' propaganda consists of promises that they will solve the land problem.

The second major factor which has shaped the pattern of contemporary China is the impact of the West and of Western ideas. For more than three thousand years the Chinese developed their own high culture and civilization, largely untouched by outside influences. . . . Then in the middle of the nineteenth century the heretofore impervious wall of Chinese isolation was breached by the West. These outsiders brought with them aggressiveness, the unparalleled development of Western technology, and a high order of culture which had not accompanied previous foreign incursions into China. Partly because of these qualities and partly because of the decay of [China's ruling dynasty], the Westerners, instead of being absorbed by the Chinese, introduced new ideas which played an important part in stimulating ferment and unrest.

By the beginning of the twentieth century, the combined force of over-population and new ideas set in motion that chain of events which can be called the Chinese revolution. It is one of the most imposing revolutions in recorded history and its outcome and consequences are yet to be foreseen. Out of this revolutionary whirlpool emerged the Kuomintang, first under

... Dr. Sun Yat-sen and later Generalissimo Chiang Kai-shek, to assume the direction of the revolution. The leadership of the Kuomintang was not challenged until 1927 by the Chinese Communist party which had been organized in the early twenties under the ideological impetus of the Russian revolution. ... To a large extent the history of the period between 1927 and 1937 can be written in terms of the struggle for power between the Kuomintang and the Chinese Communists. ...

Perhaps largely because of the progress being made in China, the Japanese chose 1937 as the departure point for the conquest of China proper, and the goal of the Chinese people became the expulsion of a brutal and hated invader. ...

In contrast ... to the unity of the people of China in the war against Japan were the divided interests of the Kuomintang and the Chinese Communists. ... Once the United States became a participant in the war, the Kuomintang was apparently convinced of the ultimate defeat of Japan and saw an opportunity to improve its position for a show-down struggle with the Communists. The Communists, for their part, seemed to see in the chaos of China an opportunity to obtain ... full power in China. This struggle for power in the latter years of the war contributed largely to the partial paralysis of China's ability to resist. ...

When peace came the United States was confronted with three possible alternatives in China:

1. it could have pulled out lock, stock and barrel;
2. it could have intervened militarily on a major scale to assist the Nationalists to destroy the Communists;
3. it could, while assisting the Nationalists to assert their authority over as much of China as possible, endeavor to avoid a civil war by working for a compromise between the two sides.

The first alternative would ... have represented an abandonment of our international responsibilities and our traditional policy of friendship with China. ... The second alternative policy, while it may look attractive theoretically and in retrospect, was wholly impracticable. ... It is obvious that the American people would not have sanctioned such a colossal commitment of our armies in 1945 or later. We therefore came to the third alternative policy whereunder we ... attempted to assist in working out a *modus vivendi* which would avert civil war but nevertheless preserve and even increase the influence of the National Government. ...

... [O]ur policy at that time was inspired by the two objectives of bringing peace to China under conditions which would permit stable government and progress along democratic lines, and of assisting the National Government to establish its authority over as wide areas of China as possible. As the event proved, the first objective was unrealizable because neither side desired it to succeed: the Communists because they refused to accept conditions which would weaken their freedom to proceed with . . . the communization of all China; the Nationalists because they cherished the illusion, in spite of repeated advice to the contrary from our military representatives, that they could destroy the Communists by force of arms.

The second objective of assisting the National Government, however, we pursued vigorously from 1945 to 1949. The National Government was the recognized government of a friendly power. Our friendship, and our right under international law alike, called for aid to the Government instead of to the Communists who were seeking to subvert and overthrow it. . . .

The reasons for the failures of the Chinese National Government appear in some detail in the attached record. They do not stem from any inadequacy of American aid. Our military observers on the spot have reported that the Nationalist armies did not lose a single battle during the crucial year of 1948 through lack of arms or ammunition. The fact was that the decay which our observers had detected . . . early in the war had fatally sapped the powers of resistance of the Kuomintang. Its leaders had proved incapable of meeting the crisis confronting them, its troops had lost the will to fight, and its Government had lost popular support. The Communists, on the other hand, through a ruthless discipline and fanatical zeal, attempted to sell themselves as guardians and liberators of the people. The Nationalist armies did not have to be defeated; they disintegrated. History has proved time and again that a regime without faith in itself and an army without morale cannot survive the test of battle. . . .

It has been urged that relatively small amounts of additional aid—military and economic—to the National Government would have enabled it to destroy Communism in China. The most trustworthy military, economic, and political information available to our Government does not bear out this view.

A realistic appraisal of conditions in China, past and present, leads to the conclusion that the only alternative open to the United States was full-scale intervention in behalf of a Government which had lost the confidence of its own troops and its own people. . . .

The unfortunate but inescapable fact is that the ominous result of the civil war in China was beyond the control of the government of the United States. Nothing that this country did or could have done within the reasonable limits of its capabilities could have changed that result; nothing that was left undone by this country contributed to it. It was the product of internal Chinese forces,

forces which this country tried to influence but could not. A decision was arrived at within China, if only a decision by default. . . .

Discussion Questions

1. Which two factors, in Acheson's view, played a key role in shaping modern China's destiny? Which did he consider more important? Why?
2. According to Acheson, why did the Nationalists fail to win the support of the Chinese people? Why and how did the Communists manage to gain the people's support?
3. What were the two main objectives of US policy in China after World War II? To what extent were they incompatible? How do you account for US failure to achieve these objectives?
4. What did Acheson see as the main reasons for the Communist victory and Nationalist defeat? How did he justify the US decision not to intervene to save the Nationalists?

19

Mao Proclaims the People's Republic of China, 1 October 1949

B Y AUTUMN OF 1949, as the Chinese Communist "People's Liberation Army" defeated the fading Nationalists and gained control of most of mainland China, their victory in the Chinese civil war was virtually assured. It was not a total triumph: Further fighting would go on for months, and the Nationalists would flee to Taiwan and continue to function there. Indeed, for the next few decades, the United Nations and the United States, plus much of the Western world, would continue to recognize the Taiwan regime as China's legitimate government.

But this could not diminish the enormity of the Communist achievement. More than a half billion Chinese people, one-fifth of all humanity, had come under their control. Coming on the heels of the recent Soviet subjugation of Eastern Europe, it created the impression that a vast Red tide was sweeping the globe.

Even before their victory was complete, the Chinese Communists moved to declare their new regime. On 1 October 1949 Mao Zedong (Mao Tse-tung), Communist Party leader and head of the new government, issued the following proclamation.

MAO'S STATEMENT PROCLAIMING THE PEOPLE'S REPUBLIC OF CHINA, 1 OCTOBER 1949

People all over China have been plunged into bitter suffering and tribulation since Chiang Kai-shek's Kuomintang reactionary government betrayed the fatherland, conspired with the imperialists and launched a counter-revolutionary war. However, the People's Liberation Army, supported by the people all over the country, fighting heroically and selflessly to . . . protect the people's lives and property and relieve the people's suffering and struggle for their rights has . . . overthrown the reactionary rule of the National Government. Now the people's liberation war has been fundamentally won and a majority of the people has been liberated.

On this foundation the first session of the Chinese People's Political Consultative Conference, composed of delegates of all democratic parties, groups, people's organizations, the People's Liberation Army in various regions, overseas Chinese and patriotic democratic elements of the whole country, has been convened. Representing the will of the people, this session of Chinese peoples:

- Enacted the organic law of the Central People's Government of the peoples of the Republic of China;
- Elected Mao Tse-tung [Mao Zedong] chairman of the Central People's Government. . . .
- Proclaimed the founding of the People's Republic of China, and
- Decided Peking [Beijing] should be the capital of the People's Republic of China.

The Central People's Government Council of the People's Republic of China took office today in this capital and unanimously made the following decisions:

- Proclamation for the formation of the Central People's Government, People's Republic of China.

- Adoption of a common program for the Chinese People's Political Consultative Conference as a policy of the Government. . . .
- Appointment of:
  - Chou En-lai [Zhou Enlai] as Premier of the State Administration Council and concurrently minister of the Ministry of Foreign Affairs,
  - Mao Tse-tung [Mao Zedong] as Chairman of the People's Revolutionary Military Council of the Central People's Government,
  - Chu Teh [Zhu De] as commander-in-chief of the People's Liberation Army. . . .

At the same time the Central People's Government Council decided to declare to the governments of all other countries that this is the sole legal Government representing all the people of the People's Republic of China. This Government is willing to establish diplomatic relations with any foreign government that is willing to observe the principles of equality, mutual benefit, mutual respect of territorial integrity and sovereignty.

Discussion Questions

1. Why did the Communists proclaim a new government, even while fighting was still going on and the Nationalists not fully defeated?
2. How did Mao justify the overthrow of the Nationalist government and the formation of the People's Republic?
3. Why did the proclamation declare the new regime the "sole legal government" of China?
4. Why did it declare that the new regime was "willing to establish diplomatic relations with any foreign government"?

20

The Soviet-Chinese Friendship Treaty, February 1950

Although the Communist victory in China was seen in the West as a huge gain for the USSR, the Soviet leader, Stalin, was not so sure. He had signed an advantageous treaty with the Nationalists in 1945 and had maintained ties with them until their defeat was assured. And China's new Communist government, despite its outward loyalty to Moscow, was not a Soviet puppet regime like most of those in Eastern Europe. Fresh from his ill-fated clash with Tito (Document 15), Stalin was wary of Communist leaders he could not control.

When Mao Zedong (Mao Tse-tung) came to Moscow in December 1949 seeking a new agreement that would be more favorable to China's new regime, it took two months of tough negotiations to hammer out a new treaty, and the Chinese Communists got less than they had wanted. Still, the Soviet-Chinese Friendship Treaty was a conspicuous achievement and a tribute to the diplomatic skills of Chinese premier Zhou Enlai (Chou En-lai), who also came to Moscow to negotiate. In addition to entering a thirty-year alliance with the new Chinese government, the Soviets agreed to provide it with economic credits and industrial equipment and to turn over to it the railways and seaports in Manchuria that the Nationalists had let them control. The treaty set the stage for a decade of cooperation, but that cooperation would later be replaced by hostility with the opening of Sino-Soviet split in the 1960s (Documents 50A–D).

A. COMMUNIQUÉ ANNOUNCING
THE SOVIET-CHINESE TREATY, 14 FEBRUARY 1950

In the course of a recent period, negotiations have taken place in Moscow between J. V. Stalin, Chairman of the Council of Ministers of the USSR, and A. Y. Vishinsky, USSR Minister of Foreign Affairs, on the one hand, and Mr. Mao Tse-tung, Chairman of the Central Government of the Chinese People's

Republic and Mr. Chou En-lai, Premier of the State Administrative Council and Foreign Minister of the People's Republic, on the other hand, during which important political and economic problems on relations between the Soviet Union and the Chinese People's Republic were discussed.

The negotiations, which took place in an atmosphere of cordiality and friendly mutual understanding, confirmed the striving of both sides to strengthen in every way and to develop relations of friendship and cooperation between them as well as their desire to cooperate for the purpose of guaranteeing general peace and the security of the nations. The negotiations were ended by the signing in the Kremlin February 14 of:

1. A Treaty of Friendship, Alliance and Mutual Aid between the Soviet Union and the Chinese People's Republic.
2. Agreements on the Chinese Changchun railway, Port Arthur and Dalny (Dairen), under which, after the signing of the peace treaty with Japan, the Chinese Changchun railway will pass into complete ownership of the Chinese People's Republic, while Soviet troops will be withdrawn from Port Arthur.
3. Agreements by which the Government of the USSR will give to the Government of the Chinese People's Republic a long term economic credit for payment of deliveries of industrial and railway equipment from the USSR.

The above-mentioned treaty and agreements were signed on the part of the USSR by Mr. A. Y. Vishinsky and on the part of the Chinese People's Republic by Mr. Chou En-lai.

In connection with the signing of the Treaty of Friendship, Alliance and Mutual Aid and agreement on the Chinese Changchun railway, Port Arthur and Dalny, Mr. Chou En-lai and A. Y. Vishinsky exchanged notes to the effect that a corresponding treaty and agreements concluded Aug. 14, 1945 between China and the Soviet Union have become invalid and that both governments affirm complete guarantee of the independent status of the Mongolian People's Republic as a result of the referendum of 1945 and the establishment with her of diplomatic relations by the Chinese People's Republic.

Simultaneously, Mr. Chou En-lai and A. Y. Vishinsky also exchanged notes regarding a decision of the Soviet Government to hand over without compensation to the Government of the Chinese People's Republic property acquired by Soviet economic organizations from Japanese owners in Manchuria, as well as on a decision of the Soviet Government to hand over without compensation to the Government of the Chinese People's Republic all buildings of the former military settlement in Peking (Peiping).

B. TREATY OF FRIENDSHIP, ALLIANCE AND MUTUAL AID BETWEEN THE USSR AND THE CHINESE PEOPLE'S REPUBLIC

. . . The high contracting parties undertake that they will undertake jointly all necessary measures at their disposal to prevent any repetition of aggression and violation of peace on the part of Japan or any other state which directly or indirectly would unite with Japan in acts of aggression. In the event of one of the agreeing parties being subjected to attack by Japan or any state allied with her, thus finding itself in a state of war, the other high contracting party will immediately render military or other aid with all means at its disposal.

The high contracting parties likewise declare their readiness, in the spirit of sincere cooperation, to take part in all international actions which have as their object to ensure peace and security throughout the entire world and will completely devote their energies to the speediest realization of these objects.

The high contracting parties undertake in the way of mutual agreement to work for the conclusion in the shortest possible space of time, jointly with other powers allied during the second World War, of a peace treaty with Japan.

The high contracting parties will not conclude any alliance directed against the other high contracting party, nor will they participate in any coalition, or in actions or measures directed against the other party.

The high contracting parties will cooperate with each other in all important international questions touching on the mutual interests of the Soviet Union and China. . . .

The high contracting parties undertake, in the spirit of friendship and cooperation and in accordance with the principles of equality, . . . with joint respect for state sovereignty and territorial integrity and non-intervention in the internal affairs of the other country to develop and strengthen economic and cultural ties between the Soviet Union and China, and to render each other every possible economic aid, and realize the necessary economic cooperation. . . .

The present agreement is to remain in force for thirty years, and unless one of the high contracting parties one year previous to the expiring of the agreement declares its desire to denounce the agreement, it will remain in force for a further period of five years. . . .

Discussion Questions

1. Why was the treaty such an important accomplishment for the Chinese Communists? Why were the negotiations so long and difficult?

2. Why did the communiqué insist that the Soviet-Chinese agreements of 1945 were no longer valid?
3. Why was the alliance directed mainly against Japan and its potential allies? What potential Japanese allies might the treaty signers have had in mind?
4. Why did the Soviets agree to hand over to China property and railways located in Manchuria? Why did they agree to grant long-term credits to China?

II

THE GLOBAL
CONFRONTATION, 1950–1960

21

McCarthy on "Communists" in the US Government, 1950

DEVELOPMENTS IN FALL OF 1949, including the Communist victory in China and the news that the Soviets had developed an atomic bomb, had a devastating impact on American morale. Searching for culprits, some Americans sought to blame these setbacks on disloyalty within the US government. Foremost among them was Joseph R. McCarthy (1909–1957), Republican senator from Wisconsin, who in February 1950 gave a speech in West Virginia charging that these reverses resulted from Communist influence among high US officials. Later that month he repeated the speech in the US Senate, displaying tactics later labeled "McCarthyism."

McCarthy's accusations, along with the disclosure of some genuine instances of espionage and betrayal, led to a "Red Scare" that swept the nation during the next few years. The loyalty of various officials, academics, writers, and performers, many of whom had belonged to left-wing organizations at one point or another, was publicly called into question. McCarthy himself continued his crusade until 1954, when he was discredited by his behavior during televised hearings on allegations of disloyalty within the US Army and was ultimately censured by the US Senate.

EXCERPTS FROM A SPEECH BY SENATOR
MCCARTHY TO THE US SENATE, 20 FEBRUARY 1950

... Today we are engaged in a final, all-out battle between communistic atheism and Christianity. The modern champions of communism have selected this as the time. And, ladies and gentlemen, the chips are down—they truly are down. ...

Six years ago . . . there was within the Soviet orbit 180,000,000 people. . . . Today, only six years later, there are 800,000,000 people under the absolute domination of Soviet Russia—an increase of over 400 percent. . . . This indicates the swiftness of the tempo of Communist victories and American defeats in the cold war. As one of our outstanding historical figures once said, "When a great democracy is destroyed, it will not be because of enemies from without, but rather because of enemies from within." The truth of this statement is becoming terrifyingly clear as we see this country each day losing on every front.

At war's end we were physically the strongest nation on earth and, at least potentially, the most powerful intellectually and morally. Ours could have been the honor of being a beacon in the desert of destruction, a shining living proof that civilization was not yet ready to destroy itself. Unfortunately, we have failed miserably and tragically to arise to the opportunity.

The reason why we find ourselves in a position of impotency is not because our only powerful potential enemy has sent men to invade our shores, but rather because of the traitorous actions of those who have been treated so well by this Nation. It has not been the less fortunate or members of minority groups who have been selling this Nation out, but rather those who have had all the benefits that the wealthiest nation on earth has had to offer—the finest homes, the finest college education, and the finest jobs in Government we can give.

This is glaringly true in the State Department. There the bright young men who are born with silver spoons in their mouths are the ones who have been worst. . . . I would like to cite one rather unusual case—the case of a man who has done much to shape our foreign policy.

When Chiang Kai-shek was fighting our war [against the Chinese Communists], the State Department had in China a young man named John S. Service. His task, obviously, was not to work for the communization of China. Strangely, however, he sent official reports back to the State Department urging that we torpedo our ally Chiang Kai-shek and stating, in effect, that communism was the best hope of China.

Later, this man—John Service—was picked up by the Federal Bureau of Investigation for turning over to the Communists secret State Department information. Strangely, however, he was never prosecuted. However, Joseph Grew, Under Secretary of State, who insisted on his prosecution, was forced to resign. Two days after Grew's successor, Dean Acheson, took over as Under Secretary of State, this man—John Service—who had been picked up by the FBI and who had previously urged that communism was the best hope of China, was not only reinstated . . . but promoted. And finally, under Acheson, placed in charge of all placements and promotions.

Today, ladies and gentlemen, this man Service is on his way to represent the State Department and Acheson in Calcutta—by far and away the most important listening post in the Far East.

Now, let's see what happens when individuals with Communist connections are forced out of the State Department. Gustave Duran, who was labeled as (I quote) "a notorious international Communist," was made assistant to the Assistant Secretary of State in charge of Latin American affairs. He was taken into the State Department from his job as a lieutenant colonel in the Communist International Brigade. Finally, after intense congressional pressure and criticism, he resigned in 1946 from the State Department—and, ladies and gentlemen, where do you think he is now? He took over a high-salaried job as Chief of Cultural Activities Section in the office of the Assistant Secretary General of the United Nations. . . .

This, ladies and gentlemen, gives you somewhat of a picture of the type of individuals who have been helping to shape our foreign policy. In my opinion the State Department, which is one of the most important government departments, is thoroughly infested with Communists.

I have in my hand 57 cases of individuals who would appear to be either card carrying members or certainly loyal to the Communist Party, but who nevertheless are still helping to shape our foreign policy.

One thing to remember in discussing the Communists in our Government is that we are not dealing with spies who get 30 pieces of silver to steal the blueprints of a new weapon. We are dealing with a far more sinister type of activity because it permits the enemy to guide and shape our policy. . . .

Discussion Questions

1. What image did McCarthy give of the world situation in 1950 and of global developments since 1945?
2. What reasons did he give for recent setbacks in US policy? What insinuations did he use to cast doubt on the loyalty of certain US officials?
3. What evidence did he provide to support his charges? What tactics did he use to gain support and sympathy for these charges?
4. Why were many Americans willing to believe McCarthy's accusations?
5. What other explanation than McCarthy's might account for the actions of John Service?

22

Acheson on the American Defense Perimeter in Asia, 1950

With Japan's defeat in 1945, Korea, which since 1910 had been a Japanese colony, was partitioned into occupation zones by the Soviet Union and the United States. In the Soviet-occupied north, a communist government was eventually established under Kim Il-Sung, a young Korean Marxist who quickly began to build up its military strength. In the south, the Americans eventually turned things over to a conservative regime led by aging nationalist Syngman Rhee. By 1949 the occupying forces had been withdrawn and Korea divided into two hostile camps, with North Korea supported by the Soviets and South Korea backed by the Americans.

That same year, responding to the Communist triumph in China, the United States began to reassess the situation in East Asia. In January 1950 Secretary of State Dean Acheson delivered a major speech before the National Press Club in which he identified a US "defense perimeter" stretching from Alaska's Aleutian Islands through Japan and the Ryukyu Islands to the Philippines. Not mentioned was South Korea, which lay outside the perimeter. This omission led to the impression that the Americas would not necessarily defend it if it were attacked. Five months later North Korea invaded the south, beginning the Korean War.

EXCERPTS FROM ACHESON'S SPEECH TO
THE NATIONAL PRESS CLUB, 12 JANUARY 1950

This afternoon I should like to discuss with you the relations between the peoples of the United States and the peoples of Asia. . . .

What is the situation in regard to the military security of the Pacific area, and what is our policy in regard to it?

In the first place, the defeat and the disarmament of Japan has placed upon the United States the necessity of assuming the military defense of Japan . . . , both in the interest of our security and in the interests of the security of the entire Pacific area. . . . We have American—and there are Australian—troops in Japan. I am not in a position to speak for the Australians, but I can assure you that there is no intention of any sort of abandoning or weakening the defenses of Japan, and that whatever arrangements are to be made, either through permanent settlement or otherwise, that defense must and shall be maintained.

This defensive perimeter runs along the Aleutians to Japan and then goes to the Ryukyus. We hold important defense positions in the Ryukyu Islands, and those we will continue to hold. In the interest of the population of the Ryukyu Islands, we will at an appropriate time offer to hold these islands under trusteeship of the United Nations. But they are essential parts of the defensive perimeter of the Pacific, and they must and will be held.

The defensive perimeter runs from Ryukyus to the Philippine Islands. Our . . . defensive relations with the Philippines are contained in agreements between us. Those agreements are being loyally carried out and will be loyally carried out. Both peoples have learned by bitter experience the vital connections between our mutual defense requirements.

So far as the military security of other areas in the Pacific is concerned, it must be clear that no person can guarantee these areas against military attack. But it must also be clear that such a guarantee is hardly sensible or necessary within the realm of practical relationship. Should such an attack occur . . . the initial reliance must be on the people attacked to resist it and then upon the commitments of the entire civilized world under the Charter of the United Nations, which so far has not proved a weak reed to lean on by any people who are determined to protect their independence against outside aggression. But it is a mistake, I think, in considering Pacific and Far Eastern problems to become obsessed with military considerations. Important as they are, there are other problems that press, and these other problems are not capable of solution through military means. These other problems arise out of the susceptibility of . . . many countries in the Pacific area, to subversion and penetration. That cannot be stopped by military means. . . .

. . . [W]hat we conclude, I believe, is that there is a new day which has dawned in Asia. It is a day in which the Asian peoples are on their own, and know it, and intend to continue on their own. It is a day in which the old relationships between east and west are gone, relationships which at their worst were exploitation and at their best were paternalism. That relationship is over, and the relationship of east and west must now be in the Far East one of mutual respect and mutual helpfulness. We are their friends. Others are their friends. We and those others are willing to help, but we can help only where we are wanted and only where conditions of help are really sensible and possible. So what we can see is that this new day in Asia, this new day which is dawning, may go on to a glorious noon or it may darken and it may drizzle out. But that decision lies within the countries of Asia and within the power of the Asian people. It is not a decision which a friend or even an enemy from the outside can make for them.

Discussion Questions

1. Why did Acheson consider it necessary to reaffirm the US commitment to the military defense of Japan?
2. Why did he not include South Korea in the US defense perimeter?
3. What did he think nations outside the perimeter should do if they were attacked? What role did he envision for the United Nations?
4. Why did he think it would be a mistake to put too much emphasis on military concerns in East Asia?
5. What did he see as the future role of the United States in East Asia? Why might his speech have given the impression that the Americans would not defend South Korea if attacked?

23

NSC-68: American Cold War Strategy, 1950

BY LATE 1949 IT LOOKED AS IF THE Communists might be winning the Cold War. That summer, much earlier than US analysts expected, the Soviets had successfully tested their first atomic bomb. That fall, much to the chagrin of the capitalistic West, Mao Zedong and the Communists had gained control of mainland China.

Early in 1950, in response to these developments and others, a group of US officials drafted a secret document called NSC (National Security Council) 68. President Truman reviewed it in April and approved it later that year, following the outbreak of the Korean War (Document 24A).

NSC-68's assessment of the Soviet threat differed substantially from that of George Kennan, who in 1947 had portrayed a paranoid, neurotic USSR, militarily weaker than the United States, obsessed with defense against another invasion, and having no desire to conquer large territories beyond its borders (Document 10). Paul Nitze, who in 1950 had succeeded Kennan as the State Department's Director of Policy Planning, cared less about the Soviets' intentions than their capabilities. Asserting that America faced a period of maximum danger if it did not rearm to wage peace, in drafting NSC-68, he and his colleagues called for vast military expenditures and substantial sacrifices, arguing that there was no other choice for the nation to maintain its freedom. Although NSC-68 was top secret, its substance soon became widely known. The actual text, however, was not declassified until 1975.

EXCERPTS FROM NSC-68
(REPORT TO THE PRESIDENT, 7 APRIL 1950)

Within the past thirty-five years the world has experienced two global wars of tremendous violence. It has witnessed two revolutions—the Russian and the Chinese—of extreme scope and intensity. It has also seen the collapse of five empires—the Ottoman, the Austro-Hungarian, the German, Italian, and Japanese—and the drastic decline of two major imperial systems, the British and the French. During the span of one generation, the international distribution of power has been fundamentally altered. . . .

Two complex sets of factors have . . . altered [the] historical distribution of power. First, the defeat of Germany and Japan and the decline of the British and French Empires have interacted with the development of the United States and the Soviet Union in such a way that power has increasingly gravitated to these two centers. Second, the Soviet Union, unlike previous aspirants to hegemony, is animated by a new fanatic faith, antithetical to our own, and seeks to impose its absolute authority over the rest of the world. Conflict has therefore become endemic and is waged, on the part of the Soviet Union, by violent or non-violent methods in accordance with the dictates of expediency. With the development of increasingly terrifying weapons of mass destruction, every individual faces the ever-present possibility of annihilation should the conflict enter the phase of total war.

On the one hand, the people of the world yearn for relief from the anxiety arising from the risk of atomic war. On the other hand, any substantial further extension of the area under the domination of the Kremlin would raise the possibility that no coalition adequate to confront the Kremlin with greater strength could be assembled. It is in this context that this Republic and its citizens in the ascendancy of their strength stand in their deepest peril.

The issues that face us are momentous, involving the fulfillment or destruction not only of this Republic but of civilization itself. . . . With conscience and resolution this Government and the people it represents must now take new and fateful decisions.

The fundamental purpose of the United States is . . . to assure the integrity and vitality of our free society, which is founded upon the dignity and worth of the individual. . . .

The fundamental design of those who control the Soviet Union and the international communist movement is to retain and solidify their absolute power, first in the Soviet Union and second in the areas now under their control. In the minds of the Soviet leaders, however, achievement of this design requires the dynamic extension of their authority and the ultimate elimination of any effective opposition to their authority. . . .

The Soviet Union is developing the military capacity to support its design for world domination. The Soviet Union actually possesses armed forces far in excess of those necessary to defend its national territory. . . . This excessive strength, coupled now with an atomic capability, provides the Soviet Union with great coercive power for use in time of peace in furtherance of its objectives and serves as a deterrent to the victims of its aggression from taking any action in opposition to its tactics which would risk war. . . .

We do not know accurately what the Soviet atomic capability is but the Central Intelligence Agency . . . estimates, concurred in by State, Army, Navy, Air Force, and Atomic Energy Commission, assign to the Soviet Union a production capability giving it a fission bomb stockpile within the following ranges:

By mid-1950 10–20
By mid-1951 25–40
By mid-1952 45–90
By mid-1953 70–135
By mid-1954 200. . . .

The Soviet Union now has aircraft able to deliver atomic bombs. Our intelligence estimates assign to the Soviet Union an atomic bomber capability already in excess of that needed to deliver all available bombs. We have at present no evaluated estimate regarding the Soviet accuracy of delivery on target. It is believed that the Soviets cannot deliver their bombs on target with a degree of accuracy comparable to ours, but a planning estimate might well place it at 40–60 percent. . . . For planning purposes, therefore, the date the Soviets possess an atomic stockpile of 200 bombs would be a critical date for the United States, for the delivery of 100 atomic bombs on targets in the United States would seriously damage this country. . . .

Several conclusions seem to emerge. First, the Soviet Union is widening the gap between its preparedness for war and the unpreparedness of the free world. . . . Second, the Communist success in China, taken with the politico-economic situation in the rest of South and South-East Asia, provides a springboard for further incursion in this troubled area. . . . Third, the Soviet Union holds positions in Europe which, if it maneuvers skillfully, could be used to do great damage to the Western European economy and to the maintenance of the Western orientation of certain countries, particularly Germany and Austria. . . .

In short, as we look into the future, the programs now planned will not meet the requirements of the free nations. . . .

It is estimated that, within the next four years, the USSR will attain the capability of seriously damaging vital centers of the United States, provided it strikes a surprise blow and provided further that the blow is opposed by no more effective force than we now have programmed. . . .

Four possible courses of action by the United States in the present situation can be distinguished. They are:

a. Continuation of current policies, with current and currently projected programs for carrying out these policies;
b. Isolation;
c. War; and
d. A more rapid building up of the political, economic and military strength of the free world than provided under *a*, with the purpose of reaching . . . a tolerable state of order among nations without war and of preparing to defend ourselves in the event that the free world is attacked. . . .

A more rapid build-up of political, economic, and military strength and thereby of confidence in the free world than is now contemplated is the only course which is consistent with progress toward achieving our fundamental purpose. The frustration of the Kremlin design requires the free world to develop a successfully functioning political and economic system and a vigorous political offensive against the Soviet Union. These, in turn, require an adequate military shield under which they can develop. It is necessary to have the military power to deter, if possible, Soviet expansion, and to defeat, if necessary, aggressive Soviet or Soviet-directed actions of a limited or total character. The potential strength of the free world is great; its ability to develop these military capabilities and its will to resist Soviet expansion will be determined by the wisdom and will with which it undertakes to meet its political and economic problems. . . .

At any rate, it is clear that a substantial and rapid building up of strength in the free world is necessary to support a firm policy intended to check and roll back the Kremlin's drive for world domination. . . .

A program for rapidly building up strength and improving political and economic conditions will place heavy demands on our courage and intelligence; it will be costly; it will be dangerous. But half-measures will be more costly and more dangerous, for they will be inadequate to prevent and may actually invite war. Budgetary considerations will need to be subordinated to the stark fact that our very independence as a nation may be at stake.

A comprehensive and decisive program to win the peace and frustrate the Kremlin design should be so designed that it can be sustained for as long as necessary to achieve our national objectives. It would probably involve:

(1) The development of an adequate political and economic framework for the achievement of our long-range objectives.
(2) A substantial increase in expenditures for military purposes. . . .
(3) A substantial increase in military assistance programs. . . .
(4) Some increase in economic assistance programs and recognition of the need to continue these programs until their purposes have been accomplished.
(5) A concerted attack on the problem of the United States balance of payments. . . .
(6) Development of programs designed to build and maintain confidence among other peoples in our strength and resolution, and to wage overt psychological warfare designed to encourage mass defections from Soviet allegiance and to frustrate the Kremlin design in other ways.
(7) Intensification of affirmative and timely measures and operations by covert means in the fields of economic warfare and political and psychological warfare with a view to fomenting and supporting unrest and revolt in selected strategic satellite countries.
(8) Development of internal security and civilian defense programs.
(9) Improvement and intensification of intelligence activities.
(10) Reduction of Federal expenditures for purposes other than defense and foreign assistance, if necessary by the deferment of certain desirable programs.
(11) Increased taxes. . . .

In summary, we must, by means of a rapid and sustained build-up of the political, economic and military strength of the free world, and by means of an affirmative program intended to wrest the initiative from the Soviet Union, confront it with convincing evidence of the determination and ability of the free world to frustrate the Kremlin design of a world dominated by its will. Such evidence is the only means short of war which eventually may force the Kremlin to abandon its present course of action and to negotiate acceptable agreements on issues of major importance. . . .

Discussion Questions

1. In what ways did NSC-68's analysis take a more pessimistic view of Soviet capabilities and intentions than that prevailing in the West before 1950?
2. In what ways did NSC-68 differ from the approach envisioned by George Kennan (Document 10) and in what ways did it continue that approach?
3. Why did NSC-68 call for a sustained military buildup? What other steps did it recommend?
4. What conditions in 1950 prompted the drafting and approval of NSC-68?
5. Why did it consider 1954 a crucial year? What assumptions about Soviet intentions were implicit in this calculation?
6. What implications might follow from a decision to commit a large share of the US budget to such an ambitious and costly program of military expenditure?

24

The Korean War, 1950–1953

On 25 June 1950 Communist North Korea invaded South Korea and quickly overran its border forces. The Truman administration, reeling from the recent Communist victory in China, quickly got the UN Security Council to call for the immediate withdrawal of invading forces. On 27 June, Truman announced a series of measures to deal with the crisis, and the Security Council passed a new resolution calling on UN members to help repel the Communist assault.

Led by the United States, a multinational UN force won a series of early victories, driving the North Koreans out of the South and pursuing them deep into their own territory. But that October, as the US-led UN forces neared the North Korean border with China, the Chinese Communists, after consultation with Soviet Premier Stalin, began sending "volunteer" forces to Korea to aid their Communist comrades. Following some Communist successes, the war bogged down into a brutal and bloody stalemate, with neither side able to make much headway, as the Americans opted not to widen the war by bombing Communist China. Negotiations were held at Panmunjom, a town near the battlefront, but they quickly bogged down over contentious issues like the UN side's unwillingness to send captured soldiers back to North Korea if they did not wish to return. The impasse was finally broken when the Communist side agreed to let such prisoners be turned over to a Neutral Nations Repatriation Commission, and the fighting ended in July of that year with an armistice signed in Panmunjom.

A. STATEMENT BY PRESIDENT TRUMAN, 27 JUNE 1950

In Korea, the Government forces, which were armed to prevent border raids and to preserve internal security, were attacked by invading forces from North Korea. The Security Council of the United Nations called upon the invading troops to cease hostilities and to withdraw to the 38th Parallel. This they have not done but, on the contrary, have pressed the attack. The Security Council called upon all members of the United Nations to render every assistance to the United Nations in the execution of this resolution. In these circumstances, I have ordered United States air and sea forces to give the Korean Government troops cover and support.

The attack upon Korea makes it plain beyond all doubt that communism has passed beyond the use of subversion to conquer independent nations and will now use armed invasion and war. It has defied the orders of the Security Council of the United Nations issued to preserve international peace and security. In these circumstances, the occupation of Formosa [Taiwan] by Communist forces would be a direct threat to the security of the Pacific area and to United States forces performing their lawful and necessary functions in that area.

Accordingly, I have ordered the Seventh Fleet to prevent any attack upon Formosa. As a corollary of this action, I am calling upon the Chinese Government on Formosa to cease all air and sea operations against the mainland.

The Seventh Fleet will see that this is done. The determination of the future status of Formosa must await the restoration of security in the Pacific, a peace settlement with Japan, or consideration by the United Nations.

I have also directed that United States forces in the Philippines be strengthened and that military assistance to the Philippine Government be accelerated.

I have similarly directed acceleration in the furnishing of military assistance to the forces of France and the Associated States in Indochina and the dispatch of a military mission to provide close working relations with those forces.

I know that all members of the United Nations will consider carefully the consequences of this latest aggression in Korea in defiance of the Charter of the United Nations. A return to the rule of force in international affairs would have far-reaching effects. The United States will continue to uphold the rule of law. . . .

B. RESOLUTION OF THE UNITED NATIONS
SECURITY COUNCIL, 27 JUNE 1950

The Security Council

Having determined that the armed attack upon the Republic of Korea by forces from North Korea constitutes a breach of the peace;

Having called for an immediate cessation of hostilities; and

Having called upon the authorities of North Korea to withdraw forthwith their armed forces to the 38th parallel; and

Having noted from the report of the United Nations Commission for Korea that the authorities in North Korea have neither ceased hostilities nor withdrawn their armed forces to the 38th parallel, and that urgent military measures are required to restore international peace and security; and

Having noted the appeal from the Republic of Korea to the United Nations for immediate and effective steps to secure peace and security,

Recommends that the Members of the United Nations furnish such assistance to the Republic of Korea as may be necessary to repel the armed attack and to restore international peace and security in the area.

C. TELEGRAM FROM MAO ZEDONG TO JOSEPH STALIN ON
SENDING CHINESE TROOPS INTO KOREA, 2 OCTOBER 1950

1) We have decided to send a part of the armed forces into Korea, under the title of Volunteer Army, to do combat with the forces of America

and its running dog Syngman Rhee, and to assist our Korean comrades. We recognize this course as necessary. If we allow the United States to occupy all of Korea, the revolutionary strength of Korea will suffer a fundamental defeat, and the American invaders will run more rampant, with negative effects for the entire Far East.

2) We recognize that since we have decided to dispatch Chinese troops to do combat in Korea: first, they must be able to solve the problem; they must be prepared to destroy and expel, within Korea itself, the armies of the United States and other countries; second, since Chinese troops will fight American troops in Korea (even though they will be using the title Volunteer Army), we must be prepared for the United States to declare . . . war with China . . . , use its air force to bomb many major cities and industrial centers in China, and use its navy to assault the coastal region.

3) Of these two problems, the primary problem is whether or not the Chinese Army can destroy the American forces within Korea itself, and effectively resolve the Korean problem. So long as our forces can destroy the American forces within Korea itself . . . , the situation will already have turned in favor of the revolutionary camp and China. This is to say, if the American forces are defeated, the Korean problem is, in fact, finished . . . ; so even if the Americans have already openly declared war on China, the scope of this war will probably not be great, and the duration will not be long. We see the least advantageous situation as the Chinese Army being unable to destroy the American forces in large number, the two armies becoming mutually deadlocked and, in addition, the United States having already entered an open state of war with China, thus leading to the resulting destruction of the economic construction plan we have already begun, and moreover, arousing dissatisfaction toward us among the national bourgeoisie and other segments of the people (they are very afraid of war).

4) Under the present situation, we have decided that on October 15 we will begin dispatching the twelve divisions that have been transferred in advance to South Manchuria. They will locate themselves in appropriate districts of North Korea. . . . While they do combat with the enemy who dares to advance and attack north of the 38th parallel, in the first period fighting a defensive war to destroy small enemy detachments and gaining a clear understanding of the situation, they will await the arrival of Soviet weapons and the equipping of our army; and then coordinate with the Korean comrades a counter-attack, destroying the invading American army. . . .

D. TELEGRAM FROM MAO TO ZHOU ENLAI IN MOSCOW ON SENDING CHINESE TROOPS INTO KOREA, 13 OCTOBER 1950

1) The result of a discussion on the part of comrades of the Politburo is that we unanimously believe that having our troops enter Korea is more advantageous [than the alternatives]. In the first period we can focus on attacking the puppet forces; our troops' countering of puppet forces is certain [of success]; we can open up a base in Korea . . . and can inspire the Korean people. In the first period, as long as we can destroy some divisions of the puppet army, the Korean situation can take a turn to our advantage.

2) The adoption of the active policy above will be extremely advantageous for China, Korea, the Far East, and the world; and, on the other hand, if we do not send troops, allowing the enemy to press to the [Chinese] border, and [allowing] the arrogance of reactionaries at home and abroad to grow, then this will be disadvantageous to all sides. Above all it will be most disadvantageous to Manchuria; all of the northeastern border defense forces will be absorbed, and South Manchurian electrical power will be controlled [by the enemy].

In summation, we recognize that we should enter the war; we must enter the war; entering the war will have great benefits; the harm inflicted by not entering the war would be great.

E. EXCERPTS FROM THE PANMUNJOM ARMISTICE AGREEMENT, 27 JULY 1953

Preamble

The undersigned, the Commander in Chief, United Nations Command, on the one hand, and the Supreme Commander of the Korean People's Army and the Commander of the Chinese People's Volunteers, on the other hand, in the interest of stopping the Korean conflict, with its great toll of suffering and bloodshed on both sides, and with the objective of establishing an armistice which will insure a complete cessation of hostilities . . . until a final peaceful settlement is achieved, do individually, collectively and mutually agree to accept and to be bound and governed by the conditions and terms of armistice set forth in the following articles and paragraphs. . . .

Article I. Military Demarcation Line and Demilitarized Zone
   1. A military demarcation line shall be fixed and both sides shall withdraw two kilometers from this line so as to establish a demilitarized zone be-

tween the opposing forces. A demilitarized zone shall be established as a buffer zone to prevent the occurrence of incidents which might lead to a resumption of hostilities. . . .

6. Neither side shall execute any hostile act within, from, or against the demilitarized zone.

7. No person, military or civilian, shall be permitted to cross the military demarcation line unless specifically authorized to do so by the Military Armistice Commission. . . .

9. No person, military or civilian, shall be permitted to enter the demilitarized zone except persons concerned with the conduct of civil administration and relief and persons specifically authorized to enter by the Military Armistice Commission. . . .

Article II. Arrangements for Cease-Fire and Armistice

12. The commanders of the opposing sides shall order and enforce a complete cessation of all hostilities in Korea by all armed forces under their control, . . . effective twelve (12) hours after this armistice agreement is signed. . . .

13. In order to insure the stability of the military armistice so as to facilitate the attainment of a peaceful settlement through the holding by both sides of a political conference . . . , the commanders of the opposing sides shall:

    (a) Within seventy-two hours after this agreement becomes effective, withdraw all of their military forces, supplies and equipment from the demilitarized zone. . . .

    (b) Within ten (10) days after this agreement becomes effective, withdraw all of their military forces, supplies and equipment from the rear and the coastal islands and waters of Korea of the other side. . . .

Article III. Arrangements Relating to Prisoners of War

51. The release and repatriation of all prisoners of war held in the custody of each side at the time this armistice agreement becomes effective shall be effected in conformity with the following provisions. . . .

    (a) Within sixty (60) days after this armistice agreement becomes effective each side shall, without offering any hindrance, directly repatriate and hand over in groups all those prisoners of war in its custody who insist on repatriation to the side to which they belonged at the time of capture. . . .

    (b) Each side shall release all those remaining prisoners of war, who are not directly repatriated, from its military control and from its custody and hand them over to the Neutral Nations Repatriation Commission. . . .

Article IV. Recommendations to the Governments

60. In order to insure the peaceful settlement of the Korean question, the military commanders of both sides hereby recommend to the Governments of the countries concerned on both sides that, within three (3) months after the armistice agreement is signed and becomes effective, a political conference of a higher level of both sides be held by the representatives appointed respectively to settle through negotiation the questions of the withdrawal of all foreign forces from Korea, the peaceful settlement of the Korean question, etc. . . .

Annex. Terms of Reference for Neutral Nations Repatriation Commission

1. In order to insure that all prisoners of war have the opportunity to exercise their right to be repatriated following an armistice, Sweden, Switzerland, Poland, Czechoslovakia and India shall each be requested by both sides to appoint a member to a Neutral Nations Repatriation Commission which shall be established to take custody in Korea of those prisoners of war who, while in the custody of the detaining powers, have not exercised their right to be repatriated. . . .

3. No force or threat of force shall be used against the prisoners of war specified in paragraph 1 above to prevent or effect their repatriation. . . .

4. All prisoners of war who have not exercised their right of repatriation following the effective date of the armistice agreement shall be released from the military control and from the custody of the detaining side . . . within 60 days . . . to the Neutral Nations Repatriation Commission. . . .

11. At the expiration of ninety (90) days after the transfer of custody of the prisoners of war to the Neutral Nations Repatriation Commission . . . the question of disposition of the prisoners of war who have not exercised their right to be repatriated shall be submitted to the political conference recommended . . . in article 60, . . . which shall endeavor to settle this question within thirty (30) days. . . . The Neutral Nations Repatriation Commission shall declare the relief from the prisoner of war status to civilian status of any prisoners of war who have not exercised their right to be repatriated and for whom no other disposition has been agreed to by the political conference within one hundred twenty (120) days after the Neutral Nations Repatriation Commission has assumed their custody. Thereafter, according to the application of each individual, those who choose to go to neutral nations shall be assisted by the Neutral Nations Repatriation Commission and the Red Cross Society of India. The operation shall be completed within thirty

(30) days, and upon its completion, the Neutral Nations Repatriation Commission shall immediately cease to function and declare its dissolution. . . .

Discussion Questions

1. Why did Truman respond so forcefully to the North Korean invasion? Why did he send forces to defend South Korea when he had not done so to defend Nationalist China?
2. Why did he work through the United Nations rather than aiding South Korea on his own?
3. Why did Mao and the Chinese Communists decide to intervene in Korea? What were their main concerns? Why did they send "volunteers" rather than openly declaring war? What help did they expect from Stalin and the Soviets?
4. Why did the Panmunjom armistice set up a "demilitarized zone"? How did the armistice finesse the issue of repatriating captured North Korean soldiers?

25

Dulles on "Massive Retaliation," 1954

T RUMAN'S APPROACH TO CONTAINMENT of communism presented several problems for his successor, Dwight D. Eisenhower, who took over as US president in 1953. For one thing, it was essentially reactive, requiring the United States and its allies to respond to apparent Communist threats in any area of the world at any time of Moscow's choosing. For another thing, it relied heavily on military force and was prohibitively expensive. Eisenhower was thus intent on finding a less reactive and less costly way to combat both communism's spread and potential Soviet advances. For him, matching Soviet ground forces in Europe would be out of the question from both a political perspective (it would mean recruiting or conscripting huge numbers of young Americans for military service) and a budgetary standpoint (it would require massive expenditures financed by higher taxation). And Eisenhower, who had spent most of his adult life in the US Army, was a hardheaded administrator who was intrinsically skeptical of military requests for large financial appropriations. Once the Korean War armistice was signed in 1953, he authorized a thorough reappraisal of American defensive strategy.

The resulting new strategy shifted US emphasis from conventional military forces to deterrence by nuclear weapons, which could deliver "a bigger bang for the buck." But such weapons would be ineffective as deterrents unless potential aggressors were convinced that the United States would actually be willing to use them. Embarking on a public campaign to assure both the Soviets and US allies of American resolve, Secretary of State John Foster Dulles addressed the Council on Foreign Relations in New York on 12 January 1954, explaining the administration's new strategy of "massive retaliation."

HIGHLIGHTS OF DULLES'S SPEECH TO THE COUNCIL ON FOREIGN RELATIONS, 12 JANUARY 1954

. . . The Soviet Communists are planning for what they call "an entire historical era," and we should do the same. They seek through many types of maneuvers gradually to divide and weaken the free nations by overextending them in efforts which, as Lenin put it, are "beyond their strength, so that they come to practical bankruptcy." Then, said Lenin, "our victory is assured." Then, said Stalin, will be "the moment for the decisive blow."

In the face of this strategy, measures cannot be judged adequate merely because they ward off an immediate danger. It is essential to do this, but it is also essential to do so without exhausting ourselves. And when the Eisenhower administration applied this test, we felt that some transformations were needed.

It is not sound military strategy permanently to commit US land forces to Asia to a degree that leaves us no strategic reserves.

It is not sound economics to support permanently other countries; nor is it good foreign policy, for in the long run, that creates as much ill will as good will.

Also, it is not sound to become permanently committed to military expenditures so vast that they lead to what Lenin called "practical bankruptcy." . . .

Take first the matter of national security. We need allies and we need collective security. And our purpose is to have them, but to have them on a basis which is more effective and . . . less costly. . . . The way to do this is to place more reliance on community deterrent power, and less dependence on local defensive power. . . . We want for ourselves and for others a maximum deterrent at a bearable cost.

Local defense will always be important. But there is no local defense which alone will contain the mighty land power of the Communist world. Local defenses must be reinforced by the further deterrent of massive retaliatory power.

A potential aggressor must know that he cannot always prescribe battle conditions that suit him. Otherwise, for example, a potential aggressor who is glutted with manpower might be tempted to attack in confidence that resistance would be confined to manpower. He might be tempted to attack in places where his superiority was decisive.

The way to deter aggression is for the free community to be willing and able to respond vigorously at places and with means of its own choosing.

Now, so long as our basic policy concepts were unclear, our military leaders could not be selective in building our military power. If the enemy could pick his time and his place and his method of warfare—and if our policy was to remain the traditional one of meeting aggression by direct and local opposition—then we had to be ready to fight in the Arctic and in the tropics; in Asia, the Near East, and in Europe; by sea, by land, and by air; by old weapons and by new weapons.

The total cost of our security efforts . . . was over $50,000,000,000 per annum, and involved, for 1953, a projected budgetary deficit of $9,000,000,000; and for 1954 a projected deficit of $11,000,000,000. This was on top of taxes comparable to wartime taxes and the dollar was depreciating in its effective value. And our allies were similarly weighed down. This could not be continued for long without grave budgetary, economic, and social consequences.

But before military planning could be changed the President and his advisers . . . had to make some basic policy decisions. This has been done. And the basic decision was . . . to depend primarily upon a great capacity to retaliate instantly by means and at places of our choosing. And now the Department of Defense and the Joint Chiefs of Staff can shape our military establishment to fit what is our policy, instead of having to try to be ready to meet the enemy's many choices. . . . And as a result it is now possible to get . . . more basic security at less cost. . . .

Discussion Questions

1. Why did Dulles single out Asia as an area where the United States should not commit massive ground forces?

2. In what ways did Dulles think it would be harmful to permanently commit US ground forces to defending other countries overseas? What did he mean when he claimed that supporting other countries permanently would create "as much ill will as good will"?
3. How would "massive retaliation" deter the Soviet Union from invading Western Europe? What role would the NATO Treaty (Document 17) play in this deterrence?
4. Why would the Soviet Union believe that the United States would use nuclear weapons to oppose a conventional military attack?
5. What were some potential drawbacks of "massive retaliation" for the United States and its allies?

26

The Geneva Accords Regarding Indochina, 1954

H o Chi Minh's declaration of independence for Vietnam (Document 4) was rejected by the French, whose efforts to reimpose a colonial regime on Indochina in 1946 were opposed by the Vietnamese Independence Brotherhood League, or Vietminh, a nationalist coalition led by that same Ho Chi Minh. Since Washington wanted to stabilize its French ally, and since Ho was a Communist, the United States provided France with financial support in the long and bloody First Indochina War (1946–1954). This support, however, did not save France from decisive defeat at the battle of Dien Bien Phu in spring 1954.

In April of that year, while the battle was going on, the French met at Geneva with representatives of Britain, the United States, the People's Republic of China, the USSR, and various Indochinese factions. Following the loss of Dien Bien Phu, a new French premier, Pierre Mendès-France, negotiated an agreement to end the war. It confirmed the division of Indochina into four states—Laos, Cambodia, North Vietnam, and South Vietnam—and called for elections to unify Vietnam in July 1956.

The United States and South Vietnam refused to sign the Geneva accords, partly out of fear that the Communist-led Vietminh, who controlled North Vietnam, would dominate the elections to unify Vietnam. Those elections were thus never held. The North Vietnamese then decided to infiltrate the South with guerrilla units known as Viet Cong, leading in 1960 to the Second Indochina (or Vietnam) War, a conflict that would continue for fifteen years.

FINAL DECLARATION OF
THE GENEVA CONFERENCE, 21 JULY 1954

FINAL DECLARATION, dated the 21st of July, 1954, of the Geneva Conference on the problem of restoring peace in Indo-China, in which the representatives of Cambodia, the Democratic Republic of Viet-Nam, France, Laos, the People's Republic of China, the State of Viet-Nam, the Union of Soviet Socialist Republics, the United Kingdom, and the United States of America took part.

1. The Conference takes note of the agreements ending hostilities in Cambodia, Laos and Viet-Nam and organizing international control and the supervision of the execution of the provisions of these agreements.
2. The Conference . . . expresses its conviction that the execution of the provisions set out in the present declaration and in the agreements on the cessation of hostilities will permit Cambodia, Laos and Viet-Nam henceforth to play their part, in full independence and sovereignty, in the peaceful community of nations. . . .
4. The Conference takes note of the clauses in the agreement on the cessation of hostilities in Viet-Nam prohibiting the introduction into Viet-Nam of foreign troops and military personnel as well as of all kinds of arms and munitions. The Conference also takes note of the declarations made by the Governments of Cambodia and Laos of their resolution not to request foreign aid, whether in war material, in personnel or in instructors except for the purpose of the effective defense of their territory. . . .
5. The Conference takes note of the clauses in the agreement on the cessation of hostilities in Viet-Nam to the effect that no military base under the control of a foreign State may be established in the regrouping zones of the two parties, the latter having the obligation to see that the zones allotted to them shall not constitute part of any military alliance and shall not be utilized for the resumption of hostilities or in the service of an aggressive policy. The Conference also takes note of

the declarations of the Governments of Cambodia and Laos to the effect that they will not enjoin in any agreement with other States if this agreement includes the obligation to participate in a military alliance not in conformity with the principles of the Charter of the United Nations or, . . . so long as their security is not threatened, the obligation to establish bases on Cambodian or Laotian territory for the military forces of foreign Powers.

6. The Conference recognizes that the essential purpose of the agreement relating to Viet-Nam is to settle military questions with a view to ending hostilities and that the military demarcation line is provisional and should not in any way be interpreted as constituting a political or territorial boundary. The Conference expresses its conviction that the execution of the provisions set out in the present declaration and in the agreement on the cessation of hostilities creates the necessary basis for the achievement in the near future of a political settlement in Viet-Nam.

7. The Conference declares that, so far as Viet-Nam is concerned, the settlement of political problems, effected on the basis of respect for the principles of independence, unity and territorial integrity, shall permit the Viet-Namese people to enjoy the fundamental freedoms, guaranteed by democratic institutions established as a result of free general elections by secret ballot. In order to ensure that sufficient progress in the restoration of peace has been made, and that all the necessary conditions obtain for free expression of the national will, general elections shall be held in July 1956, under the supervision of an international commission composed of representatives of the Member States of the International Supervisory Commission [comprised of Canada, India, and Poland] referred to in the agreement on the cessation of hostilities. . . .

8. The provisions of the agreements on the cessation of hostilities intended to ensure the protection of individuals and of property must be most strictly applied and must, in particular, allow everyone in Viet-Nam to decide freely in which zone he wishes to live.

9. The competent representative authorities of the Northern and Southern zones of Viet-Nam, as well as the authorities of Laos and Cambodia, must not permit any individual or collective reprisals against persons who have collaborated in any way with one of the parties during the war, or against members of such persons' families.

10. The Conference takes note of the declaration of the Government of the French Republic to the effect that it is ready to withdraw its troops from the territory of Cambodia, Laos and Viet-Nam, at the request of

the governments concerned and within periods which shall be fixed by agreement between the parties. . . .

12. In their relations with Cambodia, Laos and Viet-Nam, each member of the Geneva Conference undertakes to respect the sovereignty, the independence, the unity and the territorial integrity of the above mentioned states, and to refrain from any interference in their internal affairs. . . .

Discussion Questions

1. Why did the Geneva Conference decide on a temporary division of Vietnam between North and South, with elections to unify the country after two years?
2. If Vietnam's division was not meant to be permanent, why did it last more than twenty years?
3. Why did the declaration strive to preclude the military presence of outside powers in Vietnam, Laos, and Cambodia?
4. Why were the United States and South Vietnam dissatisfied with the Geneva agreement? Why were they hesitant to support the elections called for in paragraph 7?
5. Why would Ho Chi Minh and the North Vietnamese also have been dissatisfied with the Geneva accords? What more might they have expected, given their victory over France?

27

The SEATO Alliance, 1954

AFTER THE GENEVA CONFERENCE partitioned French Indochina, the United States, fearful of an eventual Communist takeover of the entire region, attempted to provide a degree of stability sufficient for Western-style democracy to take root and grow. To that end, Secretary of State John Foster

Dulles negotiated a defensive alliance called the Southeast Asia Treaty Organization (SEATO).

Modeled on the NATO alliance (Document 17), SEATO was an unimpressive imitation. Most European NATO nations bordered one another within a relatively compact area, making common defense against invasion practical. In SEATO, however, the signatories were spread out over a very wide area, much of which was covered by water. Key nations needing SEATO protection, like Burma, South Vietnam, Laos, and Cambodia, were not part of the alliance, and most SEATO members were not even in Southeast Asia! In addition, the terrain in much of the region was suitable not for the conventional forces of the United States and Western Europe, but for the sort of guerrilla warfare that had humbled the French in Indochina.

Dulles recognized these limitations but hoped that SEATO would deter future Communist aggression because of American involvement. He suspected that had the United States backed the French in Indochina with an overt military presence rather than covert financial support, the decision there might have gone the other way. Now he moved to protect the region with the strongest declaration of military support he could get through the US Congress: the Southeast Asia Collective Defense Treaty.

HIGHLIGHTS OF THE SOUTHEAST ASIA
COLLECTIVE DEFENSE TREATY, 8 SEPTEMBER 1954

Article I
The Parties undertake, as set forth in the Charter of the United Nations, to settle any international disputes in which they may be involved by peaceful means in such a manner that international peace and security and justice are not endangered, and to refrain in their international relations from the threat or use of force in any manner inconsistent with the purposes of the United Nations.

Article II
In order more effectively to achieve the objectives of this Treaty, the Parties, separately and jointly, by means of continuous and effective self-help and mutual aid will maintain and develop their individual and collective capacity to resist armed attack and to prevent and counter subversive activities directed from without against their territorial integrity and political stability.

Article III
The Parties undertake to strengthen their free institutions and to cooperate with one another in the further development of economic measures, includ-

ing technical assistance, designed both to promote economic progress and social well-being and to further the individual and collective efforts of governments toward these ends.

Article IV

1. Each Party recognizes that aggression by means of armed attack in the treaty area against any of the Parties or against any State or territory which the Parties by unanimous agreement may hereafter designate, would endanger its own peace and safety, and agrees that it will in that event act to meet the common danger in accordance with its constitutional processes. Measures taken under this paragraph shall be immediately reported to the Security Council of the United Nations.

2. If, in the opinion of any of the Parties, the inviolability or the integrity of the territory or the sovereignty or political independence of any Party in the treaty area, or of any other state or territory to which the provisions of paragraph 1 of this Article from time to time apply, is threatened in any way other than by armed attack or . . . by any fact or situation which might endanger the peace of the area, the Parties shall consult immediately in order to agree on the measures which should be taken for the common defense.

3. It is understood that no action on the territory of any State designated by unanimous agreement under paragraph 1 of this Article or on any territory so designated shall be taken except at the invitation or with the consent of the government concerned.

Article V

The Parties hereby establish a Council, on which each of them shall be represented, to consider matters concerning the implementation of this Treaty. The Council shall provide for consultation with regard to military and any other planning as the situation obtaining in the treaty area may from time to time require. The council shall be so organized as to be able to meet at any time. . . .

Article VII

Any other State in a position to further the objectives of this Treaty and to contribute to the security of the area may, by unanimous agreement of the Parties, be invited to accede to this Treaty. . . .

Article VIII

As used in this Treaty, the "treaty area" is the general area of Southeast Asia, including also the entire territories of the Asian Parties, and the general area of the Southwest Pacific not including the Pacific area north of 21 degrees 30 minutes north latitude. The Parties may, by unanimous agreement, amend this Article to include within the treaty area the territory of any State acceding to this Treaty in accordance with Article VII or otherwise to change the treaty area. . . .

Article X
This Treaty shall remain in force indefinitely, but any Party may cease to be a Party one year after its notice of denunciation has been given to the Government of the Republic of the Philippines. . . .

Understanding of the United States of America
The United States of America in executing the present Treaty does so with the understanding that its recognition of the effect of aggression and armed attack and its agreement with reference thereto in Article IV, paragraph 1, apply only to communist aggression but affirms that in the event of other aggression or armed attack it will consult under the provisions of Article IV, paragraph 2. . . .

Done at Manila, this eighth day of September, 1954.

United States	New Zealand
Great Britain	Philippine Republic
France	Thailand
Australia	Pakistan

Discussion Questions

1. What were the similarities and differences between NATO (Document 17) and SEATO? What factors accounted for the differences?
2. What were the main limitations of SEATO? Why did Dulles move ahead with it anyway?
3. How would a US policymaker assess the SEATO treaty in 1954? How would a Soviet official assess it?
4. What features of SEATO indicate its intent to protect some nations not in the alliance?

28

The Bandung Asian-African Conference, 1955

IN APRIL 1955 REPRESENTATIVES of twenty-four African and Asian nations met at Bandung in Indonesia. That country's president, Sukarno, opened the meeting with a stirring speech urging Asians and Africans to unite in ending all vestiges of colonialism and working for world peace. Later in the conference, India's prime minister Jawaharlal Nehru asserted that Asians and Africans could best exercise moral and political influence by refusing to align with either power bloc. Among its resolutions, the conference adopted a "Declaration on the Promotion of World Peace and Cooperation," whose principles included "Abstention from the use of arrangements of collective defence to serve the particular interests of any of the big powers." Nehru and Sukarno, along with Gamal Abdel Nasser of Egypt, Kwame Nkrumah of Ghana, and Josip Tito of Yugoslavia, went on to found the Nonaligned Movement, a group of nations that sought to avoid affiliation with the major power blocs.

A. EXCERPTS FROM SPEECH BY INDONESIAN PRESIDENT SUKARNO AT THE OPENING OF THE ASIAN-AFRICAN CONFERENCE IN BANDUNG, 18 APRIL 1955*

It is a new departure in the history of the world that leaders of Asian and African peoples can meet together in their own countries to discuss and deliberate upon matters of common concern. . . . Our nations and countries are colonies no more. Now we are free, sovereign and independent. . . .

We are of many different nations, we are of many different social backgrounds and cultural patterns. Our ways of life are different. Our national

---

* Reprinted from George McTurnan Kahin, *The Asian-African Conference: Bandung, Indonesia, April 1955* (Ithaca, NY: Cornell University Press, 1956), 39–51, 64–72, 84–85. Copyright © 1956 by Cornell University. Copyright renewed 1984 by George McTurnan Kahin. Used by permission of the publisher, Cornell University Press.

characters . . . are different. Our racial stock is different, and even the colour of our skin is different. But what does that matter?

. . . All of us, I am certain, are united by more important things than those which superficially divide us. We are united, for instance, by a common detestation of colonialism in whatever form it appears. We are united by a common detestation of racialism. And we are united by a common determination to preserve and stabilise peace in the world. . . .

For us, colonialism is not something far and distant. We have known it in all its ruthlessness. We have seen the immense human wastage it causes, the poverty it causes, and the heritage it leaves behind. . . .

I say to you, colonialism is not yet dead. How can we say it is dead, so long as vast areas of Asia and Africa are unfree?

. . . The battle against colonialism has been a long one; and do you know that today is a famous anniversary in that battle? On the eighteenth day of April, one thousand seven hundred and seventy-five, just one hundred and eighty years ago, Paul Revere rode at midnight through the New England countryside, warning of the approach of British troops and of the opening of the American War of Independence, the first successful anti-colonial war in history. . . . But remember, that battle which began 180 years ago is not yet completely won, and it will not have been completely won until we can survey this our own world, and can say that colonialism is dead. . . .

No task is more urgent than that of preserving peace. Without peace our independence means little. The rehabilitation and upbuilding of our countries will have little meaning. Our revolutions will not be allowed to run their course.

What can we do? The peoples of Asia and Africa wield little physical power. Even their economic strength is dispersed and slight. We cannot indulge in power politics. . . .

What can we do? We can do much! We can inject the voice of reason into world affairs. We can mobilise all the spiritual, all the moral, all the political strength of Asia and Africa on the side of peace. Yes, we! We, the peoples of Asia and Africa, 1,400,000,000 strong, far more than half the human population of the world, we can mobilise what I have called the Moral Violence of Nations in favour of peace. We can demonstrate to the minority of the world which lives on the other continents that we, the majority, are for peace, not for war, and that whatever strength we have will always be thrown on to the side of peace.

However, we cannot, we dare not, confine our interests to the affairs of our own continents. The States of the world today depend one upon the other and no nation can be an island unto itself. . . . The affairs of all the world are our affairs, and our future depends upon the solutions found to all international problems, however far or distant they may seem. . . .

If this Conference succeeds in making the peoples of the East whose representatives are gathered here understand each other a little more, . . . then this Conference . . . will have been worthwhile. . . . But I hope that this Conference will give more than understanding only. . . . I hope that this Conference will give guidance to mankind, will point out to mankind the way which it must take to attain safety and peace. I hope that it will give evidence that Asia and Africa have been reborn, nay, that New Asia and a New Africa have been born!

. . . Let us not be bitter about the past, but let us keep our eyes firmly on the future. Let us remember that no blessing of God is so sweet as life and liberty. Let us remember that the stature of all mankind is diminished so long as nations or parts of nations are still unfree. Let us remember that the highest purpose of man is the liberation of man from his bonds of fear, his bonds of human degradation, his bonds of poverty—the liberation of man from the physical, spiritual and intellectual bonds which have for too long stunted the development of humanity's majority. . . .

B. EXCERPTS FROM SPEECH BY INDIA'S PRIME MINISTER NEHRU TO THE BANDUNG CONFERENCE POLITICAL COMMITTEE, APRIL 1955*

I belong to neither [bloc] and I propose to belong to neither whatever happens in the world. . . . We do not agree with the communist teachings, we do not agree with the anti-communist teachings, because they are both based on wrong principles. . . . I am dead certain that no country can conquer India. Even the two great power blocs together cannot conquer India; not even the atom or the hydrogen bomb. I know what my people are. But I know also that if we rely on others, whatever great powers they might be, if we look to them for sustenance, then we are weak indeed. . . .

. . . I speak with the greatest respect of these Great Powers because they are not only great in military might but in development, in culture, in civilization. But I do submit that greatness sometimes brings quite false values. . . . When they begin to think in terms of military strength—whether it be the United Kingdom, the Soviet Union or the USA—then they are going away from the right track and the result of that will be that the overwhelming might of one

* Reprinted from George McTurnan Kahin, *The Asian-African Conference: Bandung, Indonesia, April 1955* (Ithaca, NY: Cornell University Press, 1956), 39–51, 64–72, 84–85. Copyright © 1956 by Cornell University. Copyright renewed 1984 by George McTurnan Kahin. Used by permission of the publisher, Cornell University Press.

country will conquer the world. Thus far the world has succeeded in preventing that; I cannot speak for the future. . . .

. . . So far as I am concerned, it does not matter what war takes place; we will not take part in it unless we have to defend ourselves. If I join any of these big groups I lose my identity. . . . If all the world were to be divided up between these two big blocs what would be the result? The inevitable result would be war. Therefore every step that takes place in reducing that area in the world which may be called the unaligned area is a dangerous step and leads to war. It reduces that objective, that balance, that outlook which other countries without military might can perhaps exercise.

. . . I am a positive person, not an 'anti' person. I want positive good for my country and the world. Therefore, are we, the countries of Asia and Africa, devoid of any positive position except being pro-communist or anti-communist? Has it come to this, that the leaders of thought who have given religions and all kinds of things to the world have to tag on to this kind of group or that and be hangers-on of this party or the other carrying out their wishes and occasionally giving an idea? It is most degrading and humiliating to any self-respecting people or nation. It is an intolerable thought to me that the great countries of Asia and Africa should come out of bondage into freedom only to degrade themselves or humiliate themselves in this way. . . .

C. PRINCIPLES OF THE BANDUNG CONFERENCE'S "DECLARATION ON THE PROMOTION OF WORLD PEACE AND COOPERATION," 24 APRIL 1955*

Free from mistrust and fear, and with confidence and goodwill towards each other, nations should practice tolerance and live together in peace . . . and develop friendly cooperation on the basis of the following principles:

1. Respect for fundamental human rights and for the purposes and principles of the Charter of the United Nations.
2. Respect for the sovereignty and territorial integrity of all nations.
3. Recognition of the equality of all races and of the equality of all nations large and small.
4. Abstention from intervention or interference in the internal affairs of another country.

---

* Reprinted from George McTurnan Kahin, *The Asian-African Conference: Bandung, Indonesia, April 1955* (Ithaca, NY: Cornell University Press, 1956), 39–51, 64–72, 84–85. Copyright © 1956 by Cornell University. Copyright renewed 1984 by George McTurnan Kahin. Used by permission of the publisher, Cornell University Press.

5. Respect for the right of each nation to defend itself singly or collectively, in conformity with the Charter of the United Nations.
6. (a) Abstention from the use of arrangements of collective defence to serve the particular interests of any of the big powers. (b) Abstention by any country from exerting pressures on other countries.
7. Refraining from acts or threats of aggression or the use of force against the territorial integrity or political independence of any country.
8. Settlement of all international disputes by peaceful means, such as negotiation, conciliation, arbitration or judicial settlement. . . .
9. Promotion of mutual interests and cooperation.
10. Respect for justice and international obligations.

Discussion Questions

1. What were Sukarno's goals for the Bandung Conference? How did he think Asian and African nations, lacking wealth and power, could advance the cause of world peace?
2. Why did Sukarno emphasize the struggle of Asians and Africans against colonialism? Why did he note that it was the 180th anniversary of the start of the American Revolution?
3. Why did Nehru see it as weakness for Asian or African nations to align with one of the big power blocs? Why did he claim that such power blocs would lead eventually to war?
4. What were the advantages and disadvantages of nonalignment for Asians and Africans?

29

The Warsaw Pact, 1955

FOR A FEW YEARS FOLLOWING the death of Joseph Stalin in March 1953, the USSR pursued a "new course" in foreign and domestic policy proclaimed by Premier Georgy Malenkov. The Soviets sought to shed their belligerent image, repair their relations with non-Communist countries, and improve living standards by shifting the emphasis of their economy from heavy industry to consumer goods. These initiatives, however, soon came under attack by Moscow hard-liners and military leaders, who combined with Malenkov's rivals in the government to force him out of office in February 1955. Although Nikolai Bulganin replaced him as premier, the real victor was Nikita S. Khrushchev, first secretary of the Soviet Communist Party,* who emerged as the Kremlin's dominant figure.

Khrushchev moved quickly to make his mark on Soviet foreign policy. On the one hand he broached some innovative arms control proposals and agreed to a peace treaty with Austria; on the other hand he moved to strengthen Soviet security and solidify the Communist bloc. In May 1955, following a Western decision to let West Germany rearm and join NATO, officials from the USSR and Eastern Europe met in Poland to form a new treaty system. The resulting alliance, called the Warsaw Pact, included Poland, Czechoslovakia, Hungary, Romania, Bulgaria, East Germany, and Albania, as well as the USSR. Ostensibly intended to counter NATO and defend Eastern Europe, it also provided a pretext for continued Soviet troop presence there and a convenient way for Moscow to keep its satellites in line. Originally designed for twenty years, it would last until 1991.

THE WARSAW SECURITY PACT, 14 MAY 1955

The Contracting Parties, reaffirming their desire for the establishment of a system of European collective security based on the participation of all European states irrespective of their social and political systems, which would make it possible to unite their efforts on safeguarding the peace of Europe; mindful . . . of the situation created in Europe by the ratification of the Paris agreements, which envisage the formation of a new military alignment in the shape of "Western European Union," with the participation of a remilitarized Western Germany and the integration of the latter in the North-Atlantic bloc, which increased the danger of another war and constitutes a threat to the national security of the peaceable states; being persuaded that in these circumstances the peaceable European states must take the necessary measures to safeguard their security and in the interests of preserving peace in Europe; guided by the objects and principles of the Charter of the United Nations Organization; being desirous of further promoting and developing friend-

---

* The main leader of the Soviet Communist Party was the head of its Central Committee, who was known from 1922 to 1952 and 1966 to 1991 as its general secretary and from 1953 to 1966 as its first secretary.

ship, cooperation and mutual assistance in accordance with the principles of respect for the independence and sovereignty of states and of non-interference in their internal affairs, have decided to conclude the present Treaty of Friendship, Cooperation and Mutual Assistance. . . .

Article 1

The Contracting Parties undertake, in accordance with the Charter of the United Nations Organization, to refrain in their international relations from the threat or use of force, and to settle their international disputes peacefully and in such manner as will not jeopardize international peace and security.

Article 2

The Contracting Parties declare their readiness to participate in a spirit of sincere cooperation in all international actions designed to safeguard international peace and security. . . . The Contracting Parties will furthermore strive for the adoption, in agreement with other states which may desire to cooperate in this, of effective measures for universal reduction of armaments and prohibition of atomic, hydrogen and other weapons of mass destruction.

Article 3

The Contracting Parties shall consult with one another on all important international issues affecting their common interests, guided by the desire to strengthen international peace and security. They shall immediately consult with one another whenever, in the opinion of any one of them, a threat of armed attack on one or more of the Parties to the Treaty has arisen, in order to ensure joint defence and the maintenance of peace and security.

Article 4

In the event of armed attack in Europe on one or more of the Parties to the Treaty by any state or group of states, each of the Parties to the Treaty, in the exercise of its right to individual or collective self-defence in accordance with Article 51 of the Charter of the United Nations Organization, shall immediately, either individually or in agreement with other Parties to the Treaty, come to the assistance of the state or states attacked with all such means as it deems necessary, including armed force. The Parties to the Treaty shall immediately consult concerning the necessary measures to be taken by them jointly in order to restore and maintain international peace and security.

Measures taken on the basis of this Article shall be reported to the Security Council in conformity with the Provisions of the Charter of the United

Nations Organization. These measures shall be discontinued immediately [when] the Security Council adopts the necessary measures to restore and maintain international peace and security.

Article 5
The Contracting Parties have agreed to establish a Joint Command of the armed forces . . . , which shall function on the basis of jointly established principles. They shall likewise adopt other agreed measures necessary to strengthen their defensive power, in order to protect the peaceful labours of their peoples, guarantee the inviolability of their frontiers and territories, and provide defence against possible aggression.

Article 6
For the purpose of the consultations among the Parties envisaged in the present Treaty, and also for the purpose of examining questions which may arise in the operation of the Treaty, a Political Consultative Committee shall be set up, in which each of the Parties to the Treaty shall be represented by a member of its Government or by another specifically appointed representative. . . .

Article 7
The Contracting Parties undertake not to participate in any coalitions or alliances and not to conclude any agreements whose objects conflict with the objects of the present Treaty. . . .

Article 8
The Contracting Parties declare that they will act in a spirit of friendship and cooperation with a view to further developing and fostering economic and cultural intercourse with one another, each adhering to the principle of respect for the independence and sovereignty of the others and non-interference in their internal affairs.

Article 9
The present Treaty is open to the accession of other states, irrespective of their social and political systems, which express their readiness by participation in the present Treaty to assist in uniting the efforts of the peaceable states in safeguarding the peace and security of the peoples. . . .

Article 11
The present Treaty shall remain in force for twenty years. . . .

Discussion Questions

1. Why were the Soviets so upset about West Germany's admission to NATO? Why would this development prompt them to form a new alliance?
2. What were the stated goals and purposes of the Warsaw Pact? What other, unstated, goals and purposes might it have had?
3. In what ways was the Warsaw Pact similar to NATO (Document 17)? In what ways did it differ?
4. What were the potential benefits to the USSR of having a joint military command with its Warsaw Pact allies?

30

Khrushchev on Peaceful Coexistence, 1956

ALTHOUGH NIKITA KHRUSHCHEV HAD RISEN to power with a reputation as a hard-liner, he had also experienced the horrors of modern war and had developed a profound conviction that a new world war in the nuclear age would be catastrophic for both sides. In 1955, following the formation of the Warsaw Pact, he took several steps to ease global tensions and lower the threshold of terror. In May his government signed the Austrian State Treaty, agreeing to remove its occupation forces from Austria and allow it to become a neutral and independent nation. He also made a trip to Yugoslavia to repair the relations with Tito that Stalin had ruptured in 1948 (Document 15). In July he went to Geneva for the Cold War era's first summit conference, meeting with the British, French, and US leaders in an effort to improve the international climate. In fall he opened diplomatic ties with West Germany and, on a goodwill visit to India, declared that socialists and capitalists must find a way to live together in peace.

Then, in a major address to the Twentieth Congress of the Soviet Communist Party in February 1956, Khrushchev called for "peaceful coexistence" between communism and capitalism, contended that communism would inevitably prevail because it was a fairer system, and declared it both possible and necessary to avoid another world war. This was a significant reinterpretation of the Marxist premise that war was inevitable as long as capitalism survived. In the years that followed, peaceful coexistence and nonviolent competition between socialism and capitalism would become major themes of Khrushchev's approach to world affairs.

EXCERPTS FROM KHRUSHCHEV'S REPORT TO THE TWENTIETH PARTY CONGRESS, 14 FEBRUARY 1956

. . . For the strengthening of world peace, it would be of tremendous importance to establish firm, friendly relations between the two biggest powers of the world, the Soviet Union and the United States. . . .

We want to be friends with and to cooperate with the United States in the effort for peace and security of the peoples as well as in the economic and cultural fields. We pursue this with good intentions, without holding a stone behind our back. . . .

If good relations are not established between the Soviet Union and the United States, and mutual distrust exists, this will lead to an arms race on a still greater scale and to a still more dangerous growth of the forces on both sides. . . .

The Leninist principle of the peaceful coexistence of states with different social systems was and remains the general line of our country's foreign policy.

It is alleged that the Soviet Union advocates the principle of peaceful coexistence exclusively from tactical considerations of the moment. However it is well known that we have advocated peaceful coexistence . . . from the very inception of Soviet power. Hence, it is not a tactical stratagem but a fundamental principle of Soviet foreign policy. . . .

When we say that in the competition between the two systems of capitalism and socialism, socialism will triumph, this by no means implies that victory will be reached by armed intervention. . . . We believe that after seeing for themselves the advantages that communism holds out, all working men and women on earth will sooner or later take to the road of the struggle to build a socialist society.

We have always asserted and continue to assert that the establishment of a new social order in any country is the internal affair of its people. Such are our positions, based on the great teachings of Marxism-Leninism.

The principle of peaceful coexistence is gaining increasingly wider international recognition. And this is logical, since there is no other way out of the present situation. Indeed, there are only two ways: either peaceful coexistence or the most devastating war in history. There is no third alternative.

We presume that countries with differing social systems cannot just simply exist side by side. There must be progress to better relations, to stronger confidence among them, to cooperation.

As will be recalled, there is a Marxist-Leninist premise which says that while imperialism exists wars are inevitable. While capitalism remains on earth the reactionary forces representing the interests of the capitalist monopolies will continue to strive for war gambles and aggression, and may try to let loose war.

But there is no fatal inevitability of war. Now there are powerful social and political forces, commanding serious means capable of preventing . . . war by the imperialists and—should they try to start it—of delivering a smashing rebuff to the aggressors and thwarting their adventuristic plans.

To this end it is necessary for all the forces opposing war to be vigilant and mobilized. It is necessary for them to act as a united front and not to slacken their efforts in the fight to preserve peace. . . .

Discussion Questions

1. What did Khrushchev mean by "peaceful coexistence," and how did he expect it to work?
2. Why did he assert that Marxists no longer considered war inevitable? What changes did he note on the world scene that made this assertion possible?
3. How did he think Communists should behave toward the capitalist world during peaceful coexistence? Why did he believe that communism would win a peaceful struggle with capitalism?
4. What benefits might he have hoped to derive for himself and his country from this speech? What potential conflicts might it arouse within the Communist camp?

31

Khrushchev's Secret Speech on Stalin and His Crimes, 1956

ALTHOUGH KHRUSHCHEV'S "peaceful coexistence" speech garnered global headlines, the most significant development of the Twentieth Party Congress occurred during its last night, when delegates were summoned back to the conference hall to hear the party boss speak again. There, in a lengthy, rambling, methodical address, he systematically exposed and condemned the crimes of the Stalin era. To the astonishment of assembled party loyalists, he denounced the late dictator for creating a personality cult, blamed him for the torture and murder of numerous party members, accused him of imprisoning multitudes of innocent people, and charged him with disastrous mistakes that damaged his country and cost millions of lives.

Khrushchev's "secret speech" did not stay secret for long. Summaries were distributed and read at private meetings throughout the USSR, and by summer 1956, the US government had obtained a copy, which it translated and published. Whatever its political benefits, the speech would soon have tragic repercussions in Poland and Hungary, where it helped trigger anti-Stalinist and anti-Soviet uprisings later that year.

HIGHLIGHTS OF KHRUSHCHEV'S SECRET SPEECH TO THE TWENTIETH PARTY CONGRESS, 25 FEBRUARY 1956

Comrades, in the report of the Central Committee of the Party at the 20th Congress . . . , a lot has been said about the cult of the individual and its harmful consequences.

After Stalin's death the Central Committee of the Party began explaining concisely and consistently that it is . . . foreign to the spirit of Marxism-Leninism to elevate one person, and to transform him into a superman possessing supernatural characteristics akin to those of a god. Such a man supposedly knows everything, sees everything, thinks for everyone, can do anything, and is infallible. . . .

Such a belief about a man, and specifically about Stalin, was cultivated among us for many years. . . .

Stalin originated the concept of enemy of the people. This term . . . made possible . . . the most cruel repression, violating all norms of revolutionary legality, against anyone who in any way disagreed with Stalin. . . . This led to glaring violations of revolutionary legality, and to the fact that many entirely innocent persons, who in the past had defended the party line, became victims.

. . . It became apparent that many party, Soviet and economic activists, who were branded in 1937–1938 as enemies, were actually never enemies, spies, wreckers, etc., but were always honest Communists; they were only so stigmatized, and often no longer able to bear barbaric tortures they charged themselves (at the order of the investigative judges-falsifiers) with all sorts of grave and unlikely crimes. . . . It was determined that of the 139 members and candidates of the party's Central Committee who were elected at the 17th Congress, 98 persons, i.e., seventy percent, were arrested and shot (mostly in 1937–1938). . . .

Even more widely was the falsification of cases practiced in the provinces. . . . Many thousands of honest and innocent Communists have died as a result of this monstrous falsification of "cases," as a result of the fact that all kinds of slanderous "confessions" were accepted, and as a result of the practice of forcing accusations against oneself and others. . . .

Facts prove that many abuses were made on Stalin's orders without reckoning with any norms of Party and Soviet legality. Stalin was a very distrustful man, sickly suspicious; we knew this from our work with him. He could look at a man and say: "Why are your eyes so shifty today?" or "Why are you turning so much today and avoiding to look me directly in the eyes?" This sickly suspicion created in him a general distrust even toward eminent party workers whom he had known for many years. Everywhere . . . he saw enemies, "two-facers," and "spies."

Possessing unlimited power, he indulged in great willfulness and choked a person morally and physically. A situation was created where one could not express one's own will.

When Stalin said that one or another should be arrested, it was necessary to accept on faith that he was an "enemy of the people." . . . And what proofs were offered? The confessions of the arrested, and the investigative judges accepted these "confessions." And how is it possible that a person confesses to crimes which he has not committed? Only in one way—because of application of physical measures of pressuring him, tortures, bringing him to a state of unconsciousness, deprivation of his judgment, taking away of his human dignity. In this manner were "confessions" acquired. . . .

During the war and after the war, Stalin put forward the thesis that the tragedy which our nation experienced in the first part of the war was the result of the "unexpected" attack of the Germans against the Soviet Union. But, comrades, this is completely untrue. . . . Documents which have now been published show that by April 3, 1941 Churchill, through his ambassador to the USSR Cripps, personally warned Stalin that the Germans had begun regrouping their armed units with the intent of attacking the Soviet Union. . . . Churchill stressed this repeatedly in his dispatches of April 18 and in the following days. However, Stalin took no heed of these warnings. . . . We must assert that information of this sort concerning the threat of German armed invasion . . . was coming in also from our own military and diplomatic sources. . . .

Despite these particularly grave warnings, the necessary steps were not taken to prepare the country properly for defense and prevent it from being caught unaware. . . .

Very grievous consequences, especially in . . . the beginning of the war, followed Stalin's annihilation of many military commanders and political workers during 1937–1941, because of his suspiciousness, and through slanderous accusations. During these years repressions were instituted against . . . military cadres beginning . . . at the company and battalion commander level and extending to the higher military centers; during this time the cadre of leaders who had gained military experience in Spain and the Far East was almost completely liquidated. The . . . large-scale repression against the military cadres led also to undermined military discipline, because for several years officers . . . were taught to unmask their superiors as hidden enemies. . . .

All this brought about the situation which existed at the beginning of the war and which was the great threat to our Fatherland. . . .

Even after the war began, the nervousness and hysteria which Stalin demonstrated, interfering with the actual military operation, caused our army serious damage. . . .

The tactics on which Stalin insisted without knowing the essence of the conduct of battle operations cost us much blood. . . . The military know that already by the end of 1941, instead of great operational maneuvers flanking the opponent and penetrating behind his back, Stalin demanded incessant frontal attacks and the capture of one village after another. Because of this, we paid with great losses. . . .

We must state that, after the war, the situation became even more complicated. Stalin became even more capricious, irritable, and brutal; in particular his suspicion grew. His persecution mania reached unbelievable dimensions. Many workers were becoming enemies before his very eyes. After the war, Stalin separated himself from the collective even more. Everything was decided by him alone without any consideration for anyone or anything. . . .

I recall the first days when the conflict between the Soviet Union and Yugoslavia began artificially to be blown up. Once, when I came from Kiev to Moscow, I was invited to visit Stalin who, pointing to the copy of a letter lately sent to Tito, asked me "Have you read this?" Not waiting for my reply, he answered, "I will shake my little finger and there will be no more Tito. He will fall."

. . . But this did not happen to Tito. No matter how much or how little Stalin shook, not only his little finger but everything else that he could shake, Tito did not fall. . . .

Let us also recall the affair of the doctor-plotters.* Actually, there was no affair outside of the declaration of the woman doctor Timashuk, who was probably influenced or ordered by someone . . . to write Stalin a letter in which she declared that doctors were applying supposedly improper methods of medical treatment. Such a letter was sufficient for Stalin to reach an immediate conclusion that there are doctor-plotters in the Soviet Union. He issued orders to arrest a group of eminent Soviet medical specialists. He personally issued advice on the conduct of the investigation and the method of interrogation of the arrested persons . . . Stalin personally called the investigative judge, gave him instructions, and advised him on which investigative methods should be used. These methods were simple—beat, beat, and once again beat.

Shortly after the doctors were arrested, we members of the Political Bureau received protocols with the doctors' confessions of guilt. After distributing these protocols, Stalin told us, "You are blind like young kittens; what will happen without me? The country will perish because you do not know how to recognize enemies." . . .

Comrades, the cult of the individual acquired such monstrous size chiefly because Stalin himself, using all conceivable methods, supported the glorification of his own person. . . .

Comrades, we must abolish the cult of the individual decisively, once and for all. . . .

Comrades, the 20th Congress of the Communist Party of the Soviet Union has manifested with a new strength the unshakable unity of our party. . . . And the fact that we present in all their ramifications the basic problems of overcoming the cult of the individual . . . is an evidence of the great moral and political strength of our party. We are absolutely certain that our party, armed with the historical resolutions of the 20th Congress, will lead the Soviet people along the Leninist path to new successes, to new victories. . . .

---

* Khrushchev refers here to the "Doctors' Plot" of 1952, which involved the arrest of a number of Soviet doctors who were charged with conspiring to end the lives of Soviet leaders. The case, which many saw as a prelude to a new set of Stalinist purges, was terminated for lack of evidence shortly after Stalin's death in March 1953.

Discussion Questions

1. Why were outsiders excluded from the session at which Khrushchev gave this speech?
2. According to Khrushchev, what was wrong with a "cult of the individual"? What did Khrushchev say were Stalin's methods for dealing with those he distrusted?
3. Why did Khrushchev claim that Stalin was to blame for massive Soviet suffering during World War II? What evidence did he provide to support this claim?
4. Why did Khrushchev give this speech? What positive benefits might he have hoped to derive? What were the risks involved?
5. What negative implications did this speech have for Khrushchev and his comrades in the Soviet leadership, all of whom had served under Stalin?

32

The Hungarian Rebellion, 1956

KHRUSHCHEV'S BLUNT DENUNCIATION of Stalin in the "Secret Speech" reverberated throughout the Soviet bloc. In some respects, this was by design—a signal by Khrushchev to his fellow Communists that his rule would be much more rational and humane than Stalin's. In other respects, however, his remarks undermined his position by calling into question the very legitimacy of the Soviet system, which had been developed largely by Stalin. This was especially true in Eastern Europe, where regimes created under Stalin still functioned in a Stalinist mode.

In June 1956 a bloody clash between demonstrators and police in the Polish city of Poznań threatened to escalate into a nationwide revolt against Soviet domination. But the Polish regime sensibly responded by ousting its hard-liners and replacing them with moderates such as Wladyslaw Gomulka, who had been purged by Stalin and had spent time in Soviet prison. Gomulka and his comrades assured Moscow that they would reform Poland without taking it out of the Warsaw Pact, and Khrushchev agreed to work with them.

Events in Hungary proved to be far more dangerous to Soviet rule, and Moscow's reaction proved to be much harsher. In October 1956, encouraged by events in Poland, students in Budapest, the capital city, demonstrated for the removal of Hungary's Stalinist rulers. Soviet forces were sent to restore order, but this only led to more uprisings, so popular reformer Imre Nagy was installed as premier to appease the people. The Soviets began withdrawing their forces, but as demonstrations continued, Nagy announced his intent to remove Hungary from the Warsaw Pact, end the Communist power monopoly, and declare neutrality in the Cold War. This went beyond what Khrushchev was willing to permit, so on the morning of 4 November, Soviet tanks rolled into Budapest. Nagy was removed and a new regime installed that was more to Soviet liking. The following excerpts provide insights into the gravity and tone of these events.

A. EXCERPTS FROM SOVIET GOVERNMENT STATEMENT, 30 OCTOBER 1956

... The Soviet Government regards it as indispensable to make a statement in connection with the events in Hungary.

The course of events has shown that the working people of Hungary, who have achieved great progress on the basis of the people's democratic order, are rightly raising the question of the necessity of eliminating serious shortcomings in the field of economic building, of the further raising of the material well-being of the population, and in the struggle against bureaucratic distortions in the state apparatus. However, this just and progressive movement of the working people was soon joined by forces of black reaction and counterrevolution, which are trying to take advantage of the discontent on the part of the working people in order to undermine the foundations of the people's democratic order in Hungary and to restore there the old landlords' and capitalists' order.

The Soviet Government, like the whole of the Soviet people, deeply regrets that the development of events in Hungary has led to bloodshed. At the request of the Hungarian people's government, the Soviet Government consented on the entry into Budapest of Soviet Army units for the purpose of assisting the Hungarian People's Army and the Hungarian organs of authority to establish order in the town.

Since it considers that the further presence of Soviet Army units in Hungary can serve as a cause for even greater deterioration of the situation, the Soviet Government has given an instruction to its military command to withdraw the Soviet Army units from Budapest as soon as this is recognized by the Hungarian Government to be necessary.

At the same time, the Soviet Government is ready to enter into corresponding negotiations with the Government of the Hungarian People's Republic and other participants of the Warsaw Treaty on the question of the presence of Soviet troops on the territory of Hungary. . . .

B. HUNGARIAN APPEALS FOR HELP, 4 NOVEMBER 1956

Statement by Premier Imre Nagy over Budapest Radio:
"Soviet troops have opened an attack on Budapest at dawn with the clear intention to overthrow the lawful, democratic government of the Hungarian people. Our troops are fighting the Soviets for right and freedom. The government is at its place! This we bring to the information of the Hungarian people and the entire world."

Teletype Message from Hungarian News Agency:
"Russian gangsters have betrayed us. The Russian troops suddenly attacked Budapest and the whole country. They opened fire on everybody in Hungary. It is a general attack. . . .

"I speak in the name of Imre Nagy. He asks help . . . Nagy and the whole government and the whole people ask help. . . .

"Long live Hungary and Europe! We shall die for Hungary and Europe. . . .

"Any news about help? Quickly, quickly, quickly. . . .

"The Russian attack was started at 4 A.M. Russian MiG fighters are over Budapest. . . .

"We have no time to lose, we have no time to lose. . . ."

Teletype Message from Budapest Newspaper:
"Since the early morning hours Russian troops are attacking Budapest and our population. . . .

"Please tell the world of the treacherous attack against our struggle for liberty. . . .

"Our troops are already engaged in fighting. . . .

"Help! Help! Help!

"S.O.S.! S.O.S.! S.O.S.!

"We have almost no weapons—only light machine guns, Russian-made long rifles and some carbines. We haven't any kind of heavy guns. The people are jumping at the tanks, throwing in hand grenades and closing the drivers' windows.

"The Hungarian people are not afraid of death. It is only a pity that we can't stand for long. . . .

"Now the firing is starting again. We are getting hits. . . .

"What is the United Nations doing? Give us a little encouragement. . . .

"The people have just turned over a streetcar to use as a barricade near the building. In the building, young people are making Molotov cocktails and hand grenades to fight the tanks. We are quiet, not afraid. . . .

"They just brought us a rumor that the American troops will be here within one or two hours. . . . We are well and fighting at 9:20 A.M."

C. EXCERPTS FROM THE PROCLAMATION OF A NEW HUNGARIAN GOVERNMENT, 4 NOVEMBER 1956

A Hungarian Workers and Peasants Government has been formed.

On October 23 a mass movement began in our country, whose noble purpose was to make good the anti-party and anti-national mistakes committed by Rakosi and his accomplices, and to defend the national independence and sovereignty of Hungary.

The weakness of Imre Nagy's government and the growing influence of counter-revolutionary elements in the revolutionary movement endangered our Socialist conquests, our people's state, our workers and peasants power, the very existence of our homeland.

This has led us, Hungarian patriots, to the creation of the Hungarian Revolutionary Workers and Peasants Government. . . .

The newly-formed Government addresses itself to the Hungarian people with the following appeal:

Brother Hungarians, workers, peasants, soldiers, comrades, our nation is living through hard times. The power of workers and peasants, the holy cause of socialism is in danger. Great danger hangs over the conquests of the last twelve years, which you Hungarian working people . . . have created with your hands by your heroic self-sacrificing labor.

The counter-revolutionary plotters are becoming increasingly daring. They are mercilessly persecuting the supporters of democracy. The Nihilists and other Fascist evil-doers are killing honest patriots and our best comrades. . . .

The reactionaries are working for their selfish aims. They have raised their hands against our people's democratic system. This signifies that they want to return the factories and works to the capitalists, and the land to the landlords. . . .

They would not have brought you freedom, prosperity and democracy had they won, but slavery, poverty, unemployment, and ruthless landlord exploitation. . . .

Exploiting the weakness of the Imre Nagy Government, the counter-revolutionary forces are marauding, murdering and robbing, and we must fear that their forces might get the upper hand. With deep sorrow and a heavy heart we see into what a terrible situation our beloved country has been dragged by counter-revolutionary elements, and often even by conscientious and progressive people, who consciously or unconsciously misused the slogans of democracy and freedom, and thus paved the road for the reactionaries.

Brothers, patriots, soldiers, and citizens. An end must be put to the misdeeds of the counter-revolutionary elements. The hour of action has struck.

We shall defend the powers of workers and peasants, the conquests of the people's democracy. We shall restore order, security and calm in our country. The interests of the people, the interests of our homeland demand that a stable and strong government be established, a government capable of bringing the country out of its present difficult position.

That is why we have formed the Hungarian Revolutionary Workers and Peasants Government. . . .

Discussion Questions

1. In what ways did the 30 October Soviet statement seem to hold out hopes for conciliation between Hungary and the USSR?
2. Why did the Soviets seem willing to compromise on October 30 but then invade on 4 November?
3. Why were the 4 November broadcasts and dispatches from Budapest so frantic? Why might the Hungarians have expected outside help?
4. Why did the outside world, and especially the United States, not come to the aid of the Hungarian rebels?
5. How did the new Hungarian government of 4 November justify taking power? What do you think were the real reasons for formation of this new government?

33

The Suez Crisis, 1956

IN THE 1950S THE MIDDLE EAST emerged as a Cold War battleground. A nationalist revolution in Egypt, headed by the dynamic and ambitious Gamal Abdel Nasser, denounced the State of Israel, aided Algerian rebels fighting against France, and recognized Communist China as a response to the United States' support for Israel. Increasingly irritated by Nasser's conduct, the United States withdrew its funding for construction of the Aswan High Dam, a project dear to Nasser. The Egyptian president responded by nationalizing the Suez Canal, whose tolls would help fund the dam project, and Moscow opportunistically offered financial and technical aid. In response to these events, Britain and France, dependent on the canal and Middle East oil, conspired with Israel to launch an attack on Egypt and seize the canal in late October 1956.

The attack misfired. Israeli forces defeated key units of Egypt's army, but British and French forces were unable to take the canal. Washington, fearing that the war would benefit the Soviets and Arab nationalists, obtained UN resolutions calling for withdrawal of all invading troops, while Moscow called for joint US-Soviet action to end the hostilities. Lacking American support, and fearful of Soviet intervention, Britain and France were forced to withdraw their troops.

Both the Americans and the Soviets had reason to wish the crisis had never occurred. Washington was placed in the awkward position of disavowing its closest allies, while Moscow was rebuffed in its efforts to arrange joint action with the United States. The Kremlin was also forced to watch as the United States enjoyed a surge of popularity among Arab states because of its opposition to Britain, France, and Israel—an opposition that was widely viewed as anticolonialist in nature. If there was a winner in the crisis, it was Nasser, who consolidated Egypt's control of the canal and whose prestige in the Arab world skyrocketed.

A. WITHDRAWAL OF US SUPPORT FOR
THE ASWAN DAM PROJECT, 19 JULY 1956

At the request of the Government of Egypt, the United States joined in December 1955 with the United Kingdom and with the World Bank in an offer to assist Egypt in the construction of a high dam on the Nile at Aswan. This project is one of great magnitude. It would require an estimated 12 to 16 years to complete at a total cost estimated at some $1,300,000,000. . . . It involves not merely the rights and interests of Egypt but of other states whose waters are contributory, including Sudan, Ethiopia, and Uganda. . . .

Developments within the succeeding 7 months have not been favorable to the success of the project, and the US Government has concluded that it is not feasible in present circumstances to participate in the project. Agreement by the riparian states has not been achieved, and the ability of Egypt to devote adequate resources to assure the project's success has become more uncertain than at the time the offer was made.

This decision in no way reflects or involves any alteration in the friendly relations of the Government and people of the United States toward the Government and people of Egypt. . . .

B. PRESIDENT NASSER'S SPEECH NATIONALIZING
THE SUEZ CANAL COMPANY, 26 JULY 1956

[Speaking of a meeting with Eugene R. Black, President of the International Bank for Reconstruction and Development, with which Egypt had been negotiating for a loan to help finance the construction of the Aswan Dam Project, President Nasser said:] I began to look at Mr. Black sitting in his chair imagining that I was sitting before Ferdinand De Lesseps. *[Ferdinand De Lesseps was the driving force behind the construction of the Suez Canal; the mention of his name in this speech was Nasser's prearranged signal to his troops to seize the Canal.]*

. . . In 1854, Ferdinand De Lesseps arrived in Egypt. He went to Mohamed Said Pasha, the Khedive. He sat beside him and told him, "We want to dig the Suez Canal. This project will greatly benefit you. It is a great project and will bring excellent returns to Egypt."

. . . The result of the words of De Lesseps in 1856, the result of friendship and loans, was the occupation of Egypt in 1882. . . .

We shall not repeat the past. We shall eradicate it by restoring our rights in the Suez Canal. This money is ours. This Canal is the property of Egypt because it is an Egyptian Joint Stock Company.

The Canal was dug by Egypt's sons and 120,000 of them died while working. The Suez Canal Company in Paris is an imposter company. It usurped our concessions. . . .

But history will never repeat itself. On the contrary, we shall build the High Dam. We shall restore our usurped rights. We shall build the High Dam as we want it. We are determined to do it. Thirty-five million Egyptian pounds the company gets every year; let Egypt take it. . . .

Therefore, I have signed today the following law which has been approved by the Cabinet: *[President Nasser then read the text of the Presidential decree on the Nationalization of the Suez Canal Company.]*

. . . Today, citizens, rights have been restored to their owners. . . .

Today, we actually achieve true sovereignty, true dignity and true pride. . . .

Today, when we regain our rights, I say in the name of the people of Egypt that we shall defend these rights and hold them fast. We shall sacrifice our lives and our blood in defending them. We shall make up for the past. . . .

Today, citizens, the Suez Canal Company has been nationalized. This order has been published in the Official Journal. It has become a matter of fact. . . .

Now, while I am speaking to you, fellow countrymen, brothers of yours are taking over the administration and the management of the Canal Company . . . for the direction of navigation in the Canal, the Canal which is situated in the territory of Egypt, cuts through the territory of Egypt, is a part of Egypt and belongs to Egypt. We now perform this task to compensate for the past and build up new edifices for pride and dignity.

May God guide you and peace be with you.

C. EXCERPTS FROM PRESIDENT EISENHOWER'S ADDRESS, 31 OCTOBER 1956

. . . The United States, through all the years since the close of World War II, has labored tirelessly to bring peace and stability to [the Middle East]. We have considered it a basic matter of United States policy to support the new state of Israel and, at the same time, to strengthen our bonds both with Israel and the Arab countries. But, unfortunately, through all these years passion in the area threatened to prevail over peaceful purpose, and in one form or another there has been almost continuous fighting.

This situation recently was aggravated by Egyptian policy, including re-armament with Communist weapons. We felt this to be a misguided policy. . . . The state of Israel, at the same time, felt increasing anxiety for its safety. And Great Britain and France feared more and more that Egyptian policies threatened their lifeline of the Suez Canal.

These matters came to a crisis on July 26 of this year when the Egyptian Government seized the Universal Suez Canal Company. For ninety years, ever since the inauguration of the canal, that company has operated the canal—largely under British and French technical supervision.

Now, there were some among our allies who urged an immediate reaction to this event by use of force. We insistently urged otherwise, and our wish prevailed, through a long succession of conferences and negotiations. . . .

But the direct relations of Egypt with both Israel and France kept worsening to a point at which first Israel, then France—and Great Britain also—determined that in their judgment there could be no protection of their vital interests without resort to force.

Upon this decision events followed swiftly. On Sunday the Israeli Government ordered total mobilization. On Monday their armed forces penetrated deeply into Egypt and to the vicinity of the Suez Canal. . . . And on Tuesday the British and French Governments delivered a twelve-hour ultimatum to Israel and Egypt, now followed up by armed attack against Egypt.

The United States was not consulted in any way about any phase of these actions. . . .

We believe these actions to have been taken in error, for we do not accept the use of force as a wise or proper instrument for the settlement of international disputes. To say this . . . is in no way to minimize our friendship with these nations. . . . And we are fully aware of the grave anxieties of Israel, of Britain, and of France. . . .

The present fact nonetheless seems clear. The action taken can scarcely be reconciled with the principles and purposes of the United Nations to which we have all subscribed. . . .

We took our first measure in this action yesterday. We went to the United Nations with a request that the forces of Israel return to their own line and that hostilities in the area be brought to a close. The proposal was not adopted because it was vetoed by Great Britain and by France. It is our hope and intent that this matter will be brought before the United Nations General Assembly. There, with no veto operating, the opinion of the world can be brought to bear in our quest for a just end to this tormenting problem. . . .

Discussion Questions

1. What reasons did the Americans give for withdrawing from the Aswan Dam project? What other reasons did they have?

2. Why did Nasser link the financial benefits of nationalizing the Canal Company to Egyptian pride and dignity? Why did he emphasize Egypt's legal rights to the canal?
3. What was Eisenhower's analysis of the Suez situation? What reasons did he give for not supporting Israel, Britain, and France? What other reasons did he have?
4. What did each of the participants gain from the Suez Crisis. What did they lose?

34

The Eisenhower Doctrine, 1957

THE UNITED STATES MANAGED to limit the damage from the Suez crisis, but President Eisenhower foresaw increased Communist pressure on Arab states in the wake of Nasser's moral victory. Hoping to forestall such pressure, he formulated the Eisenhower Doctrine, modeled on the Truman Doctrine (Document 8). Confined to the Middle East, the Eisenhower Doctrine assured nations threatened by Communist subversion or attack that the United States would provide them with economic and military aid.

Eisenhower's initiative was designed to put Nasser in his place, since the Egyptian president's successful defiance of Britain and France had made him tremendously popular throughout the region. Nasser had played a leading role at the Bandung Asian-African Conference in 1955 (Document 28) and had made no secret of his desire to unite the Arab world under his leadership. Eisenhower acted in 1957 to "contain" Arab nationalism the way Truman had acted to "contain" communism in 1947. Both doctrines were issued in response to decisions by the British to lessen their influence in a particular region—a voluntary decision in 1947, but an involuntary one following the Suez fiasco ten years later. The Eisenhower Doctrine initiated a chain of events that led to the creation of a US commitment to Middle Eastern stability, a commitment that actually outlasted the Cold War.

A. EXCERPTS FROM EISENHOWER'S MESSAGE TO CONGRESS ON THE MIDDLE EAST, 5 JANUARY 1957

... It is nothing new for the President and the Congress to join to recognize that the national integrity of other free nations is directly related to our own security.

We have joined to create and support the security system of the United Nations. We have reinforced the collective security system of the United Nations by a series of collective defense arrangements. Today we have security treaties with 42 other nations which recognize that their, and our, peace and security are intertwined. We have joined to take decisive action in relation to Greece and Turkey and in relation to Taiwan.

Thus, the United States ... has manifested in many endangered areas its purpose to support free and independent governments—and peace—against external menace, notably the menace of International Communism. Thereby we have helped to maintain peace and security during a period of great danger. It is now essential that the United States should manifest through joint action of the President and the Congress our determination to assist those nations of the Mid East area which desire that assistance.

The action which I propose would have the following features.

It would, first of all, authorize the United States to cooperate with and assist any nation or group of nations in the general area of the Middle East in the development of economic strength dedicated to the maintenance of national independence.

It would, in the second place, authorize the Executive to undertake in the same region programs of military assistance and cooperation with any nation or group of nations which desires such aid.

It would, in the third place, authorize such assistance and cooperation to include the employment of the armed forces of the United States to secure and protect the territorial integrity and political independence of such nations, requesting such aid, against overt armed aggression from any nation controlled by International Communism. ...

The present proposal would, in the fourth place, authorize the President to employ, for economic and defensive military purposes, sums available under the Mutual Security Act of 1954, as amended, without regard to existing limitations. ...

B. JOINT CONGRESSIONAL RESOLUTION TO PROMOTE PEACE AND STABILITY IN THE MIDDLE EAST, APPROVED BY THE PRESIDENT ON 9 MARCH 1957

Resolved by the Senate and House of Representatives of the United States of America in Congress assembled,

That the President be and hereby is authorized to cooperate with and assist any nation or group of nations in the general area of the Middle East desiring such assistance in the development of economic strength dedicated to the maintenance of national independence.

SEC. 2. The President is authorized to undertake, in the general area of the Middle East, military assistance programs with any nation or group of nations in that area desiring such assistance. Furthermore, the United States regards as vital to the national interest and world peace the preservation of the independence and integrity of the nations of the Middle East. To this end, if the President determines the necessity thereof, the United States is prepared to use armed forces to assist any such nation or group of such nations requesting assistance against armed aggression from any country controlled by international communism. . . .

SEC. 4. The President should continue to furnish facilities and military assistance, within the provisions of applicable law and established policies, to the United Nations Emergency Force in the Middle East, with a view to maintaining the truce in that region.

SEC. 6. This joint resolution shall expire when the President shall determine that the peace and security of the nations in the general area of the Middle East are reasonably assured by international conditions created by action of the United Nations or otherwise, except that it may be terminated earlier by a concurrent resolution of the two Houses of Congress.

Discussion Questions

1. Why did Eisenhower stress "development of economic strength dedicated to the maintenance of national independence"? What earlier Cold War documents are echoed in that phrase?
2. Why did he consider it necessary to seek congressional support for this doctrine?
3. What problems might arise from Congress's authorization for the president to use armed forces to aid any nation requesting assistance against armed aggression?
4. What was the relationship between the Truman and Eisenhower Doctrines and the gradual weakening of the British and French colonial empires?
5. How would you expect Egyptian President Nasser to react to the Eisenhower Doctrine?

35

Europe's Common Market:
The Treaty of Rome, 1957

SEEING WESTERN EUROPE'S STRENGTH and stability as essential to combating communism, the United States introduced the Marshall Plan in 1947 (Document 9) to aid Europe's economic recovery. Using this aid, nations such as West Germany, Italy, and France created "economic miracles" to regain prosperity between 1948 and 1951. Simultaneously, the Treaty of Brussels (Document 14) and the North Atlantic Treaty (Document 17) provided for military cooperation among Western European nations. As economic recovery continued, the merits of extending such cooperation to economic matters became apparent.

On 18 April 1951, six Western European nations (Belgium, the Netherlands, Luxembourg, Italy, France, and West Germany) signed a treaty establishing the European Coal and Steel Community. Since coal and steel were basic sinews of war, the signatories felt that a treaty binding them (especially France and West Germany) to peacetime cooperation in the production of these commodities would not only enhance their prosperity but also integrate their economies to make future war between them virtually impossible. Six years later, the same six nations met at Rome to create a European Economic Community (EEC) or "Common Market" covering all agricultural, industrial, and commercial production.

The 1957 Treaty of Rome had revolutionary implications. In 1833 the establishment of the Zollverein, a customs union in Central Europe, foreshadowed the eventual unification of Germany. In 1957 the creation of the EEC reflected hopes that a unified Europe could banish the scourge of war from that continent. Its anti-Soviet tone was obvious, particularly when Moscow responded to the Treaty of Rome with the creation of COMECON, a Common Market of the Communist bloc. Over the following decades, the EEC would grow into the European Community and later the European Union, bringing in numerous new members and enhancing European unity. For the moment, European nations that had recently suffered through two world wars dared to hope that the Treaty of Rome would make a third war less likely.

EXCERPTS FROM THE TREATY OF ROME, 25 MARCH 1957

HIS MAJESTY THE KING OF THE BELGIANS, THE PRESIDENT OF THE FEDERAL REPUBLIC OF GERMANY, THE PRESIDENT OF THE FRENCH REPUBLIC, THE PRESIDENT OF THE ITALIAN REPUBLIC, HER ROYAL HIGHNESS THE GRAND DUCHESS OF LUXEMBOURG, HER MAJESTY THE QUEEN OF THE NETHERLANDS,

DETERMINED to establish the foundation of an ever closer union among the European peoples,

DECIDED to ensure the economic and social progress of their countries by common action in eliminating the barriers which divide Europe,

DIRECTING their efforts to the essential purpose of constantly improving the living and working conditions of their peoples . . . ,

ANXIOUS to strengthen the unity of their economies and to ensure their harmonious development by reducing the differences existing between the various regions and by mitigating the backwardness of the less favoured,

DESIROUS of contributing by means of a common commercial policy to the progressive abolition of restrictions on international trade . . . ,

RESOLVED to strengthen the safeguards of peace and liberty by establishing this combination of resources and calling upon the other peoples of Europe who share their ideal to join in their efforts,

Have decided to create a European Economic Community. . . .

Article 1
By the present Treaty, the HIGH CONTRACTING PARTIES establish among themselves a EUROPEAN ECONOMIC COMMUNITY.

Article 2
It shall be the aim of the Community, by establishing a Common Market and progressively approximating the economic policies of Member States, to promote throughout the Community a harmonious development of economic activities, a continuous and balanced expansion, an increased stability, an accelerated raising of the standard of living and closer relations between its Member States.

Article 3

For the purposes set out in the preceding Article, the activities of the Community shall include, under the conditions and with the timing provided for in this Treaty:

(a) The elimination, as between Member States, of customs duties and of quantitative restrictions in regard to the importation and exportation of goods . . . ;

(b) The establishment of a common customs tariff and a common commercial policy toward third countries;

(c) The abolition, as between Member States, of the obstacles to the free movement of persons, services and capital;

(d) The inauguration of a common agricultural policy;

(e) The inauguration of a common transport policy;

(f) The establishment of a system ensuring that competition shall not be distorted in the Common Market;

(g) The application of procedures which shall make it possible to coordinate the economic policies of Member States and to remedy disequilibria in their balances of payments;

(h) The approximation of their respective municipal law to the extent necessary for the functioning of the Common Market;

(i) The creation of a European Social Fund in order to improve the possibilities of employment for workers and to contribute to the raising of their standard of living;

(j) The establishment of a European Investment Bank intended to facilitate the economic expansion of the Community through the creation of new resources; and

(k) The association of overseas countries and territories with the Community with a view to increasing trade and to pursuing jointly their . . . economic and social development. . . .

Article 9

1. The Community shall be based upon a customs union covering the exchange of all goods and comprising both the prohibition, as between Member States, of customs duties on importation and exportation and all charges with equivalent effect and the adoption of a common customs tariff in their relations with third countries. . . .

Signed at Rome on March 25, 1957.

Discussion Questions

1. Why was it so important to tie together the economies of France and West Germany following World War II?
2. How would the reduction of tariffs between member states and the establishment of a common external tariff against nonmembers benefit the signatories of the Treaty of Rome?
3. Which aspects of the treaty appear designed to appeal to left-wing political movements within the member states?
4. In what ways did the Treaty of Rome make eventual political unification possible in Europe?
5. Why would the USSR be unhappy about the Treaty of Rome?

36

China's "Great Leap Forward," 1958–1960

FOR MOST OF THEIR FIRST DECADE in power, the Chinese Communists took Soviet aid and followed the Soviet model, centralizing their economy and even adopting a Stalin-style Five-Year Plan to promote industrial growth. But in time China's leader, Mao Zedong, grew disenchanted with the Soviets and their system, based as it was on powerful bureaucrats who ruled in the name of the urban proletariat. Inspired by his own peasant roots and his scorn for urban elites, and impatient with the slow pace of growth, in 1958 he and his comrades launched the "Great Leap Forward," a mass campaign to remake China into an agrarian-industrial powerhouse. Peasants were herded into huge rural communes of up to ten thousand families, with collective work brigades, communal dining halls, and even their own small factories. Industry was moved from the cities to the communes, where peasants made goods in rural workshops and steel in backyard furnaces, pressured and prodded to make prodigious progress at a rate of "twenty years in a day."

But the Great Leap Forward became a great catastrophe. Rural workshops and backyard furnaces produced poor-quality goods and steel, while pressure to meet unfeasible goals led to overstated harvests and eventually to vast food shortages. Natural disasters in 1960 added to human toll, combining with a horrific famine to kill at least twenty million people.

This catastrophe also had important Cold War complications. Offended by Mao's rejection of their model and loath to continue their support for his disastrous programs, in 1960 the Soviets cut off aid, contributing to a growing rift between China and the USSR (Documents 50A–D).

The excerpts below reflect the early efforts of Chinese leaders to arouse enthusiasm for the Great Leap Forward. The first set is from a report by Communist Party Vice Chairman Liu Shaoqi that paints a rosy picture of impressive success; the second set comes from an article extolling the virtues of the "people's communes" as the basic building blocks of a glorious Communist future.

A. LIU SHAOQI ON THE PROGRESS
AND GOALS OF THE "GREAT LEAP FORWARD," 1958

. . . [T]he spring of 1958 witnessed the beginning of a leap forward on every front in our socialist construction. Industry, agriculture and all other fields of activity are registering greater and more rapid growth.

To begin with industry: The total value of industrial output for the first four months of this year was 26 percent higher than in the same period last [year]. . . . Nearly one thousand above-norm projects will be under construction this year. . . . In addition, construction work has already started on thousands of medium and small-sized coal mines, power stations, oil refineries, iron and steel plants, nonferrous mines, chemical fertilizer plants, cement plants, engineering works, and agricultural and animal products processing plants. . . . The rapid growth of the local industries is one of the outstanding features of this year's industrial upswing. . . .

In agriculture, the most striking leap took place in the campaign of the cooperative farmers to build irrigation works. From last October to April this year, the irrigated acreage throughout the country increased by . . . more than the total acreage brought under irrigation in the thousands of years before liberation. . . . This gives proof of the power to conquer nature which the masses of the people have demonstrated in the field of agriculture following the great socialist revolution. . . .

Rapid developments are also taking place in the fields of culture, education, and public health. Energetic efforts are being made in many villages throughout the country to eliminate illiteracy and establish large numbers of primary and secondary schools financed by the people. Cultural and artistic activities among the masses are advancing quickly. The public health campaign centered on the elimination of the four pests [flies, rats, mosquitoes, and sparrows] has already spread to every urban and rural district and achieved notable results. . . .

In the light of the practical experience gained in the people's struggle and of the development of Comrade Mao Zedong's thinking in the past few years, the Central Committee of the Party is of the opinion that the following are the basic points of our general line, which is to build socialism by exerting our utmost efforts, and pressing ahead consistently to achieve greater, faster, better, and more economical results:

To mobilize all positive factors and correctly handle contradictions among the people;

To consolidate and develop socialist ownership, that is, ownership by the whole people and collective ownership . . . ;

To carry out the technical revolution and cultural revolution step by step, while completing the socialist revolution on the economic, political and ideological fronts;

To develop industry and agriculture simultaneously while giving priority to heavy industry;

With centralized leadership, overall planning, proper division of labor and coordination, to develop national and local industries, and large, small, and medium-sized enterprises simultaneously; and

By means of all this, to build our country, in the shortest possible time, into a great socialist country with a modern industry, modern agriculture, and modern science and culture. . . .

B. EXCERPTS FROM "HOLD HIGH THE RED FLAG OF PEOPLE'S COMMUNES," 3 SEPTEMBER 1958

People's communes, which mark a new stage in the socialist movement in China's rural areas, are now being set up and developed in many places at a rapid rate.

This movement has been spontaneously started by the mass of peasants on the basis of great socialist consciousness. When a small number of people's communes were first established, their success at once inspired many of the agricultural producers' co-operatives to follow suit. The movement gradually gained momentum. Now, with the encouragement and guidance given by the Central Committee of the Communist Party and Chairman Mao Zedong, it is making even greater strides forward. . . .

Where the people's communes have already come into existence, the peasants, beating drums and gongs, celebrated the occasion with great joy, and their enthusiasm for production has reached a new height. The poor and lower-middle peasants, in particular, rejoice in the formation of the commune and regard it as the "realization of a long-cherished dream."

The people's commune is characterized by its bigger size and more socialist nature. With big membership and huge expanse of land the communes can carry out production and construction . . . on a large scale. They not only carry out an all-round management of agriculture, forestry, animal husbandry, side-occupations and fishery, but merge industry (the worker), agriculture (the peasant), exchange (the trader), culture and education (the student), and military affairs (the military man) into one.

People's communes so far established usually have a membership of 10,000 people each, in some cases 10,000 households. . . .

Being big, they can do many things hitherto impossible to the agricultural producers' co-operatives, such as building medium-sized water-conservancy works, setting up factories and mines requiring complicated technique, carrying out big projects of road and housing construction, establishing secondary schools and schools of higher learning, etc. . . .

The people's commune represents a much higher degree of socialist development and collectivization. . . .

As the people's commune has for its membership workers, peasants, traders, students and militiamen it is no longer a solely economic organization—it combines economic, cultural, political and military affairs into one entity. . . . This facilitates unified leadership . . . and helps the transition . . . to ownership by the whole people.

For this reason the people's commune is the most appropriate organizational form in China for accelerating socialist construction and the transition to communism. . . .

It will become the basic social unit in the future communist society as thinkers—from many outstanding utopian socialists to Marx, Engels, and Lenin—had predicted on many occasions. . . .

The establishment of people's communes has provided good conditions for the further development of the relations of production in the countryside. The expansion of the people's communes . . . makes it possible gradually to eliminate the differences between rural and urban areas, between peasants and workers, between peasants and intellectuals, as well as between collective ownership and ownership by the whole people. . . .

Discussion Questions

1. Why did China's leadership abandon the Soviet model and launch the "Great Leap Forward"? What were its main goals and objectives?
2. Why did Liu Shaoqi portray such impressive progress under the Great Leap Forward? What are the potential advantages and pitfalls of painting such a rosy picture?
3. What were the main goals and objectives of forming the "people's communes"? How were they meant to merge agriculture, industry, commerce, education, culture, and defense? How could they support the growth of Communist ideals and socialistic society?
4. Why might some peasants welcome the communes but others oppose and resist them?
5. Why was the Great Leap Forward such a catastrophic failure? Why would this program and its failure contribute to the growing rift between China and the USSR?

37

Harold Macmillan's "Wind of Change" Speech, 1960

HAROLD MACMILLAN HAD BEEN chancellor of the exchequer in Prime Minister Anthony Eden's British Cabinet at the time of the Suez Crisis (Document 33). After the fiasco he succeeded Eden as prime minister and recognized the futility of attempting to hang on to Britain's African empire. But Macmillan wanted to liberate British colonies gradually and on peaceful terms, hoping to maintain British influence in the newly independent nations. He also feared the consequences of the Union of South Africa's election of a radical nationalist government in 1948, a government that installed a brutal, rigorous segregation of the races known as apartheid.

Macmillan worried that white suppression of African nationalism would drive Africans into the arms of Moscow. When the British colonies of the Central African Federation (Northern Rhodesia, Southern Rhodesia, and Nyasa-land), which bordered the Union of South Africa to the north, adopted policies that resembled those of their southern neighbor, Macmillan worked diligently to moderate those policies. After winning a sizable parliamentary majority in the general election of October 1959, he embarked on a six-week tour of Africa, hoping to gain support for his gradual path to independence. On 3 February 1960 he spoke before a skeptical South African parliament and uttered a phrase that resonated across Africa when he spoke of "the wind of change."

African nationalists, startled at such forthrightness from a British prime minister, rejoiced at his candor. His rhetoric also moved his South African listeners, but not in the direction he intended. In 1961 South Africa withdrew from the British Commonwealth of Nations, intensified its apartheid policies, and quickly became an outcast from the international community. Not until the early 1990s, after the end of the Cold War, would South Africa acknowledge the wind of change and elect a black majority government.

EXCERPTS FROM THE SPEECH OF BRITISH PRIME MINISTER HAROLD MACMILLAN TO THE PARLIAMENT OF THE UNION OF SOUTH AFRICA, 3 FEBRUARY 1960

It is, as I have said, a special privilege for me to be here in 1960 when you are celebrating what I might call the golden wedding of the Union. At such a time it is natural and right that you should pause to take stock of your position, to look back at what you have achieved, to look forward to what lies ahead.

In the fifty years of their nationhood the people of South Africa have built a strong economy founded upon a healthy agriculture and thriving and resilient industries. No one could fail to be impressed with the immense material progress which has been achieved.

That all this has been accomplished in so short a time is a striking testimony to the skill, energy and initiative of your people. We in Britain are proud of the contribution we have made to this remarkable achievement. Much of it has been financed by British capital. According to the recent survey made by the Union Government, nearly two-thirds of the oversea investment outstanding in the Union at the end of 1956 was British. That is after two staggering wars which have bled our economy white.

But that is not all. We have developed trade between us to our common advantage, and our economies are now largely interdependent. You export to us raw materials, food and gold. We in return send you consumer goods or capital equipment. We take a third of all your exports and we supply a third of all your imports. This broad traditional pattern of investment and trade has been maintained in spite of the changes brought by the development of our two economies, and it gives me great encouragement to reflect that the economies of both our countries, while expanding rapidly, have yet remained interdependent and capable of sustaining one another.

In the twentieth century, and especially since the end of the war, the processes which gave birth to the nation states of Europe have been repeated all over the world. We have seen the awakening of national consciousness in peoples who have for centuries lived in dependence upon some other power.

Fifteen years ago this movement spread through Asia. Many countries there of different races and civilisations pressed their claim to an independent national life. Today the same thing is happening in Africa, and the most striking of all the impressions I have formed since I left London a month ago is of the strength of this African national consciousness. In different places it takes different forms, but it is happening everywhere.

The wind of change is blowing through this continent, and, whether we like it or not, this growth of national consciousness is a political fact. We must all accept it as a fact, and our national policies must take account of it.

As I have said, the growth of national consciousness in Africa is a political fact, and we must accept it as such. That means, I would judge, that we must come to terms with it. I sincerely believe that if we cannot do so we may imperil the precarious balance between the East and West on which the peace of the world depends.

The world today is divided into three main groups. First there are what we call the Western Powers. You in South Africa and we in Britain belong to this group, together with our friends and allies in other parts of the Commonwealth. In the United States of America and in Europe we call it the Free World.

Secondly there are the Communists—Russia and her satellites in Europe and China whose population will rise by the end of the next ten years to the staggering total of 800,000,000.

Thirdly, there are those parts of the world whose people are at present uncommitted either to Communism or to our Western ideas. In this context we think first of Asia and then of Africa.

As I see it the great issue in this second half of the twentieth century is whether the uncommitted peoples of Asia and Africa will swing to the East or to the West. Will they be drawn into the Communist camp? Or will the great experiments in self-government that are now being made in Asia and Africa, especially within the Commonwealth, prove so successful, and by their example so compelling, than the balance will come down in favor of freedom and order and justice?

The struggle is joined, and it is a struggle for the minds of men. What is now on trial is much more than our military strength or our diplomatic and administrative skill. It is our way of life. The uncommitted nations want to see before they choose.

Discussion Questions

1. Macmillan began his remarks with praise for South Africa's economic progress. Why might he have begun this way?
2. Macmillan treated the growth of African nationalism as a fact, neither praising nor condemning it. Why might he have spoken in this way?
3. How did Macmillan link the growth of African nationalism to the Cold War?
4. How did he attempt to convince the South African parliament that it must accommodate itself to the "wind of change"?

38

The U-2 Affair and Collapse of the Paris Summit, May 1960

THE COLD WAR BEGAN TO THAW a bit in 1959. Soviet Premier Khrushchev's September visit to the United States gave Americans their first close look at a man they would view henceforth as a human rather than an ogre. President Eisenhower, who had disliked Khrushchev when they first met at Geneva in 1955, now saw the Soviet leader as a man with whom he could cooperate to limit the nuclear arms race. Khrushchev invited Eisenhower to visit Russia in 1960, following a summit conference in Paris at which the two leaders expected to sign a treaty banning atmospheric nuclear tests. But shortly before that conference was to begin, an American spy plane crashed in Soviet territory and its pilot, Francis Gary Powers, was captured.

The United States had been conducting espionage flights over the USSR since July 1956, using a high-altitude, top-secret aircraft called the U-2. When Khrushchev visited America in September 1959, Eisenhower suspended U-2 flights out of courtesy to his visitor and did not resume them until April 1960. At that time, Eisenhower authorized two flights in an attempt to gather as much information as possible concerning Soviet missile deployments before meeting with Khrushchev in Paris. It was the second of these flights, on 1 May, that was shot down over Sverdlovsk in the Soviet Union.

The U-2 incident placed both leaders in difficult positions. Eisenhower at first denied any knowledge of the flight, not realizing that the pilot had been captured alive. Then he admitted full responsibility, which enraged Khrushchev, who had been trying to persuade hard-liners in his government that Eisenhower was trustworthy. The Soviet premier demanded an apology, which Eisenhower refused to provide, and the Paris summit broke up in confusion.

The notes and statements excerpted below provide a sense of how the crisis developed and how each side sought to handle it.

A. STATEMENT BY US DEPARTMENT OF STATE, 5 MAY 1960

The Department has been informed by NASA [the National Aeronautics and Space Administration] that, as announced May 3, an unarmed plane, a U-2 weather research plane based at Adana, Turkey, piloted by a civilian, has been missing since May 1. During the flight of the plane, the pilot reported difficulty with his oxygen equipment. Mr. Khrushchev has announced that a U.S. plane has been shot down over the USSR on that date. It may be possible that this was the missing plane. It is entirely possible that, having failure in the oxygen equipment, which could result in the pilot losing consciousness, the plane continued on automatic pilot for a considerable distance and accidentally violated Soviet airspace. The United States is taking up the matter with the Soviet Government, with particular reference to the fate of the pilot.

B. STATEMENT BY US DEPARTMENT OF STATE, 7 MAY 1960

The Department has received the text of Mr. Khrushchev's further remarks about the unarmed plane which is reported to have been shot down in the Soviet Union. As previously announced, it was known that a U-2 plane was missing. As a result of the inquiry ordered by the President it has been established that insofar as the authorities in Washington are concerned there was no authorization for any such flight as described by Mr. Khrushchev.

Nevertheless it appears that in endeavoring to obtain information now concealed behind the Iron Curtain a flight over Soviet territory was probably undertaken by an unarmed civilian U-2 plane.

It is certainly no secret that, given the state of the world today, intelligence collection activities are practiced by all countries, and postwar history certainly reveals that the Soviet Union has not been lagging behind in this field.

The necessity for such activities as measures for legitimate national defense is enhanced by the excessive secrecy practiced by the Soviet Union in contrast to the free world. One of the things creating tension in the world today is apprehension over surprise attack with weapons of mass destruction. . . .

C. SOVIET NOTE ON THE U-2 INCIDENT, 10 MAY 1960

On May 1 of this year at 5 hours 36 minutes, Moscow time, a military aircraft violated the boundary of the Union of Soviet Socialist Republics and intruded across the borders of the Soviet Union for a distance of more than 2,000 kilometers. The government of the Union of Soviet Socialist Republics naturally could not leave unpunished such a flagrant violation of Soviet state boundaries. When the intentions of the violating aircraft became apparent, it was shot down by Soviet rocket troops in the area of Sverdlovsk.

Upon examination by experts of all data at the disposal of the Soviet side, it was incontrovertibly established that the intruder aircraft belonged to the United States of America, was permanently based in Turkey, and was sent through Pakistan into the Soviet Union with hostile purposes.

As Chairman of the USSR Council of Ministers N. S. Khrushchev made public on May 7 at the final session of the USSR Supreme Soviet, exact data from the investigation leave no doubts with respect to the purpose of the flight of the American aircraft which violated the USSR border on May 1. This aircraft was specially equipped for reconnaissance and diversionary flight over the territory of the Soviet Union. It had on board apparatus for aerial photography for detecting the Soviet radar network and other special radio-technical equipment which form part of USSR anti-aircraft defenses. . . .

Pilot Powers . . . is alive . . . and will be brought to account under the laws of the Soviet state. . . .

D. EXCERPTS FROM KHRUSHCHEV'S
STATEMENT AT PARIS, 16 MAY 1960

As is generally known, a provocative act by the American air force against the Soviet Union has recently taken place. It consisted in the fact that on May 1 of this year a US military reconnaissance plane intruded into the USSR on a definite espionage mission of gathering intelligence about military and industrial installations on Soviet territory. After the aggressive purpose of the plane's flight became clear, it was shot down by a Soviet rocket unit. Unfortunately, this is not the only instance of aggressive and espionage actions by the US air force against the Soviet Union. . . .

At first the US State Department gave out an absurd version to the effect that the American plane had violated the frontiers of the Soviet Union by accident and had not had any spying or subversive assignment. When this version was shown with incontrovertible facts to be a manifest falsehood, the US State Department . . . declared on behalf of the US government that intrusions into the Soviet Union for purposes of military espionage were carried out by American aircraft in accordance with a programme approved by the US government and by the President in person. Two days later President Eisenhower himself confirmed that flights by American planes over the territory of the Soviet Union were and remained a calculated policy of the United States. . . .

The Soviet government and the entire people of the Soviet Union received with indignation these statements by the US government leaders, as did all honest people in the world who are concerned for peace. Now that the leaders of the governments of the Four Powers have come to Paris for their conference, the question arises: how is it possible to productively negotiate and examine the questions confronting the conference, when the US government and personally the President have not only failed to condemn the provocative intrusion of an American military plane into the Soviet Union, but, on the contrary, have declared that such actions remain official US policy towards the USSR? How can agreement be reached on this or that issue needing to be settled in order to lessen tension and remove suspicion and distrust between states, when the government of one of the Great Powers says outright that it is its policy to intrude into the confines of another Great Power for spying and subversive purposes, and consequently to heighten tension in the relations between the powers? Obviously, the proclamation of such a policy, which can only be adopted when nations are at war, dooms the Summit conference to total failure. . . .

E. EXCERPTS FROM EISENHOWER'S
BROADCAST ADDRESS, 25 MAY 1960

My fellow Americans—

Tonight I want to talk with you about the remarkable events last week in Paris, and their meaning to our future. . . .

You recall, of course, why I went to Paris ten days ago.

Last summer and fall I had many conversations with world leaders; some of these were with Chairman Khrushchev, here in America. Over those months a small improvement in relations between the Soviet Union and the West seemed discernible. A possibility developed that the Soviet leaders might at last be ready for serious talks about our most persistent problems—those of disarmament, mutual inspection, atomic control, and Germany, including Berlin. . . .

Our safety, and that of the free world, demand, of course, effective systems for gathering information about the military capabilities of other powerful nations, especially those that make a fetish of secrecy. This involves many techniques and methods. In these times of vast military machines and nuclear-tipped missiles, the ferreting out of this information is indispensable to free-world security. . . .

Moreover, as President, charged by the Constitution with the conduct of America's foreign relations, and as Commander-in-Chief, charged with the direction of the operations and activities of our Armed Forces . . . , I take full responsibility for approving all the various programs undertaken by our government to secure and evaluate military intelligence.

It was in the prosecution of one of these intelligence programs that the widely publicized U-2 incident occurred.

Aerial photography has been one of many methods we have used to keep ourselves and the free world abreast of major Soviet military developments. The usefulness of this work has been well established through four years of effort. The Soviets were well aware of it. Chairman Khrushchev has stated that he became aware of these flights several years ago. Only last week, in his Paris press conference, Chairman Khrushchev confirmed that he knew of these flights when he visited the United States last September.

Incidentally, this raises the natural question—why all the furor concerning one particular flight? He did not, when in America last September, charge that these flights were any threat to Soviet safety. He did not then see any reason to refuse to confer with American representatives. This he did only about the flight that unfortunately failed, on May 1, far inside Russia.

Now, two questions have been raised about this particular flight; first, as to its timing, considering the imminence of the summit meeting; second, our initial statements when we learned the flight had failed.

As to the timing, the question was really whether to halt the program and thus forgo the gathering of important information that was essential and that was likely to be unavailable at a later date. The decision was that the program should not be halted.

The plain truth is this: when a nation needs intelligence activity, there is no time when vigilance can be relaxed. Incidentally, from Pearl Harbor we learned that even negotiation itself can be used to conceal preparations for a surprise attack.

Next, as to our government's initial statement about the flight, this was issued to protect the pilot, his mission, and our intelligence processes, at a time when the true facts were still undetermined.

Our first information about the failure of this mission did not disclose whether the pilot was still alive, was trying to escape, was avoiding interrogation, or whether both plane and pilot had been destroyed. Protection of our intelligence system and the pilot, and concealment of the plane's mission, seemed imperative.... For these reasons, what is known in intelligence circles as a "covering statement" was issued. It was issued on assumptions that were later proved incorrect. Consequently, when later the status of the pilot was definitely established, and there was no further possibility of avoiding exposure of the project, the factual details were set forth....

At the four-power meeting on Monday morning, he [Khrushchev] demanded of the United States four things: First, condemnation of U-2 flights as a method of espionage; second, assurance that they would not be continued; third, a public apology on behalf of the United States; and, fourth, punishment of all those who had any responsibility respecting this particular mission.

I replied by advising the Soviet leader that I had, during the previous week, stopped these flights and that they would not be resumed. I offered also to discuss the matter with him in personal meetings, while the regular business of the summit might proceed. Obviously, I would not respond to his extreme demands. He knew, of course, by holding to those demands the Soviet Union was scuttling the summit conference.

In torpedoing the conference, Mr. Khrushchev claimed that he acted as the result of his own high moral indignation over alleged American acts of aggression. As I said earlier, he had known of these flights for a long time. It is apparent that the Soviets had decided even before the Soviet delegation left Moscow that my trip to the Soviet Union should be canceled and that nothing constructive from their viewpoint would come out of the Summit Conference....

Discussion Questions

1. Why did the Americans consider it necessary to conduct espionage flights over Soviet territory?
2. Why did the United States at first issue false statements concerning the U-2 flight? Why did it initially claim that there was "no authorization for any such flight"?
3. If Khrushchev had known of the U-2 flights for years, why had he been reluctant to expose them publicly?
4. Why was Khrushchev so angry about Eisenhower's refusal to disavow and apologize for these flights? What reasons did Khrushchev give for scuttling the Paris summit? What other reasons might he have had?
5. Why did Eisenhower "take full responsibility" for approving such flights? How did he justify this decision?

39

The Congo Crisis, 1960

ON 30 JUNE 1960 THE BELGIAN CONGO became independent, with Joseph Kasa-Vubu as president and Patrice Lumumba as prime minister. But Belgian officers still controlled the new nation's police force, and five days later Congolese police mutinied against those officers. Tens of thousands of Belgians still lived in the Congo, and violence quickly broke out on both sides. On 11 July the mineral-rich province of Katanga declared its independence, plunging the nation into chaos and raising the possibility that more of its six provinces, which had been organized along tribal lines, would break away. In violation of its Treaty of Friendship with the Congo, Belgium sent paratroops and infantry into the country, both to defend white Belgians and to support Katanga in its bid for independence.

Faced with this upheaval, Kasa-Vubu and Lumumba toured the country by plane in an effort to restore order. Their Belgian pilot refused to obey their orders, and at several stops their lives were threatened. On 13 July they appealed to the United Nations to send peacekeeping forces into the Congo but did not wait for that organization to act. On 14 July, fearing for their lives, they sent a hastily written telegram to Premier Khrushchev asking for Soviet intervention, thereby introducing the Cold War into central Africa. Khrushchev responded the following day, by which time the leaders were back in Leopoldville, the capital, and Prime Minister Lumumba was able to address the Congo's Chamber of Deputies and describe what had occurred.

All the documents reproduced below were originally written or spoken in French. In using them, students should understand several things. First, Document A was written in haste by two men in fear for their lives. French was not their native language, and their grammar and syntax are understandably shaky. They were also not highly educated, since Belgium denied university education to all but a very few Congolese. In addition, they appear to have realized near the middle of the second sentence that the telegraph office charged by the word, and it was therefore less expensive to omit words like *a, and,* and *the.* This accounts for the choppy nature of the latter part of the document.

Second, Document B was dictated by Premier Khrushchev in his native language, Russian. He was a highly intelligent but not well-educated man, and his spoken statements were sometimes ungrammatical. The Soviet Foreign Ministry cleaned up some but not all of his irregularities. His words then had to be translated into French, both because of politeness (since Kasa-Vubu and Lumumba had written to him in French) and because in 1960 French was still the basic language of diplomacy. The translation was probably done by a Russian Foreign Ministry employee who was not a native French speaker.

Third, Document C is an English translation of the official stenographic record (in French) of Lumumba's 15 July speech. But that record was made in the midst of a turbulent legislative session, with deputies shouting at one another and frequently interrupting the prime minister as he tried to make himself heard. Its authenticity is unquestionable, but its literal, word-for-word accuracy is open to debate.

None of this means these documents should not be used. It means they must be read and used with an understanding of the context in which they were written and spoken.

The Congo government's telegram and Khrushchev's response laid the foundation for one of the Cold War's most confusing crises. The mineral wealth of the provinces of Katanga and Kasai—particularly cobalt, chrome, and uranium—was valuable to the West, which feared that it might fall into Soviet hands. Moscow hoped for a foothold in the Congo as part of Khrushchev's strategy of encouraging the new states of Africa and Asia to turn to communism. This East–West confrontation led to direct UN intervention (and the death of UN Secretary General Dag Hammarskjöld in a 1961 plane crash) in an internal Congolese power struggle that lasted more than two years. Eventually, the secession of Katanga was defeated by military force, and a pro-Western government under Mobutu Sese Seko emerged in 1965.

A. TELEGRAM FROM PRESIDENT KASA-VUBU AND PRIME MINISTER LUMUMBA TO PREMIER KHRUSHCHEV, 14 JULY 1960

KINDU 14 JULY 1960

IN VIEW OF SERIOUS THREATS TO THE NEUTRALITY OF THE REPUBLIC OF THE CONGO ON THE PART OF BELGIUM AND CERTAIN WESTERN NATIONS SUPPORTING THE CONSPIRACY OF BELGIUM AGAINST OUR INDEPENDENCE, WE ASK YOU TO KINDLY BE WILLING TO FOLLOW HOUR BY HOUR UNFOLDING SITUATION IN CONGO STOP WE WOULD BE ABLE TO BE AGREEABLE TO SEEK INTERVENTION OF THE SOVIET UNION IF WESTERN CAMP DOES NOT PUT AN END TO ACT AGGRESSION AGAINST SOVEREIGNTY REPUBLIC OF THE CONGO STOP CONGOLESE NATIONAL TERRITORY TO BE THIS DAY MILITARILY OCCUPIED BY BELGIAN TROOPS AND LIFE PRESIDENT OF THE REPUBLIC AND PRIME MINISTER TO BE IN DANGER FULL STOP (SIGNED) THE PRESIDENT OF THE REPUBLIC JOSEPH KASA VUBU. THE PRIME MINISTER AND MINISTER OF NATIONAL DEFENSE PATRICE LUMUMBA.

B. REPLY OF PREMIER KHRUSHCHEV TO PRESIDENT KASA-VUBU AND PRIME MINISTER LUMUMBA, 15 JULY 1960

July 15, 1960

The Soviet Government, the peoples of the Soviet Union follow with attention the development of events in the Republic of the Congo, victim of an imperialist aggression. We understand the difficulties of your situation and we take heed of the enormous international impact of the heroic struggle of the Congolese people for the independence and territorial integrity of the Republic of the Congo.

The people are well acquainted with the colonialists, they know the innumerable atrocities that they have committed in the Congo as in the other regions of Africa, the millions of people that they have exterminated, their attempts to totally isolate the Congo from the outside world. For dozens of years, they spoke of their "civilizing mission" in the Congo, doing everything so that no Congolese could obtain higher education, nor rise to the rank of officer in the army. One can do nothing other than condemn the attitude of the ruling classes of Belgium: they signed a treaty of friendship with the independent Republic of the Congo and immediately afterwards they trampled it like a scrap of paper before the eyes of the entire world.

It is not difficult to see that those who set in motion the armed intervention against the Congo and those who pushed the Belgians to set this in motion wish to strike a blow at all the peoples of Africa, wish to preserve intact the medieval regime, the regime of slavery across a large area of the African continent. The hand raised by the aggressor against the independence of the Congo is raised at the same time against Nigeria, against Madagascar, Mali, Togo and the other countries of Africa which wish to gain independence or which should obtain it shortly.

Your struggle, is the struggle of hundreds and hundreds of millions of people in Africa, in Asia, in Latin America. Indochina, Algeria, Suez, Guatemala, Lebanon and Jordan, Guinea and Cuba, and now the Congo, they are all links in the same chain of the postwar imperialist policy. . . .

The imperialist intervention against the Republic of the Congo is an attempt to apply the brakes to the process of total liberation of Africa and, if possible, to throw it into reverse. . . . One knows that the former Congo was not only a Belgian colony. The bayonet was Belgian but the masters were the big American, Belgian, English, and West German monopolies. When the Congolese people rejected the Belgian yoke, it rejected the collective yoke of colonial imperialism on the Congo. That is the reason why the current aggression against the Congo, carried out by the Belgian units, is, at its roots, a collective imperialist aggression of powers which the big monopolies installed in the Congo and, first of all, in its rich province of Katanga.

The Soviet Union has already resolutely condemned the imperialist intervention against the Republic of the Congo. It has stated that the United Nations should take measures to end the aggression and reestablish entirely the sovereign rights of the independent Republic of the Congo.

In an atmosphere of increasing anger of peoples who have become indignant at the imperialist aggression in the Congo, the United Nations Security Council has done useful work in adopting a resolution inviting the government of Belgium to withdraw its troops from Congolese territory.

If aggression were to continue in spite of this resolution, the Soviet government declares that the necessity would arise for more effective measures to be taken, both within the framework of the United Nations and by the peace-loving states which sympathize with the Congo.

If the states which directly execute the imperialist aggression against the Republic of the Congo and those that have pushed them pursue their criminal activities, the Soviet Union will not hesitate to take resolute measures in order to put an end to the aggression . . . the cause of the Congo is that of all civilized humanity.

The demand of the Soviet Union is simple: Hands off the Republic of the Congo!

The government of the Congo may be assured that the Soviet government will grant the Republic of the Congo all the help that would be necessary for the triumph of your just cause. . . .

C. PRIME MINISTER PATRICE LUMUMBA'S ADDRESS
TO THE CHAMBER OF DEPUTIES OF THE CONGO, 15 JULY 1960

. . . After having received these reports, I decided that it was absolutely necessary for [President Kasa-Vubu and myself] to go to Elisabethville [capital of secessionist Katanga] immediately, because the chief of state had publicly sworn, before this Chamber and before the entire nation, to protect and safeguard the integrity of the territory of the nation, and if he did not take steps, the nation would hold him responsible; this is also the duty of the government. It might mean our death, but if so we would die; as leaders responsible for the nation we had to go to Katanga.

We flew to Kamina [a military base in Katanga, occupied by Belgian forces] without notifying anyone beforehand; as we got off the plane, all the Belgian military personnel present and many European civilians who were at the airfield repeatedly called us "apes." They hurled unbelievable insults at us. The commandant of the base arrived, and I said to him: "Sir, we are in a sovereign country; I am accompanying the chief of state, who in your country is called the king. It is unthinkable that your officers and all these people here who are enjoying the hospitality of our country should permit themselves to insult our chief of state in such a shameful manner."

The Commandant replied: "You should have notified us that you were coming instead of just suddenly arriving at Kamina Base out of nowhere," whereupon he took us to the entrance of the airfield where these Europeans were standing. We went into a little office and he asked us not to leave the airfield. I asked why, and he replied that there was great tension in the city. We had gone there for the express purpose of relieving that tension. . . .

The chief of state then asked the commandant of the base to put a plane from the base at our immediate disposal, along with an escort of Belgian soldiers to ensure our safety. "We are going directly to Elisabethville," the chief of state declared, and the commandant of the base replied that he could not put this plane at our disposal and would have to consult [Belgian officers in] Leopoldville.

We then said: "Sir, we have signed a treaty of friendship and cooperation with you. When the chief of state asks your help, don't waste time waiting for the approval of your government. If King Baudouin came to us to ask our help, do you think a member of our government would make him wait around for approval from the government? Where is the spirit of collaboration you have always made so much of?"

[Eventually they received a plane.] . . . We left Kamina at 8:00 P.M. for Elisabethville, and arrived there around 10:00 P.M. But the lights on the field were turned out before we could land. Why? Because Katanga was now independent. The chief of state and the prime minister were told that they would not be allowed to set foot in Katanga. . . . We were forced to turn back. . . .

Fifteen minutes after we had been refused permission to land, the [Belgian] pilot informed us that he had just received orders to take us directly to Luluabourg and not to go back to Kamina. We asked him who had any such right to order us around; we've left our plane and our pilot in Kamina and we have to go back there, we told him. . . . The pilot took us to Luluabourg, against our will, as if we had been prisoners. . . .

[The next day] we left for Stanleyville. . . . The president went to ask the pilot again what time we would arrive in Stanleyville, since it was past the time he had said. The pilot replied that he had received orders to take us directly to Leopoldville. The president ordered him to land at Stanleyville immediately.

I then talked to the pilot too: "We know you are Belgian, but this plane now belongs to the chief of state and the Congolese government. You are in the service of the Congolese government and have no right to disregard the orders of the chief of state just because you have received orders from a foreign power, that is to say, Belgium. We are independent now; and Belgium is a separate country now, just as France and America and other countries are. What you are doing is an act of high treason."

The pilot pretended to obey then, and made a long detour to lead us to believe that we were returning to Stanleyville. Then suddenly we landed at Leopoldville, against our will as if we had been prisoners. . . . We were met by a clique of the Belgian army under the command of General Cumont, who [insisted that we review a guard of Belgian troops that he had assembled].

"Sir, that is out of the question," I said. "You have brought these troops here to put our country under military occupation, in violation of our agreement, and you have the audacity to ask that the chief of state and the head of government review them? That would mean that we approve of the presence of these troops here."

General Cumont then said to the chief of state: "Are you aware that this airport is under my command and that I can take you prisoner?"

Here in Leopoldville yesterday, this Belgian general threatened to take the chief of state prisoner! I replied: "Sir, I should like you to know that you are not in your own country. You have arms and ammunition and we don't; we have only our bare hands." General Gheysen [another Belgian officer] retorted, "Sir, I should like you to know that I am in command of this airport.

We are here to protect you." "We don't need your protection," I protested. "Go protect the Belgians in your own country. . . . "

Discussion Questions

1. Why did Kasa-Vubu and Lumumba ask for Soviet intervention in the Congo? What condition did they put on their request?
2. How did Khrushchev's reply foreshadow his 6 January 1961 speech (Document 41) on the revolutionary situation in Africa and Asia? What sort of assistance did he promise to provide?
3. What is Khrushchev's opinion of the role played in the Congo Crisis by the United Nations?
4. In his speech to the chamber, Lumumba did not mention the telegram sent to Khrushchev. What might explain this omission?
5. What might explain the arrogant conduct of Belgian officials toward Kasa-Vubu and Lumumba?

40

Castro on the Cuban Revolution, 1960

IN 1959, FOLLOWING A FIVE-AND-A-HALF-YEAR struggle against the corrupt, American-supported dictatorship of Fulgencio Batista, Fidel Castro established a revolutionary regime in Cuba. Before long, it became apparent that his revolution was dedicated to reducing US influence and presence on the island, as well as purifying Cuban society from North American corruption. As time went on, he became increasingly outspoken about the Marxist nature of his revolution. By 1961 he had surrounded himself with Marxists and established close ties with Moscow, placing Cuba squarely in the midst of the Cold War.

The Eisenhower administration watched with alarm as the new Cuban government confiscated American property and executed many supporters of Batista (who had also been supporters of the United States). The US government demanded payment in full for any land expropriated and took various actions to increase economic pressure on Cuba, culminating in the suspension of the sugar quota, which had provided for American purchase of large amounts of Cuban sugar at prices above world market value. Castro responded by denouncing the United States and moving closer to Moscow, which subsequently agreed to buy Cuban sugar and, eventually, even to defend the island with Soviet weapons. In September 1960 the Cuban leader described the decline of relations between his country and the United States in a four-and-a-half-hour address to the UN General Assembly.

EXCERPTS FROM CASTRO'S ADDRESS TO THE UN GENERAL ASSEMBLY, 26 SEPTEMBER 1960

. . . First of all, the revolution found that 600,000 Cubans, able and ready to work, were unemployed. An equal number, proportionately, to the number of unemployed in the United States at the time of the great depression that shook this country and almost produced a catastrophe in the United States. This is what we met with. Permanent unemployment in my country.

What alternative was there for the revolutionary government? Betray the people? As far as the President of the United States is concerned, what we have done for our people is treason to our people. . . .

The first . . . unfriendly act perpetrated by the Government of the United States was to throw open its doors to a gang of murderers, bloodthirsty criminals that had murdered hundreds of defenseless peasants, that never tired of torturing prisoners for many, many years, that killed right and left. These hordes were received by this country with open arms. . . .

When the revolutionary government reduced by 50 per cent the rents, there were many who were upset, . . . some who owned these buildings and apartment houses. But the people rushed into the streets, rejoicing.

Without an agrarian reform our country could not have taken its first tottering step toward development. And we were able, finally, to take that step.
. . .

What did the American State Department put to us as its aspirations for its affected interests? They put three things to us: speedy payment, efficient payment, and just payment. Speedy, efficient and just! That means: "Pay! Now! Cash! On the spot! And what we ask, for our lands!"

We weren't 150 per cent Communists at that time. We were just pink at that time, slightly pink. We were not confiscating lands. We simply proposed to . . . pay for them over a period of twenty years. And the only way in which we could pay for them was by bonds, bonds which would mature in twenty years at four-and-a-half per cent and that would be amortized yearly.

How were we able to pay for this land in dollars? How were we going to pay cash on the spot, and how could we pay for them what they asked? It was ludicrous. It is obvious that at that time we had to choose between an agrarian reform and nothing.

By our honor we swear that we had then not even exchanged letters with the Prime Minister of the Soviet Union, Mr. Nikita Khrushchev. We had not even written one another. [However,] as far as the United States press was concerned . . . , Cuba then was a Red government—a Red danger ninety miles off the coast of the United States. . . .

But hysteria can reach any pitch. Hysteria can lead one to make the most unbelievable statements and the most absurd ones. Don't for one moment believe that we're going to intone a *mea culpa* here. We have to apologize to no one.

And the threats began—the threats on our sugar quota. And the cheap philosophy was spouted by imperialism.

Planes went and came back. . . . These planes were obviously leaving the United States. . . .

At least we expected the Organization of American States to condemn the political aggression against Cuba and . . . the economic aggressions of which we had been the victims.

The Government of the United States was not condemned . . . for the sixty overflights of pirate planes. The United States was not condemned for the economic and other aggressions of which we had been the victim. No. The Soviet Union was condemned.

Now this is really bizarre. We had not been attacked by the Soviet Union. We were not victims of aggression on the part of the Soviet Union. No Soviet plane had flown over our territory. . . . The Soviet Union had limited itself to saying that in the case of a military aggression against our country Soviet [artillerymen] . . . could support the victim with rockets. . . .

What was yesterday a hopeless land, a land of misery and a land of illiterates, is gradually becoming one of the most enlightened and advanced and developed peoples of the continent. . . .

Discussion Questions

1. According to Castro, what problems did he confront when he took power in Cuba? How did he deal with them?
2. According to Castro, why did the steps he took lead to conflict with the United States? What reasons did he provide to explain the hostility of the US government toward the Cuban revolution?

3. How did Castro justify the expropriation of land owned by American companies? Why would US corporations have been reluctant to accept Cuban government bonds in payment for the land taken from them?
4. How did Castro explain the developing relationship between Cuba and the Soviet Union?

III

CRISIS AND CONFLICT, 1961–1969

41

Khrushchev on "Wars of National Liberation," January 1961

A WARE THAT DIRECT MILITARY conflict with the West could be cata-strophic, Soviet leader Khrushchev opted instead for indirect conflict by helping nations in Asia, Africa, and Latin America emerge from Western domination. Early in 1961 he spelled out his approach. Professing that his goal of "peaceful coexistence" meant avoiding wars between superpowers, he nonetheless promised to support "wars of national liberation." These wars, he asserted, were revolutionary struggles by oppressed peoples against "rotten reactionary" imperialist regimes. In aiding such struggles in Vietnam, Cuba, and elsewhere, he claimed, Communists could combat capitalist imperialism and deter US intervention.

EXCERPTS FROM ADDRESS BY SOVIET PREMIER
KHRUSHCHEV TO A MEETING OF COMMUNIST PARTY
ORGANIZATIONS IN MOSCOW, 6 JANUARY 1961

. . . In modern conditions the following categories of wars should be distin-guished: World wars, local wars, liberation wars, and popular uprisings. This is necessary to work out the correct tactics with regard to these wars.

Let us begin with the question of world wars. Communists are the most determined opponents of world wars, just as they are generally opponents of wars among states. These wars are needed only by imperialists to seize the territories of others, and to enslave and plunder other peoples. . . .

Imperialists can unleash a war, but they must think hard about the conse-quences. . . . In conditions where a mighty Socialist camp exists, possessing powerful armed forces, the peoples, by mobilization of all their forces for active struggle against the warmongering imperialist, can indisputably prevent war and thus insure peaceful coexistence.

A word or two about local wars. . . . Certain imperialist circles, fearing that world war might end in the complete collapse of capitalism, are putting their money on unleashing local wars.

There have been local wars and they may occur again in the future, but opportunities for imperialists to unleash these wars too are becoming fewer and fewer. A small imperialist war, regardless of which imperialist begins it, may grow into a world thermonuclear rocket war. We must therefore combat both world wars and local wars. . . .

Now a word about national liberation wars. The armed struggle by the Vietnamese people or the war of the Algerian people . . . serve as examples of such wars. These wars began as an uprising by the colonial peoples against their oppressors. . . . Liberation wars will continue to exist as long as imperialism exists, as long as colonialism exists. These are revolutionary wars. Such wars are not only admissible but inevitable, since the colonialists do not grant independence voluntarily. Therefore, the peoples can attain their freedom and independence only by struggle, including armed struggle.

How is it that the US imperialists, while desirous of helping the French colonialists . . . , decided against direct intervention in the war in Vietnam? They did not intervene because they knew that if they did . . . , Vietnam would get relevant aid from China, the Soviet Union, and other Socialist countries, which could lead to a world war. . . .

At present, a similar war is taking place in Algeria. . . . It is the uprising of the Arab people in Algeria against the French colonizers. . . . The imperialists in the United States and Britain render assistance to their French allies with arms. . . . The Algerian people, too, receive assistance from neighboring and other countries that sympathize with their peace-loving aspirations. But it is a liberation war of a people for its independence, it is a sacred war. We recognize such wars, we help and will help the peoples striving for their independence.

Or let us take the Cuban example. A war took place there too. But it also started as an uprising against the internal tyrannical regime supported by US imperialism. . . . However, the United States did not interfere in that war directly with its armed forces. The Cuban people, under the leadership of Fidel Castro, have won.

Can such wars flare up in the future? They can. Can there be such uprisings? There can. But these are wars which are national uprisings. . . . What is the attitude of the Marxists toward such uprisings? A most positive one. These uprisings must not be identified with wars among states, with local wars, since in these uprisings the people are fighting for implementation of their right for self-determination, for independent social and national development. These are uprisings against rotten reactionary regimes, against the colonizers. The Communists fully support such just wars and march in the front rank with the peoples waging liberation struggles. . . .

Discussion Questions

1. Why and how did Khrushchev think Communists should support national liberation wars? Why did he think such wars were inevitable?
2. Why did he identify capitalism with imperialism? Why did he see socialists and national liberation movements as natural allies in a global struggle against capitalist imperialism?
3. What were the potential benefits and risks for the Soviets in supporting such wars?

42

Kwame Nkrumah on the Need for African Unity, 1961

KWAME NKRUMAH, A NATIVE of the British West African colony of Gold Coast, earned two bachelor's and two master's degrees in the United States and returned to his homeland in 1947 to become principal organizer of an anticolonial pressure group, the United Gold Coast Convention. Gifted with formidable organizational skills and boundless energy, Nkrumah proved much too radical for the convention's tastes, and in 1949 he broke away from it to form the Convention People's Party. By October of that year he was imprisoned for sedition, only to be released in 1951 when the colony's British governor, plagued by strikes and riots among the general public, decided that a peaceful transition to independence was possible only with Nkrumah's cooperation. By 1953 Nkrumah was chief minister of an autonomous Gold

Coast government, wearing a traditional British powdered wig in the colony's parliament. London granted full independence to the new nation under the name of Ghana on 6 March 1957, and Nkrumah was the logical choice as its first prime minister.

Nkrumah had served as co-treasurer of the Fifth Pan-African Congress in Manchester, England, in 1945 and had become convinced that an independent Africa could fulfill its destiny in the world only through transcending tribalism and nationalism in favor of continent-wide political unity. His commitment to pan-Africanism never wavered, and in December 1958 he hosted an All-African People's Conference in Ghana's capital, Accra. Attended by nationalist leaders from throughout Africa, the conference inspired, among others, the young Congolese Patrice Lumumba, who less than two years later would become the first prime minister of an independent Congo (Document 39). In the following excerpt from his book *I Speak of Freedom*, Nkrumah set forth his vision of African unity, a vision he hoped would permit the continent to pursue economic and political development without becoming entangled in the increasingly tension-filled Cold War.

EXCERPT FROM KWAME NKRUMAH, *I SPEAK OF FREEDOM: A STATEMENT OF AFRICAN IDEOLOGY*, 1961

. . . For centuries, Europeans dominated the African continent. The white man arrogated to himself the right to rule and to be obeyed by the non-white; his mission, he claimed, was to "civilise" Africa. Under this cloak, the Europeans robbed the continent of vast riches and inflicted unimaginable suffering on the African people. All this makes a sad story, but now we must be prepared to bury the past with its unpleasant memories and look to the future. All we ask of the former colonial powers is their goodwill and co-operation to remedy past mistakes and injustices and to grant independence to the colonies in Africa. . . .

It is clear that we must find an African solution to our problems, and that this can only be found in African unity. Divided we are weak; united, Africa could become one of the greatest forces for good in the world.

Although most Africans are poor, our continent is potentially extremely rich. Our mineral resources, which are being exploited with foreign capital only to enrich foreign investors, range from gold and diamonds to uranium and petroleum. Our forests contain some of the finest woods to be grown anywhere. Our cash crops include cocoa, coffee, rubber, tobacco, and cotton. . . . Africa contains over 40% of the total potential water power of the world, as compared with about 10% in Europe and 13% in North America. Yet so far, less than 1% has been developed. This is one of the reasons why we have in Africa the paradox of poverty in the midst of plenty, and scarcity in the midst of abundance.

Individually, the independent states of Africa, some of them rich, others poor, can do little for their people. Together, by mutual help, they can achieve much. But the economic development of the continent must be planned and pursued as a whole. . . . Only a strong political union can bring about full and effective development of our natural resources for the benefit of our people.

The emergence of such a mighty stabilizing force in this strife-torn world should be regarded not as the shadowy dream of a visionary, but as a practical proposition, which the peoples of Africa can, and should, translate into reality. There is a tide in the affairs of every people when the moment strikes for political action. Such was the moment in the history of the United States of America when the Founding Fathers saw beyond the petty wranglings of the separate states and created a Union. This is our chance. We must act now. Tomorrow may be too late and the opportunity may have passed, and with it the hope of free Africa's survival.

Discussion Questions

1. How did Nkrumah characterize the impact of European colonization on Africa?
2. Why did Nkrumah consider Africa to be a potentially rich continent?
3. Why did Nkrumah believe that unifying the entire continent was the best route to African economic development?
4. Like Ho Chi Minh (Document 4) and Sukarno (Document 28A), Nkrumah spoke glowingly of the United States. What similarities and differences can you detect in the uses these three men made of the American example?

43

Eisenhower's Farewell Address on the Military-Industrial Complex, 17 January 1961

THE U-2 AFFAIR AND COLLAPSE of the Paris summit in May 1960 (Documents 38A–E) delivered a serious setback to hopes for an easing of global tensions that year. With US presidential elections impending in November, Khrushchev gave up on efforts to work with Eisenhower and opted instead to wait and try to work with his successor. Frustrated and disturbed, Eisenhower had to drop any dreams of leaving behind a more peaceful world as he ended his illustrious career.

The old soldier and outgoing president looked for other ways to enhance his legacy. On 17 January 1961, three days before leaving office, Eisenhower delivered a televised farewell address to the American people. After extolling his nation's values and lamenting the threat to them posed by Soviet communism, he warned Americans of a potential domestic threat to their freedom: the growing size and influence of America's massive "military-industrial complex." Noting the necessity of a powerful defense establishment and supportive arms industries, he nonetheless called for vigilance lest this potent combination acquire "unwarranted influence" that could "endanger our liberties or democratic processes." Then the former general, who had directly "witnessed the horrors of war," finished his address with an eloquent plea for peace among peoples of all races, faiths, and nations. The Eisenhower era was over.

EXCERPTS FROM PRESIDENT EISENHOWER'S TELEVISED SPEECH, 17 JANUARY 1961

My fellow Americans:

. . . This evening I come to you with a message of leave-taking and farewell, and to share a few final thoughts with you. . . .

... America is today the strongest, the most influential and most productive nation in the world. Understandably proud of this pre-eminence, we yet realize that America's leadership and prestige depend, not merely upon our unmatched material progress, riches and military strength, but on how we use our power in the interests of world peace and human betterment.

Throughout America's adventure in free government, our basic purposes have been to keep the peace; to foster progress in human achievement, and to enhance liberty, dignity and integrity among people and among nations. ...

Progress toward these noble goals is persistently threatened by the conflict now engulfing the world. It commands our whole attention, absorbs our very beings. We face a hostile ideology—global in scope, atheistic in character, ruthless in purpose, and insidious in method. Unhappily the danger it poses promises to be of indefinite duration. To meet it successfully, there is called for, not so much the emotional and transitory sacrifices of crisis, but rather those which enable us to carry forward steadily, surely, and without complaint the burdens of a prolonged and complex struggle—with liberty the stake. ...

A vital element in keeping the peace is our military establishment. Our arms must be mighty, ready for instant action, so that no potential aggressor may be tempted to risk his own destruction.

Our military organization today bears little relation to that known by any of my predecessors in peacetime. ...

Until the latest of our world conflicts, the United States had no armaments industry. ... But now ... we have been compelled to create a permanent armaments industry of vast proportions. Added to this, three and a half million men and women are directly engaged in the defense establishment. We annually spend on military security more than the net income of all United States corporations.

This conjunction of an immense military establishment and a large arms industry is new in the American experience. The total influence—economic, political, even spiritual—is felt in every city, every State house, every office of the Federal government. We recognize the imperative need for this development. Yet we must not fail to comprehend its grave implications. ...

In the councils of government, we must guard against the acquisition of unwarranted influence, whether sought or unsought, by the military industrial complex. The potential for the disastrous rise of misplaced power exists and will persist.

We must never let the weight of this combination endanger our liberties or democratic processes. We should take nothing for granted. Only an alert and knowledgeable citizenry can compel the proper meshing of the huge industrial and military machinery of defense with our peaceful methods and goals, so that security and liberty may prosper together.

Disarmament, with mutual honor and confidence, is a continuing imperative. Together we must learn how to compose differences, not with arms, but with intellect and decent purpose. Because this need is so sharp and apparent I confess that I lay down my official responsibilities in this field with a definite sense of disappointment. As one who has witnessed the horror and the lingering sadness of war—as one who knows that another war could utterly destroy this civilization . . . —I wish I could say tonight that a lasting peace is in sight.

Happily, I can say that war has been avoided. Steady progress toward our ultimate goal has been made. But, so much remains to be done. . . .

So—in this my last good night to you as your President—I thank you for the many opportunities you have given me for public service in war and peace. . . .

To all the peoples of the world, I once more give expression to America's prayerful and continuing aspiration:

We pray that peoples of all faiths, all races, all nations, may have their great human needs satisfied; that those now denied opportunity shall come to enjoy it to the full; that all who yearn for freedom may experience its spiritual blessings; that those who have freedom will understand, also, its heavy responsibilities; that all who are insensitive to the needs of others will learn charity; that the scourges of poverty, disease and ignorance will be made to disappear from the earth, and that, in the goodness of time, all peoples will come to live together in a peace guaranteed by the binding force of mutual respect and love. . . .

Discussion Questions

1. What did Eisenhower see as America's main values and goals? Why did he think Soviet Communists threatened those values and goals?
2. What did Eisenhower mean by the "military-industrial complex"? Why did he think it was necessary? Why did he think it was dangerous?
3. Why did he think that mutual disarmament by the superpowers was imperative? Why did he say he was leaving office with a "sense of disappointment"?
4. What positive elements did Eisenhower note as he bid his farewell? What was he grateful for in the past? What were his hopes for the future?

44

Kennedy's Inaugural Address, 1961

O N 20 JANUARY 1961, THREE DAYS after Eisenhower's farewell address, his youthful successor, John F. Kennedy, was sworn in as president of the United States. Having narrowly defeated Richard M. Nixon, Eisenhower's vice president, Kennedy came to office as the first US president born in the twentieth century. Knowing that his inauguration would thus issue in a new era, he was determined to pursue a resolute course, despite his youth and inexperience.

Kennedy's presidency corresponded roughly with the most perilous phase of the Cold War, highlighted by dangerous confrontations with the Soviet Union over Berlin and Cuba. He began his term with a ringing inaugural address, steeped in the rhetoric of the Cold War, yet calling for sacrifice both in the name of freedom and in the cause of peace. The address set the tone for his administration's approach to foreign affairs during his first two years in office. Later, after the Cuban Missile Crisis, Kennedy would alter his rhetoric and his approach, most notably in his "Peace Speech" at American University in June 1963 (Document 47). But at the time he delivered his most famous and frequently quoted address, those changes lay in the future, hidden from the eyes and ears of the people who watched and listened on a day that, like the mood in Washington, was bright but bitterly cold.

EXCERPTS FROM KENNEDY'S
INAUGURAL ADDRESS, 20 JANUARY 1961

We observe today not a victory of party but a celebration of freedom—symbolizing an end as well as a beginning—signifying renewal as well as change. For I have sworn before you and almighty God the same solemn oath our forebears prescribed nearly a century and three quarters ago.

The world is very different now. For man holds in his mortal hands the power to abolish all forms of human poverty and all forms of human life. And yet the same revolutionary beliefs for which our forebears fought are still at issue around the globe—the belief that the rights of man come not from the generosity of the state but from the hand of God. We dare not forget today that we are the heirs of that first revolution.

Let the word go forth, from this time and place, to friend and foe alike, that the torch has been passed to a new generation of Americans—born in this century, tempered by war, disciplined by a hard and bitter peace, proud of our ancient heritage—and unwilling to witness or permit the slow undoing of those human rights to which this nation has always been committed, and to which we are committed today, at home and around the world.

Let every nation know, whether it wishes us well or ill, that we shall pay any price, bear any burden, meet any hardship, support any friend, oppose any foe to assure the survival and success of liberty. This much we pledge—and more.

To those old allies whose cultural and spiritual origins we share, we pledge the loyalty of faithful friends. United, there is little we cannot do in a host of cooperative ventures. Divided, there is little we can do—for we dare not meet a powerful challenge at odds and split asunder.

To those new states whom we welcome to the ranks of the free, we pledge our word that one form of colonial control shall not have passed away merely to be replaced by a far more iron tyranny. . . .

To those peoples in the huts and villages of half the globe struggling to break the bonds of mass misery, we pledge our best efforts to help them help themselves, for whatever period is required—not because the communists may be doing it, but because it is right. If a free society cannot help the many who are poor, it cannot save the few who are rich.

To our sister republics south of our border, we offer a special pledge—to convert our good words into good deeds—in a new alliance for progress—to assist free men and free governments in casting off the chains of poverty. But this peaceful revolution of hope cannot become the prey of hostile powers. Let all our neighbors know that we shall join with them to oppose aggression or subversion anywhere in the Americas. And let every other power know that this Hemisphere intends to remain the master of its own house. . . .

Finally, to those nations who would make themselves our adversary, we offer not a pledge but a request: that both sides begin anew the quest for peace, before the dark powers of destruction unleashed by science engulf all humanity in planned or accidental self-destruction.

We dare not tempt them with weakness. For only when our arms are sufficient beyond doubt can we be certain beyond doubt that they will never be employed. But neither can two great and powerful groups of nations take comfort from our present course—both sides overburdened by the cost of modern weapons, both rightly alarmed by the steady spread of the deadly atom, yet both racing to alter the uncertain balance of terror that stays the hand of mankind's final war.

So let us begin anew—remembering on both sides that civility is not a sign of weakness, and sincerity is always subject to proof. Let us never negotiate out of fear. But let us never fear to negotiate. . . .

In your hands, my fellow citizens, more than mine, will rest the final success or failure of our course. Since this country was founded, each generation of Americans has been summoned to give testimony to its national loyalty. The graves of young Americans who answered the call to service surround the globe.

Now the trumpet summons us again—not as a call to bear arms, though arms we need—not as a call to battle, though embattled we are—but a call to bear the burden of a long twilight struggle, year in and year out, "rejoicing in hope, patient in tribulation"—a struggle against the common enemies of man: tyranny, poverty, disease and war itself. . . .

In the long history of the world, only a few generations have been granted the role of defending freedom in its hour of maximum danger. I do not shrink from this responsibility—I welcome it. I do not believe that any of us would exchange places with any other people or any other generation. The energy, the faith, the devotion which we bring to this endeavor will light our country and all who serve it—and the glow from that fire can truly light the world.

And so, my fellow Americans: ask not what your country can do for you— ask what you can do for your country.

My fellow citizens of the world: ask not what America will do for you, but what together we can do for the freedom of man.

Finally, whether you are citizens of America or citizens of the world, ask of us here the same high standards of strength and sacrifice which we ask of you. With a good conscience our only sure reward, with history the final judge of our deeds, let us go forth to lead the land we love, asking His blessing and His help, but knowing that here on earth God's work must truly be our own.

Discussion Questions

1. Why did Kennedy begin by citing America's revolutionary heritage? What attitude did he adopt toward nations emerging from colonial rule while caught in the Cold War crossfire?
2. What messages did Kennedy's address send to America's allies? What messages did it send to the USSR and to Cuba?

3. Which parts of this address would you characterize as typical Cold War rhetoric? Why?
4. Which parts would you characterize as holding out hope for better relations between the United States and the USSR? Why?
5. What challenges did Kennedy present to Americans and other peoples of the world? What dangers were inherent in his pledge to "pay any price" and "bear any burden"?

45

The Berlin Crisis, 1961

FOR A FULL YEAR, FROM MAY 1960 to May 1961, events such as the U-2 affair and collapse of the Paris summit, the Congo Crisis, the US elections, and Kennedy's inauguration captured the world's attention. But this did not mean that the German Question had vanished. In early June 1961, Khrushchev again moved the divided city of Berlin to the center of the Cold War stage. He proposed that it should become a "demilitarized city" and that the joint military occupation, in effect since the end of World War II, should end. At a summit meeting with Kennedy in Vienna, the Soviet leader tried to bully the young president, suggesting that failure to solve the Berlin problem could result in war and threatening to unilaterally turn the city over to East Germany.

Shaken by the summit, Kennedy addressed his nation on 25 July. Painting a somber picture of Khrushchev's intentions, he revealed plans for a US military buildup and depicted Berlin as "the great testing place of Western courage."

Meanwhile, the flow of East Berliners to the West, in progress since 1948, increased. Many East Berliners crossed every morning to work in West Berlin—by car, subway, bus, or on foot—and then returned home in the evening. As the crisis heated up during 1961, more and more of them simply did not go home. Since many of these were well-educated professionals, the exodus was devastating for East Germany (the German Democratic Republic).

Unable to drive the Western powers out of West Berlin, the Soviet and East German governments finally decided to make the best of a bad situation and seal off the border between East and West Berlin. Early in the morning of 13 August 1961, East German workers erected barriers and strung barbed wire across the border running through the center of the city. US protests met a stiff Soviet response. Later these temporary fortifications would be replaced by the Berlin Wall, destined to become the Cold War's most enduring and recognizable symbol.

A. KENNEDY'S REPORT TO THE NATION ON BERLIN, 25 JULY 1961

Seven weeks ago tonight I returned from Europe to report on my meeting with Premier Khrushchev. . . . His grim warnings about the future of the world, his *aide mémoire* on Berlin, his subsequent speeches and threats . . . , and the increase in the Soviet military budget that he has announced have all prompted a series of decisions by the administration and a series of consultations with the members of the NATO organization. In Berlin, as you recall, he intends to bring to an end, through a stroke of the pen, first, our legal rights to be in West Berlin and, secondly, our ability to make good on our commitment to the 2 million free people of that city. That we cannot permit. . . .

The immediate threat to free men is in West Berlin. But that isolated outpost is not an isolated problem. The threat is worldwide. Our effort must be equally wide and strong. . . . We face a challenge in Berlin, but there is also a challenge in Southeast Asia, where the borders are less guarded, the enemy harder to find, and the danger of communism less apparent to those who have so little. We face a challenge in our own hemisphere and indeed wherever else the freedom of human beings is at stake.

Let me remind you that the fortunes of war and diplomacy left the free people of West Berlin in 1945 110 miles behind the Iron Curtain. . . . West Berlin is 110 miles within the area which the Soviets now dominate—which is immediately controlled by the so-called East German regime.

We are there as a result of our victory over Nazi Germany, and our basic rights to be there deriving from that victory include both our presence in West Berlin and the enjoyment of access across East Germany. These rights have been repeatedly confirmed . . . in special agreements with the Soviet Union. Berlin is not a part of East Germany, but a separate territory under the control of the allied powers. Thus our rights there are clear and deep-rooted. But in addition to those rights is our commitment to sustain—and defend, if need be—the opportunity for more than 2 million people to determine their own future and choose their own way of life.

Thus our presence in West Berlin, and our access thereto, cannot be ended by any act of the Soviet Government. The NATO shield was long ago extended to cover West Berlin, and we have given our word that an attack in that city will be regarded as an attack upon us all.

For West Berlin, lying exposed 110 miles inside East Germany, surrounded by Soviet troops and close to Soviet supply lines, has many roles. It is more than a showcase of liberty, a symbol, an island of freedom in a Communist sea. It is even more than a link with the free world, a beacon of hope behind the Iron Curtain, an escape hatch for refugees.

West Berlin is all of that. But above all it has now become, as never before, the great testing place of Western courage and will, a focal point where our solemn commitments . . . and Soviet ambitions now meet in basic confrontation. . . .

We do not want to fight, but we have fought before. And others in earlier times have made the same dangerous mistake of assuming that the West was too selfish and too soft and too divided to resist invasions of freedom in other lands. Those who threaten to unleash the forces of war on a dispute over West Berlin should recall the words of the ancient philosopher: "A man who causes fear cannot be free from fear."

We cannot and will not permit the Communists to drive us out of Berlin, either gradually or by force. . . .

B. US NOTE PROTESTING CLOSURE
OF EAST BERLIN BORDER, 17 AUGUST 1961

On August 13, East German authorities put into effect several measures regulating movement at the boundary of the western sectors and the Soviet sector of the city of Berlin. These measures have the effect of limiting, to a degree approaching complete prohibition, passage from the Soviet sector to the western sectors of the city. These measures were accompanied by the closing of the sector boundary by a sizable deployment of police forces and by military detachments brought into Berlin for this purpose.

All this is a flagrant, and particularly serious, violation of the quadripartite status of Berlin. Freedom of movement with respect to Berlin was reaffirmed by the quadripartite agreement of New York of May 4, 1949, and by the decision taken at Paris on June 20, 1949, by the Council of the Ministers of Foreign Affairs of the Four Powers. The United States Government has never accepted that limitations can be imposed on freedom of movement within Berlin. The boundary between the Soviet sector and the western sectors of Berlin is not a state frontier. The United States Government considers that the measures which the East German authorities have taken are illegal. It reiterates that it does not accept the pretension that the Soviet sector of Berlin forms a part of the so-called "German Democratic Republic" [East Germany] and that Berlin is situated on its territory. Such a pretension is in itself a violation of the solemnly pledged word of the USSR in the Agreement on the Zones of Occupation in Germany and the administration of Greater Berlin. Moreover, the United States Government cannot admit the right of the East German authorities to authorize their armed forces to enter the Soviet sector of Berlin.

By the very admission of the East German authorities, the measures which have just been taken are motivated by the fact that an ever increasing number of inhabitants of East Germany wish to leave this territory. The reasons for this exodus are known. They are simply the internal difficulties in East Germany. . . .

The United States Government solemnly protests against the measures referred to above, for which it holds the Soviet Government responsible. The United States Government expects the Soviet Government to put an end to these illegal measures. This unilateral infringement of the quadripartite status of Berlin can only increase existing tension and dangers.

C. SOVIET RESPONSE TO THE US PROTEST, 18 AUGUST 1961

In connection with the note of the Government of the United States of America of August 17, 1961, the Government of the Union of Soviet Socialist Republics considers it necessary to state the following:

1. The Soviet Government fully understands and supports the actions of the Government of the German Democratic Republic which established effective control on the border with West Berlin in order to bar the way for subversive activity being carried out from West Berlin against the GDR and other countries of the socialist community. In its measures on the borders the Government of the GDR merely made sure the ordinary right of any sovereign state for the protection of its interests. Any state establishes on its borders with other states such regime as it deems necessary and responsive to its legitimate interests. As is known, the regime of state borders is one of the internal questions of any state, and its decision does not require recognition or approval on the part of other governments. Attempts by the Government of the USA to interfere in the internal affairs of the GDR are therefore completely unfounded and inappropriate.

2. Doubtless the reasons are well known to the Government of the USA which made necessary and even inevitable the introduction of control over movement across the border between the GDR and West Berlin. It expended no little effort itself to evoke these reasons. West Berlin has been transformed into a center of political and economic provocations against the GDR, the Soviet Union, and other socialist countries. Former and present West Berlin municipal leaders have cynically called West Berlin an "arrow in the living body of the German Democratic Republic," a "front city," a "violator of tranquility," the "cheapest atom bomb put in the center of a socialist state." The gates of West Berlin have been opened to international criminals and provocateurs of all kinds, if only to sharpen international tension and widen the dimensions of the provocations and subversive acts against the countries of the socialist community. . . .

Discussion Questions

1. Why did Kennedy see Berlin as a testing ground for Western courage? How did he situate Berlin in the global struggle between Western democracy and communism?
2. From an American perspective, what was wrong with Khrushchev's desire to change the status of Berlin? How did Kennedy justify his resistance to this change?
3. What similarities and differences do you see between Kennedy's approach to Berlin in 1961 and Truman's in 1948? What link did Kennedy draw between Berlin and the NATO treaty?
4. Why did the Soviets and East Germans decide to seal off the border? How did they expect this to help them? In what ways might this decision be seen as a setback for them?
5. In what ways would the construction of the Berlin Wall increase global tensions? In what ways might it decrease them? In what ways was it a US setback and in what ways might it be seen as a US victory? What potential harms and benefits did it bring to each side?

46

The Cuban Missile Crisis, October 1962

IN APRIL 1961 AN AMERICAN-SPONSORED effort to overthrow Cuba's Castro regime by landing a brigade of Cuban exiles at a place called the Bay of Pigs failed miserably. Khrushchev assumed that the next invasion of Cuba would be led by US combat troops—and probably succeed. In an effort to deter such an invasion, he beefed up Soviet forces on the island and, in a perilous move, decided in 1962 to secretly install Soviet intermediate-range nuclear missiles in Cuba.

Khrushchev's aims went beyond defending Cuba. Faced with a growing US lead in long-range (intercontinental) missiles, he hoped to avoid the great time and expense of building his own large fleet of them by placing existing intermediate weapons within range of America. He also hoped, once the missiles were in place, to use them to pry concessions from the West on Berlin.

Khrushchev's hopes rested on maintaining secrecy until the missiles were operational in November, but American U-2 planes detected them on 14 October. Before revealing their presence, Kennedy consulted for days with top advisors, rejecting both the option of negotiating with Moscow and the option of trying to take out the missiles with air strikes followed by invasion. Instead, in a televised address on 22 October, he announced that the United States would impose a naval blockade, or "quarantine," of Cuba to prevent shipments of additional nuclear equipment and thus hopefully keep the missiles from becoming operational.

Following Kennedy's speech, the quarantine went into effect. Khrushchev decided not to try to break the blockade, but he refused to remove the missiles. Kennedy then considered an air attack on the missile sites, to be followed by an invasion. Since, unknown to Kennedy, many of the missiles were already operational, and since Soviet ground units were equipped with tactical nuclear weapons, such an attack could have sparked a nuclear war.

But on 26 October Kennedy received a message from Khrushchev. Undiplomatic and emotional, it contained proposals that seemed to offer a path to a peaceful settlement. The next day, however, a second Khrushchev message adopted a sterner tone and proposed that America remove its missiles from

Turkey in return for removal of Soviet missiles from Cuba. Based on an advisor's suggestion, Kennedy's response ignored the second letter and suggested that the first be the basis for negotiations. Things got very tense on 27 October when a U-2 pilot was shot down over Cuba and killed, but Kennedy held off on retaliatory strikes, warning the Soviets through private channels that an invasion was imminent, while also pledging privately to remove US missiles from Turkey. On 28 October, accepting Kennedy's assurance that the United States would not invade Cuba, Khrushchev agreed to remove the Soviet missiles, ending the missile crisis.

A. HIGHLIGHTS OF KENNEDY'S ADDRESS TO THE NATION AND THE WORLD, 22 OCTOBER 1962

This Government, as promised, has maintained the closest surveillance of the Soviet military build-up on the island of Cuba. Within the past week unmistakable evidence has established the fact that a series of offensive missile sites is now in preparation on that imprisoned island. The purpose of these bases can be none other than to provide a nuclear strike capability against the Western hemisphere. . . .

This urgent transformation of Cuba into an important strategic base by the presence of these large, long-range, and clearly offensive weapons of sudden mass destruction constitutes an explicit threat to the peace and security of all the Americas. . . . This action also contradicts the repeated assurances of Soviet spokesmen . . . that the arms build-up in Cuba would retain its original defensive character and that the Soviet Union had no need or desire to station strategic missiles on the territory of any other nation. . . .

Neither the United States of America nor the world community of nations can tolerate deliberate deception and offensive threats on the part of any nation, large or small. We no longer live in a world where only the actual firing of weapons represents a sufficient challenge to a nation's security to constitute maximum peril. Nuclear weapons are so destructive and ballistic missiles are so swift that any substantially increased possibility of their use or any sudden change in their deployment may well be regarded as a definite threat to peace. . . .

Acting, therefore, in the defense of our own security and of the entire Western Hemisphere, and under the authority entrusted to me by the Constitution as endorsed by the resolution of the Congress, I have directed that the following initial steps be taken immediately:

First, to halt this offensive buildup, a strict quarantine on all offensive military equipment under shipment to Cuba is being initiated. All ships of any kind bound for Cuba from whatever nation or port will, where they are found to contain cargoes of offensive weapons, be turned back. . . .

Second, I have directed the continued and increased close surveillance of Cuba and its military build-up. . . . Should these offensive military preparations continue, thus increasing the threat to the hemisphere, further action will be justified. I have directed the Armed Forces to prepare for any eventualities, and I trust that, in the interest of both the Cuban people and the Soviet technicians at the sites, the hazards . . . of continuing this threat will be recognized.

Third, it shall be the policy of this nation to regard any nuclear missile launched from Cuba against any nation in the Western Hemisphere as an attack by the Soviet Union on the United States, requiring a full retaliatory response upon the Soviet Union. . . .

Sixth: Under the Charter of the United Nations, we are asking tonight that an emergency meeting of the Security Council be convoked—without delay to take action against this latest Soviet threat to world peace. . . .

Seventh and finally: I call upon Chairman Khrushchev to halt and eliminate this clandestine, reckless, and provocative threat to world peace and to stable relations between our two nations. . . .

Our goal is not the victory of might, but the vindication of right; not peace at the expense of freedom, but both peace and freedom here in this hemisphere, and we hope around the world. God willing, that goal will be achieved.

B. EXCERPTS FROM KHRUSHCHEV'S
MESSAGE TO KENNEDY, 26 OCTOBER 1962

Dear Mr. President:

. . . In the name of the Soviet Government and the Soviet people, I assure you that your conclusions regarding offensive weapons in Cuba are groundless. . . .

All the means located there . . . have a defensive character, are on Cuba solely for the purpose of defense, and we have sent them to Cuba at the request of the Cuban government. . . .

You can regard us with distrust, but in any case you can be calm in this regard, that we are of sound mind and understand perfectly well that if we attack you, you will respond the same way. . . . Only lunatics or suicides, who themselves want to perish and to destroy the whole world before they die, could do this. We, however, want to live and do not at all want to destroy your country. We want something quite different: to compete with your country on a peaceful endeavor. . . .

I don't know whether you can understand me and believe me. But I should like to have you believe in yourself and agree that one cannot give way to passions; it is necessary to control them. . . .

If assurances were given by the President and the Government of the United States that the USA itself would not participate in an attack on Cuba and would restrain others from actions of this sort, if you would recall your fleet, this would immediately change everything. . . . Then, too, the question of armaments would disappear, since, if there is no threat, then armaments are a burden for every people. . . .

Armaments bring only disasters. When one accumulates them, this damages the economy, and if one puts them to use, then they destroy people on both sides. Consequently, only a madman can believe that armaments are the principal means in the life of society. . . . If people do not show wisdom, then in the final analysis, they will come to a clash, like blind moles, and then reciprocal extermination will begin.

Let us therefore show statesmanlike wisdom. I propose: we, for our part, will declare that our ships, bound for Cuba, are not carrying any kind of armaments. You would declare that the United States will not invade Cuba with its forces and will not support any kind of forces that might intend to carry out an invasion of Cuba. Then the necessity for the presence of our military specialists in Cuba would disappear.

Mr. President, I appeal to you to weigh well what the aggressive, piratical actions, which you have declared the USA intends to carry out in international waters, would lead to. . . .

If you did this as the first step towards the unleashing of war, it is evident that nothing else is left to us but to accept this challenge of yours. If, however, you have not lost your self-control and sensibly conceive what this might lead to, then, Mr. President, we and you ought not now to pull on the ends of the rope in which you have tied the knot of war, because the more the two of us pull, the tighter that knot will be tied. And a moment may come when that knot will be tied so tight that even he who tied it will not have the strength to untie it, and then it would be necessary to cut that knot. And what that would mean is not for me to explain to you, because you yourself understand perfectly of what terrible forces our countries dispose.

Consequently, if there is no intention to tighten that knot and thereby doom the world to the catastrophe of thermonuclear war, then let us not only relax the forces pulling on the ends of the rope, let us take measures to untie the knot. We are ready for this. . . .

There, Mr. President, are my thoughts, which, if you agreed with them, could put an end to the tense situation which is disturbing all peoples. These thoughts are dictated by a sincere desire to relieve the situation, to remove the threat of war.

C. EXCERPTS FROM KHRUSHCHEV'S
MESSAGE TO KENNEDY, 27 OCTOBER 1962

Dear Mr. President:

. . . I understand your concern for the security of the United States, Mr. President, because this is the primary duty of a President. But we, too, are disturbed about these same questions. . . . Our aim has been and is to help Cuba, and no one can dispute the humanity of our motives, which are oriented toward enabling Cuba to live peacefully and develop in the way its people desire.

You wish to ensure the security of your country, and this is understandable. But Cuba, too, wants the same thing; all countries want to maintain their security. But how are we . . . to assess your actions which are expressed in the fact that you have surrounded the Soviet Union with military bases; surrounded our allies with military bases; placed military bases literally around our country; and stationed your missile armaments there? . . . Your missiles are located in Britain, are located in Italy, and are aimed against us. Your missiles are located in Turkey.

You are disturbed over Cuba. You say that this disturbs you because it is 90 miles by sea from the coast of the United States of America. But Turkey adjoins us; our sentries patrol back and forth and see each other. Do you consider, then, that you have the right to demand security for your own country and the removal of the weapons you call offensive, but do not accord the same right to us? You have placed destructive missile weapons . . . in Turkey, literally next to us. . . .

I think it would be possible to end the controversy quickly and normalize the situation. . . .

I therefore make this proposal: We are willing to remove from Cuba the means which you regard as offensive. We are willing to carry this out and to make this pledge in the United Nations. Your representatives will make a declaration to the effect that the United States, for its part, considering the uneasiness and anxiety of the Soviet State, will remove its analogous means from Turkey. Let us reach agreement as to the period of time needed by you and by us to bring this about. And, after that, persons entrusted by the United Nations Security Council could inspect on the spot the fulfillment of the pledges made. . . .

We, in making this pledge, in order to give satisfaction and hope to the peoples of Cuba and Turkey and to strengthen their confidence in their security, will make a statement within the framework of the Security Council to the effect that the Soviet Government gives a solemn promise to respect the inviolability of the borders and sovereignty of Turkey, not to interfere in its internal affairs, not to invade Turkey, not to make available our territory as a bridgehead for such an invasion, and that it would also restrain those who contemplate committing aggression against Turkey, either from the territory of the Soviet Union or from the territory of Turkey's other neighboring states.

The United States Government will make a similar statement within the framework of the Security Council regarding Cuba. . . .

D. EXCERPT FROM KENNEDY'S RESPONSE TO KHRUSHCHEV, 27 OCTOBER 1962

Dear Mr. Chairman:

I have read your letter of October 26 with great care and welcomed the statement of your desire to seek a prompt solution to the problem. The first thing that needs to be done, however, is for work to cease on offensive missile bases in Cuba and for all weapons systems in Cuba capable of offensive use to be rendered inoperable, under effective United Nations arrangements.

Assuming this is done promptly, I have given my representatives in New York instructions that will permit them to work out this week . . . an arrangement for a permanent solution to the Cuban problem along the lines suggested in your letter of October 26. As I read your letter, the key elements of your proposals—which seem generally acceptable as I understand them—are as follows:

1. You would agree to remove these weapons systems from Cuba under appropriate United Nations observation and supervision; and undertake, with suitable safeguards, to halt the further introduction of such weapons systems into Cuba.
2. We, on our part, would agree—upon the establishment of adequate arrangements through the United Nations to ensure the carrying out and continuation of these commitments—(a) to remove promptly the quarantine measures now in effect and (b) to give assurances against an invasion of Cuba. I am confident that other nations of the Western Hemisphere would be prepared to do likewise.

If you will give your representatives similar instructions, there is no reason why we should not be able to complete these arrangements and announce them to the world within a couple of days. . . .

Discussion Questions

1. Why did Kennedy stress that a nuclear attack launched from Cuba against any nation in the Western Hemisphere would be considered a Soviet attack on the United States?
2. How did Kennedy justify his deployment of a naval quarantine against Cuba? What were the advantages of this approach over negotiations or invasion?
3. What did Kennedy mean when he said that, if the buildup of missiles in Cuba continued, "further action will be justified"?
4. How did Khrushchev justify the placement of missiles in Cuba? How did his two letters differ, both in tone and in the terms they proposed? How do you account for the difference?
5. How did Kennedy's response clarify the issues and offer a basis for agreement? Why did it focus on Khrushchev's first letter and ignore the proposal to remove US missiles from Turkey? Why would Kennedy insist that his eventual pledge to do so be kept private?

47

Kennedy's "Peace Speech" at American University, June 1963

THE CUBAN MISSILE CRISIS MADE a profound impression on President Kennedy, who emerged from it both relieved and sobered. The proximity of nuclear war weighed heavily on him during the months that followed. As Eisenhower had done, he renewed America's efforts to obtain a treaty with the USSR banning atmospheric testing of nuclear weapons. Levels of highly toxic radioactive elements, such as strontium-90 and cesium-139, had increased dramatically in the 1950s; cows ingested it on grass they ate and passed it to humans in their milk; fish absorbed dangerously high levels simply by living in the seas. A test ban treaty seemed essential, not necessarily to lessen the danger of nuclear war, but mainly to halt the poisoning of the planet.

With Khrushchev also chastened by the near miss in Cuba, significant progress was made. The Soviet leader, eager for an agreement that would put his nation on an equal footing with the United States, was more than willing to negotiate. Kennedy made public his hopes in an eloquent commencement address at American University in Washington. Dubbed the "Peace Speech," it startled many with its abandonment of Cold War rhetoric and its conciliatory tone. John F. Kennedy had come a long way from the clarion calls of his inaugural address.

EXCERPTS FROM KENNEDY'S COMMENCEMENT
ADDRESS AT AMERICAN UNIVERSITY, 10 JUNE 1963

. . . What kind of peace do I mean and what kind of peace do we seek? Not a Pax Americana enforced on the world by American weapons of war. Not the peace of the grave or the security of the slave; I am talking about genuine peace—the kind of peace that makes life on earth worth living—and the kind that enables men and nations to grow and to hope and to build a better life for their children—not merely peace for Americans but peace for all men and women—not merely peace in our time but peace in all time.

I speak of peace because of the new face of war. Total war makes no sense in an age when great powers can maintain large and relatively invulnerable nuclear forces and refuse to surrender without resort to those forces. It makes no sense in an age when a single nuclear weapon contains almost ten times the explosive force delivered by all the Allied air forces in the Second World War. It makes no sense in an age when the deadly poisons produced by a nuclear exchange would be carried by wind and water and soil and seed to the far corners of the globe and to generations yet unborn.

Today the expenditure of billions of dollars every year on weapons acquired for the purpose of making sure we never need them is essential to the keeping of peace. But surely the acquisition of such idle stockpiles—which can only destroy and can never create—is not the only . . . means of assuring peace.

I speak of peace, therefore, as the necessary rational end of rational men. I realize the pursuit of peace is not as dramatic as the pursuit of war—and frequently the words of the pursuer fall on deaf ears. But we have no more urgent task. . . .

No government or social system is so evil that its people must be considered as lacking in virtue. As Americans, we find Communism profoundly repugnant as a negation of personal freedom and dignity. But we can still hail the Russian people for their many achievements—in science and space, in economic and industrial growth, in culture and in acts of courage.

Among the many traits the peoples of our two countries have in common, none is stronger than our mutual abhorrence of war. Almost unique among the major world powers, we have never been at war with each other. And no nation in the history of battle ever suffered more than the Soviet Union in the Second World War. At least 20,000,000 lost their lives. Countless millions of homes and families were burned or sacked. A third of the nation's territory, including two-thirds of its industrial base, was turned into a wasteland—a loss equivalent to the destruction of this country east of Chicago.

Today, should total war ever break out again—no matter how—our two countries will be the primary targets. It is an ironic but accurate fact that the two strongest powers are the two most in danger of devastation. All we have built, all we have worked for, would be destroyed in the first 24 hours. And even in the Cold War—which brings burdens and dangers to so many countries, including this nation's closest allies—our two countries bear the heaviest burdens. For we are both devoting massive sums of money to weapons that could be better devoted to combat ignorance, poverty and disease.

We are both caught up in a vicious and dangerous cycle with suspicion on one side breeding suspicion on the other, and new weapons begetting counter-weapons.

In short, both the United States and its allies, and the Soviet Union and its allies, have a mutually deep interest in a just and genuine peace and in halting the arms race. Agreements to this end are in the interests of the Soviet Union as well as ours—and even the most hostile nations can be relied upon to accept and keep those treaty obligations . . . which are in their own interest.

So, let us not be blind to our differences—but let us also direct attention to our common interests and the means by which those differences can be resolved. And if we cannot end now our differences, at least we can help make the world safe for diversity. For, in the final analysis, our most basic common link is that we all inhabit this small planet. We all breathe the same air. We all cherish our children's future. And we are all mortal. . . .

I am taking this opportunity, therefore, to announce two important decisions: First: Chairman Khrushchev, Prime Minister Macmillan and I have agreed that high-level discussions will shortly begin in Moscow toward early agreement on a comprehensive test ban treaty. Our hopes must be tempered with the caution of history—but with our hopes go the hopes of all mankind.

Second: To make clear our good faith and solemn convictions on the matter, I now declare that the United States does not propose to conduct nuclear tests in the atmosphere so long as other states do not do so. We will not be the first to resume. Such a declaration is no substitute for a formal binding treaty—but I hope it will help us achieve it. . . .

The United States, as the world knows, will never start a war. We do not want a war. We do not now expect a war. This generation of Americans has already had enough—more than enough—of war and hate and oppression. We shall be prepared if others wish it. We shall be alert to try to stop it. But we shall also do our part to build a world of peace where the weak are safe and the strong are just.

We are not helpless before that task or hopeless of its success. Confident and unafraid, we labor on—not toward a strategy of annihilation but toward a strategy of peace.

Discussion Questions

1. How did the tone and substance of this speech differ from that of Kennedy's Inaugural Address (Document 44)? How do you account for the difference?
2. What did Kennedy see as the perils of the current world situation? What were his hopes and visions for the future?
3. What examples of conciliatory language can you find in Kennedy's speech? What examples of Cold War rhetoric remain?
4. What reasoning did Kennedy use to persuade Americans of the need for a test ban, despite their distrust for Moscow? How did he explain his contention that Moscow could be counted on to abide by such a treaty?
5. In his proposal for a treaty, how did Kennedy seek to demonstrate American good faith?

48

Kennedy's Berlin Speech, June 1963: *"Ich Bin Ein Berliner"*

JUNE 1963 WAS A TUMULTUOUS MONTH for President Kennedy. His "Peace Speech" at American University was followed the next day by a major address on civil rights. Three hours later, Medgar Evers, a prominent black civil rights leader, was assassinated in his own driveway. In the midst of this tension, Kennedy flew to Europe and paid a visit to the divided city of Berlin.

Speaking on a platform overlooking the Berlin Wall, surrounded by a huge crowd, Kennedy was in no mood to treat Moscow delicately. Hidden now was the conciliatory olive branch held out in the Peace Speech. Carried away by the drama of the occasion and his own inimitable rhetoric, Kennedy embellished the text crafted for him by his longtime speechwriter and alter ego, Theodore Sorensen. The result was an emotional rallying cry that drove the crowd into a frenzy. More than a thousand people fainted during the brief address, and its impact astonished West German Chancellor Konrad Adenauer and sobered Kennedy himself, who later said his listeners would have torn down the wall if he had urged them to do so. It was not his greatest speech, but it would be among his most widely remembered.

EXCERPTS FROM KENNEDY'S SPEECH IN BERLIN, 26 JUNE 1963

. . . Two thousand years ago the proudest boast was *"civis Romanus sum* [I am a Roman citizen]." Today in the world of freedom the proudest boast is *"Ich bin ein Berliner."*

I appreciate my interpreter translating my German.

There are many people in the world who really don't understand . . . what is the great issue between the free world and the Communist world. Let them come to Berlin.

There are some who say that Communism is the wave of the future. Let them come to Berlin.

And there are some who say in Europe and elsewhere, "We can work with the Communists." Let them come to Berlin!

And there are even a few who say that it's true that Communism is an evil system but it permits us to make economic progress. Let them come to Berlin.

Freedom has many difficulties and democracy is not perfect. But we have never had to put a wall up to keep our people in, to prevent them from leaving us. . . .

I know of no town, no city that has been besieged for 18 years that still lives with the vitality and the force and the hope and the determination of the City of West Berlin.

While the wall is the most obvious and vivid demonstration of the failures of the Communist system, all the world can see we take no satisfaction in it, for it is, as your Mayor has said, an offense not only against history, but an offense against humanity, separating families, dividing husbands and wives and brothers and sisters and dividing a people who wish to be joined together. . . .

What is true of this city is true of Germany. Real lasting peace in Europe can never be assured as long as one German out of four is denied the elementary right of free men, and that is to make a free choice. . . .

You live in a defended island of freedom, but your life is part of the main. So let me ask you as I close to lift your eyes beyond the dangers of today to the hopes of tomorrow, beyond the freedom merely of this city of Berlin and all your country of Germany . . . to the advance of freedom everywhere, beyond the wall to the day of peace with justice, beyond yourselves and ourselves to all mankind.

Freedom is indivisible and when one man is enslaved, who are free? When all are free, then we can look forward to that day when this city will be joined as one with this country and this great continent of Europe in a peaceful and hopeful globe.

When that day finally comes, as it will, the people of West Berlin can take sober satisfaction in the fact that they were in the front lines for almost two decades.

All free men, wherever they may live, are citizens of Berlin. And therefore, as a free man, I take pride in the words *"Ich bin ein Berliner."*

Discussion Questions

1. How did the tone of Kennedy's Berlin address differ from that of his speech at American University? Why would Kennedy deliver so strident an anti-Communist address so soon after his "Peace Speech"?
2. In what ways did Kennedy's speech make use of the propaganda advantage granted to the West by the building of the Berlin Wall?
3. In the context of this address, how did Kennedy define the crucial issue preventing resolution of the German Question?
4. Listening to this speech only sixteen days after Kennedy's American University speech, what might Khrushchev have thought?
5. What examples of Cold War rhetoric were present in this speech? What sort of threats were absent from it?
6. How did this address forecast the eventual solution of the German Question and the end of the Cold War?

49

The Nuclear Test Ban Treaty, August 1963

K ENNEDY'S BERLIN SPEECH, strident as it was, did not undermine efforts to achieve a nuclear test ban treaty. These efforts, in fact, had been expedited when the United States decided to drop its earlier insistence upon on-site inspections. Since underground tests could not be easily detected without such inspections, given the technological limitations of the time, these tests were excluded from the resulting agreement, making a *limited* test ban treaty.

The American action made a treaty possible by satisfying two key Soviet concerns: first, that Soviet facilities remain closed to outside inspection teams; second, that some form of testing be permitted, since Soviet nuclear technology remained several years behind that of the United States. The treaty was signed by the Soviet Union, Great Britain, and the United States, but not by France, the only other power with atomic weapons in 1963.

Eventually signed by more than one hundred countries, the Limited Nuclear Test Ban Treaty did not end the arms race, but it did help bring about a sharp reduction in the levels of toxic radioactive particles in the Earth's atmosphere.

EXCERPTS FROM THE LIMITED
NUCLEAR TEST BAN TREATY, 5 AUGUST 1963

Article I
1. Each of the Parties to this Treaty undertakes to prohibit, to prevent, and not to carry out any nuclear weapon test explosion, or any other nuclear explosion, at any place under its jurisdiction or control:
   (a) in the atmosphere; beyond its limits, including outer space; or underwater, including territorial waters or high seas; or
   (b) in any other environment if such explosion causes radioactive debris to be present outside the territorial limits of the State under whose jurisdiction or control such explosion is conducted. It is understood in this connection that the provisions of this subpara-

graph are without prejudice to the conclusion of a treaty resulting in the permanent banning of all nuclear test explosions, including all such explosions underground. . . .

2. Each of the Parties to this Treaty undertakes furthermore to refrain from causing, encouraging, or in any way participating in, the carrying out of any nuclear weapon test explosion, or any other nuclear explosion, anywhere which would take place in any of the environments described, or have the effect referred to in paragraph 1 of this article.

Article II

1. Any Party may propose amendments to this Treaty. . . .
2. Any amendment to this Treaty must be approved by a majority of the votes of all Parties to this Treaty, including the votes of all the Original Parties.

Article III

1. This Treaty shall be open to all States for signature. . . .
2. This Treaty shall be subject to ratification by signatory States. . . .
3. This Treaty shall enter into force after its ratification by all the Original Parties. . . .

Article IV

This Treaty shall be of unlimited duration. . . .

Discussion Questions

1. Why was the requirement for international inspection the focus of Soviet objections to a ban on nuclear testing?
2. Why were underground tests not covered by the treaty? Why would the Soviets be pleased with their exclusion?
3. Why were outer space tests covered by the treaty, despite the fact that existing technology could not perform such tests?
4. What was paragraph 2 of Article I attempting to prevent?
5. Why did France refuse to sign the treaty? What potential problems might this refusal cause?
6. What impact, if any, might the treaty have on nations such as China that were developing or intending to develop nuclear weapons? Why would such nations be reluctant to sign the treaty?

50

The Sino-Soviet Split, 1960–1964

THROUGHOUT THE 1950s, despite increasing tensions between them, the USSR and Communist China maintained a facade of socialist solidarity. In 1960–1963, however, the dispute between the Communist giants became an open split. In 1960 the Soviets recalled their technicians from China, and the Chinese published "Long Live Leninism," disparaging the Soviet notion of "peaceful coexistence" and obliquely assailing the USSR by maligning Yugoslavia. Soon the Soviets retaliated with verbal attacks on China's close friend Albania. In 1961, when Khrushchev assaulted both Stalin and the Albanians at the Twenty-second Congress of the CPSU (Communist Party of the Soviet Union), Chinese premier Zhou Enlai (Chou En-lai) objected and publicly laid a wreath at Stalin's tomb. In 1962 a bitter border dispute between Russia and China, combined with Chinese disgust at Khrushchev's backing down in the Cuban Missile Crisis and Soviet support for India in a border war with China, widened the breach still more.

By 1963 the two nations were publicly assailing each other by name. On 14 July of that year, the Central Committee of the CPSU issued an "open letter" that detailed the main Soviet grievances against the Chinese Communists. The following summer, the Chinese responded by publishing a diatribe, "On Khrushchev's Phony Communism and Its Historical Lessons for the World," accusing the Soviets of betraying communism and colluding with the capitalists.

A. EXCERPTS FROM CHINESE
PUBLICATION "LONG LIVE LENINISM," APRIL 1960

Editors' Note: In April of 1960, the editors of *Hongqi* (Red Flag), a journal published by the Central Committee of the Chinese Communist Party, issued an article called "Long Live Leninism" to mark the ninetieth anniversary of the birth of V. I. Lenin. Citing Lenin's identification of capitalism with imperialism as central to Leninist thought, the article criticized Communists who called for an end to war and pursued a path of peaceful cooperation with the capitalist West. According to the article, one of Leninism's basic tenets was that wars resulted inevitably from the actions of capitalist imperialists, whose relentless drive for markets, raw materials, and investment sources compelled them to seek military conquests and colonies to exploit. Wars would thus continue to occur as long as capitalist imperialist exploitation continued to exist.

The article was careful to praise the Soviet Union as the leader of the socialist camp, but it vilified Yugoslav "revisionists," whom it accused of denying this basic truth by calling for peaceful cooperation with the capitalists, naively hoping that they would give up their colonies and wealth without a fight, and dreaming that capitalism would somehow peacefully transform itself into socialism. Stressing that Communist nations had a Leninist obligation to support socialist revolutions and wars of national liberation by colonized peoples against their imperialist oppressors, the Chinese editors insisted that attempts at peaceful cooperation with the West would merely perpetuate capitalist exploitation and imperialist oppression of the colonized peoples.

Although the article ostensibly targeted Yugoslav "revisionists," there was little doubt that, as its authors later tacitly admitted, its real targets were Nikita Khrushchev and the Soviet leadership, which had been seeking "peaceful coexistence" and better relations with the capitalist West. The article thus touched off an ideological war of words between the Soviet and Chinese Communists, as the Soviets responded first by criticizing China's Albanian allies, and later by openly and publicly disparaging the Chinese Communists themselves.

Here are some excerpts that convey the flavor of the article "Long Live Leninism":

We believe in the absolute correctness of Lenin's thinking: War is an inevitable outcome of the systems of exploitation, and the imperialist system is the source of modern wars. Until the imperialist system and the exploiting classes come to an end, wars of one kind or another will still occur. . . .

To attain its aim of plunder and oppression, imperialism always has two tactics: the tactics of war and the tactics of "peace"; therefore the proletariat and the people of all countries must also use two tactics to deal with imperialism: the tactics of exposing imperialism's peace fraud and striving energetically for genuine world peace, and the tactics of being prepared to use a just war to end the imperialist unjust war if and when the imperialists should unleash it. . . .

The Yugoslav revisionists . . . deny the inherent class character of war and thereby obliterate the fundamental difference between just wars and unjust wars; they deny that imperialist war is a continuation of imperialist policies, deny the danger of imperialism unleashing another world war, deny that only after doing away with the exploiting classes will it be possible to do away with war. . . .

The modern revisionists seek to confuse the peaceful foreign policy of the socialist countries with the domestic policy of the proletariat in capitalist countries. They thus hold that peaceful coexistence of countries with different social systems means that capitalism can peacefully grow into socialism. . . .

Peaceful coexistence of different countries and people's revolutions in various countries are in themselves two different things. . . . Peaceful coexistence refers to relations between countries, revolution means the overthrow of the oppressing classes by the oppressed people within each country, while in the case of the colonies and semi-colonies, it is first and foremost a question of overthrowing alien oppressors, namely the imperialists. . . .

B. EXCERPTS FROM KHRUSHCHEV'S CLOSING REMARKS AT THE TWENTY-SECOND PARTY CONGRESS, 27 OCTOBER 1961*

. . . Some people attack us, charging that we seem to simplify or soften our assessment of the international situation when we stress the need for peaceful coexistence in present-day circumstances. They tell us that those who emphasize peaceful coexistence apparently underestimate the essence of imperialism. . . .

In our time the might of the world socialist system has grown as never before. It already unites more than a third of all humanity, and its forces are growing quickly; it is a great bastion of peace in our world. The principle of peaceful coexistence between countries with different social systems has attained vital significance in present-day circumstances.

This is not understood only by the hopeless dogmatists who, in repeating general formulas about imperialism, stubbornly turn away from life. . . .

Comrades! The report of the Central Committee, and also the remarks of delegates to the congress, spoke about the erroneous position of the leadership of the Albanian Labor Party, which set out to struggle against the tenets of the 20th Congress of our Party. . . .

It is clear that the Central Committee of our party had no choice but to tell the Congress the whole truth about the shameful position taken by the leadership of the Albanian Labor Party. If we had not done this, they would have continued to make it look as if the Central Committee of the Communist

---

* *The Current Digest of the Soviet Press*, vol. XIII, no. 46 (13 December 1961), 22–27.

Party of the Soviet Union was afraid to inform the Party about its differences with the leadership of the Albanian Labor Party. . . .

At our Congress it has been emphasized that we are prepared to normalize relations with the Albanian Labor Party on the basis of Marxist-Leninist principles. How have the Albanian leaders responded to this? They have issued a brazen statement slinging mud at our party and its Central Committee.

The leader of the delegation of the Communist Party of China, Comrade Zhou Enlai, in his remarks expressed concern about the open consideration at our Congress of the question of Albanian-Soviet relations. As far as we can see, the main concern in his statement is that the current state of our relations with the Albanian Labor Party might affect the solidarity of the socialist camp.

We share the anxiety of our Chinese friends and appreciate their concern for the strengthening of unity. If our Chinese comrades wish to devote their energies to normalizing relations between the Albanian Labor Party and fraternal parties, it is doubtful that anyone could help accomplish this task better than the Communist Party of China. This would really work to the advantage of the Albanian Labor Party, and would serve the interests of the entire commonwealth of socialist countries. . . .

C. EXCERPTS FROM OPEN LETTER OF THE CENTRAL COMMITTEE OF THE SOVIET COMMUNIST PARTY TO ALL SOVIET COMMUNISTS, 14 JULY 1963

The Central Committee of the CPSU [Communist Party of the Soviet Union] deems it necessary to address this open letter to you to set out our position on the fundamental questions of the international Communist movement in connection with the letter of the CPC [Communist Party of China] of June 14, 1963. . . .

For many years the relations between our parties were good. But some time ago, serious differences came to light between the CPC on the one hand and the CPSU and other fraternal parties on the other. . . .

For nearly half a century the Soviet country, under the leadership of the Communist Party, has been leading a struggle for the triumph of the ideas of Marxism-Leninism. . . .

The Soviet people generously shared with their Chinese brothers all their many years of long experience in Socialist construction, and their achievements in the field of science and technology. Our country has rendered and is rendering substantial aid to the development of the economy of People's China. . . . Our party—all Soviet people—rejoiced at the successes of the great Chinese people in the building of a new life, and took pride in them. . . .

This was how matters stood until the Chinese leaders began retreating from the general line of the world Communist movement.

In April 1960, the Chinese comrades openly disclosed their differences with the world Communist movement by publishing a collection of articles called "Long Live Leninism!" This collection, based on distortions—truncated and incorrectly interpreted theses of the well-known works of Lenin—contained propositions actually directed . . . against the policy of peaceful coexistence of states with different social systems, against the possibility of preventing a world war in the present day, against the use of both peaceful and non-peaceful roads of the development of Socialist revolutions.

The leaders of the CPC began imposing their views on all fraternal parties. . . . Furthermore, the Chinese comrades made their differences with the CPSU and other fraternal parties an object of open discussion in nonparty organizations. Such steps by the leadership of the CPC aroused and seriously troubled the fraternal parties. . . .

Unfortunately, the CPC leadership . . . continued pursuing its erroneous course and deepened its differences with the fraternal parties. . . .

In October 1961, the CPSU Central Committee undertook new attempts to normalize relations with the CPC. Comrades N. S. Khrushchev, F. R. Kozlov and A. I. Mikoyan had talks with Comrades Chou En-lai [Zhou Enlai], Peng Cheng and other leading officials who arrived for the 22nd CPSU Congress. Comrade N. S. Khrushchev set forth to the Chinese delegation in detail the position of the CPSU Central Committee on the questions of principle which were discussed at the 22nd Congress, and stressed our invariable desire to strengthen friendship and cooperation with the Communist Party of China.

In its letters of February 22 and May 31, 1962, the CPSU Central Committee drew the attention of the CPC Central Committee to the dangerous consequences for our common cause that might be brought about by the weakening of the unity of the Communist movement. . . .

But the Chinese leaders, every time, ignored the comradely warnings of the CPSU, further exacerbating Chinese-Soviet relations. . . .

What is the gist of the differences between the CPC on the one hand, and the CPSU and the international Communist movement on the other hand? . . .

In point of fact . . . questions that bear on the vital interests of the peoples are in the center of the dispute. These are the questions of war and peace, the question of the role and development of the world Socialist system; these are the questions of struggle against the ideology and practice of the "personality cult"; these are the questions of strategy and tactics of the world labor movement and the national liberation struggle. . . .

Our party, in the decisions of the 20th and 22nd Congresses . . . set before Communists as a task of extreme importance the task of struggling for peace, for averting a world thermonuclear catastrophe. . . . Suffice it to say that the explosion of only one powerful thermonuclear bomb surpasses the explosive force of all ammunition used during all previous wars, including World Wars I and II. And many thousands of such bombs have been accumulated! Do Communists have the right to ignore this danger? Do we have to tell the people all the truth about the consequences of thermonuclear war? We believe that undoubtedly we must. . . .

And what is the position of the CPC leadership? What do the theses that they propagate mean? An end cannot be put to wars as long as imperialism exists; peaceful coexistence is an illusion; . . . the struggle for peace hinders the revolutionary struggle? These theses mean that the Chinese comrades . . . do not believe in the possibility of preventing a new world war; they underestimate the forces of peace and Socialism and overestimate the forces of imperialism; they actually ignore the mobilization of the popular masses to the struggle with the war danger. . . .

The Chinese comrades obviously underestimate all the danger of thermonuclear war. "The atomic bomb is a paper tiger; it is not terrible at all," they contend. . . .

We would like to ask the Chinese comrades—who suggest building a bright future on the ruins of the old world destroyed by thermonuclear war—if they have consulted the working class of the countries where imperialism predominates. . . . The working class, the working people, will say to such "revolutionaries": "What right do you have to settle for us the questions of our existence and our class struggle? We are in favor of Socialism, but we want to gain it through the class struggle and not by unleashing a world war." . . .

The deep difference . . . on the questions of war, peace, and peaceful coexistence, was manifested with particular clarity during the 1962 crisis in the Caribbean Sea. . . . The Chinese comrades allege that in the period of the Caribbean crisis we made an "adventurist" mistake by introducing rockets in Cuba, and then "capitulated to American imperialism" when we removed the rockets from Cuba. . . . Such assertions utterly contradict the facts.

What was the actual state of affairs? The . . . Soviet Government possessed trustworthy information that an armed aggression of United States imperialism against Cuba was about to start. We realized . . . that the most resolute steps were needed to rebuff aggression, to defend the Cuban revolution effectively. . . .

The delivery of missiles to Cuba signified that an attack on her would meet resolute rebuff, with the employment of rocket weapons against the organizers of the aggression. . . .

Inasmuch as the point in question was not simply a conflict between the United States and Cuba but a clash between two major nuclear powers . . . , a real danger of world thermonuclear war arose. There was one alternative in the prevailing situation: either to . . . embark upon the road of unleashing a world thermonuclear war or, profiting by the opportunities offered by the delivery of missiles, to take all measures to reach an agreement on the peaceful solution of the crisis and prevent aggression against the Cuban Republic. We have chosen . . . the second road, and we are convinced that we have done the right thing. . . .

Agreement on the removal of missile weapons, in reply to the United States Government's commitment not to invade Cuba . . . have made possible the frustration of the plans of the extreme adventuristic circles of American imperialism, which were ready to go whole hog. As a result, it was possible to defend revolutionary Cuba and save peace. . . .

D. EXCERPTS FROM "ON KHRUSHCHEV'S PHONY COMMUNISM AND ITS HISTORICAL LESSONS FOR THE WORLD," 1964

At the 22nd Congress of the CPSU, the revisionist Khrushchev clique developed their revisionism . . . not only by rounding off their anti-revolutionary theories of "peaceful coexistence" and "peaceful transition" but also by declaring that the dictatorship of the proletariat is no longer necessary in the Soviet Union. . . .

The program put forward by the revisionist Khrushchev clique . . . is a program of phony communism, a revisionist program against proletarian revolution and for the abolition of the dictatorship of the proletariat. . . .

As long as imperialism exists, the proletariat in the socialist countries will have to struggle both against the bourgeoisie at home and against international imperialism. Imperialism will seize every opportunity and try to undertake armed intervention against the socialist countries or to bring about their peaceful disintegration. It will do its utmost to destroy the socialist countries or to make them degenerate into capitalist countries. The international class struggle will inevitably find its reflection within the socialist countries. . . .

The internal task consists mainly of completely abolishing all the exploiting classes, developing socialist economy to the maximum . . . , eliminating any possibility of . . . the restoration of capitalism, and providing conditions for the realization of a communist society. . . .

The international task consists mainly of preventing attacks by international imperialism (including armed intervention and disintegration by peaceful means), and of giving support to the world revolution until the peoples of all countries finally abolish imperialism, capitalism and the system of exploitation. . . .

In these circumstances, the abolition of the dictatorship of the proletariat by the revisionist Khrushchev clique is nothing but a betrayal of socialism and communism. . . .

On the pretext of "combating the personality cult," Khrushchev has defamed the dictatorship of the proletariat and the socialist system and thus in fact paved the way for the restoration of capitalism in the Soviet Union. In completely negating Stalin, he has in fact negated Marxism-Leninism which was upheld by Stalin. . . .

Khrushchev sabotages the socialist planned economy, applies the capitalist principle of profit . . . , and undermines socialist ownership by the whole people. . . . Eager to learn from the big proprietors of American farms, he is encouraging capitalist management . . . and undermining the socialist collective economy. . . . The rotten bourgeois culture of the West is now fashionable in the Soviet Union. . . .

Under the signboard of "peaceful coexistence," Khrushchev has been colluding with U.S. imperialism, wrecking the socialist camp and the international communist movement, opposing the revolutionary struggles of the oppressed peoples and nations, practicing great-power chauvinism . . . , and betraying proletarian internationalism. All this is being done for the protection of the vested interests of a handful of people, which he places above the fundamental interests of the peoples of the Soviet Union, the socialist camp, and the whole world. . . .

The revisionist Khrushchev clique know the paramount importance of controlling state power. They need it for clearing the way for the restoration of capitalism in the Soviet Union. These are Khrushchev's real aims. . . .

Discussion Questions

1. What were the main issues involved in the Sino-Soviet dispute? Why were the Chinese upset about Soviet policies?
2. Who were the actual "revisionists" referred to in "Long Live Leninism"? Why did the Chinese think it was harmful for Communists to pursue peaceful cooperation with the capitalist West?
3. At the Twenty-second Party Congress, why did Khrushchev attack Albania? Why did he not criticize China directly? Why did the Chinese object to the attack on Albania?
4. How did the Soviets defend themselves against Chinese criticism (especially with regard to "peaceful coexistence" and the Cuban Missile Crisis)? How and why did the Chinese claim that Khrushchev's "phony

communism" was really betraying communism and restoring capitalism?

5. What were the implications of the Sino-Soviet split for both the Communist movement and the Cold War? What potential advantages and disadvantages did it provide the West?

51

The Gulf of Tonkin Resolution, 1964

DURING THE EARLY 1960s, in an effort to bolster the government of South Vietnam against a Communist insurgency, President Kennedy sent increasing numbers of American military advisors to that embattled land. After Kennedy's assassination in November 1963, his successor, Lyndon Johnson, continued to expand the US role, especially after Communist North Vietnam began sending troops to join the fray in August 1964.

That same month, American surveillance ships in the Gulf of Tonkin, off the coast of North Vietnam, were reportedly attacked by North Vietnamese patrol boats. What actually occurred was not clear, but following the incident Johnson obtained congressional approval of a joint resolution giving him extensive authority to use military force in Southeast Asia.

This resolution became the main legal basis for American involvement in the Vietnam War. It enabled Johnson, who presented himself as a peace candidate in the 1964 elections, to avoid asking Congress for a declaration of war while gaining the powers he needed to fight one. Later it allowed him to continue the war without having to jeopardize congressional support for his ambitious domestic agenda by seeking a formal declaration. He used the resolution to fight an undeclared war, refusing to raise taxes or call up the reserves. The resulting economic and political pressures drove up the rate of inflation, weakened the US economy, and helped convince Johnson not to seek reelection in 1968.

THE GULF OF TONKIN RESOLUTION, 10 AUGUST 1964

Whereas naval units of the Communist regime in Vietnam, in violation of the Charter of the United Nations and of international law, have deliberately and repeatedly attacked United States naval vessels lawfully present in international waters, and have thereby created a serious threat to international peace; and

Whereas these attacks are part of a deliberate and systematic campaign of aggression that the Communist regime in North Vietnam has been waging against its neighbors and the nations joined with them in the collective defense of their freedom; and

Whereas the United States is assisting the peoples of southeast Asia to protect their freedom and has no territorial, military or political ambitions in that area, but desires only that these peoples should be left in peace to work out their own destinies in their own way; Now, therefore, be it RESOLVED BY THE SENATE AND HOUSE OF REPRESENTATIVES OF THE UNITED STATES OF AMERICA IN CONGRESS ASSEMBLED, That the Congress approves and supports the determination of the President, as Commander in Chief, to take all necessary measures to repel any armed attack against the forces of the United States and to prevent further aggression.

SEC. 2. The United States regards as vital to its national interest and to world peace the maintenance of international peace and security in Southeast Asia. Consonant with the Constitution and the Charter of the United Nations and in accordance with its obligations under the Southeast Asia Collective Defense Treaty, the United States is, therefore, prepared to take all necessary steps, including the use of armed force, to assist any member or protocol state of the Southeast Asia Collective Defense Treaty requesting assistance in defense of its freedom.

SEC. 3. This resolution shall expire when the President shall determine that the peace and security of the area is reasonably assured by international conditions created by action of the United Nations or otherwise, except that it may be terminated earlier by concurrent resolution of the Congress.

Discussion Questions

1. What was so unusual about the way President Johnson used the Gulf of Tonkin Resolution?
2. What alleged events does the resolution use to justify American actions? Why?

3. To what external documents does the resolution refer in providing a context for American actions? Why?

4. Why did Johnson decide to seek a congressional resolution rather than a declaration of war? What were the potential advantages and disadvantages of this decision?

52

Lin Biao, "Long Live the Victory of People's War," 1965

L IN BIAO WAS THE FOREMOST military hero of China's Communist revolution. His skillfully orchestrated campaigns against the Nationalists in 1947–1949 were instrumental in bringing victory to the Communist People's Liberation Army (PLA). He grew in political stature throughout the 1950s and by 1965 was one of the closest confidants of Chairman Mao Zedong (Mao Tse-tung). Later, becoming impatient for the demise of the aging Mao and disagreeing with the decision of Mao and Zhou Enlai to seek better relations with the United States, Lin mounted an unsuccessful coup attempt in September 1971. He was killed when his plane crashed as he fled toward exile in the Soviet Union.

In 1965, ostensibly to commemorate the twentieth anniversary of China's victory over Japan, Lin published a noteworthy article, "Long Live the Victory of People's War." It celebrated the crucial role of guerrilla warfare in bringing about the triumph of Communist revolution. But since guerrilla warfare had not played a decisive role in the defeat of Japan, his article was seen as having been motivated by the guerrilla war then raging in Vietnam. While carefully paying homage to the thought of Mao Zedong, Lin stressed the importance of unconventional combat in the emerging nations of Asia, Africa, and Latin America in assisting the inevitable triumph of communism throughout the world.

EXCERPTS FROM "LONG LIVE THE
VICTORY OF PEOPLE'S WAR," 3 SEPTEMBER 1965

. . . If they are to defeat a formidable enemy, revolutionary armed forces should not fight with a reckless disregard for the consequences when there is a great disparity between their own strength and the enemy's. If they do, they will suffer serious losses and bring heavy setbacks to the revolution. Guerrilla warfare is the only way to mobilize and apply the whole strength of the people against the enemy, . . . to expand our forces in the course of the war, deplete and weaken the enemy, gradually change the balance of forces between the enemy and ourselves, switch from guerrilla to mobile warfare, and finally defeat the enemy. . . .

Comrade Mao Tse-tung has provided a masterly summary of the strategy and tactics of people's war: You fight in your way and we fight in ours; we fight when we can win and move away when we can't.

In other words, you rely on modern weapons and we rely on highly conscious revolutionary people; you give full play to your superiority and we give full play to ours; you have your way of fighting and we have ours. When you want to fight us, we don't let you and you can't even find us. But when we want to fight you, we make sure that you can't get away and we hit you squarely on the chin and wipe you out. When we are able to wipe you out, we do so with a vengeance; when we can't, we see to it that you don't wipe us out. . . .

The history of people's war in China and other countries provides conclusive evidence that the growth of the people's revolutionary forces from weak and small beginnings into strong and large forces is a universal law of development of class struggle, a universal law of development of people's war. A people's war inevitably meets with many difficulties, with many ups and downs and setbacks in the course of its development, but no force can alter its general trend toward inevitable triumph. . . .

In the final analysis, the whole cause of world revolution hinges on the revolutionary struggles of the Asian, African and Latin American peoples who make up the overwhelming majority of the world's population. The socialist countries should regard it as their internationalist duty to support the people's revolutionary struggles in Asia, Africa and Latin America. . . .

All peoples suffering from US imperialist aggression, oppression and plunder, unite! Hold aloft the just banner of people's war and fight for the cause of world peace, national liberation, people's democracy and socialism! Victory will certainly go to the people of the world! Long live the victory of people's war!

Discussion Questions

1. Why did Lin Biao and the Chinese Communists publish this article? What potential goals and audience do you think they had in mind?
2. How do the views expressed in this article compare with those expressed in Andrei Zhdanov's report to the Cominform (Document 12A) and Deng Xiaoping's "Three Worlds" speech (Document 66)?
3. How might this article have been related to the emerging conflict in Vietnam (Document 53)?
4. What did Mao and Lin mean by the phrase, "You fight in your way and we fight in ours"?
5. How can you tell that this article was written by a Marxist?

53

Lyndon Johnson and the Vietnam War, 1965–1968

FOLLOWING THE GULF OF TONKIN RESOLUTION, US involvement in the Vietnam War escalated as President Johnson sent in more and more troops. In April 1965, in a major speech at Johns Hopkins University, the president sought to explain and justify this conflict.

As time went on, however, increasing numbers of Americans began to question the US role. Protest marches and demonstrations, at first isolated and small, gradually became larger and more significant. The Senate Foreign Relations Committee held a series of public hearings designed to cast doubt on the wisdom of war. Demonstrations, teach-ins, and other forms of domestic protest began in 1965 and escalated to serious proportions by spring 1968. Johnson made numerous overtures to North Vietnam to begin negotiations, but since his offers were predicated on the continued independence of South Vietnam (a condition Hanoi would not accept), his efforts were frustrating and futile.

In 1968 the American antiwar movement found a champion in Senator Eugene McCarthy of Minnesota, who challenged Johnson in the New Hampshire presidential primary. McCarthy won 42 percent of the vote against an incumbent president, instantly legitimizing the political viability of the peace movement. Senator Robert F. Kennedy of New York, younger brother of the slain president, saw the implications of McCarthy's showing and entered the race himself. Many who opposed the war but did not consider McCarthy presidential material switched to Kennedy. Meanwhile, Johnson came under pressure from his aides and from elder statesmen like Dean Acheson to pull America out of the war. Disillusioned and exhausted, he addressed the nation on Sunday evening, 31 March 1968, to proclaim a new peace initiative. Then, in a surprise ending that stunned many listeners, he announced that he was withdrawing from the presidential race. The war had claimed yet another victim: Johnson's political career.

A. JOHNSON'S SPEECH AT
JOHNS HOPKINS UNIVERSITY, 7 APRIL 1965

. . . Tonight Americans and Asians are dying for a world where each people may choose its own path to change. This is the principle for which our ancestors fought in the valleys of Pennsylvania. It is the principle for which our sons fight in the jungles of Vietnam.

Vietnam is far from this quiet campus. We have no territory there, nor do we seek any. The war is dirty and brutal and difficult. And some 400 young men—born into an America bursting with opportunity and promise—have ended their lives on Vietnam's steaming soil.

Why must we take this painful road? Why must this nation hazard its ease, its interest and its power for the sake of a people so far away? . . .

Why are we in South Vietnam? We are there because we have a promise to keep. Since 1954 every American President has offered support to the people of South Vietnam. We have helped to build and we have helped to defend. Thus, over many years, we have made a national pledge to help South Vietnam defend its independence. I intend to keep our promise. To dishonor that pledge, to abandon this small and brave nation to its enemy—and the terror that must follow—would be an unforgivable wrong.

We are also there to strengthen world order. Around the globe, from Berlin to Thailand, are people whose well-being rests, in part, on the belief that they can count on us if they are attacked. To leave Vietnam to its fate would shake the confidence of all these people in the value of American commitment. The result would be an increased unrest and instability, or even war.

We are also there because there are great stakes in the balance. Let no one think that retreat from Vietnam would bring an end to conflict. The battle would be renewed in one country and then another. The central lesson of our time is that the appetite of aggression is never satisfied. To withdraw from one battlefield means only to prepare for the next. We must say in Southeast Asia—as we did in Europe—in the words of the Bible: "Hitherto shalt thou come, but no further." . . .

Our objective is the independence of South Vietnam, and its freedom from attack. We want nothing for ourselves—only that the people of South Vietnam be allowed to guide their own country in their own way. We will do everything necessary to reach that objective. And we will do only what is necessary. . . .

We will not be defeated. We will not grow tired. We will not withdraw, either openly or under the cloak of a meaningless agreement. . . .

B. JOHNSON'S ADDRESS TO THE NATION, 31 MARCH 1968

. . . Tonight, I renew the offer I made last August: to stop the bombardment of North Vietnam. We ask that talks begin promptly, that they be serious talks on the substance of peace. We assume that during those talks, Hanoi will not take advantage of our restraint.

We are prepared to move immediately toward peace through negotiations. So tonight, in the hope that this action will lead to early talks, I am taking the first step to de-escalate the conflict. We are reducing—substantially reducing—the present level of hostilities, and we are doing so unilaterally and at once.

Tonight I have ordered our aircraft and our naval vessels to make no attacks on North Vietnam except in the area north of the demilitarized zone where the continuing enemy buildup directly threatens allied forward positions and where the movement of their troops and supplies are clearly related to that threat. The area in which we are stopping our attacks includes almost 90 percent of North Vietnam's population, and most of its territory. Thus there will be no attacks around the principal populated areas, or in the food-producing areas of North Vietnam. . . .

Now let me give you my estimate of the chances for peace—the peace that will one day stop the bloodshed in South Vietnam [so that] all the Vietnamese people will be permitted to rebuild and develop their land. . . .

I cannot promise that the initiative that I have announced tonight will be completely successful in achieving peace any more than the thirty others that we have undertaken and agreed to in recent years. . . . But it is our fervent hope that North Vietnam, after years of fighting that has left the issue unresolved, will now cease its efforts to achieve a military victory and will join with us in moving toward the peace table. And there may come a time when . . . Vietnamese—on both sides—are able to work out a way to settle their own differences by free political choice rather than by war. . . .

During the past four and a half years, it has been my fate and my responsibility to be Commander-in-Chief. I have lived daily and nightly with the cost of this war. I know the pain that it has inflicted. I know perhaps better than anyone the misgivings it has aroused. And throughout this entire long period I have been sustained by a single principle: that what we are doing now in Vietnam is vital not only to the security of Southeast Asia but it is vital to the security of every American. . . .

And the larger purpose of our involvement has always been to help the nations of Southeast Asia become independent, and stand alone, self-sustaining as members of a great world community, at peace with themselves, at peace with others. And with such a nation our country—and the world—will be far more secure than it is tonight. . . .

With America's sons in the fields far away, with America's future under challenge right here at home, with our hopes and the world's hopes for peace in the balance every day, I do not believe that I should devote an hour or a day of my time to any personal partisan causes or to any duties other than the awesome duties of this office—the Presidency of your country.

Accordingly, I shall not seek, and I will not accept, the nomination of my party for another term as your President. But let men everywhere know, however, that a strong and a confident and a vigilant America stands ready tonight to seek an honorable peace; and stands ready tonight to defend an honored cause, whatever the price, whatever the burden, whatever the sacrifice that duty may require. . . .

Discussion Questions

1. According to President Johnson's Johns Hopkins speech, what principle was America seeking to defend in Vietnam?
2. What were the three reasons he listed to explain American presence in Southeast Asia? How might Americans have differed in their perceptions of the validity of those three reasons?
3. Why would Johnson's stated objectives—the independence of South Vietnam and its freedom from attack—be difficult to attain?

4. What evidence of President Johnson's frustration can you find in his address to the nation of 31 March 1968?
5. Why did Johnson decide to withdraw from the presidential race? How did he expect this to help his peace efforts?

54

China's Great Proletarian Cultural Revolution, 1966–1969

IN 1966 CHINA'S MAO ZEDONG launched a spectacular campaign of mass mobilization called the Great Proletarian Cultural Revolution. Millions of young people heeded his call to form radical militias called Red Guards that disrupted businesses and closed universities, forcing managers and professors to labor in the fields with the peasants. For the next few years, the Chinese largely withdrew from world affairs as their energies focused inward. The Red Guards vilified not only capitalists but also the Soviet system, calling it bureaucratic and elitist, and even besieged the Soviet embassy in Beijing in 1967. They also held mass rallies to glorify their leader, waving copies of his "Little Red Book," *Quotations from Chairman Mao Tse-tung,* a collection of excerpts from his writings and sayings, which his youthful followers could recite by heart.

A. DECISION OF THE CENTRAL COMMITTEE OF THE CHINESE COMMUNIST PARTY CONCERNING THE GREAT PROLETARIAN CULTURAL REVOLUTION, 8 AUGUST 1966

The Great Proletarian Cultural Revolution now unfolding is a great revolution that touches people to their very souls and constitutes a new stage in the development of the socialist revolution. . . .

At present, our objective is to struggle against and overthrow those persons in authority who are taking the capitalist road, to criticize and repudiate the reactionary bourgeois academic "authorities" and . . . to transform education, literature and art and all other parts of [our society] . . . , so as to facilitate the consolidation and development of the socialist system. . . .

Large numbers of revolutionary young people, previously unknown, have become courageous and daring path-breakers. They are vigorous in action and intelligent. . . . [T]hey argue things out, expose and criticize thoroughly, and launch resolute attacks on the open and hidden representatives of the bourgeoisie. . . .

What the Central Committee of the Party demands of the Party committees . . . is that they persevere in giving correct leadership, put daring above everything else, boldly arouse the masses . . . and dismiss from their leading posts all those in authority who are taking the capitalist road. . . .

In the Great Proletarian Cultural Revolution, the only method is for the masses to liberate themselves. . . . Trust the masses, rely on them and respect their initiative. . . .

Concentrate all forces to strike at the handful of ultra-reactionary bourgeois rightists and counter-revolutionary revisionists, and expose and criticize to the full their crimes against the Party, against socialism, and against Mao Zedong's thought. . . . The main target of the present movement is those within the Party who are in authority and are taking the capitalist road. . . .

The Cultural Revolutionary groups, committees and other organizational forms created by the masses in many schools and units . . . are excellent new forms of organization whereby the masses educate themselves under the leadership of the Communist Party. They are an excellent bridge to keep our Party in close contact with the masses. . . .

In the Great Proletarian Cultural Revolution a most important task is to transform the old educational system and the old principles and methods of teaching. . . . In every kind of school we must apply thoroughly the policy advanced by Comrade Mao Zedong of education serving proletarian politics and education being combined with productive labor. . . . While their main task is to study, students should also learn other things. . . . [I]n addition to their studies they should also learn industrial work, farming and military affairs, and take part in the struggles of the Cultural Revolution. . . .

In the Great Proletarian Cultural Revolution, it is imperative to hold aloft the great red banner of Mao Zedong's thought and put proletarian politics in command. The movement for the creative study and application of Chairman

Mao Zedong's works should be carried forward among the masses . . . and Mao Zedong's thought should be taken as the guide to action. . . .

B. EXCERPTS FROM THE "LITTLE RED BOOK," *QUOTATIONS FROM CHAIRMAN MAO TSE-TUNG*

A revolution is not a dinner party, or writing an essay, or painting a picture, or doing embroidery; it cannot be so refined, so leisurely and gentle, so temperate, kind, courteous, restrained and magnanimous. A revolution is an insurrection, an act of violence by which one class overthrows another.

Whoever sides with the revolutionary people is a revolutionary. Whoever sides with imperialism, feudalism and bureaucrat-capitalism is a counter-revolutionary. . . .

Every Communist must grasp the truth, "Political power grows out of the barrel of a gun."

All reactionaries are paper tigers. In appearance, the reactionaries are terrifying, but in reality they are not so powerful. From a long-term point of view, it is not the reactionaries but the people who are really powerful. . . .

There are two winds in the world today, the East Wind and the West Wind. There is a Chinese saying, "Either the East Wind prevails over the West Wind or the West Wind prevails over the East Wind." I believe . . . that the East Wind is prevailing over the West Wind. That is to say, the forces of socialism have become overwhelmingly superior to the forces of imperialism.

The revolutionary war is a war of the masses; it can be waged only by mobilizing the masses and relying on them.

The people, and the people alone, are the motive force in the making of world history. The masses are the real heroes, while we ourselves are often childish and ignorant. . . .

The atom bomb is a paper tiger which the US reactionaries use to scare people. It looks terrible, but . . . the outcome of a war is decided by the people, not by . . . new types of weapon.

Every comrade must . . . understand that as long as we rely on the people, believe firmly in the inexhaustible creative power of the masses and hence trust and identify ourselves with them, we can surmount any difficulty, and no enemy can crush us while we can crush any enemy.

We should be modest and prudent, guard against arrogance and rashness, and serve the Chinese people heart and soul. . . .

Be resolute, fear no sacrifice and surmount every difficulty to win victory.

We Communists are like seeds and the people are like the soil. Wherever we go, we must unite with the people, take root and blossom among them.

You young people, full of vigour and vitality, are in the bloom of life, like the sun at eight or nine in the morning. Our hope is placed on you. . . . The world belongs to you. China's future belongs to you.

The young people are the most active and vital force in society. They are the most eager to learn and the least conservative in their thinking. . . .

Discussion Questions

1. Why did the Cultural Revolution initially rely on the revolutionary fervor of young people? Why did so many Chinese youths respond to Mao's call to form and join Red Guards?
2. What benefits could China hope to gain from the Cultural Revolution? What potential dangers did it pose for Chinese society and national security?
3. Why did the Cultural Revolution and the Red Guards rely heavily on Mao's sayings? How did some of these sayings relate to the Cold War?
4. What were the Cultural Revolution's potential impacts on Chinese society? What were its potential impacts on the Cold War and on Sino-Soviet relations?

55

The Nuclear Non-Proliferation Treaty, July 1968

IN OCTOBER 1964 PREMIER KHRUSHCHEV was removed from power in the Soviet Union. In a simultaneous but unconnected event, China successfully tested an atomic bomb, thereby joining the "nuclear club" and frightening both the Soviets and the West. India and Pakistan were rumored to be developing such weapons, and Israel was believed to have secretly done so (although the Israeli government remained silent on the matter).

In an effort to prevent the further spread of nuclear weapons, the United States, Great Britain, and the USSR began to discuss a treaty to halt nuclear proliferation, finally reaching agreement in 1968. Many other nations signed it, but France and China refused to do so until 1993, when the treaty was amended and renewed. For the duration of the Cold War, only one additional nation openly tested an atomic device: India, in 1974.

TREATY ON THE NON-PROLIFERATION OF NUCLEAR WEAPONS, 1 JULY 1968

The States concluding this Treaty, hereinafter referred to as the "Parties to the Treaty."

Considering the devastation that would be visited upon all mankind by a nuclear war and the consequent need to make every effort to avert the danger of such a war . . . ,

Believing that the proliferation of nuclear weapons would seriously enhance the danger of nuclear war,

In conformity with resolutions of the United Nations General Assembly calling for the conclusion of an agreement on the prevention of wider dissemination of nuclear weapons. . . .

Desiring to further the easing of international tension and the strengthening of trust between States in order to facilitate the cessation of the manufacture of nuclear weapons, the liquidation of all their existing stockpiles, and the elimination from national arsenals of nuclear weapons and the means of their delivery . . . ,

Have agreed as follows:

Article I
Each nuclear-weapon State Party to the Treaty undertakes not to transfer to any recipient whatsoever nuclear weapons or other nuclear explosive devices or control over such weapons or explosive devices directly, or indirectly; and not in any way to assist, encourage, or induce any non-nuclear-weapon State to manufacture or otherwise acquire nuclear weapons or other nuclear explosive devices, or control over such weapons or explosive devices.

Article II
Each non-nuclear-weapon State Party to the Treaty undertakes not to receive the transfer from any transferor whatsoever of nuclear weapons or other nuclear explosive devices or of control over such weapons or explosive devices directly, or indirectly; not to manufacture or otherwise acquire nuclear weapons or other nuclear explosive devices; and not to seek or receive any assistance in the manufacture of nuclear weapons or other nuclear explosive devices.

Article III

... 2. Each State Party to the Treaty undertakes not to provide: (a) source or special fissionable material, or (b) equipment or material especially designed or prepared for the processing, use or production of special fissionable material, to any non-nuclear-weapon State for peaceful purposes, unless the source or special fissionable material shall be subject to the safeguards required by this article. ...

Article IV

1. Nothing in this Treaty shall be interpreted as affecting the inalienable right of all the Parties to the Treaty to develop research, production and use of nuclear energy for peaceful purposes without discrimination and in conformity with Articles I and II of this Treaty. ...

Discussion Questions

1. Why did the British, Americans, and Soviets all favor a nuclear nonproliferation treaty?
2. Why did France and China initially refuse to sign it?
3. What was the treaty's potential effect on nuclear research and peaceful uses of atomic energy?
4. What did the treaty mean by "nuclear weapons or other nuclear explosive devices"?

56

The Soviet Invasion of Czechoslovakia, August 1968

IN SPRING 1968 ALEXANDER DUBČEK, the new head of the Czechoslovak Communist Party, began enacting reforms designed to bring his nation a measure of freedom and democracy. For months Moscow closely watched the situation and tried to pressure Czech leaders to moderate their reforms. Finally, on the evening of 20–21 August, the USSR attacked its socialist ally with troops and tanks, eventually reversing the reforms and reasserting Soviet control. The invasion sparked international outrage, even in such Communist countries as Romania and Yugoslavia.

No country was more appalled than the People's Republic of China. If the Kremlin could justify an invasion of Czechoslovakia, which had pursued fairly modest reforms, what was to preclude an attack on China, which for several years had been undergoing the radical upheavals of the Great Proletarian Cultural Revolution? A few days after the invasion, wasting little time on diplomatic niceties, Premier Zhou Enlai took advantage of a reception given by the Romanian ambassador in China to deliver a broadside against the USSR.

A. STATEMENT OF CZECHOSLOVAK COMMUNIST PARTY PRESIDIUM, 21 AUGUST 1968

. . . Yesterday . . . troops of the Soviet Union, Polish People's Republic, the GDR [East Germany], the Hungarian People's Republic, and the Bulgarian People's Republic crossed the frontiers of the Czechoslovak Socialist Republic.

This happened without the knowledge of the President of the Republic . . . or the First Secretary of the Czechoslovak Communist party Central Committee. . . .

The . . . Presidium appeals to all citizens of our republic to maintain calm and not to offer resistance to the troops on the march. Our army, security corps and people's militia have not received the command to defend the country.

The . . . Presidium regard this act as contrary not only to the fundamental principles of relations between Socialist states but also as contrary to the principles of international law. . . .

B. STATEMENT OF SOVIET NEWS AGENCY (TASS), 21 AUGUST 1968

TASS is authorized to state that party and Government leaders of the Czechoslovak Socialist Republic have asked the Soviet Union and other allied states to render the fraternal Czechoslovak people urgent assistance, including assistance with armed forces. This request was brought about by the threat

... emanating from the counterrevolutionary forces which have entered into a collusion with foreign forces hostile to Socialism. ...

The further aggravation of the situation in Czechoslovakia affects the vital interests of the Soviet Union and other Socialist states ... [and] constitutes at the same time a threat to the mainstays of European peace. ...

The actions which are being taken are not directed against any state and in no measure infringe state interests of anybody. They serve the purpose of peace and have been prompted by concern for its consolidation.

The fraternal countries firmly and resolutely counterpose their unbreakable solidarity to any threat from outside. Nobody will be ever allowed to wrest a single link from the community of socialist states.

C. EXCERPTS FROM ZHOU ENLAI'S SPEECH AT THE ROMANIAN EMBASSY, 23 AUGUST 1968

Comrades and friends! A few days ago, the Soviet revisionist leading clique and its followers brazenly dispatched massive armed forces to launch a surprise attack on Czechoslovakia and swiftly occupied it ..., thus perpetrating towering crimes against the Czechoslovak people.

This is the most barefaced and most typical specimen of fascist power politics played by the Soviet revisionist clique of renegades and scabs against its so-called allies. It marks the total bankruptcy of Soviet modern revisionism.

The Chinese Government and people strongly condemn the Soviet revisionist leading clique and its followers for their crime of aggression—the armed occupation of Czechoslovakia—and firmly support the Czechoslovak people in their heroic struggle of resistance to Soviet military occupation. ...

Discarding all its fig-leaves, its so-called "Marxism-Leninism," "internationalism," etc., the Soviet revisionist leading clique has brazenly resorted to direct armed aggression and intervention and is trying to create puppets with the help of guns. It is exactly what Hitler did in the past in his aggression against Czechoslovakia and the U.S. imperialism of today is doing in its aggression against Vietnam. ...

The Soviet revisionist leading clique has all along pursued the counter-revolutionary policy of U.S.-Soviet collaboration for world domination. ... U.S. imperialism and Soviet revisionism have struck a series of dirty deals on such important questions as Vietnam, the Middle East and the prevention of nuclear proliferation. The present Czechoslovak incident is no exception. It is a result of the sharpening contradictions in the scramble for and division of spheres of influence by U.S. imperialism and Soviet revisionism in Eastern Europe; it is, moreover, a result of the U.S.-Soviet collusion in a vain attempt to redivide the world. . . . That a big nation should have so willfully trampled a small nation underfoot serves as a most profound lesson for those harbouring illusions about U.S. imperialism and Soviet revisionism.

The armed aggression by Soviet revisionism has brought calamity to the Czechoslovak people, but it has also educated them, enabling them to realize gradually that revisionism is the root cause of this calamity. This is likewise a very good lesson for the people of the Soviet Union, the other East European countries and the rest of the world. . . .

We are convinced that the Czechoslovak people with their glorious revolutionary tradition will never submit to the Soviet revisionist military occupation but will surely continue to rise and carry on the revolutionary struggle against the Soviet revisionist leading clique . . . , whereas by their perverse acts the Soviet revisionist leading clique and its followers will only hasten their complete downfall as well as the total collapse of the entire modern revisionist bloc.

Discussion Questions

1. How did the Czechoslovak Communist Party Presidium react to the Soviet invasion of Czechoslovakia? What sort of resistance did it recommend?
2. How did the Soviet Union justify its invasion of Czechoslovakia? Why would this invasion upset other Communist countries?
3. According to Zhou Enlai, why was the USSR so anxious to crush the Czechoslovak reform movement? What did he see as the true aims of Soviet policy? Why did he accuse the Soviets of collusion with the Americans in trying to redivide the world?
4. What dangers did Zhou see arising from the Soviet invasion of Czechoslovakia? What potential benefits did he see?

57

The Brezhnev Doctrine, 1968

IN FALL 1968, STUNG BY THE GLOBAL outcry against its invasion of Czecho-slovakia, the USSR sought to justify its actions. An article in *Pravda*, the Soviet Communist newspaper, declared that no Communists had the right to take actions detrimental to international socialism, implying that the Czecho-slovaks had done so and that Moscow had been obliged to stop them. Later, in Poland, Soviet leader Brezhnev elaborated by asserting that a threat to social-ism in any socialist nation was a threat to the security of the entire "socialist commonwealth." Implicit was the presumption, soon called the Brezhnev Doctrine, that as leader of the socialist commonwealth, the USSR had a right to intervene in other Communist countries when it perceived their policies as detrimental to world socialism. Although Brezhnev denied its existence, this doctrine was not explicitly renounced by Moscow until 1989.

A. EXCERPT FROM "SOVEREIGNTY AND THE INTERNATIONAL OBLIGATIONS OF SOCIALIST COUNTRIES," *PRAVDA*, 26 SEPTEMBER 1968*

. . . The peoples of the socialist countries and Communist parties certainly do have and should have freedom for determining the ways of advance of their respective countries. However, none of their decisions should damage either socialism in their country or the fundamental interests of other social-ist countries, and the whole working class movement, which is working for socialism.

This means that each Communist party is responsible not only to its own people, but also to all the socialist countries, to the entire Communist move-ment. Whoever forgets this, in stressing only the independence of the Com-munist party, becomes one-sided. He deviates from his international duty. . . .

---

* "Sovereignty and International Duties of Socialist Countries," originally published in *Pravda* on 26 September 1968 and translated by Novosti, Soviet Press Agency. Reprinted in the *New York Times*, 27 September 1968.

Each Communist party is free to apply the basic principles of Marxism-Leninism and of socialism in its country, but it cannot depart from these principles. . . .

Concretely, this means, first of all, that in its activity, each Communist party cannot but take into account such a decisive fact of our time as the struggle between two opposing social systems—capitalism and socialism. . . .

The system of socialism exists in concrete form in some countries, which have their own definite state boundaries; this system is developing according to the specific conditions of each country. Furthermore, nobody interferes in the concrete measures taken to improve the socialist system in the different socialist countries.

However, the picture changes fundamentally when a danger arises to socialism itself in a particular country. As a social system world socialism is the common gain of the working people of all lands; it is indivisible and its defense is the common cause of all Communists and all progressives in the world, in the first place, the working folk of the socialist countries. . . .

The interests of the socialist community and of the whole revolutionary movement, the interests of socialism in Czechoslovakia demand complete exposure and political isolation of the reactionary forces in that country, consolidation of the working people and consistent implementation of the Moscow agreement between the Soviet and Czechoslovak leaders. . . .

B. EXCERPT FROM BREZHNEV'S REMARKS
TO THE POLISH PARTY CONGRESS, 12 NOVEMBER 1968*

. . . It is well known that the Soviet Union has done much to really strengthen the sovereignty and independence of socialist countries. The CPSU has always asserted that every socialist country must determine the concrete forms of its own development on the path to socialism, in accordance with the specific features of its national circumstances. But it is also known, comrades, that there exist general laws of socialist development, deviation from which could lead to deviation from socialism as such. And when internal and external forces hostile to socialism seek to turn the development of any socialist country toward restoring the capitalist order, when there arises a threat to the cause of socialism in that country—a threat to the security of the socialist commonwealth as a whole—this already becomes not only a problem for the

* *The Current Digest of the Soviet Press*, vol. XX, no. 46 (4 December 1968), 3–5.

people of that country, but also a common problem, the concern of all social-ist countries. Clearly, such action as military aid to a fraternal country to sup-press a threat to the socialist order—this is an extraordinary, forced measure which can be provoked only by the direct activity of the enemies of socialism inside the country and beyond its borders, actions which create a threat to the general interests of the socialist camp. . . .

Discussion Questions

1. Why did Moscow feel compelled to justify its actions in Czechoslova-kia? Why did *Pravda* say that all Communist parties were responsible to the entire Communist movement?
2. Why did Brezhnev say that a threat to socialism in any socialist country was a threat to the whole socialist commonwealth? Under what condi-tions did he think that one socialist country should intervene in the affairs of another?
3. Why would the Brezhnev Doctrine increase tensions between the USSR and China? Why would it increase tensions between the USSR and the West?
4. What were the similarities and differences between the Brezhnev Doc-trine and the Truman Doctrine (Document 8)?

58

The Soviet-Chinese Border Conflict, 1969

ON 2 MARCH 1969 A CLASH OCCURRED between Chinese and Soviet troops over an island in the river separating Russia from Manchuria. More than thirty Soviet soldiers were killed, prompting Moscow to launch a powerful counterattack. The documents excerpted here provide two very different accounts of what happened. By frightening both sides and inducing both to seek better relations with the West, these events had a profound impact on the Cold War.

A. NOTE FROM THE CHINESE MINISTRY OF FOREIGN AFFAIRS TO THE SOVIET EMBASSY IN CHINA, 2 MARCH 1969*

On the morning of March 2, 1969, Soviet frontier guards intruded into the area of Chenpao [Zhen Bao] Island, Heilunkiang Province, China, and killed and wounded many Chinese frontier guards by opening fire on them, thus creating an extremely grave border armed conflict. Against this, the Ministry of Foreign Affairs of the People's Republic of China is instructed to lodge the strongest protest with the Soviet Government.

At 0917 hours on March 2, large numbers of fully armed soldiers, together with four armored vehicles and cars, sent out by the Soviet frontier authorities, flagrantly intruded into the area of Chenpao Island which is indisputable Chinese territory, carried out blatant provocations against the Chinese frontier guards on normal patrol duty and were the first to open cannon and gun fire, killing and wounding many Chinese frontier guards.

The Chinese frontier guards were compelled to fight back in self-defence when they reached the end of their forbearance after their repeated warnings to the Soviet frontier guards had produced no effect. This grave incident of bloodshed was entirely and solely created by the Soviet authorities . . . which have long been deliberately encroaching upon China's territory, carrying out armed provocations and creating ceaseless incidents of bloodshed. The Chinese Government firmly demands that the Soviet Government punish the culprits of this incident and immediately stop its encroachment upon China's territory and its armed provocations, and reserves the right to demand compensation from the Soviet side for all the losses suffered by the Chinese side. The Chinese Government once again sternly warns the Soviet Government: China's sacred territory brooks no violation; if you should willfully cling to your reckless course and continue to provoke armed conflicts along the Sino-Soviet border, you will certainly receive resolute counterblows from the Chinese people; and it is the Soviet Government that must bear full responsibility for all the grave consequences arising therefrom.

B. STATEMENT BY SOVIET GOVERNMENT, 29 MARCH 1969†

Recently on the Ussuri River in the region of Damanskii [Zhen Bao] Island there have occurred armed border incidents provoked by the Chinese side.

---

* "Note of the Ministry of Foreign Affairs of the People's Republic of China to the Soviet Embassy in China, March 2, 1969,"*Beijing Review*, vol. 12, no. 10 (7 March 1969), 5, 7.

† "Statement of USSR Government (*Pravda*, March 30, p. 1, *Izvestia*, pp. 1–2)," *The Current Digest of the Soviet Press*, vol. XXI, no. 13 (16 April 1969), 3–5.

The Chinese authorities did not and cannot have any justification for the organization of these incidents or for the resulting clashes and bloodshed. Such events can only gladden those who want by any means to dig an abyss of enmity between the Soviet Union and the People's Republic of China. They have nothing in common with the basic interests of the Soviet and Chinese peoples.

The circumstances of the armed attacks on Soviet border guards on the Ussuri River are well known. These were premeditated and previously planned actions.

On the morning of 2 March of this year, an observation post detected a transgression of the Soviet border at Damanskii Island by approximately 30 Chinese soldiers. A group of Soviet border guards headed by an officer made their way toward the transgressors with the aim of filing a protest . . . and insisting that they leave Soviet territory. The Chinese soldiers allowed the Soviet border guards to approach within several meters and then suddenly, without any warning, opened fire at them from pointblank range.

At the same time, from an ambush on Damanskii Island where the Chinese soldiers had earlier secretly moved under cover of darkness, and from the Chinese shore, artillery guns, mortars, and automatic weapons opened fire on another group of Soviet border guards located near the Soviet shore. They joined the battle and, with the support of a neighboring border post, drove the transgressors out of Soviet territory. As a result of this treacherous attack there were dead and wounded on both sides.

In spite of a warning from the Soviet government and a call to refrain from such provocations, on 14–15 March in this same region the Chinese side launched new attempts at armed intrusion into the Soviet Union. Elements of the regular Chinese army, supported by artillery and mortar fire, attacked the Soviet border troops protecting Damanskii Island. The attack was decisively repelled, and the transgressors were driven from Soviet territory. This provocation by the Chinese side generated new casualties.

Now the Chinese authorities in their statements are trying to avoid responsibility for the armed clashes. They claim that it was not the Chinese but the Soviet border guards who transgressed the state frontier, and that this island supposedly does not belong to the Soviet Union. The Chinese side does not dispute the fact that its military personnel acted according to a prepared plan, although by having recourse to a false assertion, it presents the use of arms by the Chinese transgressors as a "necessary measure." . . .

Discussion Questions

1. In what ways do the Soviet and Chinese versions of this episode differ? How do you account for these differences?
2. Why did these border clashes become such important international incidents?
3. In the long run, why were the Chinese and the Soviets each anxious to avoid war?
4. Why would these border clashes lead each side to seek better relations with the West?

59

The Nixon Doctrine, 1969

WHEN RICHARD NIXON BECAME president in January 1969, the United States was in the midst of a disastrous and unpopular conflict. The Vietnam War, and the growing realization that America was not winning, had sapped the people's morale and left the country deeply divided. In line with his campaign promises, Nixon was eager to end the war and avoid the involvement of US troops in any more such ventures. But as a staunch anti-Communist and devout Cold Warrior, he was also determined to protect US interests and prevent Communist expansion.

One aspect of his approach was the Nixon Doctrine, which he first put forth in July 1969 while conversing with reporters on the island of Guam during a trip to Asia. Ruminating on America's role in Asia once the war in Vietnam was over, he speculated that the increasing independence and nationalism of Asian nations portended a more limited and less visible American presence. Then, in response to a question, he set forth the heart of his new doctrine: The United States would expect its friends and clients in Asia to take increasing responsibility for their own internal security and military defense.

In November of that year, in a major speech on the Vietnam War, he spelled out this new approach. The United States would continue to uphold its treaty commitments and provide a nuclear shield for its allies and friends. However, in the event of conflict, although America would still supply extensive economic aid and military equipment, it would henceforth expect the nation involved to provide the troops and personnel for its own defense. This was embodied in his Vietnamization program, designed to gradually turn over the actual fighting in Southeast Asia to the forces of South Vietnam. But it was also intended as a general policy principle to preclude Vietnam-type debacles elsewhere in the future.

A. EXCERPTS FROM NIXON'S REMARKS AT GUAM, 25 JULY 1969

The United States is going to be facing, we hope before too long . . . a major decision: What will be its role in Asia and in the Pacific after the end of the war in Vietnam? We will be facing that decision, but also the Asian nations will be wondering about what that decision is. . . .

This is a decision that will have to be made, of course, as the war comes to an end. But the time to develop the thinking which will go into that decision is now. I think that one of the weaknesses in American foreign policy is that too often we react rather precipitately to events as they occur. We fail to have the perspective and the long range view which is essential for a policy that will be viable. . . .

Now, one other point I would make very briefly . . . as far as the role we should play, we must recognize that there are two great, new factors which you will see, . . . particularly when you arrive in the Philippines—something . . . that we didn't see in 1953, to show you how quickly it has changed: a very great growth of nationalism, nationalism . . . vis-a-vis the United States, as well as other countries in the world. And, also, at the same time that national pride is becoming a major factor, regional pride is becoming a major factor.

The second factor is one that is going to . . . have a major impact on the future of Asia. . . . Asians will say in every country that we visit that they do not want to be dictated to from the outside, Asia for the Asians. And that is what we want, and that is the role we should play. We should assist, but we should not dictate.

At this time, the political and economic plans that they are gradually developing are very hopeful. We will give assistance to those plans. We, of course, will keep the treaty commitments that we have. But as far as our role is concerned, we must avoid that kind of policy that will make countries in Asia so dependent upon us that we are dragged into conflicts such as the one that we have in Vietnam. . . .

. . . I believe that the time has come when the United States, in our relations with all of our Asian friends, [must] be quite emphatic on two points: One, that we will keep our treaty commitments, our treaty commitments, for example, with Thailand under SEATO; but, two, that as far as the problems of internal security are concerned, as far as the problems of military defense, except for the threat of a major power involving nuclear weapons, that the United States is going to encourage and has a right to expect that this problem will be increasingly handled by . . . the Asian nations themselves.

I believe, incidentally, from my preliminary conversations with several Asian leaders over the past few months that they are going to be willing to undertake this responsibility. It will not be easy. But if the United States just continues down the road of responding to requests for assistance, of assuming the primary responsibility for defending these countries when they have internal problems or external problems, they are never going to take care of themselves.

B. EXCERPTS FROM NIXON'S ADDRESS TO THE NATION, 3 NOVEMBER 1969

At the time we launched our search for peace I recognized we might not succeed in bringing an end to the war through negotiation. I, therefore, put into effect another plan to bring peace—a plan which will bring the war to an end regardless of what happens on the negotiating front.

It is in line with a major shift in US foreign policy which I described in my press conference at Guam on July 25. Let me briefly explain what has been described as the Nixon Doctrine—a policy which not only will help end the war in Vietnam, but which is an essential element of our program to prevent future Vietnams.

We Americans are a do-it-yourself people. We are an impatient people. Instead of teaching someone else to do a job, we like to do it ourselves. And this trait has been carried over into our foreign policy. In Korea and again in Vietnam, the United States furnished most of the money, most of the arms, and most of the men to help the people of those countries defend their freedom against Communist aggression.

Before any American troops were committed to Vietnam, a leader of another Asian country expressed this opinion to me when I was traveling in Asia as a private citizen. He said: "When you are trying to assist another nation to defend its freedom, US policy should be to help them fight the war but not to fight the war for them."

Well, in accordance with this wise counsel, I laid down in Guam three principles as guidelines for future American policy toward Asia:

- First, the United States will keep all of its treaty commitments.
- Second, we shall provide a shield if a nuclear power threatens the freedom of a nation allied with us or of a nation whose survival we consider vital to our security.
- Third, in cases involving other types of aggression, we shall furnish military and economic assistance when requested in accordance with our treaty commitments. But we shall look to the nation directly threatened to assume the primary responsibility of providing the manpower for its defense.

After I announced this policy, I found that the leaders of the Philippines, Thailand, Vietnam, South Korea, and other nations which might be threatened by Communist aggression, welcomed this new direction in American foreign policy.

The defense of freedom is everybody's business—not just America's business. And it is particularly the responsibility of the people whose freedom is threatened. . . .

Discussion Questions

1. Why did Nixon first float his new approach in a meeting with reporters rather than proclaiming it at once as a basic policy doctrine?
2. According to Nixon, what was wrong with US policy in Asia prior to the Nixon Doctrine?
3. What reasons did he give for the promulgation of the Nixon Doctrine? What other reasons might he have had that he did not mention?
4. How did Nixon expect the Asian nations to respond to his new doctrine? How did he expect the American people to respond?

IV
THE ERA OF DÉTENTE: 1969–1979

60

Salvador Allende's Freely Elected Marxist Government in Chile, 1970–1973

IN 1958 A MARXIST PHYSICIAN named Salvador Allende came close to winning the presidency of Chile. No Marxist candidate had ever won a free election for president or prime minister anywhere in the world, and Allende's narrow defeat, coming as it did during one of the more icy periods of the Cold War, caused concern in Washington. Chile elects its presidents to a single, nonrenewable term every six years, and in 1964 the US Central Intelligence Agency invested money and time to help secure the election of Eduardo Frei, a Christian Democrat and close friend of the United States.

Frei defeated Allende by 56 to 38 percent, and his landslide victory lulled Washington into complacency. Allende clearly could not win a two-candidate race, but the 1970 election featured three candidates, and the CIA assumed that the conservative candidate would win. That was dangerously wishful thinking, since if Allende's 38 percent support held, it would be enough for him to win a three-way race. And win he did, by 36 to 34 to 27 percent, in September 1970. Belated US efforts to orchestrate a coup or to prevent Allende's election in other ways gained no traction, and he was inaugurated as president of Chile in November (Document 60A).

US president Richard Nixon and his national security advisor, Dr. Henry Kissinger, immediately initiated a program designed to destabilize Chile's economy through denial of credit from US banks and from the World Bank and International Monetary Fund. Allende had stated that he respected the democratic process and would leave office peacefully when his term ended in 1976, but few in Washington believed him. Indeed, had he been telling the truth, the United States would have been even more alarmed: If a Marxist president relinquished power voluntarily, that would mean that Communist parties would not insist on monopolizing political power, and ordinary voters would be more likely to vote for Communist candidates. It is important to realize that the Cold War was not only a struggle between competing political systems, but between competing social and economic systems as well. Marxist and Communist social and economic victories were no more welcome in Washington than political victories.

Nixon's economic warfare weakened Chile's economy, but Allende's own poorly conceived economic policies crippled it further; by late 1972 inflation was escalating and living standards were declining. Allende's address to the UN General Assembly (Document 60B) was clearly a cry for help, but the Soviet Union, having learned from the failure of Khrushchev's placement of missiles in Cuba (Document 46), was unwilling to challenge the United States in the Western Hemisphere. Only Fidel Castro's Communist regime in Cuba stepped forward to support Allende unreservedly, and that support was rhetorical rather than material. By mid-1973 inflation topped 500 percent, strikes by professional people and truckers paralyzed Chile's economy, and the Chilean armed forces overthrew Allende on 11 September 1973 (Document 60C). Allende committed suicide rather than accept exile, and Chile embarked on a seventeen-year military dictatorship that became notorious for its brutality.

A. EXCERPTS FROM SALVADOR ALLENDE'S INAUGURAL ADDRESS, 5 NOVEMBER 1970

Today, inspired by the heroes of our country, we gather here to celebrate our victory—Chile's victory—and to mark the start of the liberation of the people, who are at last in power and are taking over control of their national destiny.

But what kind of Chile are we inheriting?

We were colonies in the agrarian-mercantile civilization. We are barely neocolonial nations in the urban-industrial civilization, and, in the new civilization which threatens to continue our dependency, we have been the exploited peoples—those who existed not for themselves, but rather to contribute to the prosperity of others.

And what is the reason for our backwardness? Who is responsible for our underdevelopment?

After many deformations and deceptions, the people have understood. We know from our own experience that the real reasons for our backwardness are to be found in the system, in this dependent capitalist system which counterposes the rich minority to the needy majority internally and the powerful nations to the poor nations externally, a system in which the many make possible the prosperity of the few.

We have received a society torn by social inequality; a society divided into antagonistic classes of the exploited and exploiting; a society in which violence is part of the institutions themselves, which condemn man to a never-satisfied greed, the most inhuman form of cruelty and indifference in the face of the suffering of others. . . .

What is people's power?

People's power means that we will do away with the pillars on which the minorities have found support—those minorities that always condemned our nation to underdevelopment. We will do away with the monopolies, through which a handful of families control the economy. We will put an end to a fiscal system that serves those who seek lucre, a system which has always borne down hard on the people and touched but lightly on the rich, a system which has concentrated the nation's savings in the hands of the bankers in their greed for amassing greater riches. We will nationalize money lending and place it at the service of the prosperity of Chile and the people.

We will put an end to the *latifundia*, which condemn thousands of peasants to subjugation and poverty and keep the nation from getting from the land all the foodstuffs we need. A true agrarian reform will make it possible to do just what we are saying—feed the people. We will call a halt to the ever more massive process of denationalization of our industries and sources of work, a process which subjects us to foreign exploitation. We will reclaim Chile's basic wealth. We are going to reclaim the large copper, coal, iron and nitrate mines for the people. . . .

B. EXCERPTS FROM ALLENDE'S ADDRESS
TO THE UN GENERAL ASSEMBLY, 4 DECEMBER 1972

. . . [T]hrough the Chilean case, a new stage in the battle between imperialism and the weak countries of the Third World is being waged.

The battle in defence of natural resources is but a part of the battle being waged by the countries of the Third World against underdevelopment. There is a very clear dialectical relationship: imperialism exists because under-development exists; underdevelopment exists because imperialism exists. The aggression we are being made the object of today makes the fulfilment of the promises made in the last few years as to a new large-scope action aimed at overcoming the conditions of underdevelopment and want in the nations of Africa, Asia and Latin America appear illusory. Two years ago, on the occasion of the 25th anniversary of the founding of the United Nations, the UN General Assembly solemnly proclaimed the strategy for a second decade of development. In keeping with this strategy, all UN member states pledged to spare no efforts to transform, via concrete measures, the present unfair international division of labour and to close the vast economic and technological gap that separates the wealthy countries from the developing ones.

We have seen that none of those aims ever became a reality. On the contrary, the situation has worsened. . . .

From the very moment of our election victory on 4 September 1970, we were affected by the development of large-scale foreign pressures, aimed at blocking the inauguration of a government freely elected by the people and then overthrowing it. There have been efforts to isolate us from the world, strangle the economy and paralyze the sale of copper, our main export product, and keep us from access to sources of international financing. . . .

The Chilean people are a people that have reached the political maturity to decide by a majority the replacement of the capitalist economic system by a socialist one. Our political regime has institutions that have been open enough to channel that revolutionary will without violent clashes. It is my duty to warn this assembly that the reprisals and the blockade, aimed at producing contradictions and the resultant economic distortions, threaten to have repercussions on peace and internal coexistence in my country. . . .

C. EXCERPTS FROM SALVADOR ALLENDE'S LAST WORDS, BROADCAST OVER RADIO MAGALLANES, 11 SEPTEMBER 1973

Surely this will be the last opportunity for me to address you. The Air Force has bombed the antennas of Radio Portales and Radio Corporación.

My words do not have bitterness but disappointment. May they be a moral punishment for those who have betrayed their oath: soldiers of Chile, titular commanders in chief, Admiral Merino, who has designated himself Commander of the Navy, and Mr. Mendoza, the despicable general who only yesterday pledged his fidelity and loyalty to the Government. . . .

Given these facts, the only thing left for me is to say to workers: I'm not going to resign! Placed in a historic transition, I will pay for the loyalty of the people with my life. And I say to them that I am certain that the seeds which we have planted in the good conscience of thousands and thousands of Chileans will not be shriveled forever.

They have force and will be able to dominate us, but social processes can be arrested by neither crime nor force. History is ours, and people make history.

Workers of my country: I want to thank you for the loyalty that you always had, the confidence that you deposited in a man who was only an interpreter of great yearnings for justice, who gave his word that he would respect the Constitution and the law and did just that. At this definitive moment, the last

234 60. Salvador Allende's Freely Elected Marxist Government in Chile, 1970–1973

moment when I can address you, I wish you to take advantage of the lesson: foreign capital, imperialism, together with the reaction, created the climate in which the Armed Forces broke their tradition, the tradition taught by General Schneider and reaffirmed by Commander Araya, victims of the same social sector who today are hoping, with foreign assistance, to re-conquer the power to continue defending their profits and their privileges.

I address you, above all, the modest woman of our land, the countrywoman who believed in us, the mother who knew our concern for children. I address professionals of Chile, patriotic professionals who continued working against the sedition that was supported by professional associations, classist associations that also defended the advantages of capitalist society. I address the youth, those who sang and gave us their joy and their spirit of struggle. I address the man of Chile, the worker, the farmer, the intellectual, those who will be persecuted, because in our country fascism has been already present for many hours—in terrorist attacks, blowing up the bridges, cutting the railroad tracks, destroying the oil and gas pipelines, in the face of the silence of those who had the obligation to act. They were committed. History will judge them.

Surely Radio Magallanes will be silenced, and the calm metal of my voice will no longer reach you. It does not matter. You will continue hearing it. I will always be next to you. At least my memory will be that of a man of dignity who was loyal to his country.

The people must defend themselves, but they must not sacrifice themselves. The people must not let themselves be destroyed or riddled with bullets, but they cannot be humiliated either.

Workers of my country, I have faith in Chile and its destiny. Other men will overcome this dark and bitter moment when treason seeks to prevail. Go forward knowing that, sooner rather than later, the great avenues will open again and free men will walk through them to construct a better society.

Long live Chile! Long live the people! Long live the workers!

These are my last words, and I am certain that my sacrifice will not be in vain, I am certain that, at the very least, it will be a moral lesson that will punish felony, cowardice, and treason.

Discussion Questions

1. How did President Allende explain Chile's underdevelopment?
2. What evidence of Marxism can you find in Allende's inaugural address?
3. How did Allende explain Chile's intensifying difficulties to the United Nations?

4. What sort of support might he have hoped would be forthcoming from the United Nations?
5. What sort of hope for the future did Allende's final words offer the Chilean people?

61

The Berlin Accords, September 1971

THE CONSTRUCTION OF THE BERLIN WALL in 1961 (Document 45) increased resentment in the divided city but actually lessened superpower tension over its continuing division. It staunched the hemorrhage of trained professionals from East to West, thus satisfying the Soviet bloc, and it handed the West a tailor-made propaganda victory by enabling the "free world" to portray East Berlin as a prison. By the mid-1960s the central issue concerning Berlin's status had come to be the painful separation of friends, families, and generations on opposite sides of the wall.

The 1969 general election in West Germany brought the Social Democratic Party to power and made Willy Brandt chancellor. Brandt had impeccable anti-Nazi credentials and had served as mayor of West Berlin. At once he set about to regularize relations with the Warsaw Pact, negotiating with Poland and the USSR as part of his "Eastern Policy," or *Ostpolitik*. He also opened discussions with East Germany in an effort to reduce the misery caused by the Berlin Wall. In 1971 his labors paid off when the four powers occupying Germany—the United States, Britain, France, and the USSR—signed an agreement on the status of West Berlin. The Berlin Accords removed the threat of East German harassment of traffic on highways linking West Berlin to West Germany, thus lessening the prospects of a repetition of the 1948–1949 Berlin Blockade (Document 16). In return for this restriction on its sovereignty over access routes, East Germany received de facto Western recognition as an independent state when its name appeared seven times in the document. Two years later, in 1973, West and East Germany were both admitted to the United Nations. The German Question was still not settled, but it was certainly easier to live with once the Berlin Accords were signed.

QUADRIPARTITE AGREEMENT ON BERLIN, 3 SEPTEMBER 1971

The Governments of the United States of America, the French Republic, the Union of Soviet Socialist Republics, and the United Kingdom of Great Britain and Northern Ireland,

Represented by their Ambassadors, who held a series of meetings in the building formerly occupied by the Allied Control Council in the American sector of Berlin,

Acting on the basis of their quadripartite rights and responsibilities, and of the corresponding wartime and postwar agreements and decisions of the four powers, which are not affected,

Taking into account the existing situation in the relevant area,

Guided by the desire to contribute to practical improvements of the situation,

Without prejudice to their legal positions,

Have agreed on the following. . . .

Part II: Provisions Relating to the Western Sectors of Berlin

A. The Government of the Union of Soviet Socialist Republics declares that transit traffic by road, rail and waterways through the territory of the German Democratic Republic [East Germany] of civilian persons and goods between the western sectors of Berlin and the Federal Republic of Germany [West Germany] will be unimpeded; that such traffic will be facilitated so as to take place in the most simple and expeditious manner; and that it will receive preferential treatment. . . .

B. The Governments of the French Republic, the United Kingdom and the United States of America declare that the ties between the Western sectors of Berlin and the Federal Republic of Germany will be maintained and developed, taking into account that these sectors continue not to be a constituent part of the Federal Republic of Germany and not to be governed by it. . . .

C. The Government of the Union of Soviet Socialist Republics declares that communications between the Western sectors of Berlin and areas bordering on these sectors and those areas of the German Democratic Republic which do not border on these sectors will be improved. Permanent residents of the Western sectors of Berlin will be able to travel to and visit such areas for compassionate, family, religious, cultural or commercial reasons, or as tourists, under conditions comparable to those applying to other persons entering these areas. . . .

Discussion Questions

1. What did West Berlin gain from the Berlin Accords? What did East Germany gain?
2. Why did the treaty reassert that West Berlin was not a constituent part of West Germany?
3. How did the treaty seek to prevent a repetition of the Berlin Blockade?
4. Why would the USSR be willing to accept this agreement?

62

Nixon's China Visit: The Shanghai Communiqué, February 1972

BY THE EARLY 1970S THE DEEPENING discord between China and the USSR, combined with the gradual withdrawal of American forces from Vietnam, had created a new situation in East Asia. As the US presence diminished, the Chinese grew less concerned about the American threat and increasingly convinced that the Soviets posed a more immediate and serious danger. And the Americans, worried that Moscow might move to fill the void left by the US withdrawal from Southeast Asia, began to look to China as a potential bulwark against Soviet expansion there.

As a result, Beijing and Washington began gradually to move toward rapprochement. The fact that they had been bitter foes for decades, combined with the ongoing US presence in Vietnam and Taiwan, made this a slow and tentative process. Still, using Romania and Pakistan as intermediaries, President Nixon sent signals to the Chinese leaders, who responded in spring 1971 by hosting the US table tennis team and that summer by welcoming a surreptitious visit by Nixon's national security advisor, Henry Kissinger. Finally, in July 1971, the president publicly announced that he would visit China, sending shockwaves across the globe.

Nixon's official visit, in February 1972, created enormous excitement. With the whole world looking on, Nixon met with Premier Zhou and Chairman Mao, visited China's Great Wall, and was entertained by his Chinese hosts. In private discussions, however, it became clear that continued US support for the Nationalist regime on Taiwan would preclude full normalization of relations between Washington and Beijing. On 27 February, as Nixon prepared to leave, the two governments issued a joint communiqué outlining their agreements and differences (especially regarding Taiwan), and pledging to work together to improve relations and relax tensions.

EXCERPTS FROM THE
COMMUNIQUÉ ISSUED AT SHANGHAI, 27 FEBRUARY 1972

. . . There are essential differences between China and the United States in their social systems and foreign policies. However, the two sides agreed that countries, regardless of their social systems, should conduct their relations on the principles of respect for the sovereignty and territorial integrity of all states, nonaggression against other states, noninterference in the internal affairs of other states, equality and mutual benefit, and peaceful coexistence. International disputes should be settled on this basis, without resorting to the use or threat of force. The United States and the People's Republic of China are prepared to apply these principles to their mutual relations.

With these principles of international relations in mind the two sides stated that:

- Progress toward the normalization of relations between China and the United States is in the interests of all countries.
- Both wish to reduce the danger of international military conflict.
- Neither should seek hegemony in the Asia-Pacific region and each is opposed to the efforts by any other country or group of countries to establish such hegemony; and
- Neither is prepared to negotiate on behalf of any third party or to enter into agreements or understandings with the other directed at other states.

Both sides are of the view that it would be against the interests of the peoples of the world for any major country to collude with another against other countries, or for major countries to divide up the world into spheres of interest.

The sides reviewed the long-standing serious disputes between China and the United States.

The Chinese side reaffirmed its position: the Taiwan question is the crucial question obstructing the normalization of relations between China and the United States; the Government of the People's Republic of China is the sole legal government of China; Taiwan is a province of China . . . ; the liberation of Taiwan is China's internal affair in which no other country has the right to interfere; and all US forces and military installations must be withdrawn from Taiwan. The Chinese government firmly opposes any activities which aim at the creation of "one China, one Taiwan," "one China, two governments," "two Chinas," and "independent Taiwan" or advocate that "the status of Taiwan remains to be determined."

The US side declared: The United States acknowledges that all Chinese on either side of the Taiwan Strait maintain there is but one China and that Taiwan is a part of China. The United States Government does not challenge that position. It reaffirms its interest in a peaceful settlement of the Taiwan question by the Chinese themselves. With this prospect in mind, it affirms the ultimate objective of the withdrawal of all US forces and military installations from Taiwan. In the meantime, it will progressively reduce its forces and military installations on Taiwan as the tension in the area diminishes.

The two sides agreed that it is desirable to broaden the understanding between the two peoples. To this end, they discussed specific areas in such fields as science, technology, culture, sports, and journalism, in which people-to-people contacts and exchanges would be mutually beneficial. Each side undertakes to facilitate the further development of such contacts and exchanges.

Both sides view bilateral trade as another area from which mutual benefits can be derived, and agree that economic relations based on equality and mutual benefit are in the interest of the peoples of the two countries. They agree to facilitate the progressive development of trade between their two countries.

The two sides agree that they will stay in contact through various channels, including the sending of a senior US representative to Peking [Beijing] from time to time for concrete consultations to further the normalization of relations between the two countries and continue to exchange views on issues of common interest.

The two sides expressed the hope that the gains achieved during this visit would open up new prospects for the relations between the two countries. They believe that the normalization of relations between the two countries is not only in the interest of the Chinese and American peoples, but also contributes to the relaxation of tension in Asia and the world. . . .

Discussion Questions

1. What factors prompted the Americans and Chinese to seek improved relations? Why was Nixon in a better position to take this step than other US leaders?

2. Why did the two sides issue this communiqué at the end of Nixon's visit? What implicit message did it contain for the USSR?
3. Why was the Taiwan issue so important to China and such an obstacle to normalized relations with America?
4. What were the main similarities and differences between the Chinese and American positions concerning Taiwan?
5. Even without normalized relations, what steps did the two sides agree could be taken to improve relations between them?

63

The ABM Treaty and SALT I, 1972

IN THE EARLY 1970S THE BREAKTHROUGH in relations between China and the United States was accompanied by a decrease in tension between Moscow and Washington that came to be known as détente. As the United States disengaged from Vietnam and lost its lead in strategic missiles, and as the USSR watched its conflict with China grow and its economy deteriorate, the two sides began to work toward accord in areas of common interest.

One such area was the effort to halt the arms race. Beginning in 1969, Strategic Arms Limitation Talks (SALTs) were conducted in Helsinki and Vienna. The aim was to get both superpowers to limit their strategic missiles to the number they already had. Disputes arose, however, over whether US missiles in Europe and submarine-based missiles on both sides should be included in the pact, and whether restrictions should be placed on the number of warheads each missile could carry. So the talks dragged on for two and a half years.

Finally, in May 1972, President Nixon flew to Moscow for a summit conference with Soviet leader Brezhnev. This was a momentous occasion, marking the first peacetime visit by a US president to Russia, and the onset of the era of détente. There, on 26 May, the superpower leaders signed two landmark agreements: the ABM Treaty, which restricted each side to two missile-defense systems (one to protect its capital and one to defend a missile site), and the Interim SALT I Agreement, which sought to freeze strategic missiles at 1972 levels for five years.

A. TREATY ON THE LIMITATION OF
ANTI-BALLISTIC MISSILE SYSTEMS, 26 MAY 1972

Article I

1. Each Party undertakes to limit anti-ballistic missile (ABM) systems and to adopt other measures in accordance with the provisions of this Treaty.
2. Each Party undertakes not to deploy ABM systems for a defense of the territory of its country and not to provide a base for such a defense, and not to deploy ABM systems for defense of an individual region except as provided for in Article III of this Treaty. . . .

Article III

Each Party undertakes not to deploy ABM systems or their components except that:

(a) within one ABM system deployment area having a radius of 150 kilometers and centered on the Party's national capital, a Party may deploy:
  (1) no more than one hundred ABM launchers and no more than 100 ABM interceptor missiles at launch sites, and
  (2) ABM radars within no more than six ABM radar complexes, the area of each complex being circular and having a diameter of no more than three kilometers; and
(b) within one ABM system deployment area having a radius of 150 kilometers and containing ICBM silo launchers, a Party may deploy:
  (1) no more than one hundred ABM launchers and no more than 100 ABM interceptor missiles at launch sites,
  (2) two large phased-array ABM radars operational or under construction on the date of signature of the Treaty in an ABM system deployment area containing ICBM silo launchers, and
  (3) no more than eighteen ABM radars each having a potential less than the potential of the smaller of the above-mentioned two large phased-array ABM radars. . . .

Article V

1. Each Party undertakes not to develop, test, or deploy ABM systems or components which are sea-based, air-based, space-based, or mobile land-based.
2. Each Party undertakes not to develop, test, or deploy ABM launchers for launching more than one ABM interceptor missile at a time from

each launcher . . . , nor to develop, test, or deploy automatic or semiautomatic or other similar systems for rapid reload of ABM launchers. . . .

Article XII

1. For the purpose of providing assurance of compliance with the provisions of this Treaty, each Party shall use national technical means of verification at its disposal in a manner consistent with generally recognized principles of international law.
2. Each Party undertakes not to interfere with the national technical means of verification of the other Party operating in accordance with paragraph 1 of this Article.
3. Each Party undertakes not to use deliberate concealment measures which impede verification by national technical means of compliance with the provisions of this Treaty. . . .

Article XV

1. This Treaty shall be of unlimited duration.
2. Each Party shall, in exercising its national sovereignty, have the right to withdraw from this Treaty if it decides that extraordinary events related to the subject matter of this Treaty have jeopardized its supreme interests. It shall give notice of its decision to the other Party six months prior to withdrawal from the Treaty. Such notice shall include a statement of the extraordinary events the notifying Party regards as having jeopardized its supreme interests. . . .

B. INTERIM AGREEMENT ON CERTAIN MEASURES WITH RESPECT TO THE LIMITATION OF STRATEGIC OFFENSIVE ARMS (SALT I), 26 MAY 1972

Article I

The Parties undertake not to start construction of additional fixed land-based intercontinental ballistic missile (ICBM) launchers after July 1, 1972. . . .

Article III

The Parties undertake to limit submarine-launched ballistic missile (SLBM) launchers and modern ballistic missile submarines to the numbers operational and under construction on the date of signature of this Interim Agreement, and in addition to launchers and submarines constructed under procedures established by the Parties as replacements for an equal number of ICBM launchers of older types deployed prior to 1964 or for launchers on older submarines.

Article IV

Subject to the provisions of this Interim Agreement, modernization and replacement of strategic offensive ballistic missiles and launchers covered by this Interim Agreement may be undertaken.

Article V

[This article repeats verbatim the provisions of Article XII of the ABM Treaty, above.]

Article VII

The Parties undertake to continue active negotiations for limitations on strategic offensive arms. The obligations provided for in this Interim Agreement shall not prejudice the scope or terms of the limitations on strategic offensive arms which may be worked out in the course of further negotiations.

Article VIII

1. This Interim Agreement shall enter into force upon exchange of written notices of acceptance by each Party, which exchange shall take place simultaneously with the exchange of instruments of ratification of the Treaty on the Limitation of Anti-Ballistic Missile Systems.
2. This Interim Agreement shall remain in force for a period of five years unless replaced earlier by an agreement on more complete measures limiting strategic offensive arms. It is the objective of the Parties to conduct active follow-on negotiations with the aim of concluding such an agreement as soon as possible.
3. Each Party shall, in exercising its national sovereignty, have the right to withdraw from this Interim Agreement if it decides that extraordinary events related to the subject matter of this Interim Agreement have jeopardized its supreme interest. It shall give notice of its decision to the other Party six months prior to withdrawal from this Interim Agreement. . . .

Protocol to the Interim Agreement

. . . The Parties understand that, under Article III of the Interim Agreement for the period during which that Agreement remains in force:

The US may have no more than 710 ballistic missiles launchers on submarines (SLBMs) and no more than 44 modern ballistic missile submarines.

The Soviet Union may have no more than 950 ballistic missile launchers on submarines and no more than 62 modern ballistic missile submarines.

Additional ballistic missile launchers on submarines up to the above-mentioned levels, in the US—over 656 ballistic missile launchers on nuclear-powered submarines, and in the USSR—over 740 ballistic missile launchers on nuclear-powered submarines, operational and under construction, may become operational as replacements for equal numbers of ballistic missile launchers of older types deployed prior to 1964 or of ballistic missile launchers on older submarines.

The deployment of modern SLBMs on any submarine, regardless of type, will be counted against the total level of SLBMs permitted for the US and the USSR.

Discussion Questions

1. Why were the Americans eager to restrict ABM development? Why was the ABM treaty considered essential to controlling the arms race?
2. Why did the treaty permit each side to construct two ABM sites?
3. What was the main significance of the SALT I agreement? What were its main shortcomings?
4. How did the development and use of spy satellites (referred to in the treaties under "national technical means") help make these treaties possible?

64

The US Withdrawal
from Vietnam, January 1973

AFTER PRESIDENT NIXON TOOK OFFICE in 1969, he began searching for an honorable way out of the Vietnam War through a backstairs deal with the Soviets or the Chinese, the two main suppliers of arms to the Vietnamese

Communists. Meanwhile, National Security Advisor Henry Kissinger began meeting secretly in Paris with Le Duc Tho, a special emissary of North Vietnam. By October 1972 it appeared that a deal was close, but North Vietnamese recalcitrance following Nixon's reelection in November led him to order a massive bombing campaign in December. This "Christmas bombing" caused widespread damage to North Vietnamese cities and ports, and to Nixon's standing at home, making clear to both sides the cost of further combat. Kissinger and Le Duc Tho continued to negotiate and soon reached agreement. In a nationwide address on 23 January, Nixon announced that "peace with honor" had been achieved. Four days later, the Paris Peace Accords were signed, ending US involvement in Vietnam.

The honor of a great power is not easy to define. For Bismarck it was very different from prestige: A great power was obliged before God to act in accordance with its genuine rather than its *apparent* national interests. In modern times, "honor" is an overused term that seems almost indistinguishable from "prestige." Nixon himself feared that America would be viewed as "a pitiful, helpless giant" if it did not fulfill its commitments. Others argued that a truly great power must be willing to swallow its pride and alter its course if its prior commitments were jeopardizing its genuine national interests. The question remains open, but Nixon's speech and the Paris Peace Accords may both be read in this context.

A. NIXON'S ADDRESS TO THE NATION, 23 JANUARY 1973

Good evening. I have asked for this radio and television time tonight for the purpose of announcing that we today have concluded an agreement to end the war and bring peace with honor in Vietnam and Southeast Asia. . . .

In my addresses to the nation . . . on January 25 and May 8, I set forth the goals that we considered essential for peace with honor. In the settlement that has now been agreed to, all the conditions that I laid down then have been met. A cease-fire internationally supervised will begin at 7 P.M. this Saturday, January 27, Washington time. Within 60 days from this Saturday all Americans held prisoners of war throughout Indochina will be released.

There will be the fullest possible accounting for all of those who are missing in action. During the same 60-day period all American forces will be withdrawn from South Vietnam.

The people of South Vietnam have been guaranteed the right to determine their own future without outside interference. . . .

The United States will continue to recognize the Government of the Republic of Vietnam as the sole legitimate government of South Vietnam. We shall continue to aid South Vietnam within the terms of the agreement, and we shall support efforts for the people of South Vietnam to settle their problems peacefully among themselves.

We must recognize that ending the war is only the first step toward building the peace. All parties must now see to it that this is a peace that lasts and also a peace that heals, and a peace that not only ends the war in Southeast Asia but contributes to the prospects of peace in the whole world. This will mean that the terms of the agreement must be scrupulously adhered to. We shall do everything the agreement requires of us, and we shall expect the other parties to do everything it requires of them. We shall also expect other interested nations to help insure that the agreement is carried out and peace is maintained. . . .

Now that we have achieved an honorable agreement, let us be proud that America did not settle for a peace that would have betrayed our allies, that would have abandoned our prisoners of war or that would have ended the war for us but would have continued the war for the 50 million people of Indochina.

Let us be proud of the two and a half million young Americans who served in Vietnam, who served with honor and distinction in one of the most selfless enterprises in the history of nations.

And let us be proud of those who sacrificed, who gave their lives, so that the people of South Vietnam might live in freedom, and so that the world might live in peace. . . .

B. THE PARIS PEACE ACCORDS, 27 JANUARY 1973

Article 1
The United States and all other countries respect the independence, sovereignty, unity and territorial integrity of Vietnam as recognized by the 1954 Geneva Agreements on Vietnam.

Article 2
A cease-fire shall be observed throughout South Vietnam as of 2400 hours G.M.T. on Jan. 27, 1973. At the same hour, the United States will stop all its military activities against the territory of the Democratic Republic of Vietnam [North Vietnam] by ground, air and naval forces . . . , and end the mining of the territorial waters, ports, harbors and waterways of the Democratic Republic of Vietnam. The United States will remove, permanently deactivate or destroy all the mines in the territorial waters, ports, harbors and waterways of North Vietnam as soon as this agreement goes into effect.

The complete cessation of hostilities mentioned in this article shall be durable and without limit of time. . . .

Article 4
The United States will not continue its military involvement or intervene in the internal affairs of South Vietnam.

Article 5
Within 60 days of the signing of this agreement, there will be a total withdrawal from South Vietnam of troops, military personnel, including technical military personnel and military personnel associated with the pacification program, armaments, munitions and war material of the United States. . . .

Article 6
The dismantlement of all military bases in South Vietnam of the United States and . . . other foreign countries . . . shall be completed within 60 days of the signing of this agreement. . . .

Article 8
    (a) The return of captured military personnel and foreign civilians of the parties shall be carried out simultaneously with and completed not later than the same day as the troop withdrawal mentioned in Article 5. . . .
    (b) The parties shall help each other to get information about those military personnel and foreign civilians of the parties missing in action. . . .

Article 9
The Government of the United States of America and the Government of the Democratic Republic of Vietnam undertake to respect the following principles for the exercise of the South Vietnamese people's right to self-determination:

    (a) The South Vietnamese people's right to self-determination is sacred, inalienable and shall be respected by all countries.
    (b) The South Vietnamese people shall decide themselves the political future of South Vietnam through genuinely free and democratic general elections under international supervision.
    (c) Foreign countries shall not impose any political tendency or personality on the South Vietnamese people. . . .

Article 15
The reunification of Vietnam shall be carried out step by step through peaceful means on the basis of discussions and agreements between North and South Vietnam, without coercion or annexation by either party, and without foreign interference. The time for reunification will be agreed upon by North and South Vietnam. . . .

Discussion Questions

1. How did Nixon define "peace with honor"? What sort of settlement would he have seen as dishonorable? What US commitments to South Vietnam are reaffirmed in the speech?
2. What did Nixon expect North Vietnam to do after the Paris Peace Accords?
3. Which articles of the Paris accords reflected American interests? Which reflected North Vietnamese interests? How and why did they do so?
4. Which of the signatories would have insisted on Articles 4 and 6? Which would have insisted on Articles 8 and 9? Why?
5. How did the Paris accords handle the question of Vietnam's eventual reunification?

65

The October War in the Middle East, 1973

ON 6 OCTOBER 1973, COINCIDING with the Jewish feast of Yom Kippur and Islamic holy month of Ramadan, Egypt and Syria launched a surprise attack on Israel. From the start, this conflict had serious Cold War implications. Egypt won the early battles, forcing Israel to ask for massive supplies of weapons from America. This enabled Israel to reverse the momentum, which in turn led Egypt to complain to Moscow that US aid was unfairly affecting the war. Soviet leader Brezhnev responded by asking US Secretary of State Kissinger to fly to Moscow, where the two sides agreed on cease-fire language that became UN Security Council Resolution 338.

But the crisis was not over. Although Israel and Egypt accepted the cease-fire, both violated it. On 24 October Brezhnev placed Soviet airborne divisions on alert and proposed a joint US-Soviet military intervention, failing which Moscow might intervene alone. Washington responded by alerting its military forces to move to DEFCON 3, "the highest state of readiness for essentially peacetime conditions." The alert had an immediate effect: The Egyptians and Soviets accepted a large UN observer force to separate the warring sides, and the United States ended its alert at midnight on 25 October, after pressing the Israelis to observe the cease-fire.

A. UN SECURITY COUNCIL RESOLUTION 338, PASSED ON 22 OCTOBER 1973

The Security Council,

1. Calls upon all parties to the present fighting to cease all firing and terminate all military activity immediately, no later than 12 hours after the moment of the adoption of this decision, in the positions they now occupy. . . .
3. Decides that immediately and concurrently with the cease-fire, negotiations start between the parties concerned under appropriate auspices aimed at establishing a just and durable peace in the Middle East.

B. ISRAEL ACCEPTS THE CEASE-FIRE, 22 OCTOBER 1973

At its meeting this morning (Monday), the Cabinet decided unanimously to accept the proposal of the US Government and President Nixon, and to announce its readiness to agree to a cease-fire in accordance with proposed Security Council Resolution 338.

Under the terms of this proposed Resolution, the military forces will remain in the positions they occupy upon the coming into effect of the cease-fire. Israel will insist on an exchange of prisoners.

The implementation of the cease-fire is conditional upon reciprocity. . . .

The Minister of Defence and the Chief of Staff reported on the situation on the battle fronts.

At 4 P.M. the Government issued the following statement: The Government of Israel has been informed that the Government of Egypt has instructed the armed forces of Egypt to cease hostilities in accordance with the Security Council Resolution concerning the cease-fire.

Following upon this, the Government of Israel has issued orders to the Israeli Defence Forces on the Egyptian front to stop firing at 1850 hours Israeli time today, 22 October, provided it is confirmed that the Egyptians have indeed ceased hostilities.

The cease-fire will therefore come into effect at the end of the 12-hour period stipulated by the Security Council Resolution.

C. EGYPT ACCEPTS THE CEASE-FIRE, 22 OCTOBER 1973

President Sadat has studied with great care the Security Council resolution adopted this morning, calling for a cease-fire within a 12-hour delay and immediate and full implementation of the UN Resolution of 22 November 1967.

The Arab armed forces have confirmed their courage, skill, and martyrdom on the battlefield and it was this great action alone that has broken the deadlock in the crisis.

President Sadat also has studied with great care details of the Security Council debate and noted the following points:

1. The draft Resolution debated by the Security Council was submitted by the two super Powers, the Soviet Union and the United States, after intensive contacts between them at the highest levels and bearing in mind their special responsibility toward current international situations.
2. The Security Council adopted the draft Resolution without objections from any of its members.
3. The debate which took place in the Council was of great importance and shed necessary light on its attitudes. In this connection the statements of the French and Indian delegates were of particular importance.

Other important factors to be taken into consideration include the following:

1. The peace plan which President Sadat broadcast to the nation and the world in his speech to the People's Assembly and the Central Committee of the Arab Socialist Union on October 16, in which the President made complete Israeli withdrawal a basic point of any political action.
2. Talks held by President Sadat and Soviet Premier Alexei Kosygin in Cairo on 16–19 October, when five working sessions were held.

3. Assurances which President Sadat received from Soviet Leader Leonid Brezhnev and which were conveyed to Sadat in a special message by the Soviet ambassador to Cairo on the night of October 21.

4. Contacts which took place with a number of Arab capitals directly concerned in the battle.

President Sadat also took into consideration that the powerful factor which has changed the nature and circumstances of the entire Middle East crisis was highlighted and strengthened by the great action in which the Arab armed forces have carried out and are carrying out, and in which they confirmed their courage, skill and martyrdom on the field of battle.

This great action alone has broken the deadlock in the crisis, changed the fait accompli and the whole map of the Middle East crisis and ended forever the arrogance and power which the Israeli enemy had been displaying for the past 25 years.

In accordance with the above considerations, President Sadat, in his capacity as Supreme Commander of the Armed Forces, has issued an order to the general command to observe a ceasefire at the time laid down by the Security Council Resolution, provided the enemy is also committed to observe it.

President Sadat, in taking this decision on his own historic responsibility, considers that the main credit in this first stage of a decisive phase in the pan-Arab and Egyptian struggle is due to the firm stand taken by the whole Arab nation and to the deep awareness of its peoples as well as, above all, to the heroism of the men who accepted the challenge of fire and blood on the battlefield. God's victory for them was certain.

Discussion Questions

1. Why did Israel cite "the US Government and President Nixon" in accepting Resolution 338?
2. Why did Egypt refer to Soviet leaders Brezhnev and Kosygin in accepting Resolution 338?
3. Why did Sadat emphasize the courage and skill of his armies, which were losing the war?
4. How did the language of Sadat's acceptance demonstrate his eagerness to work toward a long-term solution of the Middle East crisis?

66

Deng Xiaoping's
"Three Worlds" Speech, April 1974

B Y THE 1970S IT WAS OBVIOUS that the Cold War was far more complex than the "two worlds" image of Communist East versus capitalist West portrayed in Stalin's 1946 "election speech" (Document 5). The Communist world had split wide apart, deep divisions had emerged in the capitalist West, and many developing "Third World" nations remained nonaligned. In a notable address to the UN General Assembly in April 1974, China's vice premier Deng Xiaoping asserted that this "drastic division and realignment" had created "three worlds," deftly depicting both the Soviets and Americans as exploiters and oppressors seeking "world hegemony," while adroitly identifying China with the Third World.

HIGHLIGHTS OF SPEECH BY CHINESE VICE-PREMIER DENG XIAOPING TO THE UN GENERAL ASSEMBLY, 10 APRIL 1974

. . . At present, the international situation is most favourable to the developing countries and the peoples of the world. More and more, the old order based on colonialism, imperialism and hegemonism is being undermined and shaken to its foundations. International relations are changing drastically. The whole world is in turbulence and unrest. The situation is one of "great disorder under heaven," as we Chinese put it. . . .

In this situation of "great disorder under heaven," all the political forces in the world have undergone drastic division and realignment. . . . A large number of Asian, African and Latin American countries have achieved independence one after another and they are playing an ever greater role in international affairs. As a result of the emergence of social-imperialism, the socialist camp which existed for a time after World War II is no longer in existence. Owing to the law of the uneven development of capitalism, the Western imperialist bloc, too, is disintegrating. Judging from the changes in international relations, the world today actually consists of three parts, or three worlds, that are both interconnected and in contradiction to one another. The United States and the Soviet Union make up the First World. The developing countries in Asia, Africa, Latin America and other regions make up the Third World. The developed countries between the two make up the Second World.

The two superpowers, the United States and the Soviet Union, are vainly seeking world hegemony. Each in its own way attempts to bring the developing countries of Asia, Africa and Latin America under its control and, at the same time, to bully the developed countries that are not their match in strength.

The two superpowers are the biggest international exploiters and oppressors of today. They are the source of a new world war. They both possess large numbers of nuclear weapons. They carry on a keenly contested arms race, station massive forces abroad and set up military bases everywhere, threatening the independence and security of all nations. They both keep subjecting other countries to their control, subversion, interference or aggression. They both exploit other countries economically, plundering their wealth and grabbing their resources. . . .

The numerous developing countries have long suffered from colonialist and imperialist oppression and exploitation. They have won political independence, yet all of them still face the historic task of clearing out the remnant forces of colonialism, developing the national economy and consolidating national independence. These countries cover vast territories, encompass a large population and abound in natural resources. Having suffered the heaviest oppression, they have the strongest desire to oppose oppression and seek liberation and development. . . .

Since the two superpowers are contending for world hegemony, the contradiction between them is irreconcilable. . . . Their compromise and collusion can only be partial, temporary and relative, while their contention is all-embracing, permanent and absolute. In the final analysis, the so-called "balanced reduction of forces" and "strategic arms limitation" are nothing but empty talk. . . . Every day, they talk about disarmament but are actually engaged in arms expansion. Every day, they talk about "detente" but are actually creating tension. Wherever they contend, turbulence occurs. So long as imperialism and social-imperialism exist, there definitely will be no tranquility in the world. . . .

The two superpowers have created their own antithesis. Acting in the way of the big bullying the small, the strong domineering over the weak and the rich oppressing the poor, they have aroused strong resistance among the Third World and the people of the whole world. The people of Asia, Africa and Latin America have been winning new victories in their struggles against colonialism, imperialism, and particularly hegemonism. . . . The struggles of the Asian, African and Latin American countries and people, advancing wave upon wave, have exposed the essential weakness of imperialism, and particularly the superpowers, which are outwardly strong but inwardly feeble, and dealt heavy blows at their wild ambitions to dominate the world.

Innumerable facts show that all views that overestimate the strength of the two hegemonic powers and underestimate the strength of the people are groundless. It is not the one or two superpowers that are really powerful; the really powerful are the Third World and the people of all countries uniting together and daring to fight and daring to win. . . .

China is a socialist country, and a developing country as well. China belongs to the Third World. Consistently following Chairman Mao's teachings, the Chinese Government and people firmly support all oppressed peoples and oppressed nations in their struggle to win or defend national independence, develop the national economy and oppose colonialism, imperialism and hegemonism. . . . We are convinced that, so long as the Third World countries and people strengthen their unity, ally themselves with all forces that can be allied with and persist in a protracted struggle, they are sure to win continuous new victories.

Discussion Questions

1. What did Deng Xiaoping mean by "great disorder under heaven"? Why did he say the world situation favored developing countries?
2. Why did he lump the Soviets and Americans together as exploiters and oppressors? Why did he dismiss their efforts at détente as "temporary and relative"?
3. Why did he identify China with the Third World?
4. In what ways was his address an accurate analysis of the world situation? In what ways was it a clever bit of anti-Soviet, anti-American, and pro-Chinese propaganda?

67

The Vladivostok Summit, 1974

B Y 1974 THE SPIRIT OF DÉTENTE had begun to fade. The SALT II discussions, designed to replace the interim five-year SALT I accord with a long-term agreement, had drifted into deadlock, and the Middle East crisis of October 1973 had exposed the limits of superpower cooperation. In August 1974 Richard Nixon, one of détente's key architects, was forced by the Watergate scandal to resign as US president.

Soon after Nixon left office, a summit conference was arranged between his successor, Gerald R. Ford, and Soviet leader Brezhnev. Their meeting, at Vladivostok in Soviet East Asia, exceeded most expectations and breathed new life into détente. The two leaders, assisted by Soviet Foreign Minister Gromyko and US Secretary of State Kissinger, managed to overcome the SALT impasse by agreeing to establish "ceilings" for the sum total of missiles and bombers each side could have and for the number of these that could be fitted with multiple warheads. They also discussed many other issues and agreed to meet again the next year.

A. AGREEMENT CONCLUDED
AT VLADIVOSTOK, 24 NOVEMBER 1974

During their working meeting in the area of Vladivostok on Nov. 23–24, 1974, the President of the USA, Gerald R. Ford, and General Secretary of the Central Committee of the CPSU, L. I. Brezhnev, discussed in detail the question of further limitations of strategic offensive arms.

They reaffirmed the great significance that both the United States and the USSR attach to the limitation of strategic offensive arms. They are convinced that a long-term agreement on this question would be a significant contribution to improving relations between the US and the USSR, to reducing the danger of war and to enhancing world peace. Having noted the value of previous agreements on this question, including the interim agreement of May 26, 1972, they reaffirm the intention to conclude a new agreement on the limitation of strategic offensive arms to last through 1985.

As a result of the exchange of views on the substance of such a new agreement, the President . . . and the General Secretary . . . concluded that favorable prospects exist for completing the work on this agreement in 1975.

Agreement was reached that further negotiations will be based on the following provisions:

1. The new agreement will incorporate the relevant provisions of the interim agreement of May 26, 1972, which will remain in force until October, 1977.
2. The new agreement will cover the period from October, 1977, through Dec. 31, 1985.
3. Based on the principle of equality and equal security, the new agreement will include the following limitations:
   A. Both sides will be entitled to have a certain agreed aggregate number of strategic delivery vehicles.
   B. Both sides will be entitled to have a certain agreed aggregate number of ICBM's [intercontinental ballistic missiles] and SLBM's [submarine-launched ballistic missiles] equipped with multiple independently targetable warheads (MIRV's).
4. The new agreement will include a provision for further negotiations beginning no later than 1980–1981 on the question of further limitations and possible reductions of strategic arms in the period after 1985.
5. Negotiations between the delegations of the US and USSR to work out the new agreement incorporating the foregoing points will resume in Geneva in January, 1975.

B. EXCERPT FROM PRESIDENT FORD'S STATEMENT, 2 DECEMBER 1974

My meetings at Vladivostok with General Secretary Brezhnev were a valuable opportunity to review Soviet-American relations and chart their future course. Although this was our original purpose, Secretary Brezhnev and I found it possible to go beyond this get-acquainted stage. Building on the achievements of the past three years we agreed that prospects were favorable for more substantial, and may I say, very intensive negotiations on the primary issue of limitation of strategic arms. In the end, we agreed on the general framework for a new agreement that will last through 1985.

We agreed it is realistic to aim at completing this agreement next year. This is possible because we made major breakthroughs on two critical issues.

(1) We agreed to put a ceiling of 2,400 each on the total number of intercontinental ballistic missiles, submarine-launched missiles and heavy bombers.

(2) We agreed to limit the number of missiles that can be armed with multiple warheads (MIRV's). Of each side's total of 2,400, 1,320 can be so armed.

These ceilings are well below the force levels which would otherwise have been expected over the next 10 years, and very substantially below the forces which would result from an all-out arms race over that same period.

What we have done is to set firm and equal limits on the strategic forces of each side, thus preventing an arms race with all its terror, instability, war-breeding tension and economic waste. We have in addition created the solid basis from which future arms reductions can be . . . and hopefully will be . . . negotiated.

It will take more detailed negotiations to convert this agreed framework into a comprehensive accord. But we have made a long step forward toward peace, on a basis of equality, the only basis on which agreement was possible. . . .

Discussion Questions

1. Why were Soviet leaders eager to restore détente's momentum after Nixon's resignation? Why were US leaders eager to continue their dialogue with Moscow?

2. What were the basic conditions agreed to at Vladivostok? How did they differ from SALT I?

3. Why did the agreement lump together ICBMs, SLBMs, and long-range bombers rather than establishing separate ceilings for each?

4. According to President Ford, what expectations did he have going into this meeting? What expectations did he have as a result of it?

68

The Helsinki Final Act, 1975

IN SUMMER 1975 LEADERS of thirty-five nations gathered in Helsinki, Finland, to sign the Helsinki Final Act. It was a crowning achievement of the Conference on Security and Cooperation in Europe (CSCE), which had begun in 1973. It represented the centerpiece of European détente, the final peace settlement of World War II in Europe, and the culmination of Moscow's efforts to gain international recognition of its territorial gains. Along with its provisions on European security, economic cooperation, and scientific collaboration, the Final Act also established guidelines regarding human rights. These guidelines, grouped together in "Basket Three," provided specific standards concerning freedom of emigration and freedom of information. In future years, Soviet failure to comply with these standards would be monitored by Western governments, human rights advocates, and dissident groups in the USSR, creating serious headaches for Moscow.

EXCERPTS FROM DECLARATION
SIGNED AT HELSINKI, 1 AUGUST 1975

Questions Relating to Security in Europe
    The states participating in the Conference on Security and Cooperation in Europe. . . .
    Declare their determination to respect and put into practice the following principles, which all are of primary significance, guiding their mutual relations:
    The participating states will respect each other's sovereign equality and individuality as well as all the rights inherent in and encompassed by its sovereignty, including in particular the right of every state to juridical equality, to territorial integrity and to freedom and political independence. They will also respect each other's right freely to choose and develop its political, social, economic and cultural systems as well as its right to determine its laws and regulations. . . .

The participating states will refrain in their mutual relations, as well as in their international relations in general, from the threat or use of force against the territorial integrity or political independence of any state. . . .

The participating states regard as inviolable all one another's frontiers as well as the frontiers of all states in Europe, and therefore they will refrain now and in the future from assaulting these frontiers. . . .

The participating states will settle disputes among them by peaceful means in such a manner as not to endanger international peace and security and justice. They will endeavor in good faith and a spirit of cooperation to reach a rapid and equitable solution on the basis of international law. . . .

The participating states will refrain from any intervention, direct or indirect, individual or collective, in the internal or external affairs falling within the domestic jurisdiction of another participating state, regardless of their mutual relations.

The participating states will refrain from direct or indirect assistance to terrorist activities or to subversive or other activities directed towards the violent overthrow of the regime of another participating state.

The participating states will respect human rights and fundamental freedoms, including the freedom of thought, conscience, religion or belief, for all without distinction as to race, sex, language or religion.

Within this framework the participating states will recognize and respect the freedom of the individual to profess and practice, alone or in community with others, religion or belief acting in accordance with the dictates of his own conscience.

The participating states on whose territory national minorities exist will respect the right of persons belonging to such minorities to equality before the law, will afford them the full opportunity for the actual enjoyment of human rights and fundamental freedoms and will, in this manner, protect their legitimate interests in this sphere.

The participating states recognize the universal significance of human rights and fundamental freedoms, respect for which is an essential factor for the peace, justice and well-being necessary to insure the development of friendly relations and cooperation among themselves as among all states. They will constantly respect these rights and freedoms in their mutual relations. . . .

Documents on Confidence-Building Measures and Certain Aspects of Security and Disarmament

The participating states . . .

Recognizing the need to contribute to reducing the dangers of armed conflict and of misunderstanding or miscalculation of military activities which could give rise to apprehension, particularly in a situation where the participating states lack clear and timely information about the nature of such activities . . . , have adopted the following:

They will notify their major military maneuvers to all other participating states through usual diplomatic channels in accordance with the following provisions:

Notification will be given of major military maneuvers exceeding a total of 25,000 troops, independently or combined with any possible air or naval components. . . .

Notification will be given of major military maneuvers which take place on the territory, in Europe, of any participating state as well as, if applicable, in the adjoining sea area and airspace. . . .

Notification will be given 21 days or more in advance of the start of the maneuver, or in the case of a maneuver arranged at shorter notice, at the earliest possible opportunity prior to its starting date.

Notification will contain information of the designation, if any, of the general purpose of and the states involved in the maneuver, the type or types and numerical strength of the forces engaged, the area and estimated time frame of its conduct. . . .

The participating states will invite other participating states, voluntarily and on a bilateral basis . . . , to send observers to attend military maneuvers. . . .

Cooperation in the Field of Economics, of Science and Technology, and of the Environment

The participating states will encourage the expansion of trade on as broad a multilateral basis as possible, thereby endeavoring to utilize the various economic and commercial possibilities.

They will endeavor to reduce or progressively eliminate all kinds of obstacles to the development of trade; will foster a steady growth of trade while avoiding as far as possible abrupt fluctuations in their trade.

The participating states will promote the publication and dissemination of economic and commercial information at regular intervals and as quickly as possible. . . .

Cooperation in Humanitarian and Other Fields

The participating states,

Will make it their aim to facilitate freer movement and contacts . . . among persons, institutions and organizations of the participating states.

In order to promote further development of contacts on the basis of family ties the participating states will favorably consider applications for travel with the purpose of allowing persons to enter or leave their territory temporarily and on a regular basis if desired, in order to visit members of their families. . . .

The participating states will deal in a positive and humanitarian spirit with the applications of persons who wish to be reunited with members of their family, with special attention given to requests of an urgent character. They will deal with applications in this field as expeditiously as possible. . . .

The participating states will examine favorably and on the basis of humanitarian considerations requests for exit or entry permits from persons who have decided to marry a citizen from another participating state. . . .

The participating states intend to facilitate wider travel by their citizens for personal or professional reasons and to this end they intend in particular:

- Gradually to simplify and to administer flexibly the procedures for exit and entry;
- To ease regulations concerning movement of citizens from the other participating states in their territory with due regard to security requirements. . . .

By way of further developing contacts among governmental institutions and non-governmental organizations and associations, including women's organizations, the participating states will facilitate the convening of meetings as well as travel by delegations, groups and individuals.

The participating states,

Make it their aim to facilitate the freer and wider dissemination of information of all kinds, to encourage cooperation in the field of information and the exchange of information with other countries, and to improve the conditions under which journalists from one participating state exercise their professions in another participating state, and express their intention in particular:

- To facilitate the dissemination of oral information through the encouragement of lectures and lecture tours by personalities and specialists from the other participating states, as well as exchanges of opinions at round-table meetings, seminars, symposia, summer schools, congresses and other bilateral and multilateral meetings.
- To facilitate the improvement of the dissemination, on their territory, of newspapers and printed publications, periodical and non-periodical, from the other participating states. For this purpose they will encourage their competent firms and organizations to conclude agreements and contracts designed gradually to increase the quantities and the number of titles of newspapers and publications imported from the other participating states.

The participating states express the intention to promote the improvement of the dissemination of filmed and broadcast information.

The participating states note the experience in the dissemination of information broadcast by radio and express the hope for the continuation of this process so as to meet the interest of mutual understanding among peoples and the aims set forth by this conference.

To encourage cooperation in the field of information on the basis of short or long term agreements or arrangements, in particular:

They will favor increased cooperation among mass media organizations, including press agencies, as well as among publishing houses and organizations.

They will favor cooperation among public or private national or international radio and television organizations, in particular through the exchange of both live and recorded radio and television programs. . . .

The participating states are disposed to increase substantially their cultural exchanges, with regard both to persons and to cultural works, and to develop among them an active cooperation, both at the bilateral and the multilateral level, in all fields of culture.

The participating states express their intention to promote wider dissemination of books and artistic works, in particular by facilitating . . . international contacts and communications between authors and publishing houses as well as other cultural institutions, with a view to a more complete mutual access to cultural achievements.

The participating states express their intention to contribute, by appropriate means, to the development of contacts and cooperation in the various fields of culture, especially among creative artists and people engaged in cultural activities.

Discussion Questions

1. In what sense was the Helsinki Final Act the final peace settlement of World War II in Europe?
2. How did it seek to improve European security and cooperation?
3. Why was the USSR eager to have Europe's current frontiers recognized as permanent? Why would Moscow have reason to be pleased with the Final Act?
4. Why did its provisions on human rights present potential problems for Moscow?

69

The Cambodian Genocide, 1975–1979

THE US WITHDRAWAL FROM Vietnam in 1973 (Documents 64A–B) ended America's military involvement, but it by no means put an end to the agonies of Southeast Asia. In 1975, with the US forces gone, the North Vietnamese forces launched an offensive that conquered the South and united Vietnam under Communist rule. That same year Communist regimes came to power in neighboring Laos and Cambodia.

Over the next few years, led by radical Maoists Pol Pot and Ieng Sary, Cambodia's new ruling party, the Communist Khmer Rouge, conducted a mass mobilization campaign modeled on Mao's earlier "Great Leap Forward" and "Great Proletarian Cultural Revolution" in China (Documents 36A–B and 54A–B). In an effort to create a rural socialist utopia, the Khmer Rouge rounded up masses of people and forced them at gunpoint to work in rural agrarian communes. Those who resisted were murdered by the thousands, while tens of thousands of others died of exhaustion and starvation in what came to be called the Cambodian genocide.

In December 1978 recently reunified Communist Vietnam invaded Cambodia and eventually ousted the Khmer Rouge regime, which fled to neighboring Thailand. In 1979 a new, more moderate Communist government took power in Cambodia. Among other things, it proceeded to form a "People's Revolutionary Tribunal" that tried the Khmer Rouge leaders in absentia. Presented here are some excerpts from the judgment of that tribunal.

GENOCIDE IN CAMBODIA: JUDGMENT OF THE "PEOPLE'S REVOLUTIONARY TRIBUNAL," 19 AUGUST 1979

Judgment of the Tribunal, August 19, 1979 . . .

. . . [D]uring their nearly four years in power [1975–1979], the accused Pol Pot and Ieng Sary . . . committed the following criminal acts.

I. Systematic implementation of a plan to kill many strata of the population on an increasingly ferocious scale. . . .

II. Killing of clergy and believers, and eradication of religion; systematic killing of members of ethnic minorities to force them to assimilate; extermination of foreign residents. . . .

III. Forcible evacuation of the population from [the capital] Phnom Penh and other liberated towns and villages; the breaking and upsetting of family and social structures; mass killing and mass executions. . . .

IV. The herding of the population into "people's communes," which were disguised concentration camps, where they were forced to work and live in physically and morally destructive conditions that caused deaths in large numbers. . . .

. . . Pol Pot and Ieng Sary set up in our country a most brutal dictatorial militarist regime that . . . killed people in bloody mass killings and by methods of torture. . . . In many areas of the country, they killed the entire population of a village or sub-district, and in some cases they killed nearly the entire population of a district, including children, the elderly, pregnant women, invalids, and the war wounded.

After examining the investigation reports presented at the hearing, the findings of a sample census conducted in a number of villages and sub-districts, and other information in the case file, the tribunal finds well founded the estimate that more than three million persons were killed or otherwise succumbed because of torture or the poor conditions of life. . . .

The approximately four million who were left alive were herded into huge concentration camps where they were forced to work like animals. Their lot was worse than that of slaves. Hungry, clad in rags and without medical care, they were doomed to physical degeneration. On the mental side, they were constantly threatened and spied upon by secret agents. They might be arrested and killed at any moment together with their close relatives. . . .

The crime of genocide committed by the accused . . . is . . . far in excess of what is required for genocide in the December 9, 1948 [United Nations] Convention. The accused not only wiped out the intellectuals, the officers, and civil servants of the previous regime, religious believers, and ethnic minorities . . . , they also killed, *en masse* and in a planned way, innocent people of different social strata. The accused sought to exterminate their own people, their own nation, pushing the people of different social strata to the point of extinction. . . .

For the above-mentioned reasons . . . , the judge and jury of the People's Revolutionary Tribunal in Phnom Penh decides:

1. That the accused . . . are guilty of genocide.
2. That the accused . . . be sentenced to death in absentia.
3. That all the property of the accused . . . be confiscated. . . .

Discussion Questions

1. What were the probable goals and motivations of the Khmer Rouge regime? How were its leaders influenced by Mao's policies in China?
2. Why did the Vietnamese Communists invade Communist Cambodia? Why might they want to replace the Khmer Rouge with a more moderate Communist regime?
3. Why would Cambodia's new Communist regime establish a revolutionary tribunal to try the ousted and departed Khmer Rouge leaders?
4. What were the main findings of the revolutionary tribunal? To what extent can its findings and judgments be considered impartial?

70

Carter on Human Rights, 1977

IN PURSUING DÉTENTE, the Soviet leaders worked reasonably well with presidents Nixon and Ford. Despite his strident anti-communism, Nixon was a realistic politician who put pragmatism above principle. When Nixon resigned in 1974, Moscow was at first alarmed but was quickly reassured when Nixon's successor, Gerald Ford, proved equally practical. But Jimmy Carter's election in 1976 changed the rules and left the Soviets uncertain of how to proceed.

Carter, an enigma to many in America and around the world, was a born-again Christian peanut farmer from Georgia with a degree in nuclear engineering from the US Naval Academy. As if his background was not sufficiently unusual, he proceeded to introduce a new variable into American foreign policy. Since the Declaration of Independence in 1776, American politics had often been filled with references to human rights, but those rights were not always honored at home and rarely emphasized in Washington's dealings abroad. Now, as Americans finished celebrating the bicentennial of their independence, Carter proposed to create a "human rights" standard by which the United States would judge other nations. A government wishing to remain friendly with Washington would have to meet that standard. The

USSR was both perplexed and annoyed, given its problems with the human rights provisions of the Helsinki Final Act.

CARTER'S ADDRESS TO THE UNITED NATIONS, 17 MARCH 1977

... It's now eight weeks since I became President. I've brought to office a firm commitment to a more open foreign policy. And I believe that the American people expect me to speak frankly about the policies that we intend to pursue and it is in that spirit that I speak to you tonight about our own hopes for the future.

I see a hopeful world, a world dominated by increasing demands for basic freedoms, for fundamental rights, for higher standards of human existence. We are eager to take part in the shaping of that world.

But in seeking such a better world, we are not blind to the reality of disagreement nor to the persisting dangers that confront us all. Every headline reminds us of bitter divisions, of national hostilities, of territorial conflicts, of ideological competition. In the Middle East peace is a quarter century overdue. A gathering racial conflict threatens Southern Africa, new tensions are rising in the horn of Africa; disputes in the eastern Mediterranean remain to be resolved.

Perhaps even more ominous is the staggering arms race. The Soviet Union and the United States have accumulated thousands of nuclear weapons. Our two nations have almost five times as many missile warheads today as we had eight years ago. Yet we are not five times more secure! On the contrary, the arms race has only increased the risk of conflict.

We can only improve this world if we are realistic about its complexities. The disagreements we face are deeply rooted, and they often raise difficult philosophical as well as territorial issues. They will not be solved easily; they will not be solved quickly. The arms race is now embedded in the very fabric of international affairs and can only be contained with the greatest difficulty. Poverty, inequality are of such monumental scope that it will take decades of deliberate and determined effort even to improve the situation substantially.

I stress these dangers and these difficulties because I want all of us to dedicate ourselves to a prolonged and persistent effort designed:

First, to maintain peace and to reduce the arms race;

Second, to build a better and more cooperative international economic system;

And third, to work with potential adversaries as well as our close friends to advance the cause of human rights. . . .

The search for peace and justice also means respect for human dignity. All the signatories of the UN Charter have pledged themselves to observe and to respect basic human rights. Thus, no member of the United Nations can claim that mistreatment of its citizens is solely its own business. Equally, no member can avoid its responsibilities to review and to speak when torture or unwarranted deprivation occurs in any part of the world.

The basic thrust of human affairs points toward a more universal demand for fundamental human rights. The United States has a historical birthright to be associated with this process.

We in the United States accept this responsibility in the fullest and the most constructive sense. Ours is a commitment, and not just a political posture. I know . . . that our own ideals in the area of human rights have not always been attained in the United States, but the American people have an abiding commitment to the full realization of these ideals. We are determined, therefore, to deal with our deficiencies quickly and openly. We have nothing to conceal. . . .

The United Nations is the global forum dedicated to the peace and well-being of every individual—no matter how weak or how poor. But we have allowed its human rights machinery to be ignored and sometimes politicized. There is much that can be done to strengthen it. . . .

Strengthened international machinery will help us to close the gap between promise and performance in protecting human rights. When gross or widespread violation takes place—contrary to international commitments—it is of concern to all. The solemn commitments of the UN Charter, of the UN's Universal Declaration of Human Rights, of the Helsinki Accords and of many other international instruments must be taken just as seriously as commercial or security agreements. . . .

These then are our basic priorities as we work with other members to strengthen and improve the United Nations:

First, we will strive for peace in the troubled areas of the world.

Second, we will aggressively seek to control the weaponry of war.

Third, we will promote a new system of international economic progress and cooperation.

And fourth, we will be steadfast in our dedication to the dignity and well-being of people throughout the world. . . .

Discussion Questions

1. President Carter asserted that no nation could claim that "mistreatment of its citizens is solely its own business." Why not?
2. What did he mean by claiming that the United States had a "historical birthright to be associated with this process"?

3. When Carter said that the United States had not always lived up to its human rights ideals, to what might he have been referring?
4. What counterarguments might other UN members have used against Carter?

71

Peace between Egypt and Israel, 1977–1979

ALTHOUGH HE SIGNED A TREATY OF PEACE and Friendship with Moscow in 1971 and accepted large amounts of Soviet aid in preparation for the Arab-Israeli War of 1973, Egypt's president Anwar el-Sadat grew increasingly dissatisfied with Soviet support and concluded that only Washington had enough clout to pressure Israel into making real concessions. In 1972 he expelled Soviet advisors from Egypt, and in 1976 he abrogated the treaty with the USSR. The following year, in a dramatic break with precedent, he flew to Israel and made a historic speech on 20 November to the Israeli parliament (the Knesset).

It is difficult to exaggerate the impact of Sadat's action. No leader of an Arab state had ever visited Israel. No Arab state had granted diplomatic recognition to Israel. Since 1948, most Arabs had refused to recognize Israel's right to exist. Sadat's bold gesture astounded Israelis and enraged much of the Arab world.

His initiative led to a return visit by Israeli prime minister Menachem Begin to Egypt later that year. Extensive diplomatic contacts then took place behind the scenes. In September 1978, President Carter invited both Sadat and Begin to the United States to negotiate a framework for an eventual treaty, underscoring America's importance as a power broker in the Middle East.

Sadat and Begin met for twelve days at Camp David, the presidential retreat in Maryland's Catoctin Mountains. Carter was present for much of that period and saved the conference from collapse on 16 September, when he prevailed on the two men to make one last attempt to reach agreement, with himself as mediator. The effort proved successful, and the historic Camp David Agreements were announced the next day.

Although the Camp David Framework envisioned a treaty within three months, several issues, including that of the Palestinian Arabs living in Israeli-occupied territory on the West Bank and in the Gaza Strip, delayed its conclusion until March 1979. Finally the two parties agreed to leave the Palestinian problem for another day and were able to reach agreement on issues affecting themselves. The final document, signed on a bright spring day in Washington, afforded one of the great photo opportunities of the twentieth century, with Sadat and Begin joining hands that were clasped by a beaming Jimmy Carter, as the flags of Egypt, Israel, and the United States rippled in a stiff breeze. It remained to be seen if this treaty would lead to a general Middle East peace or remain an isolated example of what can be accomplished when statesmen set out to break the chains of past ideas and animosities.

A. EXCERPT FROM SADAT'S SPEECH IN ISRAEL, 20 NOVEMBER 1977

I have chosen to set aside all precedents and traditions known by warring countries. In spite of the fact that occupation of Arab territory is still there, the declaration of my readiness to proceed to Israel came as a great surprise that stirred many feelings and confounded many minds. Some of them even doubted its intent. . . .

I have chosen to come to you with an open heart and an open mind. I have chosen to give this great impetus to all international efforts exerted for peace. I have chosen to present you in your own home, the realities, devoid of any scheme or whim. Not to maneuver, to win a round, but for us to win together, the most dangerous of rounds embattled in modern history, the battle of permanent peace based on justice.

It is not my battle alone. Nor is it the battle of the leadership in Israel alone. It is the battle of all and every citizen in our territories, whose right it is to live in peace. It is the commitment of conscience and responsibility in the hearts of millions.

When I put forward this initiative, many asked what is it that I conceived as possible to achieve during this visit and what my expectations were. And as I answer these questions, I announce before you that I have not thought of carrying out this initiative from the precepts of what could be achieved during this visit. I have come here to deliver a message. I have delivered the message and may God be my witness.

I repeat with Zacharia: Love right and justice. From the holy Qu'ran I quote the following verses: "We believe in God and in what has been revealed to us and what was revealed to Abraham, Ishmael, Isaac, Jacob and the 13 Jewish tribes. And in the books given to Moses and Jesus and the prophets from their Lord, who made no distinction between them." So we agree, Salam Aleikum—peace be upon you.

B. FRAMEWORK FOR PEACE AGREED
TO AT CAMP DAVID, 17 SEPTEMBER 1978

Muhammad Anwar el-Sadat, president of the Arab Republic of Egypt, and Menachem Begin, prime minister of Israel, met with Jimmy Carter, president of the United States of America, at Camp David from September 5 to September 17, 1978, and have agreed on the following framework for peace in the Middle East. They invite other parties to the Arab-Israeli conflict to adhere to it.

. . . The parties are determined to reach a just, comprehensive, and durable settlement of the Middle East conflict. . . . Their purpose is to achieve peace and good neighborly relations. They recognize that for peace to endure, it must involve all those who have been most deeply affected by the conflict. They therefore agree that this framework as appropriate is intended by them to constitute a basis for peace not only between Egypt and Israel, but also between Israel and each of its other neighbors which is prepared to negotiate peace with Israel on this basis. With that objective in mind, they have agreed to proceed as follows:

A. *West Bank and Gaza*
   1. Egypt, Israel, Jordan and the representatives of the Palestinian people should participate in negotiations on the resolution of the Palestinian problem in all its aspects. . . .
      (a) Egypt and Israel agree that, in order to ensure a peaceful and orderly transfer of authority, and taking into account the security concerns of all the parties, there should be transitional arrangements for the West Bank and Gaza for a period not exceeding five years. In order to provide full autonomy to the inhabitants, under these arrangements the Israeli military government and its civilian administration will be withdrawn as soon as a self-governing authority has been freely elected by the inhabitants of these areas to replace the existing military government. To negotiate the details of a transitional arrangement, the government of Jordan will

be invited to join the negotiations on the basis of this framework. These new arrangements should give due consideration both to the principle of self-government by the inhabitants of these territories and to the legitimate security concerns of the parties involved. . . .

B. *Egypt-Israel*

1. Egypt and Israel undertake not to resort to the threat or the use of force to settle disputes. Any disputes shall be settled by peaceful means in accordance with the provisions of Article 33 of the Charter of the United Nations.

2. In order to achieve peace between them, the parties agree to negotiate in good faith with a goal of concluding within three months from the signing of this framework a peace treaty between them, while inviting the other parties to the conflict to proceed simultaneously to negotiate and conclude similar peace treaties with a view to achieving a comprehensive peace in the area. The Framework for the Conclusion of a Peace Treaty Between Egypt and Israel will govern the peace negotiations between them. The parties will agree on the modalities and the timetable for the implementation of their obligations under the treaty.

C. *Associated Principles*

1. Egypt and Israel state that the principles and provisions described below should apply to peace treaties between Israel and each of its neighbors—Egypt, Jordan, Syria and Lebanon.

2. Signatories shall establish among themselves relationships normal to states at peace with one another. To this end, they should undertake to abide by all the provisions of the Charter of the United Nations. Steps to be taken in this respect include:

   (a) full recognition;

   (b) abolishing economic boycotts;

   (c) guaranteeing that under their jurisdiction the citizens of the other parties shall enjoy the protection of the due process of law. . . .

Signed by Sadat and Begin, with Carter signing as a witness.

C. TREATY BETWEEN EGYPT AND ISRAEL, 26 MARCH 1979

Article I

1. The state of war between the parties will be terminated and peace will be established between them upon the exchange of instruments of ratification of this treaty.

2. Israel will withdraw all its armed forces and civilians from the Sinai behind the international boundary between Egypt and mandated Palestine . . . , and Egypt will resume the exercise of its full sovereignty over the Sinai.
3. Upon completion of the interim withdrawal . . . , the parties will establish normal and friendly relations, in accordance with Article III (3).

Article II

The permanent boundary between Egypt and Israel is the recognized international boundary between Egypt and the former mandated territory of Palestine . . . without prejudice to the issue of the status of the Gaza Strip. The parties recognize this boundary as inviolable. Each will respect the territorial integrity of the other, including their territorial waters and airspace.

Article III

1. The parties will apply between them the provisions of the Charter of the United Nations and the principles of international law governing relations among states in time of peace. In particular:
    A. They recognize and will respect each other's sovereignty, territorial integrity and political independence.
    B. They recognize and will respect each other's right to live in peace within their secure and recognized boundaries.
    C. They will refrain from the threat or use of force, directly or indirectly, against each other and will settle all disputes between them by peaceful means.
2. Each party undertakes to insure that acts or threats of belligerency, hostility or violence do not originate from and are not committed from within its territory, or by any forces subject to its control or by any other forces stationed on its territory, against the population, citizens or property of the other party. Each party also undertakes to refrain from organizing, instigating, inciting, assisting or participating in acts or threats of belligerency, hostility, subversion or violence against the other party, anywhere, and undertakes to insure that perpetrators of such acts are brought to justice.
3. The parties agree that the normal relationship established between them will include full recognition, diplomatic, economic and cultural relations, termination of economic boycotts and discriminatory barriers to the free movement of people and goods, and will guarantee the mutual enjoyment by citizens of the due process of law. . . .

Discussion Questions

1. Why would many Israelis distrust Sadat? How did Sadat attempt to overcome this distrust?
2. Why did Sadat conclude that Soviet support was less valuable to him than US support?
3. Why did Carter work so hard for peace between Egypt and Israel? What benefits might such a peace bring to the United States?
4. Why were the West Bank and Gaza such difficult situations for Egypt and Israel to settle? How did the treaty deal with the issue of Gaza?
5. What concessions did Israel make to Egypt? What concessions did Egypt make to Israel?

72

The Normalization of US-Chinese Relations, 1978–1979

IN DECEMBER 1978 PRESIDENT CARTER made the dramatic announcement that, as of 1 January 1979, the United States would establish formal diplomatic relations with the People's Republic of China. This event marked the culmination of the process that had begun with President Nixon's trip to China in 1972. It also represented a decision by the Carter administration to strengthen its hand against Moscow by improving US ties with Beijing.

From the time of Nixon's visit, the main obstacle to normalized relations had been the Taiwan issue. For decades the United States had maintained close ties with the Nationalist regime ("Republic of China") and had continued to recognize it as China's official government, even though since 1949 it had controlled only Taiwan. From Beijing's perspective, however, Taiwan was part of China, and US support for the Nationalists was blatant interference in Chinese internal affairs. In the Shanghai Communiqué of 1972 (Document 62), the Nixon administration acknowledged that Taiwan was considered part of China by both Communists and Nationalists and gradually decreased the US military presence there. But it had been unwilling to terminate US diplomatic relations with the Taiwan government.

By 1978, however, the Carter administration was willing to take that step. Nationalist leader Chiang Kai-shek (Jiang Jieshi), America's old wartime ally, had died in 1975, and was followed to the grave the next year by Mao Zedong. Since then, led by Deng Xiaoping, the Chinese Communists had moved away from Mao's frenetic radicalism and had adopted a more pragmatic approach to domestic and foreign affairs. They also had joined the United States in vehement denunciations of the USSR. So, in return for unspecified assurances from Beijing that the Taiwan issue would be resolved by peaceful means, the United States agreed to cut diplomatic ties with Taiwan and formally recognize the People's Republic.

A. CARTER'S STATEMENT ON
OPENING TIES WITH CHINA, 15 DECEMBER 1978

Good evening. I would like to read a joint communique which is being simultaneously issued . . . at this very moment by the leaders of the People's Republic of China:

A Joint Communique on the Establishment of Diplomatic Relations Between the United States of America and the People's Republic of China, January 1, 1979.

The United States of America and the People's Republic of China have agreed to recognize each other and to establish diplomatic relations as of January 1, 1979. The United States recognizes the Government of the People's Republic of China as the sole legal Government of China. Within this context the people of the United States will maintain cultural, commercial and other unofficial relations with the people of Taiwan.

The United States of America and the People's Republic of China reaffirm the principles agreed on by the two sides in the Shanghai Communique of 1972 and emphasize once again that both sides wish to reduce the danger of international military conflict. Neither should seek hegemony—that is the dominance of one nation over others—in the Asia-Pacific region or in any other region of the world and each is opposed to efforts by any other country or group of countries to establish such hegemony. Neither is prepared to negotiate on behalf of any other third party or to enter into agreements or understandings with the other directed at other states.

The Government of the United States of America acknowledges the Chinese position that there is but one China and Taiwan is part of China. Both believe that normalization of Sino-American relations is not only in the interest of the Chinese and American people but also contributes to the cause of peace in Asia and in the world. The United States of America and the People's Republic of China will exchange ambassadors and establish embassies on March 1, 1979.

Yesterday, our country and the People's Republic of China reached this final historic agreement. On Jan. 1, 1979, a little more than two weeks from now, our two Governments will implement full normalization of diplomatic relations.

As a nation of gifted people who comprise about one-fourth of the total population of the Earth, China plays, already, an important role in world affairs—a role that can only grow more important in the years ahead.

We do not undertake this important step for transient tactical or expedient reasons. In recognizing the People's Republic of China—that it is a single Government of China, we're recognizing simple reality. But far more is involved in this decision than just the recognition of a fact. . . .

The change that I'm announcing tonight will be of great long-term benefit to the peoples of both our country and China and I believe for all the peoples of the world.

Normalization and expanded commercial and cultural relations that it will bring will contribute to the well-being of our nation to our own national interest. And it will also enhance the stability of Asia.

These more positive relations with China can beneficially affect the world in which we live and the world in which our children will live.

We have already begun to inform our allies and other nations and the members of the Congress of the details of our intended action, but I wish also tonight to convey a special message to the people of Taiwan.

I have already communicated with the leaders in Taiwan, with whom the American people have had, and will have, extensive, close and friendly relations. This is important between our two peoples. As the United States asserted in the Shanghai Communique of 1972, issued on President Nixon's historic visit, we will continue to have an interest in the peaceful resolution of the Taiwan issue.

I have paid special attention to insuring that normalization of relations between our country and the People's Republic will not jeopardize the well-being of the people of Taiwan.

The people of our country will maintain our current commercial, cultural, trade and other relations with Taiwan through nongovernmental means. Many other countries of the world are already successfully doing this.

These decisions and these actions open a new and important chapter in our country's history and also in world affairs. To strengthen and to expedite the benefits of this new relationship between China and the United States, I am pleased to announce that Vice Premier Teng [Deng Xiaoping] has accepted my invitation and will visit Washington at the end of January. His visit will give our Governments the opportunity to consult with each other on global issues and to begin working together to enhance the cause of world peace.

These events are the final result of long and serious negotiations begun by President Nixon in 1972 and continued under the leadership of President Ford. The results bear witness to the steady, determined, bipartisan effort of our own country to build a world in which peace will be the goal and the responsibility of all nations.

The normalization of relations between the United States and China has no other purpose than the advancement of peace. It is in this spirit, at this season of peace, that I take special pride in sharing this good news with you tonight.

B. STATEMENT BY THE PEOPLE'S REPUBLIC OF CHINA

As of Jan. 1, 1979, the People's Republic of China and the United States of America recognize each other and establish diplomatic relations, thereby ending the prolonged abnormal relationship between them. This is an historic event in Sino-United States relations.

As is known to all, the Government of the People's Republic of China is the sole legal Government of China and Taiwan is a part of China. The question of Taiwan was the crucial issue obstructing the normalization of relations between China and the United States. It has now been resolved between the two countries in the spirit of the Shanghai Communique and through their joint efforts, thus enabling the normalization of relations so ardently desired by the people of the two countries.

As for the way of bringing Taiwan back to the embrace of the motherland and reunifying the country, it is entirely China's internal affair.

At the invitation of the US Government, Teng Hsiao-ping [Deng Xiaoping], Deputy Prime Minister of the State Council of the People's Republic of China, will pay an official visit to the United States in January 1979, with a view to further promoting the friendship between the two peoples and good relations between the two countries.

Discussion Questions

1. What reasons did Carter give for establishing diplomatic relations with China? What other reasons might he have had?
2. Why were the Chinese interested in establishing diplomatic relations with the United States?

3. What concessions did the Americans make in order to establish ties with China? What concessions did the Chinese make?
4. Why was the Taiwan issue so important to the Chinese?
5. Why was it difficult for the US government to break off diplomatic relations with Taiwan?

73

The SALT II Agreement, 1979

THE SALT I AGREEMENT SIGNED by Nixon and Brezhnev in 1972 (Document 63) was an interim treaty, intended only to restrain the arms race for five years, during which the superpowers would negotiate a more comprehensive accord. After the 1974 Vladivostok summit, at which agreement was reached on the main issues (Document 67), it seemed that a new treaty was within reach. However, due to the worsening international climate and the complexity of the remaining issues, things took longer than expected. They were further delayed in 1977, when President Carter took office and insisted on pushing for extensive arms reductions, far beyond what was agreed at Vladivostok. As a result, the treaty was not completed until 1979.

The SALT II agreement, signed by Carter and Brezhnev during their Vienna summit meeting of June 1979, followed the Vladivostok guidelines. It placed a ceiling of 2,400 (to be reduced to 2,250 in 1981) on the overall number of strategic missiles and bombers each side could possess, with a sublimit of 1,320 on the number that could have multiple warheads. As a result, although the arms race was slowed, each side retained vast quantities of ICBMs (intercontinental ballistic missiles), SLBMs (submarine-launched ballistic missiles), ASBMs (air-to-surface ballistic missiles), and MIRVs (multiple independently-targeted reentry vehicles).

The SALT II accord was destined to remain unratified. In the US Senate, a determined opposition was led by Senator Henry Jackson of Washington, who had blasted the treaty as "appeasement" even before it was signed. Moscow's continuing deployment of its new SS-20, a mobile triple-warhead intermediate-range missile that was not covered under SALT (because it could not reach the United States and was thus not considered "strategic"), raised concerns among many senators. So did the 1979 revolution in Iran, which cost the United States some of its best facilities for monitoring Russian compliance. In January 1980, following the Soviet invasion of Afghanistan, Carter asked the Senate to postpone further action on the treaty. Still, although it did not have Senate approval, both Washington and Moscow professed to abide by it up to and beyond its stated expiration at the end of 1985.

TREATY ON THE LIMITATION OF STRATEGIC OFFENSIVE ARMS (SALT II), 18 JUNE 1979

Article I
Each Party undertakes, in accordance with the provisions of this Treaty, to limit strategic offensive arms quantitatively and qualitatively, to exercise restraint in the development of new types of strategic offensive arms, and to adopt other measures provided for in this Treaty. . . .

Article III
1. Upon entry into force of this Treaty, each Party undertakes to limit ICBM launchers, SLBM launchers, heavy bombers, and ASBMs to an aggregate number not to exceed 2,400.
2. Each Party undertakes to limit, from January 1, 1981, strategic offensive arms referred to in paragraph 1 of this Article to an aggregate number not to exceed 2,250, and to initiate reductions of those arms which as of that date would be in excess of this aggregate number.
3. Within the aggregate numbers provided for in paragraphs 1 and 2 of this Article . . . , each Party has the right to determine the composition of these aggregates. . . .

Article V
1. Within the aggregate numbers provided for in paragraphs 1 and 2 of Article III, each Party undertakes to limit launchers of ICBMs and SLBMs equipped with MIRVs, ASBMs equipped with MIRVs, and heavy bombers equipped for cruise missiles capable of a range in excess of 600 kilometers to an aggregate number not to exceed 1,320.
2. Within the aggregate number provided for in paragraph 1 of this Article, each Party undertakes to limit launchers of ICBMs and SLBMs equipped with MIRVs and ASBMs equipped with MIRVs to an aggregate number not to exceed 1,200.
3. Within the aggregate number provided for in paragraph 2 of this Article, each Party undertakes to limit launchers of ICBMs equipped with MIRVs to an aggregate number not to exceed 820. . . .

Article XIV

The Parties undertake to begin, promptly after the entry into force of this Treaty, active negotiations with the objective of achieving, as soon as possible, agreement on further measures for the limitation and reduction of strategic arms. It is also the objective of the Parties to conclude well in advance of 1985 an agreement limiting strategic offensive arms to replace this Treaty upon its expiration.

Article XV

1. For the purpose of providing assurance of compliance with the provisions of this Treaty, each Party shall use national technical means of verification at its disposal in a manner consistent with generally recognized principles of international law.
2. Each Party undertakes not to interfere with the national technical means of verification of the other Party operating in accordance with paragraph 1 of this Article.
3. Each Party undertakes not to use deliberate concealment measures which impede verification by national technical means of compliance with the provisions of this Treaty. . . .

Article XVI

1. Each Party undertakes, before conducting each planned ICBM launch, to notify the other Party well in advance on a case-by-case basis that such a launch will occur, except for single ICBM launches from test ranges or from ICBM launcher deployment areas, which are not planned to extend beyond its national territory. . . .

Discussion Questions

1. Why did it take so long to negotiate the SALT II agreement?
2. What were the similarities and differences between this treaty and the SALT I agreement?
3. What impact would this treaty have on the arms race? What impact would it have on the size of the arsenals of the superpowers?
4. Why was there so much opposition to this treaty in the United States?
5. Why did the US Senate not ratify SALT II? Why would both superpowers adhere to the treaty even though it was not ratified?

V

THE RENEWAL OF
THE COLD WAR, 1979–1985

74

The Creation of an Islamic Republic in Iran, 1979

From 1953 through 1979, the Shah of Iran was a reliable ally of the United States in the Cold War. In return for massive amounts of US military aid, the Shah permitted the CIA and other US intelligence agencies to use Iranian territory to establish "listening posts" that were used to monitor events and conversations within the Soviet Union. But this close relationship, along with the materialism that enormous oil revenues brought to a strongly Islamic society, alienated many of the Shah's subjects. A number of developments in late 1978 and early 1979 fostered a revolution that ousted the Shah and brought to power his principal adversary, Ayatollah Ruhollah Khomeini, a Shiite Islamic cleric exiled since 1963.

Khomeini's triumph over the Shah was made possible by an unlikely coalition of well-educated, upper-middle-class Iranians, Islamic fundamentalists, and Communists. Once in power, Khomeini united the first two groups against the third, isolated and destroyed the Communists, and then instituted a theocratic "Islamic Republic" that quickly marginalized the middle classes that had initially supported the revolution. In the final year of his life, as Mikhail Gorbachev was initiating far-reaching changes within both the USSR and the Communist bloc, Khomeini wrote a most unusual letter to the Soviet leader. It was the only letter Khomeini ever wrote to the head of another nation, and it called upon Gorbachev to abandon Marxist atheism and convert the USSR to Islam.

EXCERPTS FROM KHOMEINI'S LETTER TO GORBACHEV, 1989

In the Name of Allah, the Compassionate, the Merciful

Your Excellency Mr. Gorbachev, Chairman of the Presidium of the Union of Soviet Socialist Republics

With due wishes for the happiness and prosperity of Your Excellency and the people of the Soviet Union.

Since your assumption of office there has been the impression that Your Excellency, in analyzing world political events, particularly those pertaining to the Soviet Union, have found yourself in a new era of reassessment, change and confrontation; and your boldness and initiative in dealing with the realities of the world is quite likely to bring about changes that would result in upsetting the equations of power dominating the world. I have therefore found it necessary to bring certain matters to your attention.

Even if your new approach and decisions are merely used as a means to overcome the party crisis, and to solve some of the problems confronting your people, your courage in reappraising a school of thought that has for decades enchained the revolutionary youth of the world behind its iron curtain is indeed worthy of praise. If, however, you are considering taking a further step forward, the first thing that will ensure your success is that you reevaluate your predecessors' policy of obliterating God and religion from society, a policy that has no doubt given the heaviest blow to the Soviet people. Rest assured that this is the only way whereby world problems can be dealt with realistically.

Of course it is possible that as a result of wrong economic policies of former communist authorities, the Western world, an illusory heaven, will appear to be fascinating; but the truth lies elsewhere. If you hope, at this juncture, to cut the economic Gordian knots of socialism and communism by appealing to the center of Western capitalism, you will, far from remedying any ill of your society, commit a mistake which those to come will have to erase. For, if Marxism has come to a deadlock in its social and economic policies, capitalism has also bogged down, in this as well as in other respects though in a different form.

Mr. Gorbachev,

Reality must be faced. The main problem confronting your country is not one of private ownership, freedom and economy; your problem is the absence of true faith in God, the very problem that has dragged, or will drag, the West to vulgarism and an impasse. Your main problem is the prolonged and futile war you have waged against God, the source of existence and creation.

Mr. Gorbachev,

It is clear to everybody that from now on communism will only have to be found in the museums of world political history, for Marxism cannot meet any of the real needs of mankind. Marxism is a materialistic ideology and materialism cannot bring humanity out of the crisis caused by a lack of belief in spirituality—the prime affliction of the human society in the East and the West alike.

Mr. Gorbachev,

You may have not in theory turned your back on certain aspects of Marxism—and may continue to profess your heartfelt loyalty to it in interviews—but you know that, in practice, the reality is not so. The leader of China struck the first blow to communism and you have struck the second and, apparently, final blow. Today we have no such thing as communism in the world. . . .

Mr. Gorbachev,

When after 70 years the call, "Allah is Great" and the testimony to the prophethood of the Seal of the Prophets, Muhammad (peace be upon him and his posterity) were heard from the minarets of the mosques in some of your Republics, all the followers of the pure Muhammadan Islam were moved to tears out of ecstasy. Therefore, I have found it necessary to remind you to reflect once again on the materialistic and theistic worldviews. Materialists consider sense to be the sole criterion of knowledge and are of the opinion that whatever cannot be known through the senses falls outside the realm of knowledge. They identify existence with matter and consider as nonexistent anything that has no material body. Inevitably, they regard the world of the unseen—God Almighty, Divine Revelation, Prophethood, and the Resurrection—as mere fiction. On the other hand, theists consider both sense and reason to be the criteria of knowledge, and maintain that whatever can be known through reason lies within the realm of knowledge, although it is not perceptible. To theists, therefore, existence is inclusive of both the unseen and the manifest. For a thing to exist it is not necessary to have a material body. In the same way that a material thing depends on an incorporeal thing, sensory perception is dependent on rational perception.

The Holy Qur'an reprobates the fundamentals of materialistic thought and, addressing those who say: "We shall never believe in thee until we see God manifestly," proclaims: "Vision comprehends Him not, and He comprehends all vision; and He is the Knower of subtleties, the Aware." I should not like to present here Qur'anic arguments concerning Divine Revelation, Prophethood and the Resurrection which from your point of view are debatable. In fact, I do not wish to entangle you in the twists and turns of philosophical arguments, particularly those of Islamic philosophy. I will content myself by presenting one or two simple, intuitive examples of which even politicians can avail themselves.

It is self-evident that matter, whatever its nature, has no awareness of self. Consider a stone statue: each side is ignorant of the other side, whereas human beings and animals, we clearly observe, are aware of their surroundings. They know where they are and are aware of what goes on around them. There must be, then, an element in men and animals that transcends matter and is separate from it, living beyond the life of matter. Intrinsically, man seeks to attain absolute perfection. He strives, as you well know, for absolute power over the world; he is not attached to any power that is defective. If he has the entire world at his command, he naturally feels inclined to have command of another world once he is informed of its existence. No matter how learned a person may be if he learns of some other branch of knowledge, he naturally feels inclined to attain mastery of that branch of knowledge as well. Therefore, there must be some Absolute Power and Absolute Knowledge to which man is attached. It is God we all seek although we may not be aware of it. Man strives to attain Absolute Truth, so that he may be annihilated in God. Basically, the desire for eternal life that is inherent in every individual is proof of the existence of an Eternal World to which destruction cannot find its way. . . .

Mr. Gorbachev,

After mentioning these problems and preliminary points, let me call on you to study Islam earnestly, not because Islam and the Muslims may need you but because Islam has exalted universal values which can bring comfort and salvation to all nations and remove the basic problems of mankind. A true understanding of Islam may forever release you from the problem of Afghanistan and other similar involvements. We treat Muslims of the world as Muslims of our own country and will ever share in their destiny. . . .

In conclusion, I declare outright that the Islamic Republic of Iran as the greatest and most powerful base of the Islamic world can easily fill the vacuum of religious faith in your society. In any case, our country, as in the past, honors good neighborhood and bilateral relations.

Peace be upon those who follow the guidance.

Rūhullāh al-Mūsawī al-Khomeinī

Discussion Questions

1. How did Khomeini identify the central problem facing the Soviet Union?
2. Why did Khomeini believe that Marxism was inadequate to meet the real needs of humanity?
3. How did Khomeini contrast the materialistic and spiritual worldviews?
4. What advice did Khomeini give Gorbachev on spiritual matters?
5. Why did Khomeini caution Gorbachev against adopting a Western worldview?

75

The Euromissile Controversy, 1979

IN 1977 THE STRATEGIC BALANCE of forces in Europe was tested when the USSR deployed new SS-20 nuclear missiles. These intermediate-range missiles carried three warheads each and could be moved from place to place and fired at Western European targets from mobile launchers. Since the SS-20 could not reach the United States, Moscow contended that its deployment did nothing to alter the balance of forces between the superpowers. Privately, many American leaders agreed. But the Soviet move alarmed Europeans who might be the targets of those missiles, and this gave Washington an opportunity to reassert its leadership of NATO after more than a decade of US absorption in Southeast Asian affairs. The United States suggested that outmoded Pershing IA missiles deployed in West Germany be replaced by modern two-stage Pershing IIs and Tomahawk cruise missiles, both of which could reach targets in the USSR.

The Soviet reaction was negative and swift. From Moscow's perspective, a NATO decision to station missiles in West Germany that could reach the USSR in six to twelve minutes would destabilize the strategic balance. NATO might argue that since both SS-20s and Pershing IIs were intermediate-range missiles, the balance remained, but to the Soviets this ignored the fact that Pershing missiles in Germany would be able to hit them, while their SS-20s could not hit America. Soviet leader Brezhnev denounced the impending NATO deployment in a speech in East Berlin in October 1979. Two months later NATO announced a "dual track" policy: The missiles would be deployed as planned, but not until 1983; in the meantime, negotiations could begin with the objective of reducing not only intermediate range but also intercontinental nuclear systems. However, in the hostile climate engendered by the Soviet invasion of Afghanistan (Document 76), those talks went nowhere, and the NATO missiles were deployed in 1983.

A. BREZHNEV'S CONDEMNATION
OF NATO'S PLANS, 6 OCTOBER 1979

The dangerous plans for the deployment of new types of American missile nuclear weapons in the territory of Western Europe—about which Western propaganda is trumpeting already now—give cause for serious concern. To put it straight, implementation of these designs would change essentially the strategic situation on the continent. Their aim is to upset the balance of forces that has taken shape in Europe and to try to insure military superiority for the NATO bloc.

As to military superiority—that we shall see. The Socialist countries would not, of course, watch indifferently the efforts of the NATO militarists. We would have in such a case to take the necessary extra steps to strengthen our security. There would be no other way out left for us. But one thing is absolutely clear: realization of NATO plans would inevitably aggravate the situation in Europe and vitiate in many respects the international atmosphere in general.

It is no secret that the Federal Republic of Germany, alongside of the USA, is assigned not the least part in the preparation of these dangerous plans.

Frankly speaking, those who shape the policy of that country are facing a very dangerous choice. They will have to decide which is the best for the FRG: to help strengthen peace in Europe and develop peaceful, mutually beneficial cooperation among European states in the spirit of good neighborliness and growing mutual confidence, or to contribute to a new aggravation of the situation in Europe and the world by deploying in its territory American missile nuclear arms spearheaded against the USSR and its allies.

It is clear that in this latter case, the position of the FRG itself would considerably worsen. It is not hard to see what consequences the FRG would have in store for itself if these new weapons were to be put to use by their owners one day.

The above said also applies, of course, to other European NATO countries which would be "lucky" enough to have American medium-range missile nuclear arms deployed in their territories.

As for the Soviet Union, I repeat again and again that we do not seek military superiority. We have never intended and do not intend to threaten any state or a group of states. Our strategic doctrine is purely defensive in nature. The assertions that the Soviet Union is building up its military might in the European continent above its defense needs have nothing in common with reality. This is a deliberate deception of the broad public.

As chairman of the Defense Council of the USSR, I am most definitely stating that the number of medium-range carriers of nuclear arms on the territory of the European part of the Soviet Union has not been increased by a single missile, by a single plane during the past 10 years. On the contrary, the number of launchers of medium-range missiles and also the yield of the nuclear charges of these missiles have even been somewhat decreased. The number of medium-range bombers, too, has diminished. As to the territory of other states, the Soviet Union does not deploy such means there at all. It is already for a number of years that we are not increasing the number of our troops stationed in Central Europe as well.

I will say more. We are prepared to reduce the number of medium-range nuclear means deployed in western areas of the Soviet Union as compared to the present level, but of course, only in the event if no additional medium-range nuclear means are deployed in Western Europe.

I also want to confirm solemnly that the Soviet Union will never use nuclear arms against those states that renounce the production and acquisition of such arms and do not have them on their territory.

Motivated by a sincere desire to take out of the impasse the efforts of many years to achieve military détente in Europe, to show an example of transition from words to real deeds, we have decided, in agreement with the leadership of the GDR and after consultations with other member-states of the Warsaw Treaty, to unilaterally reduce the number of Soviet troops in Central Europe. Up to 20,000 Soviet servicemen, 1,000 tanks and also a certain amount of other military hardware will be withdrawn from the territory of the German Democratic Republic in the course of the next 12 months.

We are convinced that this new concrete manifestation of the peaceableness and good will of the Soviet Union and its allies will be approved by the peoples of Europe and the whole world. We call upon the governments of NATO countries to properly assess the initiatives of Socialist states and to follow our good example.

The Soviet Union comes out for a further expansion of measures of trust in Europe. In particular, we are prepared to reach agreement that notification about big exercises of ground forces, provided for by the Helsinki Final Act, be made even earlier and not from the level of 25,000 men, as is the case now, but from a smaller one, for instance, from the level of 20,000 men. We also are prepared, on the basis of reciprocity, not to conduct military exercises involving more than 40,000 to 50,000 men. . . .

Consideration could be given also to other ideas directed at strengthening trust between states, at lessening the danger of the outbreak of war in Europe. We continue to regard a European conference held on the political level as the most suitable place for discussing a broad complex of measures of military détente in Europe. . . .

Lying ahead, as is known, are also important talks on SALT III. We are for commencing them immediately after the entry into force of the SALT II treaty. Within the framework of these talks we agree to discuss the possibilities of limiting not only intercontinental but also other types of armaments, but with due account, of course, for all related factors and strict observance of the principle of the equal security of the sides.

B. NATO COMMUNIQUÉ ON
"DUAL TRACK" APPROACH, 12 DECEMBER 1979

1. At a special meeting of the Foreign and Defense Ministers in Brussels on 12 December 1979:

2. Ministers recalled the May 1978 Summit where governments expressed the political resolve to meet the challenges to their security posed by the continuing momentum of the Warsaw Pact military build-up.

3. The Warsaw Pact has over the years developed a large and growing capability in nuclear systems that directly threaten Western Europe and have a strategic significance for the Alliance in Europe. This situation has been especially aggravated over the last few years by Soviet decisions to implement programs modernizing and expanding their long-range nuclear capability substantially. In particular, they have developed the SS-20 missile, which offers significant improvements over previous systems in providing greater accuracy, more mobility, and greater range, as well as having multiple warheads, and the Backfire bomber, which has a much better performance than other Soviet aircraft deployed hitherto in a theater role. During this period, while the Soviet Union has been reinforcing its superiority in LRTNF [long range theatre nuclear forces] both quantitatively and qualitatively, Western LRTNF capabilities have remained static. Indeed these forces are increasing in age and vulnerability and do not include land-based, long-range theater nuclear missile systems.

4. At the same time, the Soviets have also undertaken a modernization and expansion of their shorter-range TNF [theatre nuclear forces] and greatly improved the overall quality of their conventional forces. These developments took place against the background of increasing Soviet inter-continental capabilities and achievement of parity in inter-continental capability with the United States.

5. These trends have prompted serious concern within the Alliance, because, if they were to continue, Soviet superiority in theater nuclear systems could undermine the stability achieved in inter-continental systems and cast doubt on the credibility of the Alliance's deterrent strategy by highlighting the gap in the spectrum of NATO's available nuclear response to aggression.

6. Ministers noted that these recent developments require concrete actions on the part of the Alliance if NATO's strategy of flexible response is to remain credible. After intensive consideration . . . , Ministers concluded that the overall interest of the Alliance would best be served by pursuing two parallel and complementary approaches of TNF modernization and arms control.

7. Accordingly Ministers have decided to modernize NATO's LRTNF by the deployment in Europe of US ground-launched systems comprising 108 Pershing II launchers, which would replace existing US Pershing I-A, and 464 Ground Launched Cruise Missiles (GLCM), all with single warheads. . . .

9. Ministers consider that . . . , taking account of the expansion of Soviet LRTNF capabilities of concern to NATO, arms control efforts to achieve a more stable overall nuclear balance at lower levels of nuclear weapons on both sides should therefore now include certain US and Soviet long-range theater nuclear systems. This would reflect previous Western suggestions to include such Soviet and US systems in arms control negotiations and more recent expressions by Soviet President Brezhnev of willingness to do so. Ministers fully support the decision taken by the United States following consultations within the Alliance to negotiate arms limitations on LRTNF and to propose to the USSR to begin negotiations as soon as possible along the following lines. . . .

A. Any future limitations on US systems principally designed for theater missions should be accompanied by appropriate limitations on Soviet theater systems.

B. Limitations on US and Soviet long-range theater nuclear systems should be negotiated bilaterally in the SALT III framework in a step-by-step approach.

   C. The immediate objective of these negotiations should be the establishment of agreed limitations on US and Soviet land-based long-range theater nuclear missile systems.

   D. Any agreed limitations on these systems must be consistent with the principle of equality between the sides. . . .

   E. Any agreed limitations must be adequately verifiable. . . .

11. The Ministers have decided to pursue these two parallel and complementary approaches in order to avert an arms race in Europe caused by the Soviet TNF buildup, yet preserve the viability of NATO's strategy of deterrence and defense and thus maintain the security of its member states. A modernization decision, including a commitment to deployments, is necessary to meet NATO's deterrence and defense needs, to provide a credible response to unilateral Soviet TNF deployments, and to provide the foundation for the pursuit of serious negotiations on TNF. Success of arms control in constraining the Soviet build-up can enhance Alliance security, modify the scale of NATO's TNF requirements, and promote stability and détente in Europe. . . .

Discussion Questions

1. Did Soviet deployment of SS-20s alter the strategic balance between the USSR and the United States? Why or why not?
2. Moscow considered the NATO deployment equivalent to Khrushchev's decision to place missiles in Cuba in 1962. Is this a reasonable comparison? Why or why not?
3. What did Brezhnev mean when he spoke of possible "consequences" for West Germany?
4. What did Brezhnev offer in return for a NATO decision not to deploy Pershing II missiles?
5. What reasons did NATO give in support of its contention that the SS-20 deployment altered the strategic balance?

76

The Soviet Invasion of Afghanistan, December 1979

B Y LATE 1979 DÉTENTE WAS IN critical condition. In Europe, NATO's decision to upgrade its missiles in response to Moscow's SS-20 deployment (Document 75) cast a pall over East–West relations. In Iran the seizure of American hostages triggered a protracted crisis that would distract and dominate Washington for the next fourteen months. In the US Senate, hopes faded for approval of the SALT II agreement (Document 73). But the death blow came in late December, when the USSR began a massive invasion of neighboring Afghanistan.

The crisis in Afghanistan had been in the making for months. In April 1978 a Communist coup there had brought to power a pro-Soviet regime led by Nur Muhammad Taraki. By the fall of 1979, however, an extreme faction under Hafizullah Amin had overthrown Taraki and, in trying to force radical socialism upon the Muslim Afghans, had triggered an anti-Communist rebellion. As the situation deteriorated, Moscow decided to move. During the last week of 1979, Soviet troops invaded Afghanistan, killed Amin, and installed a moderate socialist regime led by Babrak Karmal. By January 1980 more than eighty-five thousand Soviet troops were in Afghanistan, and for the next nine years the USSR found itself bogged down in a debilitating war against fiercely independent rebels.

The Soviet intervention triggered a vehement reaction in the West. President Carter, who had dedicated much effort to improving relations with Moscow, felt outraged and betrayed. First, he issued a statement denouncing the invasion and dispatched a protest note to Soviet leader Brezhnev. Then, in a revealing interview, he declared that events in Afghanistan had caused him to rethink his entire attitude toward the USSR. In January 1980 he effectively withdrew the SALT II agreement from Senate consideration and announced an embargo on shipments of grain and transfers of electronic technology to the USSR. His actions and words, and Brezhnev's angry response, left little doubt that the era of détente was over.

A. CARTER'S STATEMENT ON IRAN
AND AFGHANISTAN, 28 DECEMBER 1979

Thank you. Secretary of State Vance will proceed to the United Nations tomorrow to press the world's case against Iran in order to obtain the speediest possible release of American hostages in accordance with demands which have already been made earlier by the United Nations Security Council and the International Court of Justice. . . .

Another serious development which has caused increased concern about peace and stability in the same region of the world is the recent Soviet military intervention in Afghanistan, which has now resulted in the overthrow of the established Government and the execution of the President of that country.

Such gross interference in the internal affairs of Afghanistan is in blatant violation of accepted international rules of behavior. This is the third occasion since World War II that the Soviet Union has moved militarily to assert control over one of its neighbors, and this is the first such venture into a Moslem country by the Soviet Union since the Soviet occupation of Iranian Azerbaijan in the 1940's. The Soviet action is a major matter of concern to the entire international community.

Soviet efforts to justify this action on the basis of the United Nations Charter are a perversion of the United Nations. They should be rejected immediately by all its members. I have discussed this serious matter personally today with several other heads of government, all of whom agree that the Soviet action is a grave threat to peace. I will be sending the Deputy Secretary of State to Europe this weekend to meet with representatives of several other nations to discuss how the world community might respond to this unwarranted Soviet behavior.

Soviet military action beyond its own borders gives rise to the most fundamental questions pertaining to international stability, and such close and extensive consultation[s] between ourselves and with our allies are urgently needed. Thank you very much.

B. CARTER'S INTERVIEW CONCERNING THE
SOVIET RESPONSE TO HIS PROTEST NOTE ON
THE INVASION OF AFGHANISTAN, 31 DECEMBER 1979

A. He [Brezhnev] responded in what I consider to be an inadequate way. He claimed that he had been invited by the Afghan Government to come in and protect Afghanistan from some outside third nation threat. This was obviously false because the person that he claimed invited him in, President

Amin, was murdered or assassinated after the Soviets pulled their coup. He also claimed that they would remove their forces from Afghanistan as soon as the situation should be stabilized and the outside threat to Afghanistan was eliminated. So that was the tone of his message to me, which, as I say, was completely inadequate and completely misleading.

Q. Well, he's lying, isn't he, Mr. President?

A. He is not telling the facts accurately, that's correct.

Q. Have you changed your perception of the Russians in the time that you've been here? You started out, it seemed to a great many people, believing that if you expressed your good will and demonstrated it that they would reciprocate.

A. My opinion of the Russians has changed most drastically in the last week than even the previous two and a half years before that. It's only now dawning on the world the magnitude of the action that the Soviets undertook in invading Afghanistan. This is a circumstance that I think is now causing even former close friends and allies of the Soviet Union to re-examine their opinion of what the Soviets might have in mind.

And I think it's imperative . . . that in the next few days when we, after we consult with one another, that the leaders of the world make it clear to the Soviets that they cannot have taken this action to violate world peace not only in that region but throughout the world without paying severe political consequences. And what we will do about it I cannot yet say.

But to repeat myself, this action of the Soviets has made a more dramatic change in my own opinion of what the Soviets' ultimate goals are than anything they've done in the previous time I've been in office.

Q. But what we and the other nations allied with us do will involve more than stiff notes of protest?

A. Yes it will.

Q. It will? Action will be taken?

A. Yes. . . .

C. BREZHNEV'S EXPLANATION OF THE
SOVIET ROLE IN AFGHANISTAN, 12 JANUARY 1980

It has been clear for some time that the leading circles of the United States and of some other NATO countries have embarked on a course hostile to the cause of détente, a course of spiraling the arms race and leading to a growth of the war danger. . . .

Today the opponents of peace and détente are trying to speculate on the events in Afghanistan. Mountains of lies are being built up around these events and a shameless anti-Soviet campaign is being mounted. What has really happened in Afghanistan?

A revolution took place there in April 1978. The Afghan people took its destiny into its hands and embarked on the road of independence and freedom. As it has always been in history, the forces of the past ganged up against the revolution. The people of Afghanistan, of course, could have coped with them itself. But from the very first days of the revolution it encountered an external aggression, rude interference from outside into its internal affairs.

Thousands and tens of thousands of insurgents, armed and trained abroad, whole armed units were sent into the territory of Afghanistan. In effect, imperialism together with its accomplices launched an undeclared war against revolutionary Afghanistan.

Afghanistan persistently demanded an end to the aggression, that it be allowed to build its new life in peace. Resisting the external aggression, the Afghan leadership . . . repeatedly asked the Soviet Union for assistance. On our part, we warned those concerned that if the aggression would not be stopped we would not abandon the Afghan people at a time of trial. As is known, we stand by what we say. . . .

The unceasing armed intervention, the well advanced plot by external forces of reaction created a real threat that Afghanistan would lose its independence and be turned into an imperialist military bridgehead on our country's southern border.

In other words, the time came when we no longer could fail to respond to the friendly request of the Government of friendly Afghanistan. To have acted otherwise would have meant leaving Afghanistan a prey to imperialism, allowing the aggressive forces to repeat in that country what they had succeeded in doing, for instance, in Chile where the people's freedom was drowned in blood. To act otherwise would have meant to watch passively the origination on our southern border of a seat of serious danger to the security of the Soviet state. . . .

It was no simple decision for us to send Soviet military contingents to Afghanistan. But the Party's Central Committee and the Soviet Government acted in full awareness of their responsibility and took into account the entire sum total of circumstances. The only task set to the Soviet contingents is to assist the Afghans in repulsing the aggression from outside. They will be fully withdrawn from Afghanistan once the causes that made the Afghan leadership request their introduction disappear.

It goes without saying that there has been no Soviet "intervention" or "aggression" at all. There is another thing: we are helping the new Afghanistan on the request of its Government to defend the national independence, freedom and honor of its country from armed aggressive actions from outside. . . .

Finally, the entire sum total of the American Administration's steps in connection with the events in Afghanistan—the freezing of the SALT II treaty, refusal to deliver to the USSR a whole number of commodities, including grain, in accordance with some already concluded contracts, the termination of talks with the Soviet Union on a number of questions of bilateral relations, and so on, shows that Washington again, like decades ago, is trying to speak with us in the language of the Cold War. . . .

Discussion Questions

1. Why was Carter outraged by the Soviet invasion of Afghanistan? What impact did it have on his attitude toward the USSR?
2. Why did Carter respond so forcefully? To what extent were his actions justified?
3. What reasons did Brezhnev give for Soviet actions? What other reasons might he have had? How did his description of events in Afghanistan contrast with Carter's?
4. Why was the invasion of Afghanistan a fatal blow to détente?

77

The Carter Doctrine, January 1980

PRESIDENT CARTER'S RESPONSE to the Soviet invasion of Afghanistan was dictated not only by his personal outrage but also by his fear that Moscow was moving to establish a presence on the Indian Ocean near the Persian Gulf, where it could threaten the vital oil shipments on which the West depended. Since his tenure in office had been marked by energy shortages and rising oil prices, the president was acutely sensitive to any threat that might endanger US energy supplies. He thus moved resolutely to preclude Soviet expansion into this region. On 23 January 1980, in his annual state of the union address, he declared that the Persian Gulf would henceforth be considered a vital US interest and that America would use military force if necessary to prevent an outside power from gaining control there.

This declaration, soon called the Carter Doctrine, effectively served notice that the United States would go to war if necessary to protect the Persian Gulf from outside interference by anyone, including the USSR. It was followed by a concerted effort to thwart the Soviets in Afghanistan, including a global buildup of US forces, increased military aid to the neighboring nation of Pakistan, and surreptitious assistance to the anti-Soviet Afghan rebels.

EXCERPT FROM CARTER'S STATE OF THE UNION ADDRESS, 23 JANUARY 1980

. . . Since the end of the Second World War, America has led other nations in meeting the challenge of mounting Soviet power. This has not been a simple or a static relationship. Between us there has been cooperation—there has been competition—and at times there has been confrontation. . . .

But now the Soviet Union has taken a radical and an aggressive new step. It's using its great military power against a relatively defenseless nation. The implications of the Soviet invasion of Afghanistan could pose the most serious threat to the peace since the Second World War.

The vast majority of nations on earth have condemned this latest Soviet attempt to extend its colonial domination of others and have demanded the immediate withdrawal of Soviet troops. The Moslem world is especially and justifiably outraged by this aggression against an Islamic people. No action of a world power has ever been so quickly and so overwhelmingly condemned.

But verbal condemnation is not enough. The Soviet Union must pay a concrete price for their aggression. While this invasion continues, we and the other nations of the world cannot continue business as usual with the Soviet Union.

That's why the United States has imposed stiff economic penalties on the Soviet Union. I will not issue any permits for Soviet ships to fish in the coastal waters of the United States. I've cut Soviet access to high technology equipment and to agricultural products. I've limited other commerce with the Soviet Union, and I've asked our allies and friends to join with us in restraining their own trade with the Soviets and not to replace our own embargoed items. And I have notified the Olympic Committee that with Soviet invading forces in Afghanistan, neither the American people nor I will support sending an Olympic team to Moscow.

The Soviet Union is going to have to answer some basic questions: Will it help promote a more stable international environment in which its own legitimate, peaceful concerns can be pursued? Or will it continue to expand its military power far beyond its genuine security needs, and use that power for colonial conquest?

The Soviet Union must realize that its decision to use military force in Afghanistan will be costly to every political and economic relationship it values.

The region which is now threatened by Soviet troops in Afghanistan is of great strategic importance. It contains more than two-thirds of the world's exportable oil. The Soviet effort to dominate Afghanistan has brought Soviet military forces to within 300 miles of the Indian Ocean and close to the Straits of Hormuz—a waterway through which most of the world's oil must flow. The Soviet Union is now attempting to consolidate a strategic position therefore that poses a grave threat to the free movement of Middle East oil.

The situation demands careful thought, steady nerves and resolute action—not only for this year, but for many years to come. It demands collective efforts to meet this new threat to security in the Persian Gulf and in Southwest Asia. It demands the participation of those who rely on oil from the Middle East and who are concerned with global peace and stability. And it demands consultation and close cooperation with countries in the area which might be threatened.

Meeting this challenge will take national will, diplomatic and political wisdom, economic sacrifice and, of course, military capability. We must call on the best that is in us to preserve the security of this crucial region.

Let our position be absolutely clear: An attempt by any outside force to gain control of the Persian Gulf region will be regarded as an assault on the vital interests of the United States of America. And such an assault will be repelled by any means necessary, including military force. . . .

Discussion Questions

1. What motives did Carter see behind the Soviet invasion of Afghanistan? What justification did he give for the steps he was taking?
2. Why was Carter so concerned about a threat to the Persian Gulf? Why did he consider it a vital American interest?
3. How did the Carter Doctrine compare to the Nixon Doctrine of 1969 (Documents 59A–B)? How do you account for the differences?
4. To what extent was Carter justified in taking the actions he did? Why or why not?
5. How would you expect the Soviets to react to the measures announced by Carter? Why would they react that way?

78

Reagan's Anti-Soviet Rhetoric, 1981–1983

IN NOVEMBER 1980, against the backdrop of the Soviet-Afghan War, the ongoing hostage crisis in Iran, and a faltering US economy, presidential elections were held in the United States. Rejecting the reelection bid of President Jimmy Carter, whom many blamed for the apparent decline of US power and prestige, Americans instead chose as their president a committed Cold Warrior and ardent opponent of détente.

The inauguration of Ronald Reagan in January 1981 brought to power a man who not only was passionately anti-Communist but who also characterized the Cold War as a conflict between the forces of good and evil. As a result, the international climate became even more contentious during his first few years in office. Deeply distrustful of Moscow, the new president intensified the arms race and used his notable rhetorical skills to depict the US buildup as a crusade against the powers of darkness. In his very first press conference, Reagan complained that Americans were at a disadvantage because the Soviets were ready to "commit any crime; to lie; to cheat" in order to advance their cause. Two years later, in the most widely quoted speech of his presidency, directed to a group of Protestant ministers, he characterized the USSR as an "evil empire" and the "focus of evil in the modern world." He went on to proclaim, almost prophetically, "Communism is another sad, bizarre chapter in history whose last pages even now are being written."

A. EXCERPT FROM PRESIDENT REAGAN'S
FIRST PRESS CONFERENCE, 29 JANUARY 1981

Q. Mr. President, what do you see as the long-range intentions of the Soviet Union? Do you think . . . the Kremlin is bent on world domination that might lead to a continuation of the cold war? Or do you think that under other circumstances détente is possible?

A. Well, so far détente's been a one-way street the Soviet Union has used to pursue its own aims. I don't have to think of an answer as to what I think their intentions are: They have repeated it. I know of no leader of the Soviet Union, since the revolution and including the present leadership, that has not more than once repeated . . . their determination that their goal must be the promotion of world revolution and a one world Socialist or Communist state—whichever word you want to use.

Now, as long as they do that and as long as they, at the same time, have openly and publicly declared that the only morality they recognize is what will further their cause: meaning they reserve unto themselves the right to commit any crime; to lie; to cheat, in order to obtain that and that is moral, not immoral, and we operate on a different set of standards, I think when you do business with them—even at a détente—you keep that in mind.

B. EXCERPT FROM REAGAN'S
"EVIL EMPIRE" SPEECH, 8 MARCH 1983

During my first press conference as president . . . I pointed out that as good Marxist-Leninists the Soviet leaders have openly and publicly declared that the only morality they recognize is that which will further their cause, which is world revolution. I think I should point out I was only quoting Lenin, their guiding spirit, who said in 1920 that they repudiate all morality that proceeds from supernatural ideas or ideas that are outside class conceptions; morality is entirely subordinate to the interests of class war; and everything is moral that is necessary for the annihilation of the old exploiting social order and for uniting the proletariat.

I think the refusal of many influential people to accept this elementary fact of Soviet doctrine illustrates a historical reluctance to see totalitarian powers for what they are. We saw this phenomenon in the 1930s; we see it too often today.

This does not mean we should isolate ourselves and refuse to seek an understanding with them. I intend to do everything I can to persuade them of our peaceful intent; to remind them that it was the West that refused to use its nuclear monopoly in the forties and fifties for territorial gain and which now proposes fifty percent cuts in strategic ballistic missiles and the elimination of an entire class of land-based, intermediate-range nuclear missiles.

At the same time, however, they must be made to understand we will never compromise our principles and standards. We will never give away our freedom. We will never abandon our belief in God. And we will never stop searching for a genuine peace. But we can assure none of these things America stands for through the so-called nuclear freeze solutions proposed by some. The truth is that a freeze now would be a very dangerous fraud, for that is merely the illusion of peace. The reality is that we must find peace through strength. . . .

Let us pray for the salvation of all those who live in totalitarian darkness, pray they will discover the joy of knowing God. But until they do, let us be aware that while they preach the supremacy of the state, declare its omnipotence over individual man, and predict its eventual domination of all peoples of the earth—they are the focus of evil in the modern world. . . .

If history teaches anything, it teaches: simple-minded appeasement or wishful thinking about our adversaries is folly—it means the betrayal of our past, the squandering of our freedom. So, I urge you to speak out against those who would place the United States in a position of military and moral inferiority. . . . In your discussions of the nuclear freeze proposals, I urge you to beware the temptation of pride—the temptation of blithely declaring yourselves above it all and label both sides equally at fault, to ignore the facts of history and the aggressive impulses of an evil empire, to simply call the arms race a giant misunderstanding and thereby remove yourself from the struggle between right and wrong, good and evil. . . .

I believe we shall rise to the challenge. I believe that Communism is another sad, bizarre chapter in history whose last pages even now are being written. . . .

Discussion Questions

1. How did Reagan's Cold War approach differ from that of the previous three presidents? From Reagan's perspective, what had been wrong with détente?
2. Why was Reagan's rhetoric so appealing to many Americans?
3. According to Reagan, why were Americans at a disadvantage in dealing with the USSR? What might they do to overcome this disadvantage?
4. What arguments did Reagan use to try to persuade his listeners that the USSR was an evil empire, and that the Cold War was thus a contest between good and evil? Why do you think he chose to deliver this speech to a group of Christian ministers?
5. What were the advantages and disadvantages of Reagan's anti-Soviet rhetoric? What implications did Reagan's rhetoric have for US foreign policy?

79

Reagan's Arms Control Proposals, November 1981

W HEN RONALD REAGAN FIRST TOOK OFFICE, arms control was not one of his priorities. Unlike his immediate predecessors, the new president was deeply skeptical of the value of weapons treaties. Indeed, he and his advisors saw them as harmful to US interests, claiming that they reduced Western vigilance, solidified Moscow's gains, fostered Soviet cheating, and eased pressure on the overstressed Russian economy. So the Reagan team focused instead on enlarging the US arsenal, investing billions in new weapons systems.

The resulting escalation of the arms race, however, combined with the president's strident rhetoric, heightened anxieties and led to widespread criticism. In November 1981, to alleviate such fears and objections, he put forth his own arms control proposals. In the arena of intermediate-range nuclear forces (INF), he offered what came to be called the "zero option": NATO would cancel its installation of new missiles in Europe (Document 75B) if Moscow would eliminate all its intermediate-range missiles, especially the multiple-warhead mobile SS-20s. In the realm of strategic arms, he proposed replacing SALT with START (Strategic Arms *Reduction* Talks), thus changing the focus from mere limitation to deep and sweeping cuts. Both the Kremlin and Reagan's critics saw these as public relations gimmicks rather than serious proposals, since they required the Soviets to make disproportionate sacrifices. Still, in the long run, they helped pave the way for the INF Treaty of 1987 (Document 88) and the START agreement of 1991 (Document 95).

EXCERPT FROM REAGAN'S ADDRESS
ON ARMS REDUCTION, 18 NOVEMBER 1981

. . . Now let me turn now to our hopes for arms control negotiations. There's a tendency to make this entire subject overly complex; I want to be clear and concise. I told you of the letter I wrote to President Brezhnev last April? Well, I've just sent another message to the Soviet leadership.

It's a simple, straightforward yet historic message. The United States proposes the mutual reduction of conventional, intermediate-range nuclear and strategic forces. Specifically, I have proposed a four-point agenda to achieve this objective. . . .

The first and most important point concerns the Geneva negotiations. As part of the 1979 two-track decision, NATO made a commitment to seek arms control negotiations with the Soviet Union on intermediate-range nuclear forces. . . . We're now ready to set forth our proposal.

I have informed President Brezhnev that when our delegation travels to the negotiations on intermediate-range land-based nuclear missiles in Geneva on the 30th of this month, my representatives will present the following proposal:

The United States is prepared to cancel its deployment of Pershing 2 and ground-launched missiles if the Soviets will dismantle their SS-20, SS-4 and SS-5 missiles. This would be an historic step. With Soviet agreement, we could together substantially reduce the dread threat of nuclear war which hangs over the people of Europe. This, like the first footstep on the moon, would be a giant step for mankind.

Now we intend to negotiate in good faith and go to Geneva willing to listen to and consider the proposals of our Soviet counterparts. But let me call to your attention the background against which our proposal is made. During the past six years, while the United States deployed no new intermediate-range missiles and withdrew 1,000 nuclear warheads from Europe, the Soviet Union deployed 750 warheads on mobile, accurate ballistic missiles. They now have 1,100 warheads on the SS-20's, SS-4's and 5's. And the United States has no comparable missiles. . . .

As we look to the future of the negotiations, it's also important to address certain Soviet claims which, left unrefuted, could become critical barriers to real progress in arms control. The Soviets assert that a balance of intermediate-range nuclear forces already exists; that assertion is wrong. By any objective measure . . . the Soviet Union has developed an increasing, overwhelming advantage. They now enjoy a superiority on the order of 6 to 1. . . .

Now Soviet spokesmen have suggested that moving their SS-20's behind the Ural Mountains will remove the threat to Europe. Well, . . . the SS-20's, even if deployed behind the Urals, will have a range that puts almost all of Western Europe . . . , all of the Middle East, all of Northern Africa—all within range of these missiles, which, incidentally, are mobile and can be moved on shorter notice. . . .

The second proposal that I've made to President Brezhnev concerns strategic weapons. . . .

. . . I have informed President Brezhnev that we will seek to negotiate substantial reductions in nuclear arms, which would result in levels that are equal and verifiable. Our approach with verification will be to emphasize openness and creativity rather than the secrecy and suspicion which have undermined confidence in arms control in the past.

While we can hope to benefit from work done over the past decade in strategic arms negotiations, let us agree to do more than simply begin where these previous efforts left off. We can and should attempt major qualitative and quantitative progress. Only such progress can fulfill the hopes of our own people and the rest of the world. And let us see how far we can go in achieving truly substantial reductions in our strategic arsenals.

To symbolize this fundamental change in direction, we will call these negotiations START—Strategic Arms Reduction Talks.

The third proposal I've made to the Soviet Union is that we act to achieve equality at lower levels of conventional forces in Europe. The defense needs of the Soviet Union hardly call for maintaining more combat divisions in East Germany today than were in the whole allied invasion force that landed in Normandy on D-Day. The Soviet Union could make no more convincing contribution to peace in Europe and in the world than by agreeing to reduce its conventional forces significantly and constrain the potential for sudden aggression.

Finally, I have pointed out to President Brezhnev that to maintain peace we must reduce the risks of surprise attack and the chance of war arising out of uncertainty or miscalculation. I am renewing our proposal for a conference to develop effective measures that would reduce these dangers.

At the current Madrid meeting of the Conference on Security and Co-operation in Europe we're laying the foundation for a western-proposed conference on disarmament in Europe. This conference would discuss new measures to enhance stability and security in Europe. . . . I urge the Soviet Union to join us and many other nations who are ready to launch this important enterprise.

All of these proposals are based on the same fair-minded principles: substantial, militarily significant reduction in forces, equal ceiling for similar types of forces, and adequate provisions for verification.

My Administration, our country and I are committed to achieving arms reductions agreements based on these principles.

Discussion Questions

1. Why was Reagan initially reluctant to enter arms control talks with Moscow? Why did he want to build up the US arsenal before holding such talks?

2. How did Reagan's approach to arms control differ from that of his predecessors?
3. Why did he advance the "zero-option"? Why did he change SALT to START? Why would Moscow object to these proposals?
4. Why did he propose deep cuts in conventional forces in Europe? Why would Moscow object?
5. To what extent do you think Reagan's proposals were serious? To what extent do you think they were they propaganda ploys? How do you think he expected Moscow to respond?

80

The Polish Imposition of Martial Law, December 1981

IN 1981, AS THE REAGAN REVOLUTION was transforming US policy, and as Brezhnev's declining years were being blighted by economic stagnation and the Afghan war, a dangerous situation developed in Poland. The preceding year, a series of strikes, triggered by severe economic crisis, had led to formation of an independent workers' trade union movement called Solidarity. As the union grew in size and audacity, it began organizing mass demonstrations and pushing for political as well as economic changes.

As the situation deteriorated and the Communist government began to lose control, the Soviet military started staging maneuvers near the Polish border. For a while it looked as if the USSR would invade, as it had in Hungary in 1956 and Czechoslovakia in 1968. But in December 1981, after unsuccessfully seeking a Soviet pledge to intervene militarily if its efforts to restore order failed, the Polish regime led by General Wojciech Jaruzelski took matters into its own hands and declared martial law. It imposed curfews, suspended liberties, banned public demonstrations, arrested Solidarity leaders, and eventually outlawed the union.

The Polish declaration of martial law helped to ease the crisis and prevent a possible bloodbath, but it did not really solve the problems faced by the Polish government. Indeed, as the United States imposed economic sanctions to protest the crackdown, and as trade and tourism suffered under military rule, the Polish economy continued to decline. And the outlawed Solidarity movement simply went underground, only to reemerge at the decade's end and help lead Poland to full independence and freedom from Soviet control.

A. GENERAL JARUZELSKI'S RADIO ADDRESS, 13 DECEMBER 1981

Citizens of the Polish People's Republic, I address you today as a soldier, as the chief of the Polish Government. I address you on the most important matters.

Our country is on the edge of the abyss. Achievements of many generations, raised from the ashes, are collapsing into ruin. State structures no longer function. New blows are struck each day at our flickering economy. Living conditions are burdening people more and more.

Through each place of work, many Polish people's homes, there is a line of painful division. The atmosphere of unending conflict, misunderstanding and hatred sows mental devastation and damages the tradition of tolerance.

Strikes, strike alerts, protest actions have become standard. Even students are dragged into it.

Last night, many public institutions were occupied. There are calls for physical debate with "Reds," with people of different opinions. There are more and more examples of terror, threats, moral lynching and direct assaults. Crimes, robberies and break-ins are spreading like a wave through the country. Fortunes of millions are being made by the sharks of the economic underground.

Chaos and demoralization have reached the level of defeat. The nation has reached the borderline of mental endurance, many people are desperate. Now, not days but hours separate us from a nationwide catastrophe. . . .

We have to declare today, when we know the forthcoming day of mass political demonstrations, including the ones in the center of Warsaw called in connection with the anniversary of the December events—that tragedy cannot be repeated. It must not. We cannot let these demonstrations be a spark causing a fire in the country.

The self-preservation instinct of the nation must be taken into account. We must bind the hands of adventurers before they push the country into civil war. Citizens of Poland, heavy is the burden of responsibility which lies upon me at this very dramatic moment in Polish history. But it is my duty to take it. . . .

I declare that today the Martial Council for National Redemption has been constituted, and the Council of State obeying the Polish Constitution declared a state of emergency at midnight on the territory of Poland.

I want everybody to understand my motives and aims for action. We do not aim at a military takeover, a military dictatorship. The nation is strong and wise enough to develop a democratic system of socialist government. And in such a system, military forces could stay where their place is. None of Poland's problems can be solved by force.

The Martial Council for National Redemption is not a substitute for the constitutional government. Its only task is to protect law in the country, to guarantee reestablishment of order and discipline. That is the way to start coming out of the crisis, to save the country from collapsing. . . .

. . . The declaration of the Martial Council for National Redemption and other decrees published today define the terms and standards of public order for the duration of the state of emergency. The military council would be disbanded when law governs the country and when the conditions for the functioning of civilian administration and representative bodies are created. As the situation stabilizes itself gradually, the limits on freedom in public life will be overruled. But nobody can count on weakness or indecision. . . .

In the name of national interests, a group of people threatening the safety of the country has been interned. The extremists of Solidarity are included in this group as well as other members of illegal organizations.

On the demand of the military council, several people responsible personally for pushing the country into crisis during the 1970's and abusing the posts for personal profit have been interned. . . . The full list will be published. We will consequently clean Polish life from evil no matter where it arises. . . .

B. EXCERPTS FROM THE DECREE IMPOSING MARTIAL LAW

The convening and holding of all kinds of gatherings, processions and demonstrations is banned, as well as the organizing and conducting of public gatherings and artistic, entertainment and sports events without first obtaining the consent of the appropriate regional organ of the state administration. Excepted are religious services and rites taking place on the premises of churches, chapels or other places designated exclusively for these purposes.

The dissemination of all kinds of publications or information by any means is banned. The public performance of works of art and the use of any kind of printing equipment, without first obtaining the permission of the appropriate organ is also banned.

In connection with the introduction of martial law, the Interior Minister has introduced a ban on movement by citizens in public places during the hours from 2200 to 0600. The curfew has been introduced throughout the country. Persons who spend the daytime in public places must carry personal identity documents.

People wanting to change their permanent residence or their temporary residence for a period longer than 48 hours must first obtain permission from the regional authorities. On arrival in a given locality they must report to the authorities within 12 hours. . . .

All citizens are asked to restrict to a minimum their movements in public places so as to prevent violations of public order.

Civil, military and other public-order officials may use direct coercion with regard to persons failing to observe the above restrictions.

The introduction of martial law entails the temporary suspension of basic civil rights defined in the Polish Constitution, in particular those of personal liberty.

Polish citizens over the age of 17 whose behavior in the past gives rise to the justified suspicion that, if left free, they would not observe the legal order or that they would engage in activity that threatens the interest, security or defense of the state, may be interned at centers of isolation for the duration of martial law. . . .

In connection with the exacerbation of the political situation caused by forces hostile to the socialist state seeking to take over the radio and television, conditions arose that made it impossible to carry out normal work and that endangered the safety of the employees of Polish radio and television. In order to insure the correct and essential functioning of the radio and television, the Council of Ministers orders the following:

1. One central radio program and one central television program will be broadcast.
2. The remaining radio programs and the second television channel will cease broadcasting.
3. The regional broadcasting stations and regional television centers will be switched off and the activity of the television center and the central radio station in Warsaw will be restricted to the essential minimum. . . .

All firearms, ammunition and explosives must be handed in to the civic militia within 24 hours. The carrying of all potentially dangerous weapons is banned. . . .

State organs are also authorized to introduce limitation of freedom of movement of inhabitants in specified times and places through the introduction of a curfew or prohibition of movement to and from specified provinces, towns and parishes. . . .

From today the sale of engine fuels is suspended immediately at all public fuel stations for all private motor vehicles. All users of private cars are asked not to drive up to fuel stations because these stations will not fill tanks for an indefinite period.

Discussion Questions

1. What reasons did Jaruzelski give for declaring martial law? What other reasons might he have had? Why did he not mention them?
2. Why would the Soviets be pleased and relieved by the imposition of martial law in Poland? Why would they want to avoid an invasion of that country?
3. What restrictions did martial law entail? How were they intended to restore order and ease the crisis?
4. Why were the Solidarity leaders arrested? How did Jaruzelski justify this action? What other sorts of persons did he say would be interned for their behavior? Why?
5. Why would the United States respond to this declaration by imposing economic sanctions? Why did the West not do more to help the people of Poland in this crisis?
6. Should General Jaruzelski be considered a traitor who did Moscow's dirty work or a patriot who saved his country from invasion? Explain.

81

Andropov's Peace Offensive, 1982

IN NOVEMBER 1982, AFTER EIGHTEEN years as Soviet leader, Leonid Brezhnev died. His successor as Soviet leader was Iurii V. Andropov, who had served as Soviet ambassador to Hungary during the 1956 rebellion (Documents 32A–C) and had later become head of the KGB, the Soviet security police. Andropov believed that the USSR had stagnated during Brezhnev's declining years and that new insights and new approaches were needed.

Apprehensive about the increasing risk of nuclear war since the collapse of détente and the rise of Reagan, and mindful that global concern about that danger was mounting, he embarked on a skillful public relations campaign—aimed not only at the United States but also at its allies in Europe—designed to respond to the Reagan challenge by depicting the Soviets as the true seekers of peace. In December 1982, as part of this "peace offensive," he delivered a speech calling for measures to reduce the threat of nuclear war, including substantial reductions in the numbers of missiles deployed by both sides in Europe.

EXCERPTS FROM ANDROPOV'S SPEECH ON REDUCTIONS IN NUCLEAR MISSILES, 21 DECEMBER 1982

A nuclear war, whether big or small, whether limited or total, must not be allowed to break out. That is why the unilateral commitment of the Soviet Union not to use nuclear weapons first was received with approval and hope all over the world. If our example is followed by the other nuclear powers, this will be a truly momentous contribution to . . . preventing nuclear war. . . .

Of course, one of the main avenues leading to a real scaling down of the threat of nuclear war is that of reaching a Soviet-American agreement on limitation and reduction of strategic nuclear armaments. . . .

We are prepared to reduce our strategic arms by more than 25 percent. US arms, too, must be reduced accordingly, so that the two states have the same number of strategic delivery vehicles. We also propose that the number of nuclear warheads should be substantially lowered and that improvement of nuclear weapons should be maximally restricted. . . .

And, while the negotiations are under way, we offer what is suggested by common sense: to freeze the strategic arsenals of the two sides. The US Government does not want this and now everyone can understand why: it has embarked on a new, considerable buildup of nuclear armaments. . . .

The Soviet Union is prepared to go very far. As everybody knows, we have suggested an agreement renouncing all types of nuclear weapons . . . designed to strike targets in Europe. But this proposal has come up against a solid wall of silence. Evidently they do not want to accept it, but are afraid to reject it openly. . . .

We have also suggested . . . that the USSR and the NATO countries reduce their medium-range weaponry by more than two-thirds. So far, the United States will not have it. For its part, it has submitted a proposal that, as if in mockery, is called a "zero option." It envisages elimination of all Soviet medium-range missiles not only in the European but also in the Asiatic part of the Soviet Union, while NATO's nuclear missile arsenal in Europe is to remain intact and may even be increased. Does anyone really think that the Soviet Union can agree to this? . . .

We are prepared, among other things, to agree that the Soviet Union should retain in Europe only as many missiles as are kept there by Britain and France—and not a single one more. This means that the Soviet Union would reduce hundreds of missiles, including dozens of the latest missiles known in the West as SS-20. In the case of the USSR and the USA this would be a really honest "zero option" as regards medium-range missiles. . . .

Along with this there must also be an accord on reducing to equal levels on both sides the number of medium-range nuclear-delivery aircraft stationed in this region by the USSR and the NATO countries.

We call on the other side to accept these clear and fair terms, to take this opportunity while it still exists. But let no one delude himself: we will never let our security or the security of our allies be jeopardized. It would also be a good thing if thought were given to the grave consequences that the stationing of new US medium-range weapons in Europe would entail for all further efforts to limit nuclear armaments in general. In short, the ball is now in the court of the USA.

Discussion Questions

1. Why did Andropov launch a "peace offensive"? How did his proposals differ from Reagan's (Document 79)? Why did he object to Reagan's "zero option"?
2. Why did Andropov stress the Soviet pledge not to use nuclear weapons first? Why might the Americans not want to make such a pledge?
3. Why did he propose freezing strategic arsenals at current levels during negotiations? Why was the Reagan administration unlikely to go along?
4. Why did he suggest that the USSR should retain in Europe "only as many missiles as are kept there by Britain and France"? What objections might Washington raise to this proposal?
5. What aspects of Andropov's proposals were designed to be attractive to people in Western Europe and to Reagan's critics in the United States? How and why?

82

Reagan's "Star Wars" Speech, 1983

E ARLY IN 1983, AS ANDROPOV'S "peace offensive" achieved some success in identifying Moscow with peace and Washington with militarism, the Reagan administration began to look for ways to respond. Indeed, the president's "evil empire" speech (Document 78B), delivered in early March, was largely an attempt to justify his militaristic approach by depicting it as a noble crusade against the forces of evil.

A few weeks later, however, President Reagan went on to announce his own unique peace program. Rather than basing US security on negotiations with a foe he deeply distrusted or on the deterrent threat of nuclear war, he instead placed his faith in American technology. On 23 March, in a televised address that surprised even some of his advisors, he announced a program to develop a space-based "shield" that would protect America from Soviet attack by destroying Soviet-launched missiles before they reentered the Earth's atmosphere. Although Reagan would come to call this program his Strategic Defense Initiative (SDI), it was widely referred to as "Star Wars," after a popular movie series in which the forces of good used futuristic space technology to battle an evil empire.

There were all sorts of problems with the SDI. Much of the needed technology had not yet been developed, and the cost of producing it would be very high. Even then, most scientists agreed that it could never be made foolproof, and that a clever foe could eventually create weapons to thwart or overwhelm it. The Kremlin quickly condemned it as a first-strike weapon, pointing out that by protecting the Americans from Soviet retaliation, it would free them to launch an attack on the USSR. The SDI nonetheless remained an article of faith with Ronald Reagan throughout the rest of his presidency, severely complicating arms control negotiations, but enabling him to portray himself as a man of peace who was working to reduce the threat of nuclear war.

EXCERPTS FROM REAGAN'S TELEVISED SPEECH, 23 MARCH 1983

My fellow Americans, thank you for sharing your time with me tonight. The subject I want to discuss with you, peace and national security, is both timely and important—timely because I have reached a decision that offers new hope for our children in the 21st century. . . .

We are engaged right now in several negotiations with the Soviet Union to bring about a mutual reduction of weapons. . . . If the Soviet Union will join us in our effort to achieve major arms reduction we will have succeeded in stabilizing the nuclear balance. Nevertheless, it will be necessary to rely on the specter of retaliation—on mutual threat, and that is a sad commentary on the human condition.

Wouldn't it be better to save lives than to avenge them? Are we not capable of demonstrating our peaceful intentions by applying all our abilities and our ingenuity to achieving a truly lasting stability? I think we are—indeed, we must!

After careful consultation with my advisors, including the Joint Chiefs of Staff, I believe there is a way. Let me share with you a vision of the future which offers hope. It is that we embark on a program to counter the awesome Soviet missile threat with measures that are defensive. Let us turn to the very strengths in technology that spawned our great industrial base and that have given us the quality of life we enjoy today.

What if free people could live secure in the knowledge that their security did not rest upon the threat of instant US retaliation to deter a Soviet attack; that we could intercept and destroy strategic ballistic missiles before they reached our own soil or that of our allies?

I know this is a formidable, technical task, one that may not be accomplished before the end of this century. Yet, current technology has attained a level of sophistication where it is reasonable for us to begin the effort. It will take years, probably decades, of effort on many fronts. There will be failures and setbacks just as there will be successes and breakthroughs. And as we proceed, we must remain constant in preserving the nuclear deterrent and maintaining a solid capability for flexible response. But isn't it worth every investment necessary to free the world from the threat of nuclear war? We know it is. . . .

I clearly recognize that defensive systems have limitations and raise certain problems and ambiguities. If paired with offensive systems, they can be viewed as fostering an aggressive policy, and no one wants that.

But with these considerations in mind, I call upon the scientific community in our country, those who gave us nuclear weapons, to turn their great talents now to the cause of mankind and world peace: to give us the means of rendering these nuclear weapons impotent and obsolete.

Tonight, consistent with our obligations under the ABM Treaty and recognizing the need for closer consultation with our allies, I am taking an important first step. I am directing a comprehensive and intensive effort to define a long-term research and development program to begin to achieve our ultimate goal of eliminating the threat posed by strategic nuclear missiles. This could pave the way for arms control measures to eliminate the weapons themselves. We seek neither military superiority nor political advantage. Our only purpose—one all people share—is to search for ways to reduce the danger of nuclear war.

Discussion Questions

1. What was the essence of Reagan's "Star Wars" vision? Why was it so appealing to him, and why would it be appealing to many others?
2. What were the potential advantages and disadvantages of SDI for the United States? Why might some be skeptical of its value?
3. What political benefits might Reagan derive from initiating SDI?
4. Why would Soviet leaders react negatively to SDI? What concerns would it arouse in them?
5. Why would Reagan's program complicate arms control negotiations with the Soviets? How and why could it be seen as violating the spirit of the 1972 ABM Treaty (Document 63A)?

83

The Nuclear Freeze Resolution, 1983

IN THE EARLY 1980S, as the nuclear arms race intensified, an extensive grassroots "nuclear freeze" movement emerged in Europe and America. Proposing to end the arms race by negotiating a prompt cessation of all weapons testing and production, it called for an "immediate, mutual and verifiable freeze" on the arsenals of both sides. In his 1982 "peace offensive" (Document 81), Soviet leader Andropov even sought to associate himself with this movement, hoping thereby to bring pressure on the Reagan administration to halt its weapons buildup and cancel its planned deployment of new missiles in Europe.

Meanwhile, in the United States, as the movement picked up steam, politicians climbed onboard. Despite Reagan's efforts to counter it, a nuclear freeze resolution was approved by the US House of Representatives in May 1983. Although the resolution had no binding force, it did serve as a public call to Reagan to moderate his policies and reach an agreement with Moscow.

HIGHLIGHTS OF THE NUCLEAR WEAPONS FREEZE RESOLUTION PASSED BY THE HOUSE OF REPRESENTATIVES, 4 MAY 1983

Resolved by the Senate and House of Representatives of the United States of America in Congress assembled, that, consistent with the maintenance of essential equivalence in overall nuclear capabilities now and in the future, the Strategic Arms Reduction Talks between the United States and the Soviet Union should have the following objectives:

1. Pursuing the objective of negotiating an immediate, mutual and verifiable freeze, then pursuing the objective of negotiating immediate, mutual and verifiable reductions in nuclear weapons.
2. Deciding when and how to achieve a mutual verifiable freeze on testing, production, and further deployment of nuclear warheads, missiles, and other delivery systems, and systems which would threaten the viability of sea-based nuclear deterrent forces, and to include all air defense systems designed to stop nuclear bombers. Submarines are not delivery systems as used herein.
3. Consistent with pursuing the objective of negotiating an immediate, mutual and verifiable freeze, giving special attention to destabilizing weapons, especially those which give either nation capabilities which confer upon it even the hypothetical advantage of a first strike.
4. Providing the cooperative measures of verification, including provisions for on-site inspection as appropriate to complement national technical means of verification and to ensure compliance.
5. Proceeding from this mutual and verifiable freeze, pursuing substantial, equitable and verifiable reductions through numerical ceilings, annual percentages, or any other equally effective and verifiable means of strengthening strategic stability. . . .
6. Preserving present limitations and controls on nuclear weapons and nuclear delivery systems.
7. Incorporating ongoing negotiations in Geneva on intermediate-range nuclear systems into the START negotiations.

8. Discussing the impact of comprehensive defensive systems consistent with all provisions of the Treaty on the Limitation of Anti Ballistic-Missile Systems.

In those negotiations, the United States shall make every effort to reach a common position with our North Atlantic Treaty Organization allies on any element of an agreement which would be inconsistent with existing United States commitments to those allies.

Discussion Questions

1. Why did the nuclear freeze movement become so popular in Europe in the early 1980s? Why would Soviet leader Andropov be supportive of this movement?
2. Why did the nuclear freeze movement also become popular in America? How did Reagan's policies and rhetoric contribute to the growth of this movement?
3. What were the key provisions of the freeze resolution? Which provisions would Reagan object to and why? Why, in particular, would he object to a freeze on the development of systems that would provide "even the hypothetical advantage of a first strike"?
4. What might the resolution's sponsors have hoped to accomplish in getting congressional approval? What impact, if any, was it likely to have on the Reagan administration and on the US-Soviet arms control negotiations?

84

The KAL 007 Incident, 1983

THROUGHOUT 1983 THE INTERNATIONAL climate worsened, thanks to the continuing weapons buildup on both sides, the deadlock in the arms control talks, the tensions aroused by Reagan's SDI, the impending deployment of new US missiles in Europe, and various other factors. Ostensible efforts to improve things, such as Andropov's peace offensive and the nuclear freeze movement, had little long-term impact.

Then, on 1 September 1983, a tragic incident damaged relations still further. A South Korean jetliner, on a flight from New York via Alaska to Korea (KAL flight 007), went off course and flew through Soviet airspace for a few hours, passing over sensitive military sites. As it was about to leave Soviet airspace, it was shot down with a missile fired by a Soviet pilot, killing all 269 persons aboard.

The event resulted in a wave of international outrage against the USSR and in charges and countercharges that brought superpower relations to an impasse. Moscow asserted that the Boeing 747 had been mistaken for a US spy plane and that the Americans had provoked the incident by using a passenger plane for aerial reconnaissance. Washington responded by accusing Moscow of barbarism and demanding compensation for the victims' families. In this atmosphere, hopes for progress in the arms talks dimmed and soon disappeared. In November the United States began installing its new missiles in Europe as planned, and the Kremlin responded by breaking off the weapons negotiations. Soviet-American relations had reached a new low.

STATEMENT BY SECRETARY OF STATE GEORGE SHULTZ ON SOVIET DOWNING OF KOREAN JETLINER, 1 SEPTEMBER 1983

At 1400 hours Greenwich mean time yesterday, a Korean Air Lines Boeing 747 en route from New York to Seoul, Korea, departed Anchorage, Alaska. Two-hundred sixty-nine passengers and crew were on board, including Congressman Lawrence P. McDonald.

At approximately 1600 hours Greenwich mean time, the aircraft came to the attention of Soviet radar. It was tracked constantly by the Soviets from that time.

The aircraft strayed into Soviet airspace over the Kamchatka Peninsula and over the Sea of Okhotsk and over the Sakhalin Islands. The Soviets tracked the commercial airliner for some two and a half hours.

A Soviet pilot reported visual contact with the aircraft at 1812 hours. The Soviet plane was, we know, in constant contact with its ground control.

At 1821 hours the Korean aircraft was reported by the Soviet pilot at 10,000 meters. At 1826 hours the Soviet pilot reported that he fired a missile and the target was destroyed. At 1830 hours the Korean aircraft was reported by radar at 5,000 meters. At 1838 hours the Korean plane disappeared from the radar screen.

We know that at least eight Soviet fighters reacted at one time or another to the airliner. The pilot who shot the aircraft down reported after the attack that he had in fact fired a missile, that he had destroyed the target, and that he was breaking away.

About an hour later, the Soviet controllers ordered a number of their search aircraft to conduct search and rescue activities in the vicinity of the last position of the Korean airliner as reflected by Soviet tracking. One of these aircraft reported finding kerosene on the surface of the seas in that area.

During Wednesday night, United States State Department officials . . . were in contact with Soviet officials seeking information concerning the airliner's fate. The Soviets offered no information.

As soon as US sources had confirmed the shooting down of the aircraft, the US on its own behalf and on behalf of the Republic of Korea called in the Soviet chargé d'affaires in Washington this morning to express our grave concern over the shooting down of an unarmed civilian plane carrying passengers with a number of nationalities. We also urgently demanded an explanation from the Soviet Union.

The United States reacts with revulsion to this attack. Loss of life appears to be heavy. We can see no excuse whatsoever for this appalling act.

Discussion Questions

1. Why would the Soviets shoot down a foreign aircraft that flew over their territory? Why would they wait to do so until the plane was about to leave Soviet airspace?
2. In his statement, why did Secretary Shultz provide such precise detail about the time and circumstances of the incident?
3. Why did Shultz's statement say there was no excuse for this "appalling act"? Why would Moscow accuse Washington of purposely provoking this incident?
4. Why did it have such a devastating impact on international relations? Why and how did it contribute to the cessation of arms control talks between the Americans and Soviets?

VI

THE END OF THE
COLD WAR, 1985–1991

85

The Geneva Summit, 1985

FOLLOWING THE KAL 007 INCIDENT in September 1983, Soviet leader Andropov largely disappeared from public view, sidelined by a kidney ailment that would end his life in February 1984. His replacement, Konstantin Chernenko, was an aging party functionary and former Brezhnev crony whose foreign policy was for the most part circumspect and inflexible. The war in Afghanistan persisted, and the ongoing chill in superpower relations was symbolized by a Soviet bloc boycott of the 1984 Olympic Summer Games that were held in Los Angeles.

In March 1985, however, Chernenko died and was soon replaced as general secretary of the Soviet Communist Party by the much younger Mikhail Gorbachev, marking a generational shift in the Kremlin leadership. It also marked an important change in the way Moscow did business. Energetic, outgoing, and articulate, Gorbachev looked and acted more like a Western politician than a Communist bureaucrat. Eager to improve the stagnant Soviet economy and reduce the huge costs of maintaining a mammoth military machine and a network of client states, he began to look for ways to ease international anxieties and halt the ruinous arms race.

In his efforts he met with a favorable response from President Ronald Reagan, who quickly invited him to America for a summit conference. Gorbachev, however, preferred a neutral site, so the two men met at Geneva, Switzerland, in November 1985. Their summit meeting produced no major breakthroughs, but it did generate real progress in personal relations. During a break in the formal talks, Gorbachev and Reagan held a private discussion, with no advisors present, by a fireplace in a beach house near Lake Geneva. The dynamic young Soviet Communist and the aging American Cold Warrior, so different in their backgrounds and beliefs, shared with each other their hopes and concerns and developed a rapport that would help them make real headway in the next few years.

A. EXCERPTS FROM JOINT SOVIET-AMERICAN STATEMENT ON THE GENEVA SUMMIT, 21 NOVEMBER 1985

By mutual agreement, the President of the United States, Ronald Reagan, and the General Secretary of the Central Committee of the Communist Party of the Soviet Union, Mikhail S. Gorbachev, met in Geneva November 19–21. . . .

While acknowledging the differences in their systems and approaches to international issues, some greater understanding of each side's view was achieved by the two leaders. They agreed about the need to improve US-Soviet relations and the international situation as a whole.

In this connection the two sides have confirmed the importance of an ongoing dialogue, reflecting their strong desire to seek common ground on existing problems. They agreed to meet again in the nearest future. The General Secretary accepted an invitation by the President . . . to visit the United States of America, and the President . . . accepted an invitation by the General Secretary . . . to visit the Soviet Union. Arrangements for the timing of the visits will be agreed upon through diplomatic channels.

In their meetings, agreement was reached on a number of specific issues. . . .

Security. The sides . . . have agreed that a nuclear war cannot be won and must never be fought. Recognizing that any conflict between the USSR and the US could have catastrophic consequences, they emphasized the importance of preventing any war between them, whether nuclear or conventional. They will not seek to achieve military superiority.

Nuclear and Space Talks. The President and the General Secretary discussed the negotiations on nuclear and space arms. They agreed to accelerate the work at these negotiations, with a view to . . . prevent an arms race in space and to terminate it on earth, to limit and reduce nuclear arms and enhance strategic stability. Noting the proposals recently tabled by the US and the Soviet Union, they called for early progress . . . in areas where there is common ground, including the principle of 50 percent reductions in the nuclear arms of the US and the USSR . . . , as well as the idea of an interim I.N.F. agreement. During the negotiation of these agreements, effective measures for verification . . . will be agreed upon.

Risk Reduction Centers. The sides agreed to study the question at the expert level of centers to reduce nuclear risk. . . . They took satisfaction in such recent steps in this direction as the modernization of the Soviet-US hot line.

Nuclear Nonproliferation. General Secretary Gorbachev and President Reagan reaffirmed the commitment of the USSR and the US to the Treaty on the Nonproliferation of Nuclear Weapons and their interest in strengthening together with other countries the nonproliferation regime, and in further enhancing the . . . treaty . . . by enlarging its membership. . . .

Chemical Weapons. . . . [T]he two sides reaffirmed that they are in favor of a general and complete prohibition of chemical weapons and the destruction of existing stockpiles of such weapons. They agreed to accelerate efforts to conclude an effective and verifiable international convention on this matter. . . .

Process of Dialogue. President Reagan and General Secretary Gorbachev agreed . . . to place on a regular basis dialogue at various levels. Along with meetings between the leaders of the two countries, this envisages regular meetings between the USSR Minister of Foreign Affairs and the US Secretary of State, as well as between the heads of other ministries and agencies. . . . Recognizing that exchanges of views on regional issues on the expert level have proven useful, they agreed to continue such exchanges on a regular basis. The sides intend to expand the programs of bilateral cultural, educational and scientific-technical exchanges, and also to develop trade and economic ties. . . . They agreed on the importance of resolving humanitarian cases in the spirit of cooperation. They believe that there should be greater understanding among our peoples and that to this end they will encourage greater travel and people-to-people contact. . . .

Environmental Protection. Both sides agreed to contribute to the preservation of the environment—a global task—through joint research and practical measures. In accordance with the existing US-Soviet agreement in this area, consultations will be held next year in Moscow and Washington on specific programs of cooperation. . . .

B. REMARKS BY GENERAL SECRETARY GORBACHEV

. . . The President and I have done a huge amount of work. We've gone into great detail; we've really done it in depth. And we've done it totally openly and frankly.

We've discussed several most important issues. The relations between our two countries and the situations in the world in general today—these are issues and problems the solving of which in the most concrete way is of concern both to our countries and to the peoples of other countries in the world. We discussed these issues basing our discussions on both sides' determination to improve relations between the Soviet Union and the United States of America. We decided that we must help to decrease the threat of nuclear war.

We must not allow the arms race to move off into space and we must cut it down on earth.

It goes without saying that discussions of these sorts we consider to be very useful, and in its results you find a clear reflection of what the two sides have agreed together. We have to be realistic and straightforward, and therefore the solving of the most important problems concerning the arms race and increasing hopes of peace we didn't succeed in reaching at this meeting. So of course there are important disagreements on matters of principle that remain between us. However, the President and I have agreed that this work . . . will be continued . . . by our representatives.

We're also going to seek new kinds of developing bilateral Soviet-American relations. And also we're going to have further consultations on several important questions where, for the most part, our positions again are completely different. . . .

But the significance of everything which we have agreed with the President can only, of course, be reflected if we carry it on into concrete measures. If we really want to succeed in something, then both sides are going to have to do an awful lot of work. . . . I would like to announce that the Soviet Union, for its part, will do all it can in this cooperation with the United States of America . . . to cut down the arms race, to cut down the arsenals which we've piled up and . . . produce the conditions which will be necessary for peace on earth and in space.

We make this announcement perfectly aware of our responsibility both to our own people and to the other peoples of the earth. And we would very much hope that we can have the same approach from the Administration of the United States of America. If that can be so, then the work that has been done in these days in Geneva will not have been done in vain. . . .

C. REMARKS BY PRESIDENT REAGAN

. . . We've packed a lot into the last two days. I came to Geneva to seek a fresh start in relations between the United States and the Soviet Union and we have done this. General Secretary Gorbachev and I have held comprehensive discussions covering all elements of our relationship. I'm convinced that we are heading in the right direction. We've reached some useful interim results which are described in the joint statement that is being issued this morning.

In agreeing to accelerate the work of our nuclear arms negotiators, Mr. Gorbachev and I have addressed our common responsibility to strengthen peace. I believe that we have established a process for more intensive contacts between the United States and the Soviet Union. These two days of talks should inject a certain momentum into our work . . . a momentum we can continue at the meeting that we have agreed on for next year.

Before coming to Geneva, I spoke often of the need to build confidence in our dealings with each other. Frank and forthright conversation at the summit are part of this process. But I'm certain General Secretary Gorbachev would agree that real confidence in each other must be built on deeds, not simply words. This is the thought that ties together all the proposals that the United States has put on the table in the past, and this is the criteria by which our meetings will be judged in the future.

The real report card on Geneva will not come in for months or even years. But we know the questions that must be answered.

Will we join together in sharply reducing offensive nuclear arms and moving to nonnuclear defensive strengths for systems to make this a safer world? Will we join together to help bring about a peaceful resolution of conflicts in Asia, Africa and Central America, so that the peoples there can freely determine their own destiny without outside interference? Will the cause of liberty be advanced, and will the treaties and agreements signed—past and future—be fulfilled? The people of America, the Soviet Union and throughout the world are ready to answer yes.

I leave Geneva today and our fireside summit determined to pursue every opportunity to build a safer world of peace and freedom. There's hard work ahead, but we're ready for it. General Secretary Gorbachev, we ask you to join us in getting the job done, as I'm sure you will.

Discussion Questions

1. Why did Gorbachev prefer to meet Reagan in Geneva rather than the United States?
2. Why was the establishment of personal rapport between these two men so important?
3. What was the nature and significance of the formal agreements reached at Geneva?
4. Why did Gorbachev insist that "we must not allow the arms race to move off into space"? Why did Reagan advocate "moving to nonnuclear defensive strengths for systems to make this a safer world"? What future discord between them might these statements portend?
5. Why did Reagan call for "a peaceful resolution of conflicts in Asia, Africa and Central America"? What specific conflicts did he have in mind?

6. Why did both leaders stress the importance of following up on the Geneva talks with concrete actions and accomplishments?

86

The Reykjavik Summit, 1986

FOLLOWING THE GENEVA SUMMIT conference of November 1985, Mikhail Gorbachev made some striking proposals designed to jump-start the moribund arms control talks. Among other things, he called for the elimination of all nuclear weapons in three stages over the next fifteen years, and he urged the withdrawal of all US and Soviet intermediate-range missiles from Europe—in effect supporting Reagan's earlier "zero-option" proposal (Document 79). Under his guidance, Moscow was clearly seizing the initiative in negotiations to end the arms race.

Scrambling to catch up, the Reagan administration began to refine its own positions and push for a second summit. But Gorbachev, although he had agreed in Geneva to visit the United States, now refused to do so unless and until the arms control talks made some serious headway. After further discussions, he finally agreed to preliminary talks with Reagan in the fall of 1986 at Reykjavik, Iceland.

Although the Reagan team saw this merely as a preliminary meeting to prepare for a Washington summit, Gorbachev came ready to talk turkey, bringing sweeping proposals for a 50 percent cut in all strategic arms, the elimination of intermediate-range weapons from Europe, talks on a total test ban, and mutual agreement to abide by the ABM treaty for ten more years. Struck by the scope of these proposals, the Americans eventually replied with a counterproposal to abolish all strategic missiles in the next ten years. Not to be outdone, Gorbachev came back with a plan to eliminate *all* nuclear weapons, not just missiles, by 1996. Excitement grew as the two sides worked to hammer out an accord. But the talks collapsed when Reagan refused to confine his Strategic Defense Initiative (SDI) to laboratory testing during that period. Bitterly disappointed, the two sides blamed each other, and Gorbachev made the following remarks while still in Iceland.

EXCERPTS FROM GORBACHEV'S
STATEMENT IN REYKJAVIK, 12 OCTOBER 1986

About one hour has passed since our meeting with the President of the United States of America ended. . . . And sometimes they say when you stand face to face with someone you cannot see his face. So I have just left . . . that meeting and particularly at the last stages of that meeting, the debates were very pointed and I'm still very much under the influence of those debates.

The atmosphere at the meeting was friendly. We could discuss things freely and without limitation, outlining our views as to various problems and this has made it possible for us to have a more in-depth understanding of many major issues of international politics, bilateral relations and above all, the questions of war and peace, of ending the nuclear arms race and the entire range of problems within that broad topic. . . .

We brought here a whole package of major proposals which . . . could genuinely within a short period of time make it possible to genuinely avert the threat of nuclear war and would also make it possible to begin movement toward a non-nuclear world. I proposed to the President that we should here in Reykjavik issue instructions to the agencies involved to prepare three draft agreements that we could then sign during my visit to the United States.

On strategic weapons, we proposed that they should be reduced by 50 percent, so that before the end of this century, this most deadly type of weapon would be completely eliminated. It was our belief that the world was looking for major steps, that it was expecting deep cuts rather than some cosmetic reductions, that bold and responsible decisions were necessary. . . .

But when we began discussing that question, we felt in response that the proposals which were given to us were not adequate. They were not really relevant because they only repeated what is already being bandied about, limits, sublimits, arithmetic that only makes the substance of the question very confusing.

We said, we have this recognition of the triad of strategic offensive weapons: ICBMs, missiles carried by submarines, and strategic missiles on bombers. Now let us reduce that by one half, a fifty percent reduction in land-based missiles, including the heavy missiles that so concerned the United States, a fifty percent reduction in submarine-launched missiles and fifty percent reduction in missiles on strategic aircraft. The American delegation agreed to that. We had an accord there.

We put forward a proposal to instruct delegations to prepare an agreement on medium-range missiles. I proposed to the President to give up all the options that had been discussed until then, and to really go back to the American proposals of complete elimination of US medium-range missiles in Europe and to eliminate also the Soviet medium-range missiles in Europe. At this meeting, we decided to remove from the agenda altogether the question of British and French nuclear missiles. Let them remain, let them be upgraded.

The Americans did not expect that we would make such proposals. That was not acceptable. The US side again wanted us to accept interim solutions that would preserve some American missiles in Europe and some Soviet missiles.

In the end, we made that last step. We said, in Europe we will eliminate US and Soviet medium-range missiles. In Asia, 100 warheads on missiles each. We agreed that an agreement to that effect could be signed.

In this situation, when we are entering the stage of genuine cuts, [we proposed] that in ten years the nuclear arsenals of the Soviet Union and the United States would be eliminated altogether. We said that within that period, the treaties that exist, like the ABM treaty, should not only be preserved, but they should be strengthened. We proposed that the ABM treaty should be strengthened, that both sides should undertake within the next ten years not to use their right to withdraw from that treaty. . . . We said in our proposals that . . . within those ten years, all the requirements of the ABM treaty would be strictly preserved, that the development and testing of space weapons would be banned and that only research within laboratories would be permitted.

We know the commitment of the US Administration and the President to SDI. Our agreement to the possibility of lab testing makes possible for the President to go through with the research and to see what is SDI and what it's all about. And this is really where the real fight began. The President insisted until the end that the United States retained the right to . . . test things relating to SDI not only in the laboratories but also out of the laboratories, including in space.

I said to the President that we were missing a historic chance. Never had our positions been so close together. When we were saying goodbye, the President said he was disappointed and that from the very beginning I, that is to say Gorbachev, had come to Reykjavik with no willingness to reach agreement. Why, he said, because of just one word are you so intransigent in your approach to SDI and as regards testing?

No, it's not one word that is the point here. It is the substance that is the key to what the Administration really intends. If you make an inventory of things that have happened, you will see that we have made very serious, unprecedented concessions and compromises. . . . And still there has been no agreement. The Americans came to this meeting empty-handed, with an entire set of mothballed proposals that made the situation so bad, so stuffy at the Geneva negotiations.

Discussion Questions

1. Why was Gorbachev so eager to move forward with sweeping arms cuts? What conditions in the USSR may have contributed to his haste?
2. Why was the Reagan team reluctant to move as quickly as Gorbachev wanted to?
3. Why would the Soviets dislike the US proposal to abolish all strategic missiles in ten years? Why did Gorbachev up the ante and propose elimination of *all* nuclear weapons in ten years?
4. Why did Gorbachev insist that both sides must agree to adhere to the ABM treaty for those ten years? Why did Reagan refuse to limit SDI testing to the laboratory during this period? Why was this refusal unacceptable to Gorbachev?
5. What were the main achievements and failings of the Reykjavik Summit? Despite its failure, how might it have helped to clear the way for significant future agreements?

87

Reagan's 1987 Berlin Speech: "Tear Down This Wall"

ALTHOUGH RONALD REAGAN was not an expert on Germany, like all Cold War presidents he had to deal with that divided nation. He visited Berlin for the first time in 1982, amid protests against the impending deployment there of new US missiles. Two years later, when Reagan traveled to France for ceremonies commemorating the fortieth anniversary of the Allied invasion of Germany, West German Chancellor Helmut Kohl objected to his country's exclusion from the festivities, even though they were a celebration of Europe's liberation from German rule. But Kohl was persistent, so Reagan made it up to him when he returned to Europe in 1985 to mark the fortieth anniversary of the end of World War II. That visit included a wreath-laying ceremony at a Germany military cemetery in Bitburg, which Kohl portrayed as a gesture of reconciliation. Unfortunately, the cemetery also contained the graves of a number of officers in Hitler's dreaded bodyguard, the SS, many of whose members had taken part in the Holocaust or committed other war crimes. Reagan went through with the ceremony despite a firestorm of criticism from the media and veterans' groups in the United States, but he might have been forgiven had he never returned to Germany.

But two years later he was back, this time for another visit to Berlin. By then Gorbachev's liberation of the USSR was in full swing, and Reagan took the opportunity to press for a further relaxation of tensions in Europe. There, in a stunning speech in the shadow of the Berlin Wall, evoking memories of Kennedy's 1963 Berlin speech (Document 48), he challenged Mr. Gorbachev to "tear down this wall." The wall remained standing for two more years, but Reagan's speech came to be seen as a harbinger of its collapse.

HIGHLIGHTS OF REAGAN'S BERLIN WALL SPEECH, 12 JUNE 1987

Behind me stands a wall that encircles the free sectors of this city, part of a vast system of barriers that divides the entire continent of Europe. From the Baltic south, those barriers cut across Germany in a gash of barbed wire, concrete, dog runs and guard towers. Farther south, there may be no visible, no obvious, wall. But there remain armed guards and checkpoints all the same—still a restriction on the right to travel, still an instrument to impose upon ordinary men and women the will of a totalitarian state.

Yet it is here in Berlin where the wall emerges most clearly; here, cutting across your city, where the news photo and the television screen have imprinted this brutal division of a continent upon the mind of the world. Standing before the Brandenburg Gate, every man is a German, separated from his fellow men. Every man is a Berliner, forced to look upon a scar.

[West German] President von Weizsäcker has said: The German Question is open as long as the Brandenburg Gate is closed. Today I say: As long as this gate is closed, as long as this scar of a wall is permitted to stand, it is not the German Question alone that remains open, but the question of freedom for all mankind. Yet I do not come here to lament. For I find in Berlin a message of hope—even, in the shadow of this wall, a message of triumph. . . .

From devastation—from utter ruin—you Berliners have in freedom rebuilt a city that once again ranks as one of the greatest on earth. . . .

In the 1950s, Khrushchev predicted, "We will bury you." But in the West today, we see a free world that has achieved a level of prosperity and well-being unprecedented in all human history. In the Communist world, we see failure. Technological backwardness. Declining standards of health. Even want of the most basic kind—too little food. Even today, the Soviet Union still cannot feed itself.

After these four decades, then, there stands before the entire world one great and inescapable conclusion. Freedom leads to prosperity. Freedom replaces the ancient hatreds among the nations with comity and peace. Freedom is the victor.

Now the Soviets themselves may in a limited way be coming to understand the importance of freedom. We hear much from Moscow about a new policy of reform and openness. Some political prisoners have been released. Certain foreign news broadcasts are no longer being jammed. Some economic enterprises have been permitted to operate with greater freedom from state control.

Are these the beginnings of profound changes in the Soviet state? Or are they token gestures, intended to raise false hopes in the West or to strengthen the Soviet system without changing it? We welcome change and openness. For we believe freedom and security go together—that the advance of human liberty can only strengthen the cause of world peace. There is one sign the Soviets can make that would be unmistakable, that would advance dramatically the cause of freedom and peace.

General Secretary Gorbachev, if you seek peace—if you seek prosperity for the Soviet Union and Eastern Europe—if you seek liberalization, come here, to this gate.

Mr. Gorbachev, open this gate.

Mr. Gorbachev, tear down this wall.

I understand the fear of war and the pain of division that afflict this continent—and I pledge to you my country's efforts to help overcome these burdens. To be sure, we in the West must resist Soviet expansion. So we must maintain defenses of unassailable strength. Yet we seek peace. So we must strive to reduce arms on both sides.

Beginning 10 years ago, the Soviets challenged the Western alliance with a grave new threat: hundreds of new and more deadly SS-20 nuclear missiles, capable of striking every capital in Europe. The Western alliance responded by committing itself to a counterdeployment unless the Soviets agreed to negotiate a better solution—namely, the elimination of such weapons on both sides.

For many months, the Soviets refused to bargain in earnestness. As the alliance in turn prepared to go forward with its counterdeployment, there were difficult days—days of protests like those during my 1982 visit to this city—and the Soviets later walked away from the table.

But through it all, the alliance held firm. And I invite those who protested then—I invite those who protest today—to mark this fact: Because we remained strong, the Soviets came back to the table. Because we remained strong, today we have within reach the possibility, not merely of limiting the growth of arms, but of eliminating, for the first time, an entire class of nuclear weapons from the face of the earth. . . .

Today, thus, represents a moment of hope. We in the West stand ready to cooperate with the East to promote true openness—to break down the barriers that separate people, to create a safer, freer world. And surely there is no better place than Berlin, the meeting place of East and West, to make a start. . . .

As I looked out a moment ago from the Reichstag, that embodiment of German unity, I noticed words crudely spray-painted upon the wall—perhaps by a young Berliner. "This wall will fall. Beliefs become reality." Yes, across Europe, this wall will fall. For it cannot withstand faith. It cannot withstand truth. The wall cannot withstand freedom.

Discussion Questions

1. In what ways was Reagan's speech reminiscent of Churchill's Iron Curtain speech (Document 6A) and Kennedy's Berlin speech (Document 48)? In what ways did it differ?
2. To which aspects of Soviet liberalization did Reagan call attention? To what basic human desire did he link the idea of freedom?
3. How did Reagan support his conviction that Europe's division was coming to an end?
4. Why did he issue a personal appeal to Gorbachev? What impact might this appeal have had on the Soviet leader?

88

The INF Treaty, December 1987

FOLLOWING THE COLLAPSE of the Reykjavik Summit (Document 86), Reagan's refusal to confine SDI research to laboratory testing at Gorbachev's insistence seemed to doom any hopes for arms control progress until a new US president took office. But early in 1987, faced with the continuing decline of the Soviet economy and the slow pace of his *perestroika* reforms,

Gorbachev decide he could not wait that long. Even if progress in the Strategic Arms Reduction Talks (START) was blocked by disagreement over SDI testing, he concluded, it might still be useful to reach an agreement on intermediate-range nuclear forces (INF). So he simply chose to "unpack his package" and negotiate a separate INF accord. Early in 1987 he unexpectedly announced that, no matter what happened with SDI or START, he was ready to discuss the elimination of US and Soviet intermediate-range missiles in Europe.

Suddenly, it seemed, there was hope. Since Reagan had already advocated this approach in his 1981 "zero-option" proposal (Document 79), it looked as if a deal was readily within reach. But Washington, concerned that the Soviets would still have a large number of intermediate-range missiles in Asia, pressed for a broader accord. Why not abolish all such weapons, wherever they were located? This breathtaking proposal, known as "global zero-zero," would form the basis for the INF treaty, worked out through negotiations during 1987.

In December, Gorbachev traveled to Washington to meet with Ronald Reagan and sign the new INF pact. The exhilaration was palpable as the two leaders formally agreed to eliminate all missiles with ranges of 500 to 5,500 kilometers (roughly 300 to 3,400 miles), including the American Pershing IIs and Soviet SS-20s, within the next three years. Skeptics pointed out that this would only reduce nuclear stockpiles by about 4 percent, but that failed to dim the glow. For the first time ever, the superpowers agreed not just to limit the arms race but actually to abolish a whole class of weapons.

TREATY ON INTERMEDIATE AND
SHORTER RANGE NUCLEAR FORCES, 8 DECEMBER 1987

Article I
In accordance with the provisions of this Treaty . . . each Party shall eliminate its intermediate range and shorter-range missiles, not have such systems thereafter, and carry out the other obligations set forth in this Treaty. . . .

Article II
For the purposes of this treaty:

(1) The term "ballistic missile" means a missile that has a ballistic trajectory over most of its flight path. The term "ground launched ballistic missile (GLBM)" means a ground launched ballistic missile that is a weapon-delivery vehicle.

(2) The term "cruise missile" means an unmanned, self-propelled vehicle that sustains flight through the use of aerodynamic lift over most of its flight path. The term "ground launched cruise missile (GLCM)" means a ground launched cruise missile that is a weapon-delivery vehicle. . . .

(5) The term "intermediate-range missile" means a GLBM or GLCM having a range capacity in excess of 1000 kilometers but not in excess of 5500 kilometers.

(6) The term "shorter-range missile" means a GLBM or GLCM having a range capacity equal to or in excess of 500 kilometers but not in excess of 1000 kilometers. . . .

Article IV

(1) Each Party shall eliminate all its intermediate-range missiles and launchers of such missiles, and all support structures and support equipment . . . associated with such missiles and launchers, so that no later than three years after entry into force of this Treaty and thereafter no such missiles, launchers, support structures or support equipment shall be possessed by either Party.

(2) To implement paragraph 1 of this Article, upon entry into force of this Treaty, both parties shall begin and continue throughout the duration of each phase, the reduction of all types of their deployed and non-deployed intermediate-range missiles and deployed and non-deployed launchers of such missiles and support structures and support equipment associated with such missiles and launchers. . . . These reductions shall be implemented in two phases so that:

  (a) by the end of the first phase, that is, no later than 29 months after entry into force of this treaty. . . .

    (ii) the number of deployed intermediate-range missiles for each Party shall not exceed the number of such missiles considered by the Parties to carry 180 warheads. . . .

    (iv) the aggregate number of deployed and non-deployed intermediate-range missiles for each Party shall not exceed the number of such missiles considered by the Parties to carry 200 warheads. . . .

  (b) by the end of the second phase, that is, no later than three years after entry into force of this Treaty, all intermediate-range missiles of each Party, launchers of such missiles and all support structures and support equipment . . . shall be eliminated.

Article V

(1) Each Party shall eliminate all its shorter-range missiles and launchers of such missiles, and all support equipment . . . so that no later than 18 months after entry into force of the Treaty and thereafter no such missiles, launchers or support equipment shall be possessed by either Party.

(2) No later than 90 days after entry into force of the Treaty, each Party shall complete the removal of all its deployed shorter-range missiles and deployed and non-deployed launchers of such missiles to elimination facilities and shall retain them at those locations until they are eliminated. . . . No later than 12 months after entry into force of the Treaty, each Party shall complete the removal of all its non-deployed shorter-range missiles until they are eliminated. . . .

Article XI

(1) For the purpose of ensuring verification of compliance with the provisions of this Treaty, each Party shall have the right to conduct on-site inspections. . . .

(2) . . . both within the territory of the other Party and within the territories of basing countries. . . .

Article XII

(1) For the purpose of ensuring verification of compliance with the provisions of the Treaty, each Party shall use national technical means of verification at its disposal in a manner consistent with . . . international law.

(2) Neither Party shall:
    (a) interfere with national technical means of verification of the other party . . . ; or
    (b) use concealment measures which impede verification of compliance with the provisions of the Treaty by national technical means of verification. . . .

Article XV

(1) This Treaty shall be of unlimited duration.

(2) Each Party shall, in exercising its national sovereignty, have the right to withdraw from this Treaty if it decides that extraordinary events related to the subject matter of this Treaty have jeopardized its supreme interests. It shall give notice of its decision to withdraw to the other Party six months prior to withdrawal from this Treaty. . . .

Discussion Questions

1. Why was Gorbachev willing to negotiate an INF treaty, but not a START agreement, without an agreement on SDI testing?
2. Why were missiles with a range of less than 5,500 kilometers considered "intermediate," while those with longer range were considered "strategic"?
3. Why did the treaty call for the phased elimination of intermediate-range weapons rather than their immediate destruction?
4. Why did the treaty place so much emphasis on verification procedures?
5. What was the most important accomplishment of the INF treaty? What were its main limitations? Why did its signing create such excitement?

89

The Soviet Withdrawal from Afghanistan, 1988–1989

IN FEBRUARY 1988, A FEW MONTHS after the INF treaty signing, came another very hopeful development. The USSR, frustrated by an unwinnable war that was draining its resources and sapping its soldiers' morale, decided to cut its losses and withdraw from Afghanistan.

The Afghan War had been going badly for Moscow for some time. Despite their massive firepower and superior equipment, the Soviet forces had been unable to get the better of the primitive but rugged Afghan guerrillas. After some initial Soviet successes, the conflict had bogged down into a long debilitating stalemate with no end in sight.

Since coming to power in 1985, Mikhail Gorbachev had been searching for a way to get his forces out of Afghanistan. At first he had tried to end the conflict by sending in additional forces to overwhelm the insurgents. When that failed, he had begun to work toward a negotiated settlement in Geneva, where peace talks had been going on since 1982. But the Afghan rebels, who eventually were armed with US-supplied Stinger antiaircraft missiles, saw little reason to compromise, and the talks dragged on month after month with only modest progress.

Finally Gorbachev decided that the time had come to withdraw. In the statement excerpted below, he announced that, as long as an agreement was reached barring outside interference, Soviet troops would begin pulling out in May 1988. Despite problems caused by US insistence on continuing aid to the rebels, the withdrawal was completed within the prescribed ten months.

GORBACHEV'S STATEMENT ON SOVIET WITHDRAWAL FROM AFGHANISTAN, 8 FEBRUARY 1988

The military conflict in Afghanistan has been going on for a long time now. It is one of the most bitter and painful regional conflicts. Judging by everything, certain prerequisites have now emerged for its political settlement. In this context the Soviet leadership considers it necessary to . . . make its position totally clear.

In the near future, a new round of talks conducted by Afghanistan and Pakistan through the personal representative of the United Nations Secretary General will be held in Geneva. There are considerable chances that this round will become a final one.

By now documents covering all aspects of a settlement have been almost fully worked out. . . . They include agreements between Afghanistan and Pakistan on non-interference in each other's internal affairs and on the return of Afghan refugees from Pakistan; international guarantees of non-interference in Afghanistan's internal affairs; a document on the interrelationship of all elements of political settlement. There is also agreement on establishing a verification mechanism.

So what remains to be done? It is to establish a time frame for the withdrawal of Soviet troops from Afghanistan that would be acceptable to all. Precisely that—a time frame, since the fundamental political decision to withdraw Soviet troops from Afghanistan was adopted by us, in agreement with the Afghan leadership, some time ago, and announced at that same time.

The question of time frame has both a technical and a political aspect. As for the technical aspect, it is clear that the actual withdrawal of troops will take a certain amount of time. . . . As for the political aspect of the matter, it is that the withdrawal of Soviet troops is, quite naturally, linked with precluding interference in Afghanistan's internal affairs. Prerequisites for that have now been created to a mutual satisfaction.

Seeking to facilitate a speedy and successful conclusion of the Geneva talks between Afghanistan and Pakistan, the Government of the USSR and the Republic of Afghanistan have agreed to set a specific date for beginning the withdrawal of Soviet troops—May 15, 1988—and to complete their withdrawal within 10 months. The date is set based on the assumption that agreements on the settlement would be signed no later than March 15, 1988, and that, accordingly, they would all enter into force simultaneously two months after that. If the agreements are signed before March 15, the withdrawal of troops will, accordingly, begin earlier. . . .

And now about our boys, our soldiers in Afghanistan. They have been doing their duty honestly, performing acts of self-denial and heroism.

Our people profoundly respect those who were called to serve in Afghanistan. The state provides for them, as a matter of priority, good educational opportunities and a chance to get interesting, worthy work.

The memory of those who have died a hero's death in Afghanistan is sacred to us. It is the duty of party and Soviet authorities to make sure that their families and relatives are taken care of with concern, attention and kindness.

And, finally, when the Afghan knot is untied, it will have the most profound impact on other regional conflicts too.

Whereas the arms race, which we are working so hard—and with some success—to stop, is mankind's mad race to the abyss, regional conflicts are bleeding wounds which can result in gangrenous growth on the body of mankind.

The earth is literally spotted with such wounds. Each of them means pain not only for the nations directly involved but for all—whether in Afghanistan, in the Middle East, in connection with the Iran-Iraq war, in southern Africa, in Kampuchea, or in Central America.

Who gains from those conflicts? No one except the arms merchants and various reactionary expansionist circles who are used to exploiting and turning a profit on people's misfortunes and tragedies.

Implementing political settlement in Afghanistan will be an important rupture in the chain of regional conflicts.

Just as the agreement to eliminate intermediate- and short-range missiles is to be followed by a series of further major steps towards disarmament, with negotiations on them already underway or being planned, likewise behind the political settlement in Afghanistan already looms a question: which conflict will be settled next? And it is certain that more is to follow.

States and nations have sufficient reserves of responsibility, political will and determination to put an end to all regional conflicts within a few years. This is worth working for. The Soviet Union will spare no effort in this most important cause.

Discussion Questions

1. Why was Gorbachev anxious to end Soviet involvement in the Afghan war? Why did he wish to preclude outside interference in Afghanistan as a precondition for withdrawal?
2. Why did he announce a timetable for withdrawal even before the peace talks were done?
3. What impact might his announcement be expected to have on the peace talks? What impact might it be expected to have on superpower relations?
4. Why did he think Soviet withdrawal from Afghanistan could help bring an end to other regional conflicts?
5. What factors might account for Soviet failure to win the Afghan war?

90

Gorbachev's UN Address, December 1988

IN MAY 1988, AS SOVIET FORCES were starting to withdraw from Afghanistan, Ronald Reagan traveled to Moscow for his third summit meeting with Gorbachev. Although no major new agreements were reached, the trip itself symbolized how much had changed in a few short years, as the ardent old Cold Warrior was warmly received in the heart of what he had five years earlier referred to as the "evil empire."

But the Reagan era was quickly approaching its end. In November of that year, Vice President George H. W. Bush was elected to succeed him as president, and the world waited to see what impact this would have on superpower relations.

Meanwhile, in early December, after the elections but before Bush formally took office, Gorbachev visited New York to address the UN General Assembly. In his remarkable speech, which reflected the momentous shift in Soviet behavior, he emphatically declared that all nations must be free to choose their own destiny, that ideology had no place in foreign affairs, and that great powers should renounce the use of force in international relations. He went on to pledge substantial cuts in Soviet troops and tanks, especially those stationed in Eastern Europe. The impact of his words would soon reverberate throughout the Soviet bloc.

EXCERPTS FROM GORBACHEV'S SPEECH TO THE UNITED NATIONS, 7 DECEMBER 1988

. . . The world in which we live today is radically different from what it was at the beginning or even in the middle of this century. And it continues to change as do all its components. The advent of nuclear weapons was just another tragic reminder of the fundamental nature of that change. A material symbol and expression of absolute military power, nuclear weapons at the same time revealed the absolute limits of that power. The problem of mankind's survival and self-preservation came to the fore. . . .

It is obvious, for instance, that the use or threat of force no longer can or must be an instrument of foreign policy. This applies above all to nuclear arms, but that is not the only thing that matters. All of us, and primarily the stronger of us, must exercise self-restraint and totally rule out any outward-oriented use of force. . . .

The new phase also requires de-ideologizing relations among states. We are not abandoning our convictions, our philosophy or traditions, nor do we urge anyone to abandon theirs. But neither do we have any intention to be hemmed in by our values. That would result in intellectual impoverishment, for it would mean rejecting a powerful source of development—the exchange of everything original that each nation has independently created.

In the course of such exchange, let everyone show the advantages of their social system, way of life or values—and not just by words or propaganda, but by real deeds. That would be a fair rivalry of ideologies. But it should not be extended to relations among states.

We are, of course, far from claiming to be in possession of the ultimate truth. But, on the basis of a thorough analysis of the past and newly emerging realities, we have concluded that . . . we should jointly seek the way leading to the supremacy of the universal human idea over the endless multitude of centrifugal forces, the way to preserve the vitality of this civilization, possibly the only one in the entire universe.

Could this view be a little too romantic? Are we not overestimating the potential and the maturity of the world's social consciousness? We have heard such doubts and such questions both in our country and from some of our Western partners. I am convinced that we are not floating above reality. . . .

Now let me turn to the main issue—disarmament, without which none of the problems of the coming century can be solved. . . .

Today, I can report to you that the Soviet Union has taken a decision to reduce its armed forces. Within the next two years their numerical strength will be reduced by 500,000 men. The numbers of conventional armaments will also be substantially reduced. This will be done unilaterally. . . .

By agreement with our Warsaw Treaty allies, we have decided to withdraw by 1991 six tank divisions from East Germany, Czechoslovakia and Hungary, and to disband them. Assault landing troops and several other formations and units . . . with their weapons and combat equipment, will also be withdrawn. Soviet forces stationed in those countries will be reduced by 50,000 men and their armaments, by 5,000 tanks.

All Soviet divisions remaining for the time being in the territory of our allies are being reorganized. Their structure will be different from what it is now; after a major cutback of their tanks it will become clearly defensive. At the same time, we shall reduce the numerical strength of the armed forces and the numbers of armaments stationed in the European part of the Soviet Union. In total, Soviet armed forces in this part of our country and in the territories of our European allies will be reduced by 10,000 tanks, 8,500 artillery systems and 800 combat aircraft.

Over these two years we intend to reduce significantly our armed forces in the Asian part of our country, too. By agreement with the government of the Mongolian People's Republic a major portion of Soviet troops temporarily stationed there will return home.

In taking this fundamental decision the Soviet leadership expresses the will of the people, who have undertaken a profound renewal of their entire socialist society. We shall maintain our country's defense capability at a level of reasonable and reliable sufficiency so that no one might be tempted to encroach on the security of the Soviet Union and our allies.

By this action, and by all our activities in favor of demilitarizing international relations, we wish to draw the attention of the international community to yet another pressing problem—the problem of transition from the economy of armaments to an economy of disarmament. Is conversion of military production a realistic idea? . . . We think that, indeed, it is realistic. For its part, the Soviet Union is prepared to do these things:

- In the framework of our economic reform we are ready to draw up and make public our internal plan of conversion;
- In the course of 1989 to draw up, as an experiment, conversion plans for two or three defense plants;
- To make public our experience in providing employment for specialists from military industry and in using its equipment, buildings and structures in civilian production.

It is desirable that all states, in the first place major military powers, should submit to the United Nations their national conversion plans. It would also be useful to set up a group of scientists to undertake a thorough analysis of the problem of conversion as a whole and as applied to individual countries and regions and report to the secretary-general of the United Nations, and, subsequently, to have this matter considered at a session of the General Assembly.

And finally, since I am here on American soil . . . , I have to turn to the subject of our relations with this great country. I had a chance to appreciate the full measure of its hospitality during my memorable visit to Washington exactly a year ago.

The relations between the Soviet Union and the United States of America have a history of five and a half decades. As the world changed, so did the nature, role and place of those relations in world politics. For too long a time they developed along the lines of confrontation and sometimes animosity. . . . But in the last few years the entire world could breathe a sigh of relief thanks to the changes for the better . . . in the relationship between Moscow and Washington.

No one intends to underestimate the seriousness of our differences and the toughness of outstanding problems. We have, however, already graduated from the primary school of learning to understand each other and seek solutions in both our own and common interests. The Soviet Union and the United States have built the largest nuclear and missile arsenals. But it is those two countries that, having become specifically aware of their responsibility, were the first to conclude a treaty on the reduction and physical elimination of a portion of their armaments which posed a threat to both of them and to all others. Both countries possess the greatest and the most sophisticated military secrets. But it is those two countries that have laid a basis for and are further developing a system of mutual verification both of the elimination of armaments and of the reduction and prohibition of their production. It is those two countries that are accumulating the experience for future bilateral and multilateral agreements.

We value this. We acknowledge and appreciate the contribution made by President Ronald Reagan and by the members of his administration, particularly Mr. George Shultz. All this is our joint investment in a venture of historic importance. We must not lose this investment, or leave it idle.

The next US administration, headed by President-elect George Bush, will find in us a partner who is ready—without long pauses or backtracking—to continue the dialogue in a spirit of realism, openness and good will, with a willingness to achieve concrete results working on the agenda which covers the main issues of Soviet-US relations and world politics. I have in mind, above all, these things:

- Consistent movement toward a treaty on 50 percent reductions in strategic offensive arms while preserving the ABM treaty;
- Working out a convention on the elimination of chemical weapons . . . ;
- And negotiations on the reduction of conventional arms and armed forces in Europe.

I also have in mind economic, environmental and humanistic problems. . . .

I would like to believe that our hopes will be matched by our joint effort to put an end to an era of wars, confrontation and regional conflicts, to aggressions against nature, to the terror of hunger and poverty as well as to political terrorism. This is our common goal and we can only reach it together. Thank you.

Discussion Questions

1. Why would Gorbachev choose the UN General Assembly as his forum for this address? What was the significance of him giving this speech on US soil?
2. What did he mean by "de-ideologizing relations among states"? What implications did this have for superpower relations?
3. Why did he say that "force no longer can . . . be an instrument of foreign policy"? What implications did this have for the Soviet bloc?
4. What did he mean by "transition . . . to an economy of disarmament"? How did he foresee that such a transition could occur?
5. Why did he announce specific Soviet force and weapons reductions in this speech? Why would he make unilateral cuts, without first insisting that the Americans must match them with similar reductions?
6. What did he foresee as the future role of the superpowers in the world and the future relations between them?
7. How does this speech compare and contrast with Khrushchev's "peaceful coexistence" speech in 1956 (Document 30)?

91

The Tiananmen
Square Massacre, June 1989

IN 1989, AS COLD WAR TENSIONS were subsiding in the West, a crisis developed in China. A dozen years of modernization, including capitalist-style economic freedoms and growing commerce with the West, had raised hopes among Chinese youths for more political freedom. Beginning in April, thousands of student protesters and others camped out in Beijing's vast Tiananmen Square, staging demonstrations and demanding more freedom and an end to official corruption. In May, in the midst of these demonstrations, Gorbachev paid a state visit to Beijing, during which he urged his Chinese hosts to continue on the path of openness and democratic reform.

As the protests increased, however, Chinese premier Li Peng called for "decisive measures" to restore order, including the use of armed force. Deng Xiaoping, China's main leader, eventually sided with Li Peng. On 19 May, Li Peng demanded resolute action in a starkly worded address, and on 20 May he declared martial law in Beijing. On 3–4 June, martial law units of the Chinese army forcefully cleared the square, killing hundreds of protesters. On 9 June, in a speech to these units, Deng Xiaoping lauded their efforts and blamed the massacre on a "rebellious clique" that wanted to "topple our country and overthrow our party." Stability was restored and economic modernization continued, but hopes for greater freedom in China were dashed.

A. LI PENG'S SPEECH ON BEHALF OF THE
CHINESE COMMUNIST PARTY CENTRAL
COMMITTEE AND STATE COUNCIL, 19 MAY 1989

Comrades, . . . the party Central Committee and the State Council have convened a meeting here . . . calling on everyone to mobilize in this emergency and to adopt resolute and effective measures to curb turmoil in a clear-cut manner, to restore normal order in society, and to maintain stability and unity. . . .

. . . [T]he current situation in the capital is quite grim. The anarchic state is going from bad to worse. Law and discipline have been undermined. . . . More and more students and other people have been involved in demonstrations. Many institutions of higher learning have come to a standstill. Traffic jams have taken place everywhere. The party and government leading organs have been affected, and public security has been rapidly deteriorating. All this has seriously disturbed and undermined the normal order of production, work, study, and everyday life of the people. . . .

The activities of some of the students on hunger strike at Tiananmen Square have not yet been stopped completely. Their health is seriously deteriorating and some of their lives are still in imminent danger. In fact, a handful of persons are using the hunger strikers as hostages to coerce and force the party and the government to yield to their political demands. . . .

. . . The square is packed with extremely excited crowds who keep shouting demagogic slogans. Right now, representatives of the hunger striking students say that they can no longer control the situation. If we fail to promptly put an end to such a state of affairs and let it go unchecked, it will very likely lead to serious consequences which none of us want to see.

The situation in Beijing is still developing, and has already affected many other cities in the country. In many places, the number of demonstrators and protesters is increasing. In some places, there have been many incidents of people breaking into local party and government organs, along with beating, smashing, looting, burning, and other undermining activities that seriously violated the law. . . .

All these incidents demonstrate that we will have nationwide major turmoil if no quick action is taken to turn and stabilize the situation. . . .

. . . At present, it has become more and more clear that the very, very few people who attempt to create turmoil want to achieve, under the conditions of turmoil, precisely their political goals which they could not achieve through normal democratic and legal channels. . . .

One important reason for us to take a clear-cut stand in opposing the turmoil and exposing the political conspiracy of a handful of people is to distinguish the masses of young students from the handful of people who incited the turmoil. For almost a month, we adopted an extremely tolerant and restrained attitude in handling the student unrest. No government in the world would be so tolerant. . . . However, the handful of behind-the-scenes people who were plotting and inciting the turmoil . . . took the tolerance as weakness on the part of the party and government. They continued to cook up stories to confuse and poison the masses, in an attempt to worsen the situation. This has caused the situation in the capital and many localities across the country to become increasingly acute. Under such circumstances, the CPC . . . is forced to take resolute and decisive measures to put an end to the turmoil. . . .

. . . Now, to check the turmoil with a firm hand and quickly restore order, I urgently appeal on behalf of the party Central Committee and the State Council: First, to those students now on hunger strike at Tiananmen Square to end the fasting immediately, leave the square, receive medical treatment, and recover their health as soon as possible. Second, to the masses of students and people in all walks of life to immediately stop all parades and demonstrations, and give no more so-called support to the fasting students in the interest of humanitarianism. . . .

Comrades, on behalf of the party Central Committee and the State Council, I now . . . call on the whole party, the entire army, and people of all nationalities throughout the country to unite, to pull together, and to act immediately at all their posts in an effort to stop the turmoil and stabilize the situation. . . .

B. DENG XIAOPING'S SPEECH
TO MARTIAL LAW UNITS, 9 JUNE 1989

Comrades, you have been working very hard. First, I express my profound condolences to the commanders and fighters of the People's Liberation Army [PLA], commanders and fighters of the armed police force, and public security officers and men who died a heroic death . . . , and cordial regards to all commanders and fighters of the PLA, commanders and fighters of the armed police force, and public security officers and men who took part in this struggle. I propose that we all rise and stand in silent tribute to the martyrs.

The main difficulty in handling this incident has been that we have never experienced such a situation before, where a handful of bad people mixed with so many young students and onlookers. For a while we could not distinguish them, and as a result, it was difficult for us to be certain of the correct action that we should take. . . .

. . . Actually, what we face is not simply ordinary people who are unable to distinguish between right and wrong. We also face a rebellious clique and a large number of the dregs of society, who want to topple our country and overthrow our party. . . . They have two main slogans: One is to topple the Communist Party, and the other is to overthrow the socialist system. . . .

In the course of quelling this rebellion, many of our comrades were injured or even sacrificed their lives. Their weapons were also taken from them. Why was this? It also was because bad people mingled with the good, which made it difficult to take the drastic measures we should take.

Handling this matter amounted to a very severe political test for our army, and what happened shows that our PLA passed muster. . . . Even though the losses are regrettable, this has enabled us to win over the people and made it possible for those people who can't tell right from wrong to change their viewpoint. This has made it possible for everyone to see for themselves what kind of people the PLA are, whether there was bloodbath at Tiananmen, and who were the people who shed blood.

. . . Although it is very saddening to have sacrificed so many comrades, if the . . . incident is analyzed objectively, people cannot but recognize that the PLA are the sons and brothers of the people. This will also help the people to understand the measures we used in the course of the struggle. In the future, the PLA will have the people's support for whatever measures it takes to deal with whatever problem it faces. . . .

America has criticized us for suppressing students. In handling its internal student strikes and unrest, didn't America mobilize police and troops, arrest people, and shed blood? They are suppressing students and the people, but we are quelling a counterrevolutionary rebellion. What qualifications do they have to criticize us? From now on, we should pay attention when handling such problems. As soon as a trend emerges, we should not allow it to spread. . . .

Discussion Questions

1. Why did China's economic modernization and trade with the West lead Chinese students to hope for more political freedom?
2. What impact might the easing of Cold War tensions, reforms in the USSR, and Gorbachev's visit have had on the demonstrations?
3. Why did China's leaders take so long to act against the demonstrations?
4. Why did Li Peng consider the situation so dangerous? Why did he advocate forceful steps to restore order? What dangers did he see in letting the protests continue?
5. What did Deng Xiaoping give as reasons why the crisis arose? Was his speech an accurate analysis or a self-serving justification for the actions of the Chinese leaders?
6. How did Deng justify the violent crackdown? Why did he portray the martial law units as heroes? Why did he refer to actions earlier taken in America against student protesters?

92

The Opening of the Berlin Wall, November 1989

GORBACHEV'S REFORMS IN THE USSR, which included greater freedoms and contested elections, led to increasing expectations of liberalization in the Soviet satellites of Eastern Europe. Encouraged by Gorbachev to carry out similar reforms, Hungary's leaders began opening their borders with the West in May, and Polish authorities allowed free elections in June.

These decisions in turn had a transformative effect in East Germany. After Poland's Communists had suffered a huge electoral defeat, and as it became clear that Gorbachev would not intervene to save the satellite regimes, East Germans acted with increasing boldness. That summer and fall, some began to stage massive demonstrations; others went to Hungary so that they could escape to the West through the newly opened borders.

On 9 November 1989, faced with a mass exodus of people and demonstrations throughout East Germany, that country's Communist regime took a desperate gamble. Hoping to ease the crisis, its leaders decided to ease restrictions on travel to the West. Their spokesman, however, instead announced that almost all of these restrictions were to be lifted at once. As rumors spread that the Berlin Wall would thus be opened, Berliners by the thousands gathered at the wall to celebrate its opening and eventually begin dismantling it.

Before long, inspired by these events, revolutions would overthrow Communist regimes throughout Eastern Europe. Gorbachev and the Soviets chose not to intervene, as the empire that Stalin built proceeded to crumble.

STATEMENT ALLOWING EAST GERMANS TO TRAVEL ABROAD OR EMIGRATE, 9 NOVEMBER 1989

... The Council of Ministers of East Germany has decided immediately to set in force the following stipulations for private journeys and permanent emigration until a corresponding parliamentary law comes into effect:

1. Private journeys into foreign countries can be applied for without fulfilling preconditions (reasons for travel, relatives). Permission will be given at short notice.
2. The relevant passport and registration offices of the regional offices of the People's Police in East Germany have been ordered to issue visas for permanent emigration immediately without the present preconditions for permanent emigration having been fulfilled. Application for permanent emigration is also possible as before at departments of internal affairs.
3. Permanent emigration is allowed across all border crossing points between East Germany and West Germany and West Berlin.
4. Because of this the temporary issuing of permits in East German missions abroad and permanent emigration using East German identity cards through third countries will no longer apply.

Discussion Questions

1. What did East German leaders hope to accomplish by issuing this statement?
2. What was the significance of this statement for Berliners? Why and how did it lead to the fall of the Berlin Wall?
3. Why was it difficult to keep the Berlin Wall closed once the Hungarians had opened their border with the West? What was the impact of this opening on the "iron curtain"?
4. How did the Berlin events help open the way for revolutions throughout Eastern Europe?
5. How did these events help pave the way for reunification of Germany?

93

NATO's London Declaration on the End of the Cold War, July 1990

I**N SUMMER 1990, IN THE WAKE** of the liberation of Central and Eastern Europe, and in the context of the dramatic events that were transforming those regions and the Soviet Union itself, the North Atlantic Treaty Organization held a summit conference in London, attended by the key leaders of the NATO nations. Its main result was the issuing, on 6 July 1990, of a document called the London Declaration on a Transformed North Atlantic Alliance. Asserting that Europe had entered a new era, it effectively declared that the Cold War was over and that a new role was evolving for the NATO alliance.

Although no single document or declaration formally closed the Cold War, in many ways the London Declaration signaled the termination of that conflict. It promised to extend "the hand of friendship" to the member nations of the Warsaw Pact; it called for mutual recognition that they were no longer adversaries; and it invited them to establish regular diplomatic and military ties with NATO. It also pledged to "help build the structures of a more united continent," thereby ending Europe's decades of division into armed and hostile blocs. Indeed, in the aftermath of the Cold War, the NATO alliance was destined to endure and expand, but the Warsaw Pact alliance would be dissolved by its member states in 1991.

THE LONDON DECLARATION ON A
TRANSFORMED NORTH ATLANTIC ALLIANCE, 6 JULY 1990

Europe has entered a new, promising era. Central and Eastern Europe is liberating itself. The Soviet Union has embarked on the long journey toward a free society. The walls that once confined people and ideas are collapsing. Europeans are determining their own destiny. They are choosing freedom. They are choosing economic liberty. They are choosing peace. They are choosing a Europe whole and free. As a consequence, this Alliance must and will adapt.

The North Atlantic alliance has been the most successful defensive alliance in history. As our alliance enters its fifth decade and looks ahead to a new century, it must continue to provide for the common defense. . . . Yet our alliance must be even more an agent of change. It can help build the structures of a more united continent, supporting security and stability with the strength of our shared faith in democracy, the rights of the individual, and the peaceful resolution of disputes. . . .

We recognize that, in the new Europe, the security of every state is inseparably linked to the security of its neighbors. NATO must become an institution where Europeans, Canadians and Americans work together not only for the common defense, but to build new partnerships with all the nations of Europe. The Atlantic Community must reach out to the countries of the East which were our adversaries in the cold war, and extend to them the hand of friendship.

We will remain a defensive alliance and will continue to defend all the territory of all of our members. We have no aggressive intentions and we commit ourselves to the peaceful resolution of all disputes. We will never in any circumstance be the first to use force.

The member states of the North Atlantic Alliance propose to the member states of the Warsaw Treaty Organization a joint declaration in which we solemnly state that we are no longer adversaries and reaffirm our intention to refrain from the threat or use of force against the territorial integrity or political independence of any state, or from acting in any other manner inconsistent with the purpose and principles of the United Nations Charter and with the CSCE [Conference on Security and Cooperation in Europe] Final Act. We invite all other CSCE member states to join us in this commitment to non-aggression.

In that spirit, and to reflect the changing political role of the Alliance, we today invite President Gorbachev on behalf of the Soviet Union, and representatives of the other Central and Eastern European countries, to come to Brussels and address the North Atlantic Council. We today also invite the Governments of the Union of Soviet Socialist Republics, the Czech and Slovak Federal Republic, the Hungarian Republic, the Republic of Poland, the People's Republic of Bulgaria and Romania to come to NATO, not just to visit, but to establish regular diplomatic liaison with NATO. This will make it possible for us to share with them our thinking and deliberations in this historic period of change.

Our alliance will do its share to overcome the legacy of decades of suspicion. We are ready to intensify military contacts, including those of NATO Military Commanders, with Moscow and other Central and Eastern European capitals.

We welcome the invitation to NATO Secretary General Manfred Wörner to visit Moscow and meet with Soviet leaders. . . .

The significant presence of North American conventional and US nuclear forces in Europe demonstrates the underlying political compact that binds North America's fate to Europe's democracies. But, as Europe changes, we must profoundly alter the way we think about defense.

To reduce our military requirements, sound arms control agreements are essential. That is why we put the highest priority on completing this year the first treaty to reduce and limit conventional armed forces in Europe. . . .

As Soviet troops leave Eastern Europe and a treaty limiting conventional armed forces is implemented, the Alliance's integrated force structure and its strategy will change fundamentally to include the following elements:

- NATO will field smaller and restructured active forces. These forces will be highly mobile and versatile so that Allied leaders will have maximum flexibility in deciding how to respond to a crisis. It will rely increasingly on multinational corps made up of national units.
- NATO will scale back the readiness of its active units reducing training requirements and the number of exercises.
- NATO will rely more heavily on the ability to build up larger forces if and when they might be needed.

To keep the peace, the Alliance must maintain for the foreseeable future an appropriate mix of nuclear and conventional forces, based in Europe, and kept up to date where necessary. But, as a defensive Alliance, NATO has always stressed that none of its weapons will ever be used except in self-defense and that we seek the lowest and most stable level of nuclear forces needed to secure the prevention of war.

The political and military changes in Europe, and the prospects of further changes, now allow the Allies concerned to go further. They will thus modify the size and adapt the tasks of their nuclear deterrent forces. They have concluded that, as a result of the new political and military conditions in Europe, there will be a significantly reduced role for sub-strategic nuclear systems of the shortest range. They have decided specifically that, once negotiations begin on short-range nuclear forces, the Alliance will propose, in return for reciprocal action by the Soviet Union, the elimination of all its nuclear artillery shells from Europe. . . .

Today, our Alliance begins a major transformation. Working with all the countries of Europe, we are determined to create enduring peace on this continent.

Discussion Questions

1. Why did NATO need to redefine its mission in 1990? What did it expect the "new NATO" would become?
2. Why did the London Declaration invite Warsaw Pact members to visit NATO headquarters and establish cordial relations? Why did it invite Gorbachev to come and speak?
3. What specific steps was NATO prepared to take to "overcome the legacy of decades of suspicion"?
4. How was NATO ready to respond to the withdrawal of Soviet forces from Central and Eastern Europe?
5. What sort of Europe did NATO envision in the aftermath of the Cold War?

94

The Kohl-Gorbachev Agreement on German Unification, July 1990

A CENTRAL FEATURE OF THE COLD WAR was the so-called "German Question," flowing from the failure of the four main Allied powers (the United States, Great Britain, France, and the USSR) to reach agreement on the status of Germany after World War II. Their postwar partition of that country into military occupation zones, followed by the onset of the Cold War, had resulted in its enduring division into capitalist West Germany (the Federal Republic of Germany, or FRG) and communist East Germany (the German Democratic Republic, or GDR), with the former eventually joining NATO and the latter in the Warsaw Pact. The partition was solidified by the "iron curtain" of barbed wire and fortifications that separated East from West, and later also by the Berlin Wall.

In 1989 and 1990, however, the fall of the Berlin Wall, the liberation of Eastern Europe from Soviet control, and the winding down of the Cold War removed the main obstacles to German unification. Exploiting this new situation, the Germans pressed the four powers that had divided their country to let them reunite. After some initial hesitance, a framework for discussions was approved. But the West envisioned a unified Germany that was part of NATO, while Soviets insisted that it must be neutral. In July 1990, in an effort to break the impasse, West German chancellor Helmut Kohl traveled to the USSR and persuaded Gorbachev to accept NATO membership for a united Germany, in return for major economic concessions and a pledge that the NATO military structure would not expand into eastern Germany until Soviet troops had left. This agreement removed the last major hurdle and, once appropriate treaties were completed and signed, 3 October 1990 was proclaimed the "Day of German Unity."

A. STATEMENT BY HELMUT KOHL, 16 JULY 1990

The . . . significance of our meeting lies in the results: We have agreed that significant progress could be made in central questions. This breakthrough was possible because both sides are aware that in Europe, in Germany and in the Soviet Union historic changes are taking place that give us a special responsibility. . . .

President Gorbachev and I have agreed that we have to face this historic challenge and that we have to try to be worthy of it. And we understand this task out of a special duty to our own generation, which consciously saw and witnessed the war and its consequences, and which has the great, maybe unique, chance to durably create the future of our Continent and our countries peacefully, securely and freely.

It is clear to President Gorbachev and to me that German-Soviet relations have a central significance for the future of our peoples and for the fate of Europe. We want to express this and have agreed to conclude an all-encompassing bilateral treaty immediately after unification, which shall organize our relations durably and in good-neighborliness. . . .

Today I can state the following with satisfaction and in agreement with President Gorbachev:

- The unification of Germany encompasses the Federal Republic, the GDR and Berlin.
- When unification is brought about, all the rights and responsibilities of the Four Powers will end. With that, the unified Germany, at the point of its unification, receives its full and unrestricted sovereignty.
- The unified Germany may . . . decide freely and by itself if and which alliance it wants to be a member of. . . . I have declared as the opinion of the West German Government that the unified Germany wants to be a

member of the Atlantic Alliance, and I am certain that this also complies with the opinion of the Government of the GDR.

- The unified Germany concludes a bilateral treaty with the Soviet Union for the reorganization of the troop withdrawal from the GDR, which shall be ended within three to four years. . . .
- As long as Soviet troops will remain stationed on the territory of the GDR, NATO structures will not be expanded to this part of Germany. . . .
- A unified Germany will refrain from producing, holding or commanding of atomic, biological and chemical weapons and will remain a member of the Non-Proliferation Treaty. . . .

B. STATEMENT BY MIKHAIL GORBACHEV, 16 JULY 1990

Chancellor Kohl has said a great deal about the great work we have done together. . . .

We could work so fruitfully because . . . our relations are already marked by a very high level of dialogue, and the meetings on highest levels, the telephone calls, the mutual visits have contributed to this intensive dialogue.

We have expected that there will be . . . changes, for example in the area of NATO.

The Warsaw Pact has already, as you know, changed its doctrine at its last session. That was a challenge, a call to change the structures of the blocs, from military blocs to more political ones.

We have received a very important impulse from the conference in London, NATO's most recent conference, which brought very important positive steps. . . .

If the . . . step of London had not been made, then it would have been difficult to make headway at our meeting. I want to characterize the two last days with a German expression: we made *realpolitik*. We have taken as a basis today's reality, the significance for Europe and the world.

We have reached agreement over the fact that the NATO structure is not going to be expanded to the territory of the former GDR. And if on the basis of our agreement the Soviet troops will be withdrawn in a time frame of, let us say, three to four years, then we take it that after this time period this territory will also be part of a Germany that has full sovereignty. We take it that no other foreign troops appear there; here we have trust and are aware of the responsibility of this step.

Mr. Chancellor, it was you most of all who developed this idea at this meeting. We cannot talk yet about a unified Germany, it is still an idea yet, but an idea that I welcome. . . .

Discussion Questions

1. Why would Kohl and his NATO allies insist that a unified Germany be part of NATO?
2. Why would Gorbachev have initially opposed this condition? What developments and agreements made it possible for him to accept it?
3. Why was Gorbachev so sensitive to the military status of East Germany (the GDR)?
4. How did Kohl reassure Gorbachev about NATO's role in a reunified Germany?
5. As reflected in their statements, how did Kohl's and Gorbachev's positions regarding NATO's role differ? What potential future problems might this difference portend?
6. What was the historic significance of the Kohl-Gorbachev agreement?

95

The Strategic Arms Reduction Treaty (START), July 1991

IN SUMMER 1991, GEORGE H. W. BUSH traveled to Moscow for his third summit meeting with Mikhail Gorbachev. Fresh from his success in the First Persian Gulf War, during which a US-led coalition ousted Iraqi forces from oil-rich Kuwait, Bush was at the height of his power and popularity. Gorbachev, on the other hand, was desperately trying to keep his ailing empire together, as the various republics of the USSR sought increasing independence from Moscow.

The highlight of the meeting was the signing the Strategic Arms Reduction Treaty (START), culminating over two decades of arms control negotiations. The Strategic Arms Limitation Talks, which produced the SALT I and SALT II accords in the 1970s, had sought to slow the arms race by committing both sides not to expand their arsenals beyond a certain level. Following Reagan's 1981 proposal to move from *limitation* to *reduction* of nuclear arms, SALT had given way to START. For years, however, the talks had made little progress because of disputes over which weapons to include and Reagan's commitment to his Strategic Defense Initiative (SDI).

In 1989, however, things had begun to change. Reagan was replaced by Bush, who was much less enamored of SDI; and Gorbachev, whose economic reforms were failing and whose empire was coming apart, was more and more desperate to make headway on arms control. The fall of the Berlin Wall and revolutions of Eastern Europe, moreover, reduced the tensions that had long helped fuel the arms race. At a Malta summit meeting in December of that year, the two leaders agreed to expedite START so as to conclude a treaty within twelve months.

The pact was not completed until 1991, but it was nonetheless a momentous achievement. Within seven years, according to its terms, the Soviets would eliminate half their deployed nuclear warheads, and the Americans would cut theirs by more than a third. The nuclear arms race, which had terrified the world for so long, was apparently over.

TREATY ON THE REDUCTION AND LIMITATION OF STRATEGIC OFFENSIVE ARMS, 31 JULY 1991

Article I
Each Party shall reduce and limit its strategic offensive arms in accordance with the provisions of this Treaty. . . .

Article II
1. Each Party shall reduce and limit its ICBMs [intercontinental ballistic missiles] and ICBM launchers, SLBMs [submarine-launched ballistic missiles] and SLBM launchers, heavy bombers, ICBM warheads, SLBM warheads, and heavy bomber armaments, so that seven years after entry into force of this Treaty and thereafter, the aggregate numbers, as counted in accordance with Article III of this Treaty, do not exceed:
   (a) 1600, for deployed ICBMs and their associated launchers, deployed SLBMs and their associated launchers, and deployed heavy bombers, including 154 for deployed heavy ICBMs and their associated launchers;
   (b) 6000, for warheads attributed to deployed ICBMs, deployed SLBMs, and deployed heavy bombers, including: (i) 4900, for warheads attributed to deployed ICBMs and deployed SLBMs; (ii) 1100, for warheads attributed to deployed ICBMs on mobile launchers of ICBMs; (iii) 1540, for warheads attributed to deployed heavy ICBMs.

2. Each Party shall implement the reductions pursuant to paragraph 1 of this Article in three phases, so that its strategic offensive arms do not exceed:

   (a) by the end of the first phase, that is, no later than 36 months after entry into force of this Treaty, and thereafter, the following aggregate numbers: (i) 2100, for deployed ICBMs and their associated launchers, deployed SLBMs and their associated launchers, and deployed heavy bombers; (ii) 9150, for warheads attributed to deployed ICBMs, deployed SLBMs, and deployed heavy bombers; (iii) 8050, for warheads attributed to deployed ICBMs and deployed SLBMs;

   (b) by the end of the second phase, that is, no later than 60 months after entry into force of this Treaty, and thereafter, the following aggregate numbers: (i) 1900, for deployed ICBMs and their associated launchers, deployed SLBMs and their associated launchers, and deployed heavy bombers; (ii) 7950, for warheads attributed to deployed ICBMs, deployed SLBMs, and deployed heavy bombers; (iii) 6750, for warheads attributed to deployed ICBMs and deployed SLBMs;

   (c) by the end of the third phase, that is, no later than 84 months after entry into force of this Treaty: the aggregate numbers provided for in paragraph 1 of this Article.

3. Each Party shall limit the aggregate throw-weight of its deployed ICBMs and deployed SLBMs so that seven years after entry into force of this Treaty and thereafter such aggregate throw-weight does not exceed 3600 metric tons. . . .

Article IX

1. For the purpose of ensuring verification of compliance with the provisions of this Treaty, each Party shall use national technical means of verification at its disposal in a manner consistent with . . . international law.

2. Each Party undertakes not to interfere with the national technical means of verification of the other Party operating in accordance with paragraph 1 of this Article.

3. Each Party undertakes not to use concealment measures that impede verification, by national technical means of verification, of compliance with the provisions of this Treaty. . . .

Article XI

1. For the purpose of ensuring verification of compliance with the provisions of this Treaty, each Party shall have the right to conduct inspections and continuous monitoring activities. . . .

Article XVII

1. This Treaty . . . shall be subject to ratification in accordance with the constitutional procedures of each Party. . . .

2. This Treaty shall remain in force for 15 years unless superseded earlier by a subsequent agreement on the reduction and limitation of strategic offensive arms. . . .

3. Each Party shall, in exercising its national sovereignty, have the right to withdraw from this Treaty if it decides that extraordinary events related to the subject matter of this Treaty have jeopardized its supreme interests. It shall give notice of its decision to the other party six months prior to withdrawal from this Treaty. . . .

Discussion Questions

1. Why was Gorbachev so eager to conclude an arms reduction treaty? How did the replacement of Reagan by Bush help clear the way for this treaty?

2. In what sense did the provision for equal ceilings of 1,600 delivery systems and 6,000 deployed warheads represent a US victory?

3. Why were the provisions for inspection and monitoring so crucial? Why were "national technical means" (mainly spy satellites) important in assuring compliance?

4. Why did the treaty phase in the force reductions over a seven-year period?

96

The Attempted Coup in the USSR, August 1991

ONLY THREE WEEKS AFTER THE signing of the START agreement in Moscow, a group of Soviet officials, disturbed by the deterioration of Soviet power under Gorbachev's regime, attempted to remove him from power and restore authoritarian rule. In the end, they failed, helping to pave the way for the very thing they had hoped to prevent: the disintegration of the USSR.

The August coup of 1991 was triggered by Gorbachev's efforts to conclude a new "union treaty" that would give much authority to the USSR's constituent republics. For several years, inspired in part by the 1989 revolutions in Eastern Europe, the various Soviet national republics had been seeking either full independence or at least greater autonomy. When repressive efforts from Moscow failed to keep them in line, Gorbachev put forth a compromise plan whereby the USSR would retain control of finances, transport, communication, and the military, leaving the republics to run their internal affairs. In a March 1991 referendum, more than 75 percent of the voters supported this "union treaty," although six small republics refused to take part. During the ensuing summer, eight of the remaining republics ratified the proposal, and an official signing ceremony was set for 20 August.

On 18 and 19 August, the hardliners made their move. Detaining Gorbachev at his vacation home, they set up an emergency committee to run the country and sent troops and tanks into Moscow and other major cities. But their plans unraveled when Boris Yeltsin, the flamboyant president of the Russian Republic, issued an appeal for massive popular resistance, and the troops refused to move against huge crowds that gathered around his Moscow headquarters. Within a few days, the coup collapsed. Gorbachev returned to Moscow, but it soon became clear that the real power had shifted to Yeltsin. The course of events is dramatically reflected in the documents below.

A. ANNOUNCEMENT ON GORBACHEV'S REMOVAL AND FORMATION OF EMERGENCY COMMITTEE, 19 AUGUST 1991

In view of Mikhail Sergeyevich Gorbachev's inability, for health reasons, to perform the duties of the USSR President and of the transfer of the USSR President's powers, in keeping with . . . the USSR Constitution, to USSR Vice President Gennady Ivanovich Yanayev,

With the aim of overcoming the profound and comprehensive crisis, political, ethnic and civil strife, chaos and anarchy that threaten the lives and security of the Soviet Union's citizens and the sovereignty, territory integrity, freedom and independence of our fatherland,

Proceeding from the results of the nationwide referendum on the preservation of the Union of Soviet Socialist Republics, and

Guided by the vital interests of all ethnic groups living in our fatherland and all Soviet people,

We Resolve:

1. In accordance with . . . the USSR law "on the legal regime of a state of emergency," and with demands by broad popular masses to adopt the most decisive measures to prevent society from sliding into national catastrophe and insure law and order, to declare a state of emergency in some parts of the Soviet Union for six months from 04:00 Moscow time on Aug. 19, 1991.
2. To establish that the Constitution and laws of the USSR have unconditional priority throughout the territory of the USSR.
3. To form a State Committee for the State of Emergency in the USSR in order to run the country and effectively exercise the state-of-emergency regime, consisting of:
   O. D. Baklanov, First Deputy Chairman of the USSR Defense Council
   V. A. Kryuchkov, chairman of the KGB
   V. S. Pavlov, Prime Minister of the USSR
   B. K. Pugo, Interior Minister of the USSR
   V. A. Starodubtsev, chairman of the Farmers' Union of the USSR
   A. I. Tizyakov, president of the USSR Association of State Enterprises and Industrial, Construction, Transport and Communications Facilities
   D. T Yazov, Defense Minister of the USSR
   G. I. Yanayev, Acting President of the USSR
4. To establish that the USSR State Committee for the State of Emergency's decisions are mandatory for unswerving fulfillment by all agencies of power and administration, officials and citizens throughout the territory of the USSR.

B. YELTSIN'S CALL TO RESIST
THE COUP ATTEMPT, 19 AUGUST 1991

Citizens of Russia: On the night of 18–19 August 1991, the legally elected President of the country was removed from power.

Regardless of the reasons given for his removal, we are dealing with a rightist, reactionary, anti-constitutional coup. Despite all the difficulties and severe trials being experienced by the people, the democratic process in the country is acquiring an increasingly broad sweep and an irreversible character.

The peoples of Russia are becoming masters of their destiny. The uncontrolled powers of unconstitutional organs have been considerably limited, and this includes party organs.

The leadership of Russia has adopted a resolute position toward the union treaty striving for the unity of the Soviet Union and unity of Russia. Our position on this issue permitted a considerable acceleration of the preparation of this treaty, to coordinate it with all the republics and to determine the date of signing as Aug. 20. Tomorrow's signing has been cancelled.

These developments gave rise to angry reactionary forces, pushed them to irresponsible and adventurist attempts to solve the most complicated political and economic problems by methods of force. Attempts to realize a coup have been tried earlier. We considered and consider that such methods of force are unacceptable. They discredit the union in the eyes of the whole world, undermine our prestige in the world community, and return us to the cold-war era along with the Soviet Union's isolation in the world community. All of this forces us to proclaim that the so-called committee's ascendancy to power is unlawful.

Accordingly we proclaim all decisions and instructions of this committee to be unlawful. We are confident that the organs of local power will unswervingly adhere to constitutional laws and decrees of the President of Russia. We appeal to citizens of Russia to give a fitting rebuff to the putschists [coup plotters] and demand a return of the country to normal constitutional development.

Undoubtedly it is essential to give the country's President, Gorbachev, an opportunity to address the people. Today he has been blockaded. I have been denied communications with him. We demand an immediate convocation of an extraordinary Congress of People's Deputies of the Union. We are absolutely confident that our countrymen will not permit the sanctioning of the tyranny and lawlessness of the putschists, who have lost all shame and conscience. We address an appeal to servicemen to manifest lofty civic duty and not take part in the reactionary coup. Until these demands are met, we appeal for a universal unlimited strike.

C. PRESIDENT BUSH'S STATEMENT
ON THE SOVIET COUP, 19 AUGUST 1991

We are deeply disturbed by the events of the last hours in the Soviet Union and condemn the unconstitutional resort to force. While the situation continues to evolve and information remains incomplete, the apparent unconstitutional removal of President Gorbachev, the declaration of a state of emergency, and the deployment of Soviet military forces in Moscow and other cities raise the most serious questions about the future course of the Soviet Union. This misguided and illegitimate effort bypasses both Soviet law and the will of the Soviet peoples.

Accordingly, we support President Yeltsin's call for "restoration of the legally elected organs of power and the reaffirmation of the post of USSR President M. S. Gorbachev."

Greater democracy and openness in Soviet society, including steps toward implementation of Soviet obligations under the Helsinki Final Act and the Charter of Paris, have made a crucial contribution to the welcome improvement in East-West relations during the past few years.

In these circumstances, US policy will be based on the following guidelines:

We believe the policies of reform in the Soviet Union must continue, including democratization, the process of peaceful reconciliation between the center and the republics and economic transformation.

We support all constitutionally elected leaders and oppose the use of force or intimidation [to] suppress them or restrict their right to free speech.

We oppose the use of force in the Baltic States or against any republics to suppress or replace democratically elected governments.

We call upon the USSR to abide by its international treaties and commitments, including its commitments to respect basic human rights and democratic practices under the Helsinki Accords, and the Charter of Paris.

We will avoid in every possible way actions that would lend legitimacy or support to this coup effort.

We have no interest in a new cold war or in the exacerbation of East-West tensions.

At the same time, we will not support economic aid programs if adherence to extra-constitutional means continues.

D. EXCERPTS FROM SOVIET
TELEVISION REPORT, 21 AUGUST 1991

Good evening, Comrades, Television viewers, an hour ago, the President of the USSR, Mikhail Gorbachev, made a statement for the country's radio and television. He stays fully in command of the situation and the connections which have been interrupted by the activities of the group of the emergency council have now been restored.

The President of the USSR had a telephone conversation with Comrades Yeltsin, Nazarbayev, Karimov [the leaders of the Russian, Kazakh, and Uzbek republics] and others. All of them totally denounced the attempt at a *coup d'etat* or the interruption in the legal activities of the country's Government. They stated that these anti-constitutional actions were not supported by the higher authorities of the country nor by the peoples of the country. These adventurists will bear full responsibility, liability for their illegal actions.

Mikhail Gorbachev gave directions to the general staff and the Minister of Defense Moiseyev to remove all troops presently in the cities of the country.

Today Mikhail Gorbachev had a telephone conversation with the President of the United States, Bush. The President of the United States expressed his very profound satisfaction at the fact that the extremely dangerous situation which arose because of these unconstitutional acts of this group of individuals has ended. In turn, President Gorbachev stated that the society and Government of the country had rebuffed this adventure. And the Presidents agreed to maintain continuing contact with one another and continuing cooperation in accordance with agreements reached already.

Discussion Questions

1. Why did the coup organizers depose Gorbachev? What did they hope to accomplish?
2. Why did the coup organizers declare a state of emergency? Why did they place Yanayev at the head of the emergency committee?
3. What key positions were held by the coup leaders, and what roles would they be expected to play? Why would the participation of Kryuchkov, Pugo, and Yazov seem to ensure the coup's success? Why did it fail to do so?
4. Why did Yeltsin appeal for a universal strike? Why was his resistance so effective?
5. Why did Bush denounce the coup and threaten to cut off economic aid? What risks did he take in doing so?
6. Why did the coup fail? How did it help undermine Gorbachev and empower Yeltsin?

97

Gorbachev's Resignation Speech, December 1991

A FTER THE ABORTIVE COUP ATTEMPT of August 1991, Gorbachev sought vainly to hold onto power and keep the USSR together. But Yeltsin's role in foiling the coup had strengthened him and his Russian Republic, enabling him and the heads of other republics to ignore Gorbachev and his badly weakened Soviet regime. In the Russian Republic, Yeltsin's government assumed many functions hitherto controlled by the USSR. And on 1 December, the people of Ukraine voted for complete independence, dashing any hopes of preserving the Soviet Union.

On 8 December, Yeltsin and the leaders of Ukraine and Belarus met and agreed to replace the USSR with a loose association called the Commonwealth of Independent States. When most of the other republics agreed to join this coalition, Gorbachev's cause was lost. On 25 December 1991, he formally relinquished his duties and resigned as Soviet president. A short time later, the Soviet flag was lowered from its place atop the Kremlin, and the USSR—one of history's largest and most powerful empires—officially ceased to exist.

HIGHLIGHTS OF GORBACHEV'S
RESIGNATION SPEECH, 25 DECEMBER 1991

Dear fellow countrymen, compatriots,

Due to the situation which has evolved as a result of the formation of the Commonwealth of Independent States, I hereby discontinue my activities at the post of President of the Union of Soviet Socialist Republics. . . . This being my last opportunity to address you as President of the USSR, I find it necessary to inform you of what I think of the road that has been trodden by us since 1985. . . .

Destiny so ruled that when I found myself at the helm of this state it already was clear that something was wrong in this country. We had a lot of everything—land, oil and gas, other natural resources—and there was intellect and talent in abundance. However, we were living much worse than people in the industrialized countries were living and we were increasingly lagging behind them. The reason was obvious even then. This country was suffocating in the shackles of the bureaucratic command system. Doomed to cater to ideology, and suffer and carry the onerous burden of the arms race, it found itself at the breaking point. . . .

The process of renovating this country and bringing about drastic change in the international community has proven to be much more complicated than anyone could imagine. However, let us give its due to what has been done so far.

This society has acquired freedom. It has been freed politically and spiritually, and this is the most important achievement that we have [not] yet fully come to grips with. . . . The totalitarian system has been eliminated, which prevented this country from becoming a prosperous and well-to-do country. . . .

Free elections have become a reality. Free press, freedom of worship, representative legislatures and a multi-party system have all become reality. Human rights are being treated as the supreme principle and top priority. Movement has been started toward a multitier economy and the equality of all forms of ownership. . . .

We're now living in a new world. An end has been put to the cold war and to the arms race, as well as to the mad militarization of the country, which has crippled our economy, public attitudes and morals. The threat of nuclear war has been removed. . . .

We opened up ourselves to the rest of the world, abandoned the practices of interfering in others' internal affairs and using troops outside this country, and we were reciprocated with trust, solidarity, and respect. . . . The nations and peoples of this country have acquired the right to freely choose their format for self-determination. . . .

Of course, there were mistakes made that could have been avoided, and many of the things that we did could have been done better. But I am positive that sooner or later, some day our common efforts will bear fruit and our nations will live in a prosperous, democratic society.

I wish everyone all the best.

Discussion Questions

1. Why did Gorbachev resign as Soviet president?
2. According to Gorbachev, what was wrong with the USSR when he took over as its leader?

3. Why did he insist that his reforms were necessary, despite the fact that they had helped enable the USSR's dismemberment?
4. What did Gorbachev consider to be his main achievements and legacy?
5. What do you consider to be Gorbachev's main achievements and legacy? What, if anything, do you think he could or should have done differently?